LEARN AND PRACTICE SERIES

DATA SCIENCE & MACHINE LEARNING

Scikit-Learn with Python

Edition - 1

eka PUBLISHING

SWAPNIL SAURAV

Learn Machine Learning Concept with our Expert

Unlock your potential as an AI and ML professional! This book covers basic to advanced level topics required to master the Machine Learning concepts. Machine learning is a vast field and the internet does provide plenty of resources available to get your hands on it – from books to blogs to vlogs. If you are someone looking to master the topics, you may not from where to begin with. Author felt the need to bring out a book which hand holds the reader and navigate her or him through all the concepts with easy to understand language and explaining through working programs in Python. This book covers Statistics concepts first and then takes the reader into vast world of Machine Learning. There are lot of programs implemented which goes with the explain, thats why we call it Learn and Practice.

Book uses Scikit-learn (formerly scikits.learn and also known as sklearn) is the most popular package and also a free software machine learning library for the Python programming language. It features various classification, regression and clustering algorithms including support vector machines, random forests, gradient boosting, k-means and DBSCAN, and is designed to interoperate with the Python numerical and scientific libraries NumPy and SciPy.

Happy Coding in Python

Series: Learn and Practice Series
Book 3: Data Science and Machine Learning using Python
Author: Swapnil Saurav
Cover: Aniruddh Vaidya
Price: ₹ 750
ISBN: 978-81-946334-9-5

Email ID: ekapresshyderabad@gmail.com (Send us any feedback/comments)
Online shop: www.ekapress.org

FOREWORD

During the last half decade, Machine Learning has become very important. Both as a career option, as well as potential to bring about major changes, in how our day-to-day businesses will be conducted.

I congratulate Swapnil for writing this book, to help those who want to learn Machine Learning and pursue it as a career path.

Machine Learning owes its roots in Statistics. And, it is very nice to see concepts of Statistics getting a fair amount of space in the book. Getting a good background in statistics will help ML professionals and researchers fully appreciate the algorithms' working and also provide the background when one develops enough expertise to further refine those algorithms. In this book, Swapnil has also provided several working examples in Python. Python is very popular in ML world, and hence, his choice of Python for examples is very apt. These examples provide an easy way to jump into the domain quickly.

I hope, you find this book and the examples useful, as you embark on your journey to learn Machine Learning.

- Sanjay Churiwala
Sr Director, Xilinx | Author

ABOUT THE AUTHOR

Swapnil Saurav has more than 16 years of work experience in IT industry with focus on Supply Chain Analytics. He is an ambitious, creative and highly motivated individual, who has a passion for the Supply Chain with focus on Retail and Manufacturing industries and an uncompromising commitment to quality and outstanding customer service. He has been invited to be the key note speaker at various industry forums and has a passion for teaching & developing leaders for tomorrow. His expertise lies in figuring out ways to do what others say can't be done. He holds MBA from S.P. Jain Institute of Management & Research, M.S. (BITS, Pilani) and B.E. (Visvesvaraya Technological University).

Website: www.swapnil.asia
Linked In profile: https://in.linkedin.com/in/swapnilsaurav

More books from the author:
This is part of a 5 book series published by the author

1. Book 1: Learn and Practice Python 3 Programming
2. Book 2: Learn and Practice Data Visualization using Python 3
3. **Book 3: Data Science and Machine Learning using Python**
4. Book 4: Master Deep Learning using Python
5. Book 5: Machine Learning Applications: Retail Analytics

All the books are available on Amazon and other online platforms.

Happy Learning!

TABLE OF CONTENTS

UNIT 1: INTRODUCTION TO INFERENTIAL STATISTICS

STATISTICS AND MACHINE LEARNING

Some people would have you believe that statistics and machine learning are two completely different technologies. The fact is that statistics and machine learning have a lot in common and that statistics represents one of the five tribes (schools of thought) that make machine learning feasible. The five tribes are:

- Symbolists: The origin of this tribe is in logic and philosophy. This group relies on inverse deduction to solve problems.
- Connectionists: The origin of this tribe is in neuroscience. This group relies on backpropagation to solve problems.
- Evolutionaries: The origin of this tribe is in evolutionary biology. This group relies on genetic programming to solve problems.
- Bayesians: This origin of this tribe is in statistics. This group relies on probabilistic inference to solve problems.
- Analogizers: The origin of this tribe is in psychology. This group relies on kernel machines to solve problems.

The ultimate goal of machine learning is to combine the technologies and strategies embraced by the five tribes to create a single algorithm (the master algorithm) that can learn anything. Of course, achieving that goal is a long way off.

Using the Bayesian tribe strategy, you solve most problems using some form of statistical analysis. You do see strategies embraced by other tribes described, but the main reason you begin with statistics is that the technology is already well established and understood. In fact, many elements of statistics qualify more as engineering (in which theories are implemented) than science (in which theories are created). Understanding the role of algorithms in machine learning is essential to defining how machine learning works. Analyzing the evidence proves or disapproves the hypothesis that it supports. Consequently it isn't possible to determine which disease someone has until you test all the symptoms. Example: Spam Filtering

Other Techniques:

Symbolic Reasoning, expands the realm of human knowledge. Example of this technique is if a is greater than b and b is greater than c, then we deduce that a is greater than c. Taking it to next level, lets take another example- deduction would say that if a tree is green and that green trees give oxygen, then the tree must also give oxygen.

Connections modeled on brain's neurons, strives to reproduce the brain's functions using silicon instrad of neurons. Some of deep learning techniques are based on this.

The evolutionaries rely on the principles of evolution to solve problems. In other words, this strategy is based on survival of the fittest (removing any solutions that doesn't match desired output). Tree structure where next level is built on the previous level, recursion are all examples of this.

The Analogyzers use kernel machines to recognize the patterns in data. By recognizing the pattern of one set of inputs and comparing it to the pattern of a known output, one can create problem solution. For example, the recommender systems track your pattern of buying behavior and recommends related products.

In this book, we will limit our study to Bayesian strategy using probability and statistics. Exploratory data analysis, data summarization, and data visualizations can be used to help frame your predictive modeling problem and better understand the data. That statistical methods can be used to clean and prepare data ready for modeling. That statistical hypothesis tests and estimation statistics can aid in model selection and in presenting the skill and predictions from final models.

Let's look at some of the examples of how to Use Statistical Methods in a Machine Learning Project. We will that how a working knowledge of statistics is essential for successfully working through a predictive modeling problem which is done by Machine Learning algorithms:

- Problem Framing: The framing of the problem is not always obvious. For newcomers to a domain, it may require significant exploration of the observations in the domain. For domain experts that may be stuck seeing the issues from a conventional perspective, they too may benefit from considering the data from multiple perspectives. Statistical methods that can aid in the exploration of the data during the framing of a problem include:
    - Exploratory Data Analysis. Summarization and visualization in order to explore ad hoc views of the data.
    - Data Mining. Automatic discovery of structured relationships and patterns in the data.

- Data Understanding: Data understanding means having an intimate grasp of both the distributions of variables and the relationships between variables. Some of this knowledge may come from domain expertise, or require domain expertise in order to interpret.
  Two large branches of statistical methods are used to aid in understanding data; they are:
    - Summary Statistics. Methods used to summarize the distribution and relationships between variables using statistical quantities.
    - Data Visualization. Methods used to summarize the distribution and relationships between variables using visualizations such as charts, plots, and graphs.

- Data Cleaning: Although the data is digital, it may be subjected to processes that can damage the fidelity of the data, and in turn any downstream processes or models that make use of the data. Some examples include: Data corruption, Data errors, Data loss. The process of identifying and repairing issues with the data is called data cleaning.
  Statistical methods are used for data cleaning; for example:
    - Outlier detection. Methods for identifying observations that are far from the expected value in a distribution.

  - Imputation. Methods for repairing or filling in corrupt or missing values in observations.

- Data Selection: The process of reducing the scope of data to those elements that are most useful for making predictions is called data selection.
  Two types of statistical methods that are used for data selection include:
  - Data Sample. Methods to systematically create smaller representative samples from larger datasets.
  - Feature Selection. Methods to automatically identify those variables that are most relevant to the outcome variable.

- Data Preparation: Data can often not be used directly for modeling. Some transformation is often required in order to change the shape or structure of the data to make it more suitable for the chosen framing of the problem or learning algorithms. Data preparation is performed using statistical methods. Some common examples include:
  - Scaling: Methods such as standardization and normalization.
  - Encoding: Methods such as integer encoding and one hot encoding.
  - Transforms: Methods such as power transforms like the Box-Cox method.

- Model Evaluation: A crucial part of a predictive modeling problem is evaluating a learning method. Generally, the planning of this process of training and evaluating a predictive model is called experimental design. This is a whole subfield of statistical methods.
  - Experimental Design: Methods to design systematic experiments to compare the effect of independent variables on an outcome, such as the choice of a machine learning algorithm on prediction accuracy. As part of implementing an experimental design, methods are used to resample a dataset in order to make economic use of available data in order to estimate the skill of the model. These two represent a subfield of statistical methods.
  - Resampling Methods: Methods for systematically splitting a dataset into subsets for the purposes of training and evaluating a predictive model.

- Model Configuration: A given machine learning algorithm often has a suite of hyperparameters that allow the learning method to be tailored to a specific problem. The configuration of the hyperparameters is often empirical in nature, rather than analytical, requiring large suites of experiments in order to evaluate the effect of different hyperparameter values on the skill of the model. The interpretation and comparison of the results between different hyperparameter configurations is made using one of two subfields of statistics:
  - Statistical Hypothesis Tests. Methods that quantify the likelihood of observing the result given an assumption or expectation about the result (presented using critical values and p-values).
  - Estimation Statistics. Methods that quantify the uncertainty of a result using confidence intervals.

- Model Selection: One among many machine learning algorithms may be appropriate for a given predictive modeling problem. The process of selecting one method as the solution is called model selection. This may involve a suite of criteria both from stakeholders in the project and the careful interpretation of the estimated skill of the methods evaluated for the problem. As with model configuration, two classes of statistical methods can be used to interpret the estimated skill of different models for the purposes of model selection. They are:

- Statistical Hypothesis Tests: Methods that quantify the likelihood of observing the result given an assumption or expectation about the result (presented using critical values and p-values).
- Estimation Statistics: Methods that quantify the uncertainty of a result using confidence intervals.

- Model Presentation: Once a final model has been trained, it can be presented to stakeholders prior to being used or deployed to make actual predictions on real data. A part of presenting a final model involves presenting the estimated skill of the model. Methods from the field of estimation statistics can be used to quantify the uncertainty in the estimated skill of the machine learning model through the use of tolerance intervals and confidence intervals:
  - Estimation Statistics: Methods that quantify the uncertainty in the skill of a model via confidence intervals.

- Model Predictions: Finally, it will come time to start using a final model to make predictions for new data where we do not know the real outcome. As part of making predictions, it is important to quantify the confidence of the prediction. Just like with the process of model presentation, we can use methods from the field of estimation statistics to quantify this uncertainty, such as confidence intervals and prediction intervals:
  - Estimation Statistics: Methods that quantify the uncertainty for a prediction via prediction intervals.

So, you see that, every step we will need to use our statistics knowledge. We will cover these and more in the next chapters. So get ready to take a deeper dive in Statistics. We will also learn how to use Python to implement these concepts.

INFERENTIAL STATISTICS

Descriptive statistics describes data (for example, a chart or graph) and inferential statistics allows you to make predictions ("inferences") from that data. With inferential statistics, you take data from samples and make generalizations about a population.

For detailed analysis with descriptive statistics, refer our book: Learn and Practice Data Visualization (using Python) by Swapnil Saurav. In this book, our focus is on inferential statistics.

Let's consider a scenario, you been hired as Market Rsearch manager at a company that manufactures water purifiers. You want to find out what your customers think about your products. For the data, you might stand in a mall and ask a sample of 100 people if they like your products. You could make a bar chart of yes or no answers (that would be descriptive statistics) or you could use your research (and inferential statistics) to reason that around 30-40% of the population dislike your products.

There are two main areas of inferential statistics:

- Estimating parameters. This means taking a statistic from your sample data (for example the sample mean) and using it to say something about a population parameter (i.e. the population mean).
- Hypothesis tests. This is where you can use sample data to answer research questions. For example, you might be interested in knowing if a new cancer drug is effective. Or if breakfast helps children perform better in schools.

With inferential statistics you take that sample data from a small number of people and and try to determine if the data can predict whether the drug will work for everyone (i.e. the population). There are various ways you can do this, from calculating a z-score (z-scores are a way to show where your data would lie in a normal distribution to post-hoc (advanced) testing.

A hypothesis test can show where your data is placed on a distribution like this one.

Inferential statistics use statistical models to help you compare your sample data to other samples or to previous research. Most research uses statistical models called the Generalized Linear model and include Student's t-tests, ANOVA (Analysis of Variance), regression analysis and various other models that result in straight-line ("linear") probabilities and results.

WHAT TO EXPECT IN THIS BOOK

We will talk about Probability and statistics. Probability and statistics are related areas of mathematics which concern themselves with analyzing the relative frequency of events. Probability deals with predicting the likelihood of future events, while statistics involves the analysis of the frequency of past events. This is also part of inferential statistics.

Understanding statistics, especially Bayesian probabilities, is critical to many machine learning algorithms. Aim of this book is to introduce just the right topics to you so that you are ready to learn Machine Learning at a quick pace. We have introduced core concepts, probabilities,

Bayesian ideas, and descriptive statistics in this book. We have taken every care to introduce the topics in an easy manner so that you don't need a math degree to understand. We have added Python code so that you learn this with hands-on approach. Many times, we tend to use machine learning packages directly, but its always a good practice to learn the basics first. As a data scientist, these are a very necessary part of your career, which is why you have to learn.

1. First and foremost: basic Python skills

We have followed hands-on approach in this book with lot of examples written in Python so, you need the most basic Python programming skills. If you don't have the relevant skills, you can learn python online or buy our book "***Learn and Practice Python Programming by Swapnil Saurav***". The book is available on Kindle and the physical copy can also be bought world-wide.

2. The necessity of statistics in data science

Statistics is a broad field that is used in many industries. Its definition in Wikipedia is:

> *it is the collection, analysis, interpretation, presentation and organization of data.*

So it's not surprising that data scientists need to understand statistics.

For example, data analysis requires at least descriptive statistics and probability theory. These theories will help you make better business decisions based on the data. Key concepts include probability distribution, statistical significance, hypothesis testing, and regression.

Moreover, machine learning needs to understand Bayesian probabilities, and Bayesian probabilities are the engines of many machine learning modules. Key concepts include conditional probabilities, prior probabilities, posterior probabilities, maximum likelihood estimates, and if these concepts make you fear, don't worry, once you roll up your sleeves and start learning, you'll understand.

3. The best way to learn data statistics in data science

Popular belief is that to learn a new concept or topic, one has to jump out of the classroom and directly through hands-on methods, and the statistics in data science are no exception. In this book we will see how to master the core concepts of statistics through programming.

If you don't have a formal math-related educational background, you'll find that this way you can more easily understand complex formulas. It will let you think about the logic of each calculation.

If you have some formal and relevant mathematical background, this approach will combine your theory with practice and give you a lot of interesting programming challenges.

Here are three steps that we have covered in this book to learning statistics and probability theory in the field of data science:

- ***Statistical core concept***: Descriptive statistics, distribution, hypothesis testing and regression.
- ***Bayesian probability theory***: Conditional probability, prior probability, posterior probability, maximum likelihood estimation

- ***Introducing statistics in machine learning***: Learn basic machine learning concepts and how to use statistics in machine learning

After completing these three steps, you will truly face and face more difficult machine learning problems and common data science applications. The book is divided into three parts; they are: Probability, Statistical Inference and Statistical Models and Methods.

The first step: the core concept of statistics

In order to know how to go to school statistics, first of all, to understand how it is used is very helpful for learning. Let's look at some examples of real analysis or as an application that data scientists might use:

Pilot design: Your company starts a new product line, but sells it through offline retail. You need to design an A/B test to control the differences between the different areas. You also need to estimate some meaningful results from the store from a statistical perspective.

Regression model: Your company needs to be able to better predict what the demand for a personal product line will be in all its stores. Insufficient inventory and excess inventory can be costly. You consider building a series of regular regression models.

Data conversion: In the process you are testing, there are multiple machine learning models for you to use. Some models can generate corresponding data distributions by inputting data. You need to be able to identify them and convert the input data appropriately or know under what assumptions Correlation.

A data scientist has to make hundreds of decisions every day, ranging from a module challenge to a team R&D strategy. Most decisions require a solid theoretical foundation of statistics and probability theory.
For example, data scientists need to constantly decide which data is deterministic and which data is random. In addition, they need to know if there are points of interest for further exploration.
These are the core things that are at the time of making an analysis decision (if you only know how to calculate the value, then just touch the surface).

Step 2: Bayesian Probability Theory

A philosophical debate on statistics is Frequentists and Bayesians, and Bayesian theory is more relevant when learning statistics in data science. In short, frequency theory is used near sampling modules. This means that they will only be used to describe the data that has been collected.
Bayesian theory, on the other hand, is used not only for sampling modules, but also for data that is not known before collection.

In Bayesian theory, the level of uncertainty before collecting data is called "a priori probability", and after the data, it is updated to "posterior probability". For some machine learning models, this is a very core concept. It is very important to master them.
Moreover, these concepts make sense after using them.

Step 3: Introduce statistics in machine learning

If you want to learn statistics in data science, after you have completed the core concepts of statistics and Bayesian theory, there is no better way to use statistical analysis in machine learning modules. The field of machine learning is closely related to statistics. Statistical machine learning is the most important way of machine learning now.

In this step, you will implement some machine learning modules from scratch, which will help you unravel a true understanding of its underlying technology. At this stage, even if you copy the code directly line by line, it is ok. It will help you to open up the black box of machine learning while consolidating your knowledge of statistical learning.

Please note, this book is not a replacement for any good statistics book. If you want to get deeper into statistics subject, then this is not the book for you. In this book we will cover the statistics required for Machine Learning Developer and for managers. This is not for Data scientists looking for getting deeper knowledge of the subject. If you want to understand the topics related to Machine Learning and want to learn Python code for the statistics then this is the right book for you. We will cover basic knowledge of Statistics for Machine Learning and implementation using Python.

Let's now deep dive!

***

UNIT 2: SET OPERATIONS

A set is an unordered collection of items. Every element is unique (no duplicates) and must be immutable (which cannot be changed). However, the set itself is mutable. We can add or remove items from it.

- Sets can be used to perform mathematical set operations like union, intersection, symmetric difference etc.
- A set is created by placing all the items (elements) inside curly braces {}, separated by comma or by using the built-in function set().
- It can have any number of items and they may be of different types (integer, float, tuple, string etc.). But a set cannot have a mutable element, like list, set or dictionary, as its element.

Practice Programs

```
#create set
my_set = {1, 2, 3}
print(my_set)
# set of mixed datatypes
my_set = {1.0, "Hello", (1, 2, 3)}
print(my_set)

#Using a for loop, we can iterate though each item in a set.
num_set = set([0, 1, 2, 3])
for n in num_set:
    print(n)
```

Here is a list of methods that are available with set objects along with examples. Readers are encouraged to practice them.

Method	Description	Example
add()	Add an element to a set	thisset.add("orange")
clear()	Remove all elements form a set	thisset.clear()
copy()	Return a shallow copy of a set	x = fruits.copy()
difference()	Return the difference of two or more sets as a new set	z = x.difference(y)
intersection()	Return the intersection of two sets as a new set	z = x.intersection(y)
intersection_update( )	Update the set with the intersection of itself and another	x.intersection_update(y)
difference_update()	Remove all elements of another set from this set	x.difference_update(y)
discard()	Remove an element from set if it is a member. (Do nothing if the element is not in set)	fruits.discard("banana")
isdisjoint()	Return True if two sets have a null intersection	z = x.isdisjoint(y)
issubset()	Return True if another set contains this set	z = x.issubset(y)
issuperset()	Return True if this set contains another set	z = x.issuperset(y)
pop()	Remove and return an arbitary set element. Raise KeyErrorif the set is empty	fruits.pop()
remove()	Remove an element from a set. If the element is not a member, raise a KeyError	fruits.remove("banana")

symmetric_difference()	Return the symmetric difference of two sets as a new set	z = x.symmetric_difference(y)
symmetric_difference_update()	Update a set with the symmetric difference of itself and another	x.symmetric_difference_update(y)
union()	Return the union of sets in a new set	z = x.union(y)
update()	Update a set with the union of itself and others	x.update(y)

Practice Programs

```
# # initialize Sets A and B
A = {1, 2, 3, 4, 5}
B = {4, 5, 6, 7, 8}

#Union: Union of A and B is a set of all elements from both sets.
#Union is performed using | operator.
# Same can be accomplished using the method union().
print(A | B)

# Intersection of A and B is a set of elements that are common in
both sets.
#It is performed using & operator or method intersection().
print(A & B)

#Difference of A and B (A - B) is a set of elements that are only
in A but not in B. Similarly, B - A is a set of element in B but
not in A.
# Difference is performed using - operator.
# Same can be accomplished using the method difference().
print(A - B)

#Symmetric Difference of A and B is a set of elements in both A & B
# except those that are common in both.
#Symmetric difference is performed using ^ operator.
# Same can be accomplished using the method symmetric_difference().
print(A ^ B
```

Output:
{1, 2, 3, 4, 5, 6, 7, 8}
{4, 5}
{1, 2, 3}
{1, 2, 3, 6, 7, 8}

Python Set Operations

Sets can be used to carry out mathematical set operations like union, intersection, difference and symmetric difference. We can do this with operators or methods.

Let us consider the following two sets for the following operations
>>> A = {1, 2, 3, 4, 5}
>>> B = {4, 5, 6, 7, 8}

Set Intersection

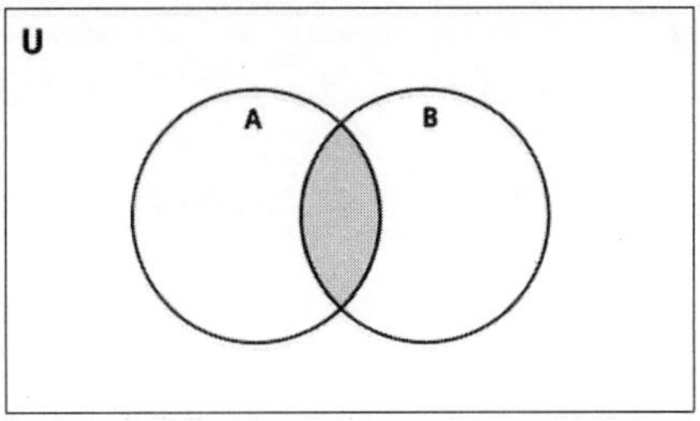

Intersection of A and B is a set of elements that are common in both sets. Intersection is performed using & operator. Same can be accomplished using the method intersection().

```
# initialize A and B
A = {1, 2, 3, 4, 5}
B = {4, 5, 6, 7, 8}

# use & operator
# Output: {4, 5}
print(A & B)
```

Set Difference

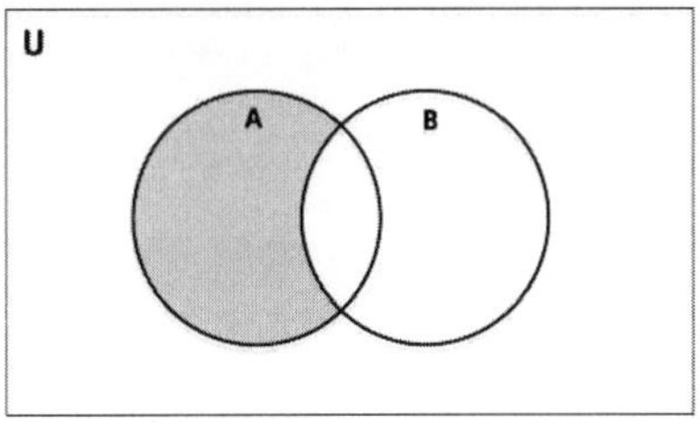

Difference of A and B (A - B) is a set of elements that are only in A but not in B. Similarly, B - A is a set of element in B but not in A. Difference is performed using - operator. Same can be accomplished using the method difference().

```
# initialize A and B
A = {1, 2, 3, 4, 5}
B = {4, 5, 6, 7, 8}

# use - operator on A
# Output: {1, 2, 3}
print(A - B)
```

Set Symmetric Difference

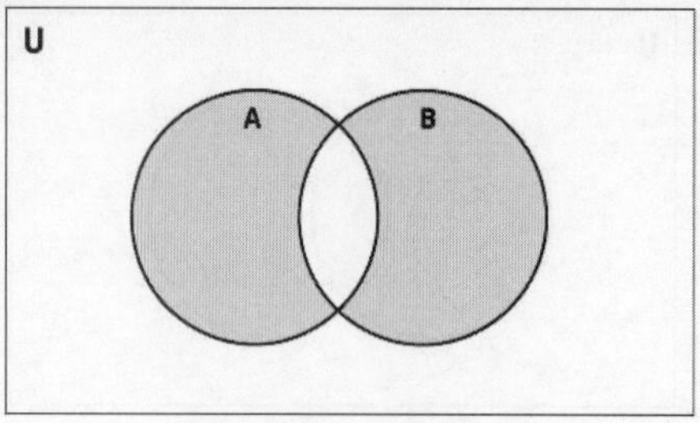

Symmetric Difference of A and B is a set of elements in both A and B except those that are common in both. Symmetric difference is performed using ^ operator. Same can be accomplished using the method symmetric_difference().

```
# initialize A and B
A = {1, 2, 3, 4, 5}
B = {4, 5, 6, 7, 8}

# use ^ operator
# Output: {1, 2, 3, 6, 7, 8}
print(A ^ B)
```

Union of sets

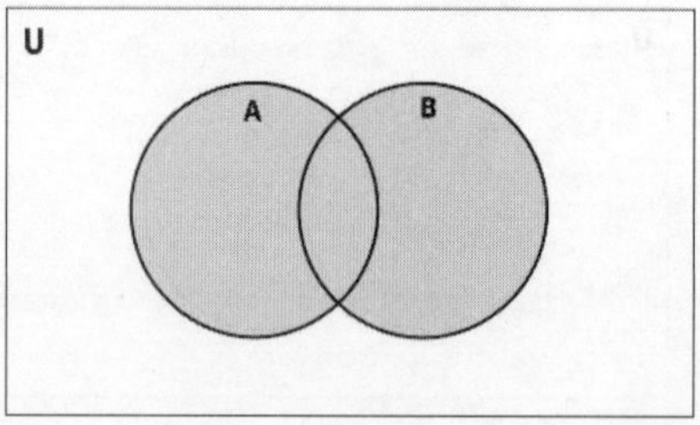

Union of A and B is a set of all elements from both sets. Union is performed using | operator. Same can be accomplished using the method union().

```
# initialize A and B
A = {1, 2, 3, 4, 5}
B = {4, 5, 6, 7, 8}

# use | operator
# Output: {1, 2, 3, 4, 5, 6, 7, 8}
print(A | B)
```

***

UNIT 3: PERMUTATION AND COMBINATION

Permutation and combination are the ways to represent a group of objects by selecting them in a set and forming subsets. It defines the various ways to arrange a certain group of data. When we select the data or objects from a certain group it is said to be permutations whereas the order in which they are represented is called combination.

Permutation Formula

A permutation is the choice of r things from a set of n things without replacement and where the order matters.

$^nP_r = (n!) / (n-r)!$

Combination Formula

A combination is the choice of r things from a set of n things without replacement and where order does not matter.

$$_nC_r = \binom{n}{r} = \frac{_nP_r}{r!} = \frac{n!}{r!(n-r)!}$$

SOLVING PERMUTATION AND COMBINATION USING SCIPY

Special Package (scipy.special)
SciPy gives functionality to calculate Permutations and Combinations.

Permutation and combination are the ways to represent a group of objects by selecting them in a set and forming subsets. It defines the various ways to arrange a certain group of data. When we select the data or objects from a certain group it is said to be permutations whereas the order in which they are represented is called combination.

Permutation Formula

A permutation is the choice of r things from a set of n things without replacement and where the order matters.

$^nP_r = (n!) / (n-r)!$

Combination Formula

A combination is the choice of r things from a set of n things without replacement and where order does not matter.

$$_nC_r = \binom{n}{r} = \frac{_nP_r}{r!} = \frac{n!}{r!(n-r)!}$$

Problem 1: In a group of 6 boys and 4 girls, four children are to be selected. In how many different ways can they be selected such that at least one boy should be there?

Solution: We have 4 options as given below:

- We can select 4 boys: 6C4
- We can select 3 boys and 1 girl: 6C3 × 4C1
- We can select 2 boys and 2 girls: 6C2 × 4C2
- We can select 1 boy and 3 girls: 6C1 × 4C3

```
from scipy.special import comb

sum=0
#find combinations of 5, 2 values using comb(N, k)
#We can select 4 boys: 6C4
com = comb(6, 4, exact = False, repetition=False)
sum+=com
#We can select 3 boys and 1 girl: 6C3 × 4C1
com = comb(6, 3) * comb(4, 1)
sum+=com
#We can select 2 boys and 2 girls: 6C2 × 4C2
com = comb(6, 2) * comb(4,2)
sum+=com
#We can select 1 boy and 3 girls: 6C1 × 4C3
com = comb(6, 1) * comb(4, 3)
sum+=com
print("Total combination possible: ",sum)
```

Output:

```
Total combination possible: 209.0
```

The number of combinations of N things taken k at a time. This is often expressed as "N choose k":

```
scipy.special.comb(N, k, exact=False, repetition=False)
```

Parameters

- Nint, ndarray - Number of things.
- kint, ndarray - Number of elements taken.
- exactbool, optional - If exact is False, then floating point precision is used, otherwise exact long integer is computed.
- repetitionbool, optional - If repetition is True, then the number of combinations with repetition is computed.

Problem 2: Three men have 4 coats, 5 waist coats, and 6 caps. In how many ways can they wear them?

Solution:

Number of ways in which 3 Men can wear 4 coats = 4!/1! = 4! = 24

Number of ways in which 3 Men can wear 5 waist coats = 5 X 4 X 3 = 60

Number of ways in which 3 Men can wear 6 caps = 6 X 5 X 4 = 120

By Fundamental Principle of Multiplication

Arrangement of 4 Coats AND Arrangement of 5 Waist Coats AND Arrangement of 6 Caps

Total number of ways = 24 X 60 X 120 = 172,800

```
from scipy.special import perm

product=1
#find permutation of 4, 3 using perm (N, k) function
#Number of ways in which 3 Men can wear 4 coats
per = perm(4, 3)
product*=per
#Number of ways in which 3 Men can wear 5 waist coats
per = perm(5, 3)
product*=per
#Number of ways in which 3 Men can wear 6 caps
per = perm(6, 3)
product*=per

print("Total Permutation possible: ",product)
```

Output:

```
Total Permutation possible:  172800.0
```

Permutations of N things taken k at a time, i.e., k-permutations of N. It's also known as "partial permutations".

```
scipy.special.perm(N, k, exact=False)
```

Parameters

- Nint, ndarray - Number of things.
- kint, ndarray - Number of elements taken.
- exactbool, optional - If exact is False, then floating point precision is used, otherwise exact long integer is computed.

SOLVING PERMUTATION AND COMBINATION USING ITERTOOLS

Finding permutations and combinations of a given sequence can also be done using python package called itertools. This is the most popular package to perform Permutation and Combinations. It involves very easy steps which are described below, you can take our Python training program for deep understanding of Permutation and Combination in python.

Step1: Importing itertools package:To implement permutation and combination, you will have to first import itertools package.

Step2: Getting all permutations/combinations: This is done by entering a list of items(defining sequence of items) as an input that will return all permutations and combinations in the form of list of tuples. You can also define a particular length of permutations and combinations.

Step3: Printing the result: Generally, for loop is used to print all the permutations and combinations.

Let's solve some examples in Permutations

Example 1: Without determining the length of the permutation

Code:

```
### Without determining the length of the permutation
# Importing itertools package
from itertools import permutations
#Getting all permutations
per = permutations(['a','b','c'])
#Printing the result
for p in list(per):
    print(p)
```

Output:

```
('a', 'b', 'c')
('a', 'c', 'b')
('b', 'a', 'c')
('b', 'c', 'a')
('c', 'a', 'b')
('c', 'b', 'a')
```

Example 2: By determining the length of the permutation.

Code:

```
# Importing itertools package
from itertools import permutations
#Getting all permutations
per = permutations(['a','b','c'],2)
#Printing the result
for p in list(per):
    print(p)
```

Output:

```
('a', 'b')
('a', 'c')
('b', 'a')
('b', 'c')
('c', 'a')
('c', 'b')
```

Let's solve some examples in Combinations

Example 1: Determining the length of the combination

Code:

```
# Importing itertools package
from itertools import combinations
#Getting all combinations by defining a particular length
com = combinations(['x','y','z'],2)
#Printing the result
for c in list(com):
    print(c)
```

Output: Combinations follows lexical order which means the output will correspond to the sorted input.

```
('x', 'y')
('x', 'z')
('y', 'z')
```

Example 2: Combinations_with_replacements is used when you want to print the combination of same elements.

Code:

```
# Importing itertools package
from itertools import combinations_with_replacement
#Getting all combinations by defining a particular length
com = combinations_with_replacement(['a','b','c'], 2)
#Printing the result
for c in list(com):
    print(c)
```

Output:

```
('a', 'a')
('a', 'b')
('a', 'c')
('b', 'b')
('b', 'c')
('c', 'c')
```

***

UNIT 4: PROBABILITY

Before you get your hands dirty, it's time to consider what probability theory is and why it's important to learn about it when you're getting into data science. You'll often wonder in real-life situations what the probabilities are of some event occurring, such as winning the lottery, the victory of your soccer team or a discount on your favorite pair of shoes. "What are the chances..." is an expression you probably use very often. Determining the chances of an event occurring is called "probability".

This type of probability is different from the mathematical way of looking at probability, which you can find in probability theory, a branch of mathematics. And in mathematics, you have two broad categories of interpretations on "probability" is - the "physical" and "evidential" probabilities.

The former are also called objective or frequency probabilities and are associated with random physical systems such as flipping coins, roulette wheels, or rolling dice. In such systems, a given type of event tends to occur at a persistent rate, or "relative frequency", in a long run of trials.

The latter is also called Bayesian probability, which can be assigned to any statement whatsoever, even when no random process is involved, as a way to represent its subjective plausibility, or the degree to which the statement is supported by the available evidence. On most accounts, evidential probabilities are considered to be degrees of belief, defined in terms of dispositions to gamble at certain odds.

Note that probability theory is mainly concerned with predicting the likelihood of future events, while statistics analyzes the frequency of past events. This also explains why probability theory is also one of the core topics that you should cover if you want to become a data scientist: as you well know, in data science and machine learning, you'll use data from events that have already occurred to predict future events.

So while probability theory is generally considered to be hard to understand intuitively, the concepts are crucial to data science and predictive analytics.

KEY CONCEPTS AND SYMBOLS

Some key concepts that you should probably be aware of for this tutorial are mostly concerned with the frequentist perspective on probability, as this tutorial works with a deck of 52 playing cards.

From that perspective, the fundamental ingredient of probability theory is an experiment that can be repeated, at least hypothetically, under essentially identical conditions. This experiment may lead to different outcomes on different trials or single performances of an experiment. The set of all possible outcomes or results of an experiment is then called a "sample space". An event is a well-defined subset of the sample space.

This is all very theoretical.

Let's consider some examples:

- A somewhat cliché example would be flipping a coin. In this case, the experiment is, in fact, the flipping of a coin. You can toss the coin multiple times, and all these trials might have different outcomes. As there are two possible outcomes -heads or tails- the sample space is 2. However, the event "tossing a coin" can, for example, consist of one outcome "Heads". Similarly, when you toss a coin twice, your event "the first toss results in a Heads" might have an outcome "Heads-Heads" or "Heads-Tails".
- Another example that is maybe less straightforward is an experiment where you spin a globe and you stop it by putting your finger on it. You can spin the globe multiple times and all these times might have different outcomes - You can either land your finger on land or on water. That means that the sample space is 2. An event "my finger is on land" might have an outcome "Land - Water" or "Land - Land".
- A last example is the experiment where you toss a die. You can toss the die multiple times and all of these throws can have different outcomes: 6 to be exact, since your die has 6 numbers (1,2,3,4,5,6). An event "The sum of the results of the two toss is equal to 10" can consist of 10, while the event "the number is even" can consist of 2, 4, or 6.

STRUCTURE OF PROBABILITY

In probability theory, an experiment or trial is any procedure that can be infinitely repeated and has a well-defined set of possible outcomes, known as the sample space. An experiment is said to be random if it has more than one possible outcome, and deterministic if it has only one. A random experiment that has exactly two (mutually exclusive) possible outcomes is known as a Bernoulli trial.

In any branch of Mathematics, developing a language of terms and symbols is helpful. The structure of probability provides a common framework within which the topics of probability can be explored.

Random Phenomena

A random variable is a variable whose possible values are numerical outcomes of a random phenomenon. There are two types of random variables, discrete and continuous.

A discrete random variable is one which may take on only a countable number of distinct values and thus can be quantified. For example, you can define a random variable X to be the number which comes up when you roll a fair dice. X can take values : [1,2,3,4,5,6] and therefore is a discrete random variable.

The probability distribution of a discrete random variable is a list of probabilities associated with each of its possible values. It is also sometimes called the probability function or the probability mass function. To have a mathematical sense, suppose a random variable X may take k different values, with the probability that X=xi defined to be P(X=xi)=pi. Then the probabilities pi must satisfy the following:

1. 0 < pi < 1 for each i
2. p1+p2+...+pk=1.

Some examples of discrete probability distributions are Bernoulli distribution, Binomial distribution, Poisson distribution etc. (Learn more about discrete probability distribution in Unit 5).

A continuous random variable is one which takes an infinite number of possible values. For example, you can define a random variable X to be the height of students in a class. Since the continuous random variable is defined over an interval of values, it is represented by the area under a curve (or the integral).

The probability distribution of a continuous random variable, known as probability distribution functions, are the functions that take on continuous values. The probability of observing any single value is equal to 0 since the number of values which may be assumed by the random variable is infinite. For example, a random variable X may take all values over an interval of real numbers. Then the probability that X is in the set of outcomes A,P(A), is defined to be the area above A and under a curve. The curve, which represents a function p(x), must satisfy the following:

1. The curve has no negative values (p(x)>0 for all x)
2. The total area under the curve is equal to 1.

A curve meeting these requirements is often known as a density curve. Some examples of continuous probability distributions are normal distribution, exponential distribution, beta distribution, etc. (Learn more about continuous probability distribution in Unit 6).

Experiment

Experiment is a process that produces outcomes. Examples:

- Auditing every 5th account to detect any errors
- Sampling every 100th bottle of ketchup from an assembly line and checking the weight
- Testing new drug on samples of Covid-19 patients and measuring the improvement
- Interviewing randomly selected 50 consumers to get a feedback on a product

Event

Event is the outcome of an experiment. For example, after inspecting 5 random financial account, 1 account has errors. Another example would be: If we assemble a deck of 52 playing cards with no jokers, and draw a single card from the deck, then the sample space is a 52-element set, as each card is a possible outcome. An event, however, is any subset of the sample space, including any singleton set (an elementary event), the empty set (an impossible event, with probability zero) and the sample space itself (a certain event, with probability one). Other events are proper subsets of the sample space that contain multiple elements. So, for example, potential events include:

- "Red and black at the same time without being a joker" (0 elements),
- "The 5 of Hearts" (1 element),

- "A King" (4 elements),
- "A Face card" (12 elements),
- "A Spade" (13 elements),
- "A Face card or a red suit" (32 elements),
- "A card" (52 elements).

Events are represented in capital letters.

Elementary Events

In probability theory, an elementary event (also called an atomic event or sample point) is an event which contains only a single outcome in the sample space. The following are examples of elementary events:

- All sets {k}, where k ∈ N if objects are being counted and the sample space is S = {0, 1, 2, 3, ...} (the natural numbers).
- {HH}, {HT}, {TH} and {TT} if a coin is tossed twice. S = {HH, HT, TH, TT}. H stands for heads and T for tails.

Sample Space

The sample space (also called sample description space or possibility space) of an experiment or random trial is the set of all possible outcomes or results of that experiment. A sample space is usually denoted using set notation, and the possible ordered outcomes are listed as elements in the set. It is common to refer to a sample space by the labels S, Ω, or U (for "universal set"). The elements of a sample space may be numbers, words, letters, or symbols. They can also be finite, countably infinite, or uncountably infinite.

For example, if the experiment is tossing a coin, the sample space is typically the set {head, tail}, commonly written {H, T}. For tossing two coins, the corresponding sample space would be {(head,head), (head,tail), (tail,head), (tail,tail)}, commonly written {HH, HT, TH, TT}.[6] If the sample space is unordered, it becomes {{head,head}, {head,tail}, {tail,tail}}.

For tossing a single six-sided die, the typical sample space is {1, 2, 3, 4, 5, 6}.

Sample space for two dice:

	1	2	3	4	5	6
1	(1, 1)	(1, 2)	(1, 3)	(1, 4)	(1, 5)	(1, 6)
2	(2, 1)	(2, 2)	(2, 3)	(2, 4)	(2, 5)	(2, 6)
3	(3, 1)	(3, 2)	(3, 3)	(3, 4)	(3, 5)	(3, 6)
4	(4, 1)	(4, 2)	(4, 3)	(4, 4)	(4, 5)	(4, 6)
5	(5, 1)	(5, 2)	(5, 3)	(5, 4)	(5, 5)	(5, 6)
6	(6, 1)	(6, 2)	(6, 3)	(6, 4)	(6, 5)	(6, 6)

Probability

Probability is a value between 0 and 1 that indicates the likelihood of a particular event. For example, the probability of getting heads when tossing as coin is ½. We assign a probability measure P(A) to an event A. This is a value between 0 and 1 that shows how likely the event is. If P(A) is close to 0, it is very unlikely that the event A occurs. On the other hand, if P(A) is close to 1, A is very likely to occur.

$$\text{probability of an event} = \frac{\text{Number of sample points that produce the event}}{\text{Total number of sample points in the sample space}}$$

```
import random
def coin_trial():
    heads = 0
    for i in range(10):
        if random.random() >= 0.5:
            heads +=1
    return heads
def simulate(n):
    trials = []
    for i in range(n):
        trials.append(coin_trial())
    return(sum(trials)/n)
#calling the function Case 1:
retv=simulate(10)
print("Sum is ", retv)
#calling the function Case 2:
retv=simulate(1000)
print("Sum is ", retv)
#calling the function Case 3:
retv=simulate(100000)
print("Sum is ", retv)
```

Output: (Your output may vary)

```
Sum is  5.5
Sum is  4.958
Sum is  4.9991
```

The coin_trial function represents a simulation of 10 coin tosses. It uses the random() function to generate random number between 0 and 1, and increments our heads count if it's equal or greater than 0.5 (rest of values assuming gives count for Tails). Then, simulate repeats these trials depending on how many times you'd like, returning the average number of heads across all of the trials. I have run this simulation for 10, 1000 and 100,000 times and observed some interesting results.

First, the data confirm that our average number of heads does approach what probability suggests it should be. Furthermore, this average improves with more trials. In 10 trials, there's some slight error, but this error almost disappears entirely with 1000,000 trials. As we get more trials, the deviation away from the average decreases. As we get more and more data, the real-world starts to resemble the ideal.

Thus, given enough data, statistics enables us to calculate probabilities using real-world observations. Probability provides the theory, while statistics provides the tools to test that theory using data. What is the chance of someone developing a disease over time? There are no easy ways to calculate probabilities, so we must fall back on using data and statistics to calculate them. Given more and more data, we can become more confident that what we calculate represents the true probability of these important events happening.

Let's Practice some of the concepts we have discussed so far:
Creating a sample space and calculating the probability for tossing a coin

```
#Creating a Sample Space of Coin-Flips
sample_space = {'Heads', 'Tails'}
#All outcomes within sample_space share an identical
# probability, which is equal to 1 / len(sample_space)
prob_heads = 1 / len(sample_space)
print(f'Probability of choosing heads is {prob_heads}')

#Let's define event conditions
# Event 1: Output is Head
def is_heads(outcome):
    return outcome == 'Heads'
# Event 2: Output is Tail
def is_tails(outcome):
    return outcome == 'Tails'
# Event 3: Output is either Head or Tail
def is_heads_or_tails(outcome):
    return outcome in {'Heads', 'Tails'}
# Event 4: Output is neither Head or Tail
def is_neither(outcome):
    return not is_heads_or_tails(outcome)
# Defining an event detection function
def get_event(event_condition, sample_space):
    '''The function iterates through generic_sample_space
    and returns the set of outcomes
    where event_condition(outcome) is True.'''
    val=[]
    for outcome in sample_space:
        if event_condition(outcome):
            val.append(outcome)
    return set(val)
```

```
#Now define probability function
def compute_probability(event_condition, generic_sample_space):
    '''The probability of an event is equal to
    len(event) / len(sample_space), but only if
    all outcomes are known to occur with equal likelihood. '''
    event = get_event(event_condition, generic_sample_space)
    return len(event) / len(generic_sample_space)
#Calling the events:
events = [is_heads_or_tails, is_heads, is_tails, is_neither]

for event_condition in events:
    prob = compute_probability(event_condition, sample_space)
    name = event_condition.__name__
    print(f"Probability of event arising from '{name}' is
{prob}")
```

Output:

```
Probability of choosing heads is 0.5
Probability of event arising from 'is_heads_or_tails' is 1.0
Probability of event arising from 'is_heads' is 0.5
Probability of event arising from 'is_tails' is 0.5
Probability of event arising from 'is_neither' is 0.0
```

Now let's look at a biased coin where the probability of getting Head is thrice that of Tail.

```
#Creating a weighted sample space
weighted_ss = {'Heads': 3, 'Tails': 1}

# Checking the weighted sample space size
#Throw assert error if sample space sum is not 4
ss_size = sum(weighted_ss.values())
assert ss_size == 4

#We can redefine event size in similar manner
# Event 1: Output is Head
def is_heads(outcome):
    return outcome == 'Heads'
# Event 2: Output is Tail
def is_tails(outcome):
    return outcome == 'Tails'
# Event 3: Output is either Head or Tail
def is_heads_or_tails(outcome):
    return outcome in {'Heads', 'Tails'}
# Event 4: Output is neither Head or Tail
def is_neither(outcome):
    return not is_heads_or_tails(outcome)
# Defining an event detection function
```

```
def get_event(event_condition, sample_space):
    '''The function iterates through generic_sample_space
    and returns the set of outcomes
    where event_condition(outcome) is True.'''
    val=[]
    for outcome in sample_space:
        if event_condition(outcome):
            val.append(outcome)
    return set(val)

def compute_weighted_probability(event_condition,
generic_sample_space):
    event = get_event(event_condition, generic_sample_space)
    if type(generic_sample_space) == type(set()):
        return len(event) / len(generic_sample_space)

    event_size = sum(generic_sample_space[outcome]
                     for outcome in event)
    return event_size / sum(generic_sample_space.values())

event = get_event(is_heads_or_tails, weighted_ss)
event_size = sum(weighted_ss[outcome] for outcome in event)
assert event_size == 4

#Calling the events:
events = [is_heads_or_tails, is_heads, is_tails, is_neither]

for event_condition in events:
    prob = compute_weighted_probability(event_condition,
weighted_ss)
    name = event_condition.__name__
    print(f"Probability of event arising from '{name}' is
{prob}")
```

Output:

```
Probability of event arising from 'is_heads_or_tails' is 1.0
Probability of event arising from 'is_heads' is 0.75
Probability of event arising from 'is_tails' is 0.25
Probability of event arising from 'is neither' is 0.0
```

The main subject of probability theory is to develop tools and techniques to calculate probabilities of different events. Probability theory is based on some axioms that act as the foundation for the theory, so let us state and explain these axioms.

Union and Intersections

Let's revisit the topic from Chapter 2 (Sets) here.

The **union** of 2 sets A and B is denoted by **U**- $A \cup B$. This is the set of all distinct elements that are in A or B. We can define the union of a collection of sets, as the set of all distinct elements that are in any of these sets. This is used when we need to find probability of occurring A or B, example: A card is drawn from a standard deck. Find the probability of drawing a heart or a 7 (Any card of heart or 7 of any trump).

The **intersection** of 2 sets A and B is denoted by $A \cap B$. This is the set of all distinct elements that are in both A and B. We define the intersection of a collection of sets, as the set of all distinct elements that are in all of these sets. This is used when we need to find probability of occurring A and B, example: A card is drawn from a standard deck. Find the probability of drawing a heart and a 7 (7 of Heart).

Example:

IF $A=\{1,3,5,7,9\}$ **AND** $B=\{2,3,5,7,\}$, **THEN**:

$A \cup B=\{1,2,3,5,7,9\}$ $A \cap B=\{3,5,7\}$.

Independent Events

Independent events are events that don't impact the probability of the other event(s). Two events A and B are independent if knowing whether event A occurred gives no information about whether event B occurred. This is true when you, for example, draw an Ace from the deck, replace the card, shuffle the deck, and then drawing another card. The probability of drawing an Ace the first draw is the same as the second.

Events A and B are independent if:

- The probability of events A and B to occur equals the product of the probabilities of each event occurring.
- the probability of event A to occur if an event B has already occurred is equal to the probability of an event A to occur.
- The probability of an event B to occur if an event A has already occurred is the same as the probability of an event B to occur.

Events A and B (which have nonzero probability) are independent if and only if one of the following equivalent statements holds:

$$P(A \cap B)=P(A)P(B)$$
$$P(A|B)=P(A)$$
$$P(B|A)=P(B)$$

Dependent Events

Dependent events, are events that have an impact on the probability of the other event(s). For example, you draw a card from the deck and then draw a second card from the deck without replacing the first card. In this case, the probability of drawing an Ace the fist draw is not the same as the probability of drawing an Ace on the second draw. After the first card is drawn, the sample space has reduced by 1, from 52 to 51. Depending on what the card was on the first draw, the number of event outcomes may have also changed. If the card was an Ace, there are now only 3 Aces remaining for the second draw.

Multiple Events

Suppose we are playing a card game, and we will win if the next card drawn is either a heart or a king. We would be interested in finding the probability of the next card being a heart or a king. The union of two events E and F, written E∪F, is the event that occurs if either or both events occur.

$$P(E\cup F)=P(E)+P(F)-P(E\cap F)$$

To calculate the probability for multiple events, you basically determine the number of events, you then determine the probability for each event occurring separately and you multiply all of these probabilities to get your final answer:

$$P(EventA\cap EventB)=P(EventA)\times P(EventA)$$

Example: A card is drawn from a standard deck. Find the probability of drawing a heart or a 7.

A standard deck contains an equal number of hearts, diamonds, clubs, and spades. So the probability of drawing a heart is 1/4. There are four 7s in a standard deck, and there are a total of 52 cards. So the probability of drawing a 7 is 1/13.

The only card in the deck that is both a heart and a 7 is the 7 of hearts, so the probability of drawing both a heart and a 7 is 1/52.

Substitute $P(H)=1/4, P(7)=1/13, and P(H\cap 7)=1/52$ into the formula.

$$P(E\cup F)=P(E)+P(F)-P(E\cap F)=1/4+1/13-1/52=4/13$$

The probability of drawing a heart or a 7 is 4/13

Mutually Exclusive Events

When you're working with multiple events, you might also have events that are mutually exclusive or disjoint: they cannot both occur. In such cases, you might want to calculate the probability (or the union) of any of multiple mutually exclusive events occurring. In such cases, you don't multiply probabilities, but you simply add together the probability of each event occurring:

$$P(EventA \cup EventB)=P(EventA) + P(EventB)$$

It's key here to understand that the "OR" component is very important: drawing a heart OR drawing a club are two mutually exclusive events. A heart is a heart and a club is a club. To determine the probability of drawing a heart or drawing a club, add the probability of drawing a heart to the probability of drawing a club.

$$P(Heart \cup Club) = (\frac{13}{52}) + (\frac{13}{52})$$

Non-Mutually Exclusive Events

Drawing a heart or drawing an ace are two non-mutually exclusive events. The ace of hearts is both an ace and a heart. When events are not mutually exclusive, you must correct for the overlap.

$$P(EventA\cup EventB)=P(EventA)+P(EventB)-P(EventA\cup EventB$$

To calculate the probability of drawing a heart or an ace, add the probability of drawing a heart to the probability of drawing an ace and then subtract the probability of drawing the ace of hearts.

$$P(Heart \cup Ace) = (\frac{13}{52}) + (\frac{4}{52}) - (\frac{1}{52})$$

Collectively Exhaustive Events

A set of events is collectively exhaustive if they cover all of the probability space: i.e., the probability of any one of them happening is 100%. If a set of statements is collectively exhaustive we know at least one of them is true. These types of events or statements may or may not be mutually exclusive, since knowing that they cover all possibilities doesn't tell us anything about whether or not they are redundant or whether two or may events may happen at the same time.

If you are rolling a six-sided die, the set of events {1, 2, 3, 4, 5, 6} is collectively exhaustive. Any roll must be represented by one of the set.

In surveys it is important that multiple choice questions offer collectively exhaustive answer choices. For example, if a questionnaire asked if the respondent was:

a. African
b. Pacific Islander
c. Latino
d. Caucasian

An Asian respondent, for instance, would have no answer to mark. This problem can be remedied if care is taken that every possible category is included, or, in cases where that is impractical, an 'other' option is included. Since 'other' includes everything but previously listed choices, questions with an 'other' option added immediately meet this criteria.

Complementary Events

Two events are said to be complementary when one event occurs if and only if the other does not. The probabilities of two complimentary events add up to 1. For example, rolling a 5 or greater and rolling a 4 or less on a die are complementary events, because a roll is 5 or greater if and only if it is not 4 or less.

Counting the Possibilities

The calculating of possible outcomes is a process for determining the number of possible results for an event. There are various methods for conducting this process. The best way to calculate the number of possible outcomes of an event is dependent on the type of event and the structure of the event. A simple example can be found in sports. In any cricket game, there are two possible outcomes: Team A wins or Team B wins. However, a possibility problem can be much more complex than determining the number of possible winners of an athletic competition between two teams. We will look at 3 possibilities here.

mn rule

Let's say that we want to order an ice cream cone from a local ice cream shop. The shop offers four flavors of ice cream (vanilla, chocolate, pistachio, and mint) and two types of cones (regular and cinnamon). We need to determine how many different types of ice cream cones we can order. There are four possibilities from just choosing an ice cream flavor. Once we choose an ice cream flavor, we need to choose a cone. There are two possible cones to choose from, so there are two possible combinations with each flavor. Therefore, the possible number of ice cream cones is 4 x 2 = 8.

This is called fundamental counting principle. This principle states that if there are p possibilities for one event and q possibilities for a second event, then the number of possibilities for both events is p x q. We can add additional events to this formula. Let's say that we can also choose a topping for our ice cream cone from among three choices of toppings. Then the possible number of ice cream cones is 4 x 2 x 3 = 24.

Sampling from a Population with Replacement

If a die is rolled three times in succession, how many different outcomes can occur? The size of the population, N, is 6 – the size sides of the die. We are sampling three dice rolss, n = 3. The sample space is:

$$N^n = 6^3 = 216$$

We see that, sampling n items from a population of size N with replacement would provide:

$$(N)^n \text{ possibilities}$$

Combinations: Sampling from a Population with Replacement

Third methdod is combination, sampling n items from a population of size N without replacement provides:

$$\binom{n}{k} = \frac{n!}{k!(n-k)!}$$

A certain lottery has a hat with the numbers 1 through 10 each written on a single scrap of paper. Three numbers are successively pulled from the hat and set aside in no particular order. If a player can pick four numbers, what is the probability that he wins the lottery?

Sample space: We know that the numbers are not replaced after they are chosen and that the order of the selection is not important; thus, the winning lottery numbers are three unique numbers.

$$\binom{10}{4} = \frac{10!}{4!(10-4)!} = \frac{10!}{4!6!} = \frac{10\cdot 9\cdot 8\cdot 7}{4\cdot 3\cdot 2\cdot 1} = \frac{5040}{24} = 210$$

Apart from the three winning numbers, there are seven other numbers that can be chosen for the fourth number. As a result, the player has seven possible winning combinations.

The probability P of the player winning is thus: $P = \frac{7}{210} = \frac{1}{30}$

FOUR TYPE OF PROBABILITY: MARGINAL, UNION, JOINT. CONDITIONAL

Marginal	Union	Joint	Conditional
$P(X)$	$P(X \cup Y)$	$P(X \cap Y)$	$P(X \mid Y)$
The probability of X occurring	The probability of X or Y occurring	The probability of X and Y occurring	The probability of X occurring given that Y has occurred
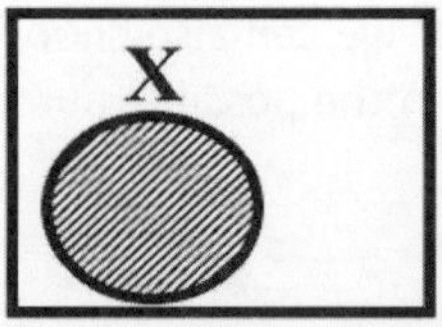	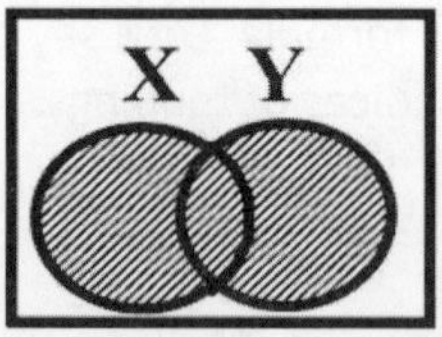	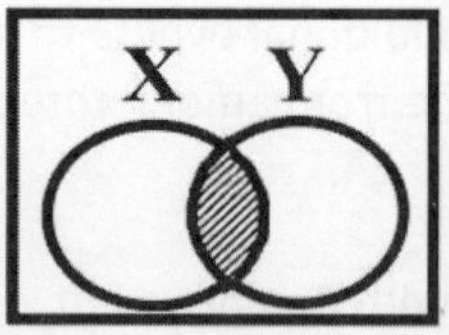	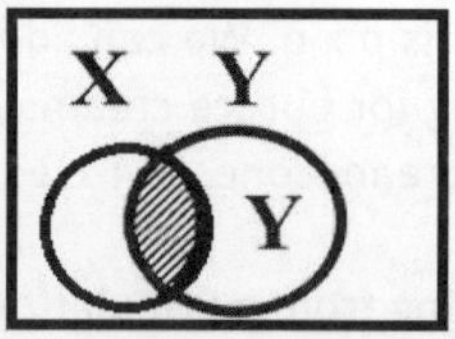

Probability quantifies the uncertainty of the outcomes of a random variable. It is relatively easy to understand and compute the probability for a single variable. Nevertheless, in machine learning, we often have many random variables that interact in often complex and unknown ways. There are specific techniques that can be used to quantify the probability for multiple random variables, such as the joint, marginal, and conditional probability. These techniques provide the basis for a probabilistic understanding of fitting a predictive model to data.

Marginal probability: the probability of an event occurring (p(A)), it may be thought of as an unconditional probability. It is not conditioned on another event. Example: the probability that a card drawn is red (p(red) = 0.5). Another example: the probability that a card drawn is a 4 (p(four)=1/13).

Union of two events: p(A or B). The probability of event A or event B occurring. It is the probability of the union of two or more events. The probability of the union of A and B may be written p(A U B). Example: the probability that a card is a four or red =p(four or red) = 4/52+ 26/52 = 30/52=15/26. (There are four fours in a deck of 52, 26 red cards).

Joint probability: p(A and B). The probability of event A and event B occurring. It is the probability of the intersection of two or more events. The probability of the intersection of A and B may be written p(A ∩ B). Example: the probability that a card is a four and red =p(four and red) = 4/52* 26/52 = 2/52=1/26. (There are two red fours in a deck of 52, the 4 of hearts and the 4 of diamonds).

Conditional probability: p(A|B) is the probability of event A occurring, given that event B occurs. Example: given that you drew a red card, what's the probability that it's a four (p(four|red))=2/26=1/13. So out of the 26 red cards (given a red card), there are two fours so 2/26=1/13.

Addition Laws

When two events, A and B, are non-mutually exclusive, there is some overlap between these events. The probability that A or B will occur is the sum of the probability of each event, minus the probability of the overlap.

$$P(A \text{ or } B) = P(A) + P(B) - P(A \text{ and } B)$$

Experiment: A single 6-sided die is rolled. What is the probability of rolling a 2 or a 5?
Possibilities:
1. The number rolled can be a 2.
2. The number rolled can be a 5.

Events: These events are mutually exclusive since they cannot occur at the same time.
Probabilities: How do we find the probabilities of these mutually exclusive events? We need a rule to guide us.

Addition Rule 1: When two events, A and B, are mutually exclusive, the probability that A or B will occur is the sum of the probability of each event.

$$P(A \text{ or } B) = P(A) + P(B)$$

Probabilities:
P(2) = 1/6
P(5) = 1/6

P(2 or 5) = P(2) + P(5): 1/6 + 1/6 = 1/3 = 0.33

Multiplication Laws

The multiplication rule states that: "The probability of occurrence of given two events or in other words the probability of intersection of two given events is equal to the product obtained by finding the product of the probability of occurrence of both events."

P (A and B) = P (A ∩∩ B) = P (A) * P (B)

Experiment: A bag contains 3 pink candies and 7 green candies. Two candies are taken out from the bag with replacement. Find the probability that both candies are pink.
Let A = event that first candy is pink and B = event that second candy is pink.

P (A) = 3/10

Since the candies are taken out with replacement, this implies that the given events A and B are independent.

P (B|A) = P (B) = 3/10

Hence by the multiplication law we get, P (A ∩ B) = P (A) * P (B|A)
P (A ∩ B) = 3/10 * 3/10

CONDITIONAL PROBABILITY

In probability theory, conditional probability is a measure of the probability of an event occurring given that another event has (by assumption, presumption, assertion or evidence) occurred.

Translation: given B is true, what is the probability that A is also true.

It's easier to understand something with concrete examples. Below are a few random examples of conditional probabilities we could calculate.
Examples:

- Event A is that it is raining outside, and it has a 0.3 (30%) chance of raining today.
- Event B is that you will need to go outside, and that has a probability of 0.5 (50%).

The formula for conditional probability is P(A|B) = P(A ∩ B) / P(B).

$$P(\mathrm{A} \mid \mathrm{B}) = \frac{P(\mathrm{A\ and\ B})}{P(\mathrm{B})}$$

- P(A|B) = probability of A occurring, given B occurs
- P(A ∩ B) = probability of both A and B occurring
- P(B) = probability of B occurring

| means "given". Meaning "in cases where something else occurs".
∩ means intersection which you can think of as and, or the overlap in the context of a Venn diagram:

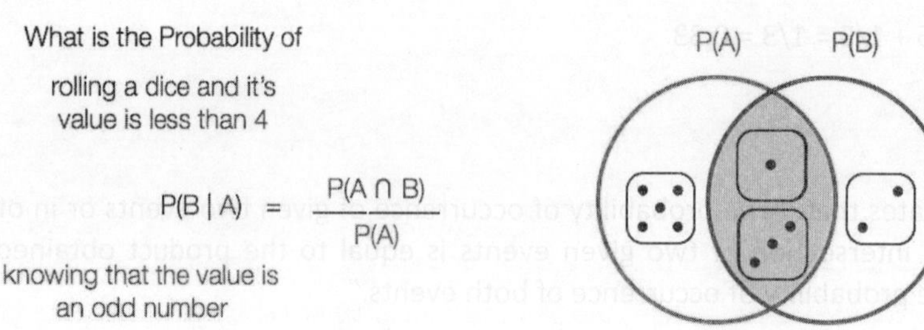

Example with Python: Calculate the probability a student gets an A (80%+) in math, given they miss 10 or more classes.

We will use student.csv dataset for this.

```
import pandas as pd
df =
pd.read_csv('https://raw.githubusercontent.com/swapnilsaurav/Da
taset/master/student.csv')
print(df.head(3))
```

Output:

```
  school sex  age address famsize Pstatus  ...  Walc  health absences G1 G2  G3
0     GP   F   18       U     GT3       A  ...     1       3        6  5  6   6
1     GP   F   17       U     GT3       T  ...     1       3        4  5  5   6
2     GP   F   15       U     LE3       T  ...     3       3       10  7  8  10

[3 rows x 33 columns]
```

We're only concerned with the columns, absences (number of absences), and G3 (final grade). Let's create a couple new boolean columns based on these columns. Add a boolean column called grade_A noting if a student achieved 80% or higher as a final score. Original values are on a 0–20 scale so we multiply by 5.

Make another boolean column called high_absenses with a value of 1 if a student missed 10 or more classes. Add one more column to make building a pivot table easier.

```
import numpy as np
df['grade_A'] = np.where(df['G3']*5 >= 80, 1, 0)
df['high_absenses'] = np.where(df['absences'] >= 10, 1, 0)
df['count'] = 1
#drop all columns we don't need
df = df[['grade_A','high_absenses','count']]
print(df.head())
```

Output:

```
   grade_A  high_absenses  count
0        0              0      1
1        0              0      1
2        0              1      1
3        0              0      1
4        0              0      1
```

Last step: We'll create a pivot table from this.

```
#Pivot table
print(
pd.pivot_table(
    df,
    values='count',
    index=['grade_A'],
    columns=['high_absenses'],
    aggfunc=np.size,
    fill_value=0
))
```

Output:

```
high_absenses      0    1
grade_A
0                277   78
1                 35    5
```

Above information from Pivot table can also be represented by a 2X2 matrix: as:

grade_A \ high_absenses	0	1
0	277	78
1	35	5

This can be translated into probability matrix, as:

grade_A \ high_absenses	0	1
0	0.70	0.20
1	0.09	0.01

If you add up all the probabilities from the 4 squares, it will total upto 1.

We now have all the data we need to do our calculation. Let's start by calculating each individual part in the formula.
In our case:

- P(A) is the probability of a grade of 80% or greater.
- P(B) is the probability of missing 10 or more classes.
- P(A|B) is the probability of a 80%+ grade, given missing 10 or more classes.

Manually calculating of parts:
P(A) = (35 + 5) / (35 + 5 + 277 + 78) = 0.1013
P(B) = (78 + 5) / (35 + 5 + 277 + 78) = 0.2101
P(A ∩ B) = 5 / (35 + 5 + 277 + 78) = 0.01266

Solution:
Per the formula, P(A|B) = P(A ∩ B) / P(B), put it together.
P(A|B) = 0.012658227848101266/ 0.21012658227848102= 0.06
There we have it. The probability of getting at least an 80% final grade, given missing 10 or more classes is 6%.

Using Python:

```
#Calculations
sample_space = len(df)
print("Sample Space: ", sample_space)
#Probability A: grade_A value is 1
a = len(df[(df['grade_A']>0)])
prob_a = a/sample_space
print("Probability of grade of 80% or greater: ",prob_a)
#Probability B: high_absenses is 1
b = len(df[(df['high_absenses']>0)])
prob_b = b/sample_space
print("Probability of missing 10 or more classes: ",prob_b)
#Probability (A and B): where grade and high_absenses =1
ab = len(df[(df['grade_A']>0) & (df['high_absenses']>0)])
prob_ab = ab/sample_space
print("Probability of a 80%+ grade, given missing 10 or more 
classes: ",prob_ab)

#Conditional probability solution:
prob_aIb = prob_ab / prob_b
print("Probability of getting at least an 80% final grade, "
      "given missing 10 or more classes is: ",prob_aIb, " or 
{:.0f}%".format(prob_aIb*100))
```

Output:

```
Sample Space:  395
Probability of grade of 80% or greater:  0.10126582278481013
Probability of missing 10 or more classes:  0.21012658227848102
Probability of a 80%+ grade, given missing 10 or more classes:  0.012658227848101266
Probability of getting at least an 80% final grade, given missing 10 or more classes is:  0.060240963855421686  or 6%
```

An understanding Conditional Probability is essential before diving into probability estimations using Bayes' theorem. Now that we know what conditional probability is, lets dive into Bayes rule.

BAYES' RULE

Bayes' rule (alternatively Bayes's theorem, Bayes's law or Bayes's rule) describes the probability of an event, based on prior knowledge of conditions that might be related to the event. For example, if the risk of developing health problems is known to increase with age, Bayes's theorem allows the risk to an individual of a known age to be assessed more accurately than simply assuming that the individual is typical of the population as a whole.

One of the many applications of Bayes's theorem is Bayesian inference, a particular approach to statistical inference. When applied, the probabilities involved in Bayes' theorem may have different probability interpretations. With Bayesian probability interpretation, the theorem expresses how a degree of belief, expressed as a probability, should rationally change to account for the availability of related evidence. Bayesian inference is fundamental to Bayesian statistics. Bayes's theorem "is to the theory of probability what the Pythagorean theorem is to geometry."

Bayes's theorem is stated mathematically as the following equation:

$$P(A \mid B) = \frac{P(B \mid A)P(A)}{P(B)}$$

where A and B are events and $P(B) \neq 0$.

- $P(A \mid B)$ is a conditional probability: the likelihood of event A occurring given that B is true.
- $P(B \mid A)$ is also a conditional probability: the likelihood of event B occurring given that A is true.
- $P(A)$ and $P(B)$ are the probabilities of observing A and B respectively; they are known as the marginal probability.

Let's look at the 2 questions below:

1. A couple has 2 children and the older child is a boy. If the probabilities of having a boy or a girl are both 50%, what's the probability that the couple has two boys? We already know that the older child is a boy. The probability of two boys is equivalent to the probability that the younger child is a boy, which is 50%.
2. A couple has two children, of which at least one is a boy. If the probabilities of having a boy or a girl are both 50%, what is the probability that the couple has two boys?

At first glance, question 2 appears to be asking the same question as question 1. But that's not correct. Let understand this:

- A couple has two children, the older of which is a boy. What is the probability that they have two boys?
- A couple has two children, one of which is a boy. What is the probability that they have two boys?

Define three events, A, B, and C, as follows:

A= both children are boys
B= the older child is a boy
C= one of their children is a boy

Question 1 is asking for P(A|B), and Question 2 is asking for P(A|C). The first is computed using the simpler version of Bayes' theorem:

P(A|B)= (P(A) * P(B|A)) / P(B) = (1/4 * 1) / (1/2) = 1/2 = 0.5

To, let's turn our attention to question 2. To find P(A|C), we must determine P(C), the prior probability that the couple has at least one boy. This is equal to 1 - P(both children are girls) = 1 - (1/2 * 1/2) = ¾ = 0.75

Therefore the desired probability is:

P(A|C)= (P(A) * P(C|A)) / P(C) = (1/4 * 1) / (3/4) = 1/3 = 0.3333

Let's take a break and look at couple of brain teasers based on probability:

1. Monty Hall Problem

The Monty Hall problem is loosely based on the American television game show "Let's Make a Deal" and named after its original host, Monty Hall. Indian version of the game show was named as "Khullja Sim Sim", first telecasted by Star Plus (2001–04) hosted by Aman Verma and then on BIG Magic (2012–13) hosted by Hussain Kuwajerwala. Back to our problem, it was originally posed (and solved) in a letter by Steve Selvin to the American Statistician in 1975. It became famous as a question from a reader's letter quoted in Marilyn vos Savant's "Ask Marilyn" column in Parade magazine in 1990

Problem:
Suppose you're on a game show, and you're given the choice of three doors: Behind one door is a car; behind the others, goats. You pick a door, say No. 1, and the host, who knows what's behind the doors, opens another door, say No. 3, which has a goat. He then says to you, "Do you want to pick door No. 2?" Is it to your advantage to switch your choice?

Assumptions:

- The host must always open a door that was not picked by the contestant (Mueser and Granberg 1999).
- The host must always open a door to reveal a goat and never the car.
- The host must always offer the chance to switch between the originally chosen door and the remaining closed door.

Answer is: Yes, you should switch to the other door. A key insight is that, under these standard conditions, there is more information about doors 2 and 3 than was available at the beginning of the game when door 1 was chosen by the player. Another insight is that switching doors is a different action than choosing between the two remaining doors at random, as the first action uses the previous information and the latter does not.

Simple solution:
Three initial configurations of the game. In two of them, the player wins by switching away from the choice made before a door was opened.
The solution presented by vos Savant (1990b) in Parade shows the three possible arrangements of one car and two goats behind three doors and the result of staying or switching after initially picking door 1 in each case:

Behind door 1	Behind door 2	Behind door 3	Result if staying at door #1	Result if switching to the door offered
Goat	Goat	**Car**	Wins goat	**WINS Car**
Goat	**Car**	Goat	Wins goat	**WINS Car**
Car	Goat	Goat	**WINS Car**	Wins goat

Under the standard assumptions, contestants who switch have a 2/3 chance of winning the car, while contestants who stick to their initial choice have only a 1/3 chance.
Most people come to the conclusion that switching does not matter because there are two unopened doors and one car and that it is a 50/50 choice. This would be true if the host opens a door randomly, but that is not the case; the door opened depends on the player's initial choice, so the assumption of independence does not hold. Before the host opens a door there is a 1/3 probability the car is behind each door.

2. Three Prisoners Problem

The Three Prisoners problem appeared in Martin Gardner's "Mathematical Games" column in Scientific American in 1959. It is mathematically equivalent to the Monty Hall problem with car and goat replaced with freedom and execution, respectively.

Problem:
Three prisoners, A, B, and C, are in separate cells and sentenced to death. The governor has selected one of them at random to be pardoned. The warden knows which one is pardoned, but is not allowed to tell. Prisoner A begs the warden to let him know the identity of one of the two who are going to be executed. "If B is to be pardoned, give me C's name. If C is to be pardoned, give me B's name. And if I'm to be pardoned, secretly flip a coin to decide whether to name B or C."

The warden tells A that B is to be executed. Prisoner A is pleased because he believes that his probability of surviving has gone up from 1/3 to 1/2, as it is now between him and C. Prisoner A secretly tells C the news, who reasons that A's chance of being pardoned is unchanged at 1/3, but he is pleased because his own chance has gone up to 2/3. Which prisoner is correct?

Solution:
The answer is that prisoner A did not gain any information about his own fate, since he already knew that the warden would give him the name of someone else. Prisoner A, prior to hearing from the warden, estimates his chances of being pardoned as 1/3, the same as both B and C. As the warden says B will be executed, it is either because C will be pardoned (1/3 chance), or A will be pardoned (1/3 chance) and the B/C coin the warden flipped came up B (1/2 chance; for an overall 1/2*1/3=1/6 chance B was named because A will be pardoned). Hence, after hearing that B will be executed, the estimate of A's chance of being pardoned is half that of C. This means his chances of being pardoned, now knowing B is not, again are 1/3, but C has a 2/3 chance of being pardoned.

Being pardoned	Warden: "not B"	Warden: "not C"	Sum
A	**1/6**	1/6	1/3
B	**0**	1/3	1/3
C	**1/3**	0	1/3

As the warden has answered that B will not be pardoned, the solution comes from the second column "not B". It appears that the odds for A vs. C to be pardoned are 1:2

Back to our learning. Let's see how we can solve such problems using Bayes' theorem.

Example: Thomas wants to get a new puppy
Conditions:

- He can choose to get his new puppy either from the pet store or the shelter home. The probability of him going to the pet store is 0.2.
- He can choose to get either a big, medium or small puppy.
- If he goes to the pet store, the probability of him getting a small puppy is 0.6. The probability of him getting a medium puppy is 0.3, and the probability of him getting a large puppy is 0.1.
- If he goes to the shelter, the probability of him getting a small puppy is 0.1. The probability of him getting a medium puppy is 0.35, and the probability of him getting a large puppy is 0.55.

Problem:

1. What is the probability of Thomas getting a small puppy?
2. Given that he got a large puppy, what is the probability that Thomas went to the pet store?
3. Given that Thomas got a small puppy, is it more likely that he went to the pet store or to the pound?

First we will solve by building a tree, this will also help us in understanding the problem better.

Given problem:

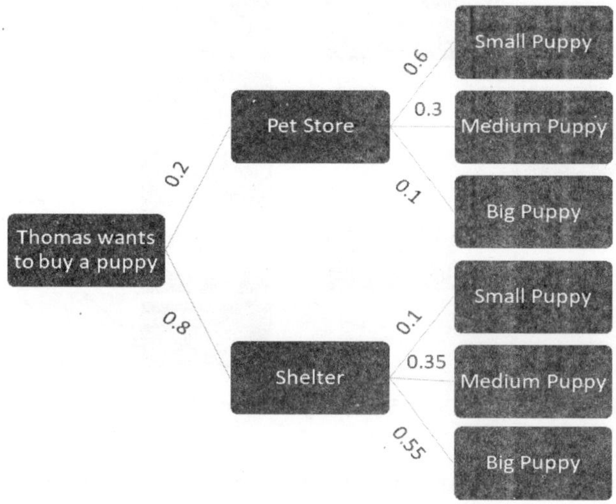

Q1. Probability of Thomas getting a small puppy:

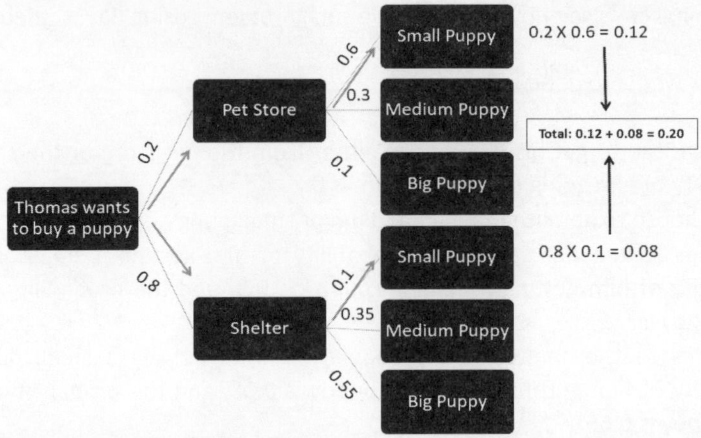

We found the probability of all possible Small Puppy purchases by taking the probability of Shelter or Pet Store, then multiplying it with the probability of buying a Small Puppy. Then we added those together to the answer to the probability of Thomas buying a Small Puppy!

Q2. Given that he got a large puppy, what is the probability that Thomas went to the pet store? Using Bayes rule formula,

$$P(\text{Pet Store}|\text{Large}) = \frac{P(\text{Large}|\text{Pet Store})*P(\text{Pet Store})}{P(\text{Large})}$$

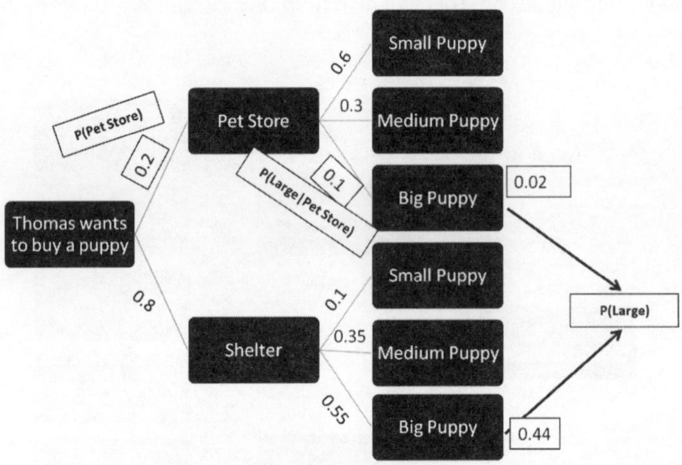

$$P(\text{Pet Store}|\text{Large}) = \frac{.10*.20}{.46}$$

Q3. Given that Thomas got a small puppy, is it more likely that he went to the pet store or to the shelter?

To answer this question, given Small Puppy, we need to find which is higher, P(Pet Store|Small Puppy) or P(Shelter | Small Puppy). To simplify things, let's look at the variables we need:

For the P(Pet Store | Small Puppy):

- P(Small Puppy| Pet Store) = .60
- P(Pet Store) = .20

- P(Small Puppy) = .20

Now plug those into Bayes' Theorem and see what numbers we get:
P(Pet Store | Small Puppy) = P(Small Puppy| Pet Store) * P(Pet Store) / P(Small Puppy)
= 0.60 * 0.20 / 0.20 = 0.60

For the P(Shelter | Small Puppy):

- P(Small Puppy | Shelter) = .10
- P(Shelter) = .80
- P(Small Puppy) = .20

Now plug those into Bayes' Theorem and see what numbers we get:
P(Shelter | Small Puppy) = P(Small Puppy | Shelter) * P(Shelter) / P(Small Puppy)
= 0.10 * 0.80 /0.20 = 0 .40

Since P(Pet Store|Small Puppy) is larger than P(Shelter|Small Puppy), given that Thomas got himself a Small Puppy, it is more likely that Thomas went to a Pet Store to get his Puppy!

Problem: Cancer Rate

Even if 100% of patients with pancreatic cancer have a certain symptom, when someone has the same symptom, it does not mean that this person has a 100% chance of getting pancreatic cancer. Assume the incidence rate of pancreatic cancer is 1/100000, while 1/10000 healthy individuals have the same symptoms worldwide, the probability of having pancreatic cancer given the symptoms is only 9.1%, and the other 90.9% could be "false positives" (that is, falsely say you have cancer; "positive" is a confusing term when, as here, the test tells you bad news).

Based on incidence rate, the following table presents the corresponding numbers per 100,000 people.

Cancer / Symptom	Yes	No	Total
Yes	1	10	11
No	0	99989	99989
Total	1	99999	100000

which can then be used to calculate the probability of having cancer when you have the symptoms:

$$\begin{aligned} P(\text{Cancer}|\text{Symptoms}) &= \frac{P(\text{Symptoms}|\text{Cancer})P(\text{Cancer})}{P(\text{Symptoms})} \\ &= \frac{P(\text{Symptoms}|\text{Cancer})P(\text{Cancer})}{P(\text{Symptoms}|\text{Cancer})P(\text{Cancer}) + P(\text{Symptoms}|\text{Non-Cancer})P(\text{Non-Cancer})} \\ &= \frac{1 \times 0.00001}{1 \times 0.00001 + (10/99999) \times 0.99999} = \frac{1}{11} \approx 9.1\% \end{aligned}$$

Problem: Factory Production

A factory produces an item using three machines—A, B, and C—which account for 20%, 30%, and 50% of its output, respectively. Of the items produced by machine A, 5% are defective; similarly, 3% of machine B's items and 1% of machine C's are defective. If a randomly selected item is defective, what is the probability it was produced by machine C?

Condition / Machine	Defective	Flawless	Total
A	10	190	200
B	9	291	300
C	5	495	500
Total	24	976	1000

Once again, the answer can be reached without using the formula by applying the conditions to a hypothetical number of cases. For example, if the factory produces 1,000 items, 200 will be produced by Machine A, 300 by Machine B, and 500 by Machine C. Machine A will produce 5% × 200 = 10 defective items, Machine B 3% × 300 = 9, and Machine C 1% × 500 = 5, for a total of 24. Thus, the likelihood that a randomly selected defective item was produced by machine C is 5/24 (~20.83%).

This problem can also be solved using Bayes' Theorem: Let Xi denote the event that a randomly chosen item was made by the i th machine (for i = A,B,C). Let Y denote the event that a randomly chosen item is defective. Then, we are given the following information:

$$P(X_A) = 0.2, \quad P(X_B) = 0.3, \quad P(X_C) = 0.5.$$

If the item was made by the first machine, then the probability that it is defective is 0.05; that is, P(Y | XA) = 0.05. Overall, we have:

$$P(Y|X_A) = 0.05, \quad P(Y|X_B) = 0.03, \quad P(Y|X_C) = 0.01.$$

To answer the original question, we first find P(Y). That can be done in the following way:

$$P(Y) = \sum_i P(Y|X_i)P(X_i) = (0.05)(0.2) + (0.03)(0.3) + (0.01)(0.5) = 0.024.$$

Hence, 2.4% of the total output is defective.

We are given that Y has occurred, and we want to calculate the conditional probability of XC. By Bayes' theorem,

$$P(X_C|Y) = \frac{P(Y|X_C)P(X_C)}{P(Y)} = \frac{0.01 \cdot 0.50}{0.024} = \frac{5}{24}$$

Given that the item is defective, the probability that it was made by machine C is 5/24. Although machine C produces half of the total output, it produces a much smaller fraction of the defective items. Hence the knowledge that the item selected was defective enables us to replace the prior probability P(XC) = 1/2 by the smaller posterior probability P(XC | Y) = 5/24.

Solving Monty Hall Problem using Python: Lets do some programming

Program 1: Playing one time

```
import random
#There are 3 doors, one has car
doors = ['car', 'goat', 'goat']

#use shuffle function to randomly select one door
```

```
random.shuffle(doors)
print("Order of doors: ",doors)

# we chose a door at random
select_index = random.choice([0, 1, 2])
print("Selected Door Index is: ",select_index)

#result of staying with our original choice,
# and remove that option from the list
stay_result = doors.pop(select_index)
print("Known to Monty but unknown to Player, Door has: 
",stay_result)

#We are left with the two doors that Monty has to choose from
print("Doors Monty has to choose from: ", doors)

#Now, lets remove the first goat value
doors.remove('goat')

#Now we have only one remaining door.
# The item behind that door is the result
# from switching from our original door.
switch_result = doors[0]
print("If switched, would have won a ",switch_result)
```

Output:

```
Order of doors:  ['goat', 'car', 'goat']
Selected Door Index is:  2
Known to Monty but unknown to Player, Door has:  goat
Doors Monty has to choose from:  ['goat', 'car']
If switched, would have won a  car
```

Now, we will run this same experiement for more 100,000 times and verify if our analysis of winning chances increases by double if the player choose to switch is also proved by the python program.

```
import random
n_trials = 100000
#declare a list to capture the original choice
stay_results = []
#declare a list to capture the switch choice
switch_results = []

for i in range(n_trials):
    #There are 3 doors, one has car
    doors = ['car', 'goat', 'goat']
```

```
    #use shuffle function to randomly select one door
    random.shuffle(doors)

    # we chose a door at random
    select_index = random.choice([0, 1, 2])

    #result of staying with our original choice,
    # and remove that option from the list
    stay_result = doors.pop(select_index)

    #We are left with the two doors that Monty has to choose
from

    #Now, lets remove the first goat value
    doors.remove('goat')

    #Now we have only one remaining door.
    # The item behind that door is the result
    # from switching from our original door.
    switch_result = doors[0]

    # Put results into result lists
    stay_results.append(stay_result)
    switch_results.append(switch_result)

#After 100,000 runs are done
#count method of the list to count the number of "car" element
#  in each list, and divide by the length of the list,
# to get the proportion of successes.
prob_stay = stay_results.count('car') / n_trials
prob_switch = switch_results.count('car') / n_trials

print("Probability of winning car with staying with original
decision: ", prob_stay)
print("Probability of winning car with switching the original
decision: ", prob_switch)
```

Output:

```
Probability of winning car with staying with original decision:  0.33356
Probability of winning car with switching the original decision:  0.66644
```

***

UNIT 5: DISCRETE PROBABILITY DISTRIBUTION

A probability distribution is the mathematical function that gives the probabilities of occurrence of different possible outcomes for an experiment. It is a mathematical description of a random phenomenon in terms of its sample space and the probabilities of events (subsets of the sample space).

A probability distribution describes how the values of a random variable is distributed. For example, the collection of all possible outcomes of a sequence of coin tossing is known to follow the binomial distribution. Whereas the means of sufficiently large samples of a data population are known to resemble the normal distribution. Since the characteristics of these theoretical distributions are well understood, they can be used to make statistical inferences on the entire data population as a whole.

For instance, if the random variable X is used to denote the outcome of a coin toss ("the experiment"), then the probability distribution of X would take the value 0.5 for X = heads, and 0.5 for X = tails (assuming the coin is fair). Examples of random phenomena include the weather condition in a future date, the height of a person, the fraction of male students in a school, the results of a survey, etc.

A probability distribution is a mathematical function that has a sample space as its input, and gives a probability as its output. The sample space is the set of all possible outcomes of a random phenomenon being observed; it may be the set of real numbers or a set of vectors, or it may be a list of non-numerical values. For example, the sample space of a coin flip would be {heads, tails} .

Probability distributions are generally divided into two classes. A discrete probability distribution is applicable to the scenarios where the set of possible outcomes is discrete (e.g. a coin toss or the roll of a dice), and the probabilities are here encoded by a discrete list of the probabilities of the outcomes, known as the probability mass function. On the other hand, continuous probability distributions are applicable to scenarios where the set of possible outcomes can take on values in a continuous range (e.g. real numbers), such as the temperature on a given day. In this case, probabilities are typically described by a probability density function.[4][5] The normal distribution is a commonly encountered continuous probability distribution. More complex experiments, such as those involving stochastic processes defined in continuous time, may demand the use of more general probability measures.

A probability distribution whose sample space is one-dimensional (for example real numbers, list of labels, ordered labels or binary) is called univariate, while a distribution whose sample space is a vector space of dimension 2 or more is called multivariate. A univariate distribution gives the probabilities of a single random variable taking on various alternative values; a multivariate distribution (a joint probability distribution) gives the probabilities of a random vector – a list of two or more random variables – taking on various combinations of values. Important and commonly encountered univariate probability distributions include the binomial distribution, the hypergeometric distribution, and the normal distribution. The multivariate normal distribution is a commonly encountered multivariate distribution.

Functions for discrete variables

- Probability function: describes the probability distribution of a discrete random variable.
- Probability mass function (pmf): function that gives the probability that a discrete random variable is equal to some value.
- Frequency distribution: a table that displays the frequency of various outcomes in a sample.
- Relative frequency distribution: a frequency distribution where each value has been divided (normalized) by a number of outcomes in a sample i.e. sample size.
- Discrete probability distribution function: general term to indicate the way the total probability of 1 is distributed over all various possible outcomes (i.e. over entire population) for discrete random variable.
- Cumulative distribution function: function evaluating the probability that X will take a value less than or equal to x for a discrete random variable.
- Categorical distribution: for discrete random variables with a finite set of values.

MEANING OF PROBABILITY DISTRIBUTION

- If we want to predict a variable accurately then the first task we need to perform is to understand the underlying behaviour of our target variable.
- What we need to do first is to determine the possible outcomes of the target variable and if the underlying outcomes are discrete (distinct values) or continuous (infinite values). For the sake of simplicity, if we are estimating the behaviour of a dice then the first step would be to consider that it can take any value from 1 to 6 (discrete).
- Then the next step would be to start assigning probabilities to the events (values). Consequently, if a value cannot occur then it is assigned a probability of 0%. If an event always occurs then it gets a probability of 100%. If you add all of the probabilities then it will sum up to 100%.
- As an instance, we can start repeating an experiment for a large number of times and start noting the values we retrieve for the variable.
- Now what we can do is to group the values into categories/buckets. And for each bucket, we can start recording the number of times the variable had the value of the bucket. For example, we can throw a dice 10000 times and can create 6 buckets as there are 6 possible values that a dice can take. After every throw, we can record the number of occurrences for each value.
- We can then plot a line-chart where the x-values would the values of the bucket and the y-axis values would represent the occurance of the bucket value. We will notice that it forms the shape of a curve. This curve is known as the probability distribution curve and the likelihood of the target variable getting a value is the probability distribution of the variable.
- Once we understand how the values are distributed then we can start estimating the probabilities of the events, even by the means of using formulas (known as probability distribution functions). As a consequence, we can start understanding the behaviour of our target variables better. The probability distribution is dependent on the moments of the sample such as mean, standard deviation, skewness, and/or kurtosis.

DISCRETE VERSUS CONTINOUS DISTRIBUTIONS

To define probability distributions for the simplest cases, it is necessary to distinguish between discrete and continuous random variables. In the discrete case, it is sufficient to specify a probability mass function p assigning a probability to each possible outcome: for example, when throwing a fair die, each of the six values 1 to 6 has the probability 1/6.

$$P(x=1)=P(x=2)=P(x=3)=P(x=4)=P(x=5)=P(x=6) = 1/6$$

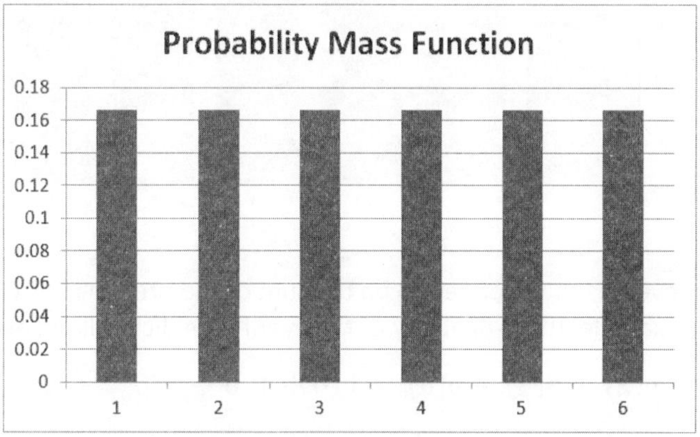

This distribution shows the same probability for each value: it is called the uniform distribution. Let's simulate this using python program:

```
import numpy as np
import matplotlib.pyplot as plt
#100000 trials we will make
num_throws = 100000
outcomes = []
for i in range(num_throws):
    # let's roll the die
    outcome = np.random.choice(['1', '2', '3', '4', '5', '6'])
    outcomes.append(outcome)

val, cnt = np.unique(outcomes, return_counts=True)
prop = cnt / len(outcomes)

# Now that we have rolled our die 10000 times,
# let's plot the results
plt.bar(val, prop)
plt.ylabel("Probability")
plt.xlabel("Outcome")
plt.show()
plt.close()
```

Output:

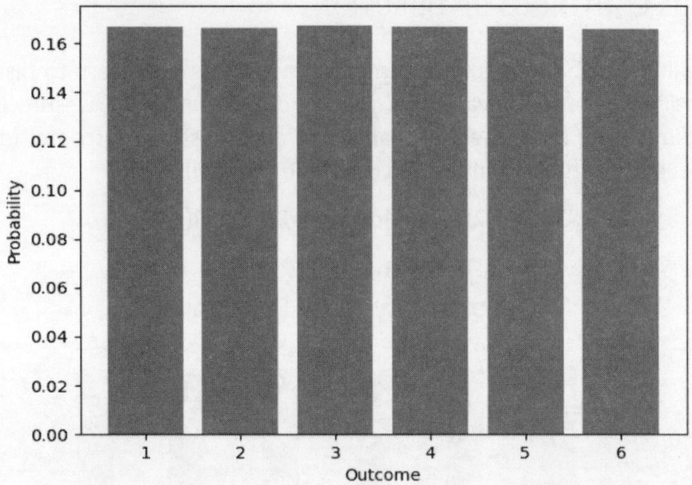

The probability of an event is then defined to be the sum of the probabilities of the outcomes that satisfy the event; for example, the probability of the event "the dice rolls an even value" is:

$$p(2) + p(4) + p(6) = 1/6 + 1/6 + 1/6 = 1/2.$$

Let's modify the above program to make measure the probability of even values:

```
outcomes_even = []
for i in range(num_throws):
    # let's roll the die
    outcome = np.random.choice(['1', '2', '3', '4', '5', '6'])
    if outcome =='2' or outcome =='4' or outcome =='6':
        outcomes_even.append("Even")
    else:
        outcomes_even.append("Odd")

#For plotting Even and Odd numbers
val, cnt = np.unique(outcomes_even, return_counts=True)
prop = cnt / len(outcomes_even)

# Now that we have rolled our die 10000 times,
# let's plot the results
plt.bar(val, prop)
plt.ylabel("Probability")
plt.xlabel("outcomes_even")
plt.show()
plt.close()
```

Output:

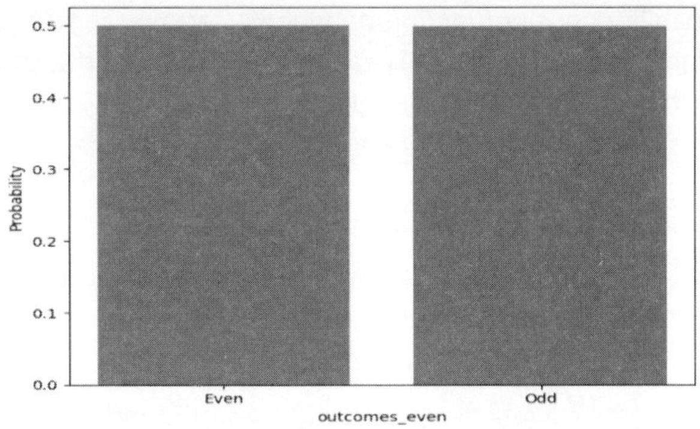

Some variables are not discrete. They can take an infinite number of values in a certain range. But we still need to describe the probability associated with outcomes, like height of Indian citizens, weight of Canadian citizens, etc. The equivalent of the probability mass function for a continuous variable is called the probability density function.

In the case of the probability mass function, we saw that the y-axis gives a probability. For instance, dice thrown once, the probability to get a [3] was equal to 1/6≈0.16 (check on the plot above). It is 1/6 because it is one possibility over 6 total possibilities.

However, we can't do this for continuous variables because the total number of possibilities is infinite. For instance, if we draw a number between 0 and 1, we have an infinite number of possible outcomes (for instance 0.320502304...). In the example above, we had 6 possible outcomes, leading to probabilities around 1/6. Now, we have each probability equal to 1/+∞≈0. Such a function would not be very useful.

For that reason, the y-axis of the probability density function doesn't represent probability values. To get the probability, we need to calculate the area under the curve. The advantage is that it leads to the probabilities according to a certain range (on the x-axis): the area under the curve increases if the range increases. Let's see a plot below:

Example: Let's say that we have a random variable x that can take values between 0 and 1. Here is its probability density function:

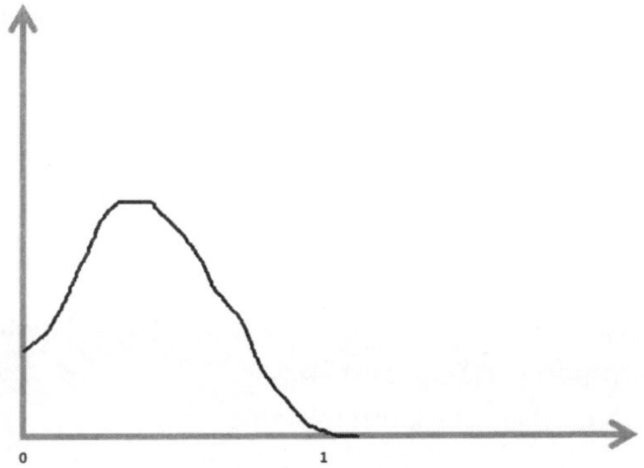

Probability at any given point will be zero. We need to find probability for a region. Finding probabilities from probability density function between a certain range of values can be done by calculating the area under the curve for this range. For example, the probability of drawing a value between 0.3 and 0.5 corresponds to the following area:

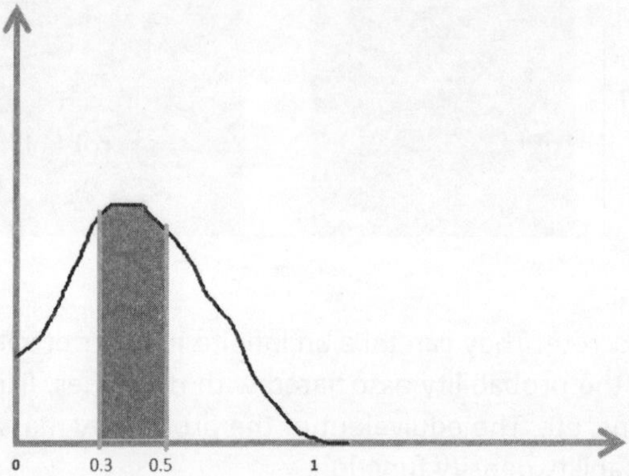

We can easily see that if we increase the range, the probability (the area under the curve) will increase as well. Continous distribution will be discussed in detail in the next unit.

DESCRIBING A DISCRETE DISTRIBUTION

A discrete random variable is a random variable that can have one of a finite set of specific outcomes. The two types of discrete random variables most commonly used in machine learning are binary and categorical.

- Binary Random Variable: x in {0, 1}
- Categorical Random Variable: x in {1, 2, ..., K}.

A binary random variable is a discrete random variable where the finite set of outcomes is in {0, 1}. A categorical random variable is a discrete random variable where the finite set of outcomes is in {1, 2, ..., K}, where K is the total number of unique outcomes.

Each outcome or event for a discrete random variable has a probability. The relationship between the events for a discrete random variable and their probabilities is called the discrete probability distribution and is summarized by a probability mass function, or PMF for short.

For outcomes that can be ordered, the probability of an event equal to or less than a given value is defined by the cumulative distribution function, or CDF for short. The inverse of the CDF is called the percentage-point function and will give the discrete outcome that is less than or equal to a probability.

There are many common discrete probability distributions. The following are examples of discrete probability distributions commonly used in statistics:

1. Bernoulli Distribution: Binary Random Variable
2. Binomial distribution: Sequence of a Binary Random Variable
3. Geometric Distribution

4. Hypergeometric distribution.
5. Multinomial Distribution: Sequence of a Categorical Random Variable
6. Negative binomial distribution.
7. Poisson distribution.

We will cover some of the popular distributions in the next section. We will cover following important concepts for each of the distributions:

1. PMF: Probability Mass Function, returns the probability of a given outcome.
2. CDF: Cumulative Distribution Function, returns the probability of a value less than or equal to a given outcome.
3. PPF: Percent-Point Function, returns a discrete value that is less than or equal to the given probability.
4. Plot: Plotting the distribution

BERNOULLI DISTRIBUTION

The Bernoulli distribution is a discrete probability distribution that covers a case where an event will have a binary outcome as either a 0 or 1 : x in {0, 1}. An event for which the probability of occurrence is p and the probability of the event not occurring is 1-p i.e., the event has only two possible outcomes (these can be viewed as Success or Failure, Yes or No and Heads or Tails). The event occurs with a probability p and 1-p respectively.

A "Bernoulli trial" is an experiment or case where the outcome follows a Bernoulli distribution. The distribution and the trial are named after the Swiss mathematician Jacob Bernoulli.

Some common examples of Bernoulli trials include:

- The single flip of a coin that may have a heads (0) or a tails (1) outcome.
- A single birth of either a boy (0) or a girl (1).
- How many shots on a goal post resulted in the goal score, and how many shots were missed. We can call a goal scored as a "success" and a missed target to be a failure.
- Rolling Dice: The probability of a roll of two dice resulting in a double six. A double six dice roll could be considered to be a success and everything else can be considered a failure.
- A common example of a Bernoulli trial in machine learning might be a binary classification of a single example as the No Buy (0) or Buy (1) behavior.

The distribution can be summarized by a single variable p that defines the probability of an outcome 1. Given this parameter, the probability for each event can be calculated as follows:

$$P(x=1) = p$$
$$P(x=0) = 1 - p$$

In the case of flipping a fair coin, the value of p would be 0.5, giving a 50% probability of each outcome.

Plot: Plotting the distribution

Bernouli's Plot: We use various functions in numpy library to mathematically calculate the values for a bernoulli distribution. Histograms are created over which we plot the probability distribution curve. We can generate a Bernoulli distributed discrete random variable using bernoulli.rvs() method from the scipy.stats module in python. The function will take the probability of success (p) as a shape parameter The size parameter decides the number of times the trials are to be repeated.

```
from scipy.stats import bernoulli
import seaborn as sb
import matplotlib.pyplot as plt

data_bern = bernoulli.rvs(size=1000,p=0.6)
ax = sb.distplot(data_bern,
                 kde=True,
                 color='crimson',
                 hist_kws={"linewidth": 25,'alpha':1})
ax.set(xlabel='Bernouli', ylabel='Frequency')
plt.show()
```

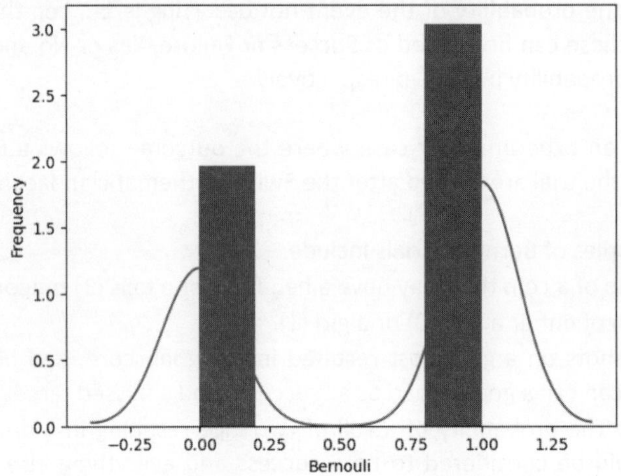

PMF: Probability Mass Function, returns the probability of a given outcome.
Since the event can be either 0 (Not desired output) or 1 (desired output), the k value in the formula of the pmf can take 0 or 1 only. Let's look at the code below, first case is for tossing a coin, k = getting a Tail and probability p is 0.5. In the second case, we will take k = getting a value 5 when you roll a dice.

```
from scipy.stats import bernoulli

#Probability mass function
#pmf(k, p, loc=0)

pmf_val = bernoulli.pmf(1,1/6) #Success
```

```
print("Probability of getting a success on rolling a dice:
",pmf_val)
pmf_val = bernoulli.pmf(0,1/6) #Failure
print("Probability of getting a failure on rolling a dice:
",pmf_val)
pmf_val = bernoulli.pmf(1,1/2) #Success
print("Probability of getting a success on tossing a coin:
",pmf_val)
pmf_val = bernoulli.pmf(0,1/2) #Failure
print("Probability of getting a failure on tossing a coin:
",pmf_val)
```

Output

```
Probability of getting a success on rolling a dice:  0.16666666666666669
Probability of getting a failure on rolling a dice:  0.8333333333333334
Probability of getting a success on tossing a coin:  0.5
Probability of getting a failure on tossing a coin:  0.5
```

CDF: Cumulative Distribution Function, returns the probability of a value less than or equal to a given outcome.

As seen from the plot, the value starts from 0 and goes all the way upto 1. Cumulative distribution will start from 0 and upto 1. CDF(0) will be same at PMF(0) and CDF(1) will be 1 as it covers all the possible values. Let's solve using Python:

```
from scipy.stats import bernoulli

#Cumulative distribution function
#cdf(k, p, loc=0)

cdf_val = bernoulli.cdf(1,1/6) #Success
print("Cumulative Probability for all results in rolling a
dice: ",cdf_val)
cdf_val = bernoulli.cdf(0,1/6) #Failure
print("Cumulative Probability for first result in rolling a
dice: ",cdf_val)
cdf_val = bernoulli.cdf(1,1/2) #Success
print("Cumulative Probability for all results in tossing a
coin: ",cdf_val)
cdf_val = bernoulli.cdf(0,1/2) #Failure
print("Cumulative Probability for first result in tossing a
coin: ",cdf_val)
```

Output:

```
Cumulative Probability for all results in rolling a dice:  1.0
Cumulative Probability for first result in rolling a dice:  0.8333333333333334
Cumulative Probability for all results in tossing a coin:  1.0
Cumulative Probability for first result in tossing a coin:  0.5
```

PPF: Percent-Point Function, returns a discrete value that is less than or equal to the given probability. It is inverse of cdf — percentiles.
In this method, we pass the probability and expect the value k.

```
from scipy.stats import bernoulli

#Generate 10 random values
data_bern = bernoulli.rvs(size=10,p=0.6)
print("10 random values: ",data_bern)

#Percent point function
#ppf(q, p, loc=0)
#Output will be k (0 or 1)
ppf_val = bernoulli.ppf(1,1/6) #Success
print("Cumulative Probability for all results in rolling a
dice: ",ppf_val)
ppf_val = bernoulli.ppf(5/6,1/6) #Failure
print("Cumulative Probability for first result in rolling a
dice: ",ppf_val)
ppf_val = bernoulli.ppf(1,1/2) #Success
print("Cumulative Probability for all results in tossing a
coin: ",ppf_val)
ppf_val = bernoulli.ppf(1/2,1/2) #Failure
print("Cumulative Probability for first result in tossing a
coin: ",ppf_val)
```

Output:

```
10 random values:  [1 1 1 0 0 1 0 1 1 1]
Cumulative Probability for all results in rolling a dice:  1.0
Cumulative Probability for first result in rolling a dice:  0.0
Cumulative Probability for all results in tossing a coin:  1.0
Cumulative Probability for first result in tossing a coin:  0.0
```

Other functions available are:

- median(p, loc=0) : Median of the distribution.
- mean(p, loc=0): Mean of the distribution.
- var(p, loc=0): Variance of the distribution.
- std(p, loc=0): Standard deviation of the distribution.
- interval(alpha, p, loc=0): Endpoints of the range that contains alpha percent of the distribution
- For detailed documentation, please refer the official documentation site at: https://docs.scipy.org/doc/scipy/reference/generated/scipy.stats.bernoulli.html

Applications of Bernoulli Outcomes

There are real-life situations that involve noting if a specific event occurs or not. Such events are recorded as a success or a failure. Let's look at the few examples:

- Success of a medical treatment
- Interviewed person being a female
- Student result(Pass/fail) in an exam
- Transmittance of a disease (transmitted/not transmitted)

BINOMIAL DISTRIBUTION

The repetition of multiple independent Bernoulli trials is called a Bernoulli process. The outcomes of a Bernoulli process will follow a Binomial distribution. As such, the Bernoulli distribution would be a Binomial distribution with a single trial. The binomial distribution is the probability distribution of a sequence of experiments where each experiment produces a binary outcome and where each of the outcomes is independent of all the others.

The probability mass function for binom is:

f(k)=(nk)pk(1−p)n−k

for `k` in `{0, 1, ..., n}`.

binom takes n and p as shape parameters.

The probability mass function above is defined in the "standardized" form. To shift distribution use the loc parameter. Specifically, binom.pmf(k, n, p, loc) is identically equivalent to binom.pmf(k - loc, n, p).

Some common examples of Bernoulli processes include:

- A sequence of independent coin flips.
- A sequence of independent births.
- Randomly picking people on the street to answer a yes or no question.
- Attempting to convince visitors of a website to buy a product — the yes or no outcome is whether they purchased or not.
- The performance of a machine learning algorithm on a binary classification problem can be analyzed as a Bernoulli process, where the prediction by the model on an example from a test set is a Bernoulli trial (correct or incorrect).

The Binomial distribution summarizes the number of successes k in a given number of Bernoulli trials n, with a given probability of success for each trial p.

We can demonstrate this with a Bernoulli process where the probability of success is 50% or P(x=1) = 0.5 (e.g. unbiased coin) and the total number of trials is 10 (k=10).

Plot: Plotting the distribution

Lets plot, explanation within the program:

E.g. Not using scipy.binom (manual process)

```
import numpy as np
import matplotlib.pyplot as plt
import seaborn as sns
# Input variables
# Number of trials
trials = 100000
# Number of independent experiments in each trial
n = 10 #Tossing the coin 10 times

# Probability of success for each experiment
p = 0.5
# Function that runs our coin toss trials
# heads is a list of the number of successes from each trial of n
experiments
def run_binom(trials, n, p):
    heads = []
    for i in range(trials):
        tosses = [np.random.random() for i in range(n)]
        heads.append(len([i for i in tosses if i>=0.50]))
    return heads
# Run the function
heads = run_binom(trials, n, p)
# Plot the results as a histogram
fig, ax = plt.subplots(figsize=(14,7))
ax = sns.distplot(heads, bins=11, label='simulation results')
ax.set_xlabel("Number of Heads",fontsize=16)
ax.set_ylabel("Frequency",fontsize=16)
```

Output:

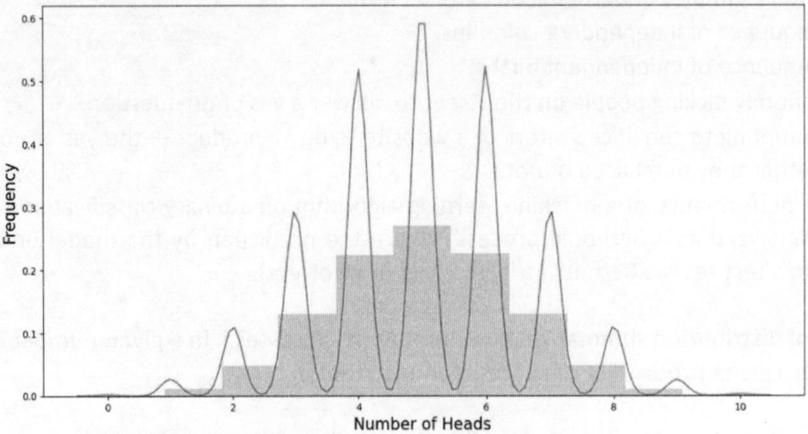

Program: Using binom function, plotting graph

```
from scipy.stats import binom
import seaborn as sb
import matplotlib.pyplot as plt

data_binom = binom.rvs(n=10,p=0.5,loc=0,size=100000)
```

```
ax = sb.distplot(data_binom,
                 kde=True,
                 color='blue',
                 hist_kws={"linewidth": 25,'alpha':1})
ax.set(xlabel='Binomial', ylabel='Frequency')
plt.show()
```

Output:

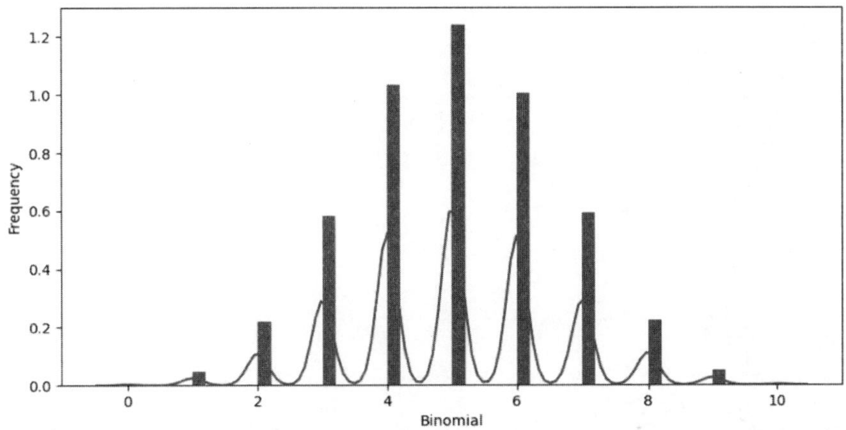

Analysis: Looking at the plots, it shows that the highest probability is for 5 outcomes when you run 10 trials with 0.5 probability. E.g. if you toss an unbiased coin 10 times, getting 5 heads (or getting 5 Tails) will have the highest probability.

PMF: Probability Mass Function, returns the probability of a given outcome.

```
from scipy.stats import binom

#Probability mass function
#pmf(k, n, p, loc=0)
# k- number of expected result,
# n: total number of experiment
# p: probability

#1. Rolling a dice
# Rolling 10 times
# probability of getting exactly 3 times number 5
pmf_val = binom.pmf(3, 10,1/6)
print("Probability of getting number 5 thrice: ",pmf_val)

#2. Tossing an unbiased coin
# Tossing 10 times
# probability of getting exactly 8 times Head
pmf_val = binom.pmf(8, 10,1/2)
print("Probability of getting 8 times Head: ",pmf_val)
```

Output:

```
Probability of getting number 5 thrice:  0.15504535957425197
Probability of getting 8 times Head:  0.04394531249999999
```

CDF: Cumulative Distribution Function, returns the probability of a value less than or equal to a given outcome.

When we say here CDF of 7, indicates the probability of getting 0 to 7 (including) times the desired result. Let's look below the Python implementation:

```
from scipy.stats import binom

#Cumulative distribution function
#cdf(k, n, p, loc=0)
# k- upto expected result,
# n: total number of experiment
# p: probability

#1. Rolling a dice
# Rolling 10 times
# probability of getting 0 or 1 or 2 or 3 times number 5
pmf_val = binom.cdf(3, 10,1/6)
print("Probability of getting 3 or less times 5: ",pmf_val)
# probability of getting 10 or less times number 5
pmf_val = binom.cdf(10, 10,1/6)
print("Probability of getting 10 or less times 5: ",pmf_val)
#2. Tossing an unbiased coin
# Tossing 10 times
# probability of getting 8 or less times Head
pmf_val = binom.cdf(8, 10,1/2)
print("Probability of getting 8 or less times Head: ",pmf_val)
# probability of getting 3<= Heads <=8
pmf_val1 = binom.cdf(8, 10,1/2)
pmf_val2 = binom.cdf(2, 10,1/2)
print("Probability of getting 3<= Heads <=8: ",(pmf_val1-
pmf_val2))
```

Output:

```
Probability of getting 3 or less times 5:  0.9302721574455114
Probability of getting 10 or less times 5:  1.0
Probability of getting 8 or less times Head:  0.9892578125
Probability of getting 3<= Heads <=8:  0.9345703125
```

PPF: Percent-Point Function, returns a discrete value that is less than or equal to the given probability.

```
from scipy.stats import binom

#ppf(q, n, p, loc=0)
#(inverse of cdf – percentiles).
# q: calculated probability
# n: total number of experiment
# p: probability

#1. Rolling a dice
ppf_val = binom.ppf(0.930272, 10,1/6, loc=0)
print("Probability of getting number 5 thrice: ",ppf_val)

#2. Tossing an unbiased coin
ppf_val = binom.ppf(0.989257, 10,1/2)
print("Probability of getting 8 times Head: ",ppf_val)
```

Output:

```
Probability of getting number 5 thrice:  3.0
Probability of getting 8 times Head:  8.0
```

Applications of Binomial Distribution

- 80% of people who purchase pet insurance are women. If 9 pet insurance owners are randomly selected, find the probability that exactly 6 are women.
- 60% of people who purchase sports cars are men. If 10 sports car owners are randomly selected, find the probability that exactly 7 are men.

POISSON DISTRIBUTION

The Poisson distribution , named after French mathematician Siméon Denis Poisson, is a discrete probability distribution that expresses the probability of a given number of events occurring in a fixed interval of time or space if these events occur with a known constant mean rate and independently of the time since the last event. The Poisson distribution can also be used for the number of events in other specified intervals such as distance, area or volume.

For instance, an individual keeping track of the amount of mail they receive each day may notice that they receive an average number of 4 letters per day. If receiving any particular piece of mail does not affect the arrival times of future pieces of mail, i.e., if pieces of mail from a wide range of sources arrive independently of one another, then a reasonable assumption is that the number of pieces of mail received in a day obeys a Poisson distribution.

Other example that may follow a Poisson distribution include the number of phone calls received by a call center per hour. The Poisson distribution is appropriate for modeling the number of phone calls an office would receive during the noon hour, if they know that they average 4 calls per hour during that time period. Although the average is 4 calls, they could theoretically get any

number of calls during that time period. The events are effectively independent since there is no reason to expect a caller to affect the chances of another person calling.
The occurrence rate may be assumed to be constant.

It is reasonable to assume that (for example) the probability of getting a call in the first half hour is the same as the probability of getting a call in the final half hour. Of course, this situation isn't an absolute perfect theoretical fit for the Poisson distribution. For instance, the office certainly cannot receive a trillion calls during the time period, as there are less than a trillion people alive to be making calls. Practically speaking, the situation is close enough that the Poisson distribution does a good job of modeling the situation's behavior.

Formula:
The Poisson distribution is popular for modeling the number of times an event occurs in an interval of time or space. A discrete random variable X is said to have a Poisson distribution with parameter λ > 0, if, for k = 0, 1, 2, ..., the probability mass function of X is given by:

$$f(k;\lambda) = \Pr(X = k) = \frac{\lambda^k e^{-\lambda}}{k!},$$

where

- *e* is Euler's number (*e* = 2.71828...)
- *k*! is the factorial of *k*.

The positive real number λ is equal to the expected value of X and also to its variance.

$$\lambda = \mathrm{E}(X) = \mathrm{Var}(X).$$

Assumptions and validity
The Poisson distribution is an appropriate model if the following assumptions are true:
k is the number of times an event occurs in an interval and k can take values 0, 1, 2, ...

- The occurrence of one event does not affect the probability that a second event will occur. That is, events occur independently.
- The average rate at which events occur is independent of any occurrences. For simplicity, this is usually assumed to be constant, but may in practice vary with time.
- Two events cannot occur at exactly the same instant; instead, at each very small sub-interval exactly one event either occurs or does not occur.

If these conditions are true, then k is a Poisson random variable, and the distribution of k is a Poisson distribution.

The Poisson distribution is also the limit of a binomial distribution, for which the probability of success for each trial equals λ divided by the number of trials, as the number of trials approaches infinity

Lets take a problem and solve using Python:
Example : If the average number of cars that cross a particular street in a day is 25, then you can find the probability of 28 cars passing the street using the poisson formula given by:

$$p = \frac{e^{-\mu}\mu^{x}}{x!} = \frac{e^{-25} \times 25^{28}}{28!} = 0.0632$$

Plot: Plotting the distribution
Let's plot the distribution and mark our solution on it

```
from scipy.stats import poisson
import matplotlib.pyplot as plt

plt.ylabel('Probability of car passing')
plt.xlabel('Number of cars')
plt.title('Probability Distribution Curve')
arr = []
posson_rate = poisson(25)
for num in range(0, 50):
    arr.append(posson_rate.pmf(num))

prob = posson_rate.pmf(28)
plt.grid(True)
plt.plot(arr, linewidth=2.0)
plt.plot([28], [prob], marker='o', markersize=6, color="red")
plt.show()
```

Output:

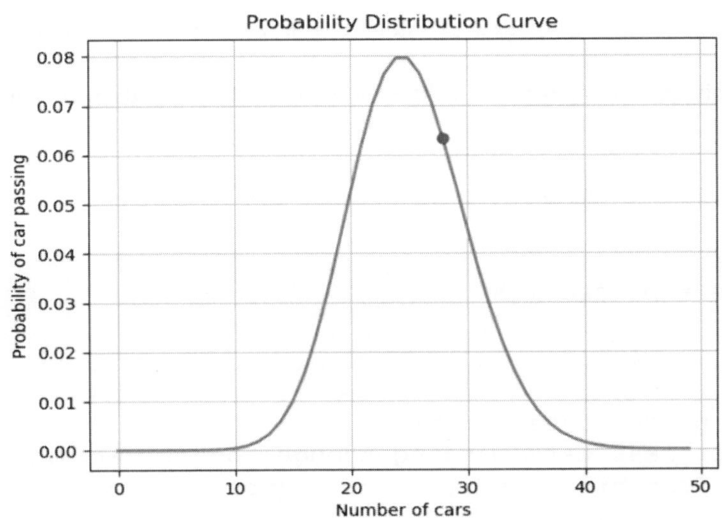

PMF: Probability Mass Function, returns the probability of a given outcome.

```
from scipy.stats import poisson
```

```
#Given mean
posson_rate = poisson(25)

#probability for 28 cars
prob = posson_rate.pmf(28)
print("Probability of 28 cars passing the street is ", prob)
```

Output:

```
Probability of 28 cars passing the street is  0.06321459690112517
```

CDF: Cumulative Distribution Function, returns the probability of a value less than or equal to a given outcome.

```
from scipy.stats import poisson

#Given mean
posson_rate = poisson(25)

#cumulative probability for 28 cars
cum_prob = posson_rate.cdf(28)
print("Probability of 28 or less cars passing the street is ",
cum_prob)
```

Output:

```
Probability of 28 or less cars passing the street is  0.763400741866402
```

PPF: Percent-Point Function, returns a discrete value that is less than or equal to the given probability.

```
from scipy.stats import poisson

#Given mean
posson_rate = poisson(25)

#cumulative probability for 28 cars
prob=0.25
ppf_cars = posson_rate.ppf(prob)
print("{} or less cars passing though the street gives a
cumulative Probability of {}".format(ppf_cars,prob))
```

Output:

```
22.0 or less cars passing though the street gives a cumulative Probability of 0.25
```

OTHER DISTRIBUTION

Other popular discrete distribution which we have not covered here but are recommended for further read:

1. Geometric Distribution
2. Hypergeometric distribution.
3. Multinomial Distribution.
4. Negative binomial distribution.

Application of Discrete Probability Distribution in Machine Learning

The probability for a discrete random variable can be summarized with a discrete probability distribution. Discrete probability distributions play an important role in applied machine learning and there are a few distributions that a practitioner must know about.

Discrete probability distributions are used in machine learning, most notably in the modeling of binary and multi-class classification problems, in evaluating the performance for binary classification models, such as the calculation of confidence intervals, and in the modeling of the distribution of words in text for natural language processing.

Knowledge of discrete probability distributions is also required in the choice of activation functions in the output layer of deep learning neural networks for classification tasks and selecting an appropriate loss function.

Please refer our book titled: Learn & Practice Series: Data Science and Machine Learning with Python by Swapnil Saurav for detailed analysis.

***

UNIT 6: CONTINOUS PROBABILITY DISTRIBUTION

A continuous distribution describes the probabilities of the possible values of a continuous random variable. A continuous random variable is a random variable with a set of possible values (known as the range) that is infinite and uncountable.

The relationship between the events for a continuous random variable and their probabilities is called the continuous probability distribution and is summarized by a probability density function or PDF for short. Probabilities of continuous random variables (X) are defined as the area under the curve of its PDF. Thus, only ranges of values can have a nonzero probability. The probability that a continuous random variable equals some value is always zero.

Unlike a discrete random variable, the probability for a given continuous random variable cannot be specified directly; instead, it is calculated as an integral (area under the curve) for a tiny interval around the specific outcome. The probability of an event equal to or less than a given value is defined by the cumulative distribution function, or CDF for short. The inverse of the CDF is called the percentage-point function and will give the discrete outcome that is less than or equal to a probability.

- PDF: Probability Density Function, returns the probability of a given continuous outcome.
- CDF: Cumulative Distribution Function, returns the probability of a value less than or equal to a given outcome.
- PPF: Percent-Point Function, returns a discrete value that is less than or equal to the given probability.
- RVS: Gives a random sample value from the distribution

There are many common continuous probability distributions. The most common is the normal probability distribution. Practically all continuous probability distributions of interest belong to the so-called exponential family of distributions, which are just a collection of parameterized probability distributions (e.g. distributions that change based on the values of parameters).

Continuous probability distributions play an important role in machine learning from the distribution of input variables to the models, the distribution of errors made by models, and in the models themselves when estimating the mapping between inputs and outputs.

In the following sections, will take a closer look at some of the more common continuous probability distributions.

DESCRIBING CONTINOUS DISTRIBUTION

The continuous normal distribution can describe the distribution of weight of adult males. For example, you can calculate the probability that a man weighs between 160 and 170 pounds.

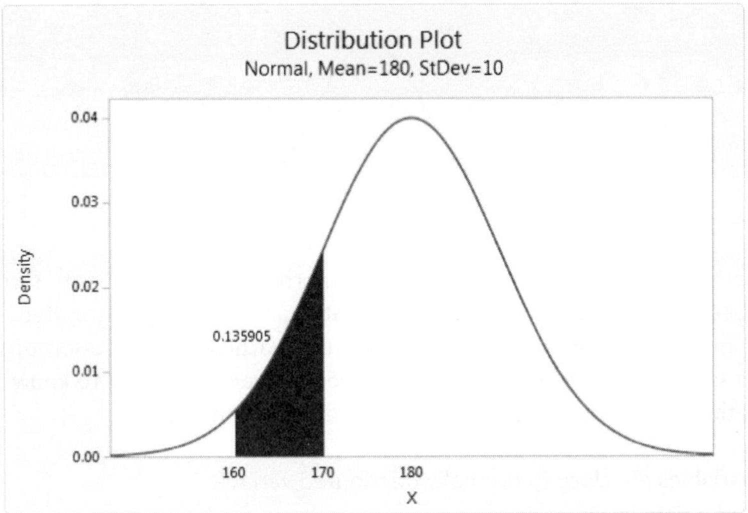

The shaded region under the curve in this example represents the range from 160 and 170 pounds. The area of this range is 0.136; therefore, the probability that a randomly selected man weighs between 160 and 170 pounds is 13.6%. The entire area under the curve equals 1.0.

However, the probability that X is exactly equal to some value is always zero because the area under the curve at a single point, which has no width, is zero. For example, the probability that a man weighs exactly 190 pounds to infinite precision is zero. You could calculate a nonzero probability that a man weighs more than 190 pounds, or less than 190 pounds, or between 189.9 and 190.1 pounds, but the probability that he weighs exactly 190 pounds is zero.

Functions for continuous variables

- *Probability density function (pdf)* function*:* whose value at any given sample (or point) in the sample space (the set of possible values taken by the random variable) can be interpreted as providing a relative likelihood that the value of the random variable would equal that sample.
- *Continuous probability distribution (cdf) function*: most often reserved for continuous random variables.
- *Percent Point function (ppf)* function: evaluating the probability X will take a value less than or equal to x for continuous variable.

NORMAL DISTRIBUTION

Normal Distribution, also known as Gaussian distribution, refers to a particularly important phenomenon in the realm of probability and statistics. The normal distribution looks like this:

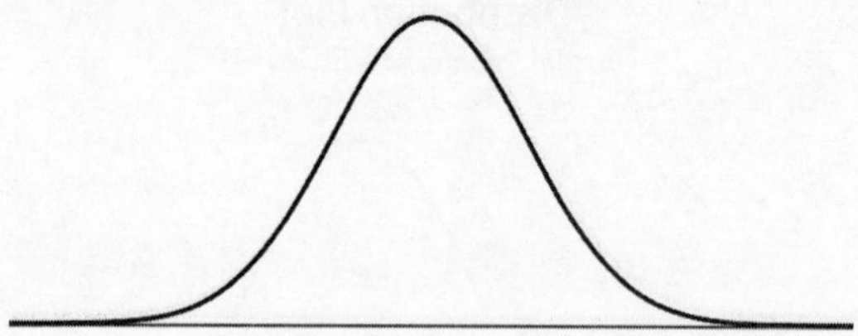

The most important qualities to notice about the normal distribution is its symmetry and its shape. We've been calling it a distribution, but what exactly is being distributed? It depends on the context. In probability, the normal distribution is a particular distribution of the probability across all of the events. The x-axis takes on the values of events we want to know the probability of. The y-axis is the probability associated with each event, from 0 to 1.

The following variables are close to normally distributed variables:

- Height of a population
- Blood pressure of adult human
- Position of a particle that experiences diffusion
- Measurement errors
- Residuals in regression
- Shoe size of a population
- Amount of time it takes for employees to reach home
- A large number of educational measures

A normal distribution has a bell-shaped density curve described by its mean μ and standard deviation σ. The density curve is symmetrical, centered about its mean, with its spread determined by its standard deviation showing that data near the mean are more frequent in occurrence than data far from the mean. The probability distribution function of a normal density curve with mean μ and standard deviation σ at a given point x is given by:

$$f(x|\mu,\sigma^2) = \frac{1}{\sqrt{2\pi\sigma^2}} e^{-\frac{(x-\mu)^2}{2\sigma^2}}$$

From the formula, we see that it's a function of mean and standard deviation. A normal distribution is a distribution that is solely dependent on two parameters of the data set: mean and the standard deviation of the sample.

- Mean — this is the average value of all the points in the sample that is computed by summing the values and then dividing by the total number of the values in a sample.
- Standard Deviation — this indicates how much the data set deviates from the mean of the sample.
- The mean, mode, and median of the distribution are equal.

The graph of a random variable X ~ N (μ, σ) is shown below:

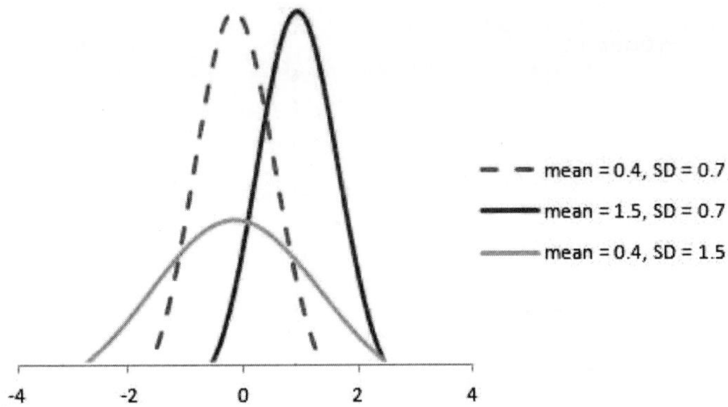

This characteristic of the distribution makes it extremely simple for statisticians and hence any variable that exhibits normal distribution is feasible to be forecasted with higher accuracy. Essentially, it can help in simplying the model.

Empirical Rule for Normal Distribution

Have you heard of the empirical rule? It's a commonly used concept in statistics (and in a lot of performance reviews as well):

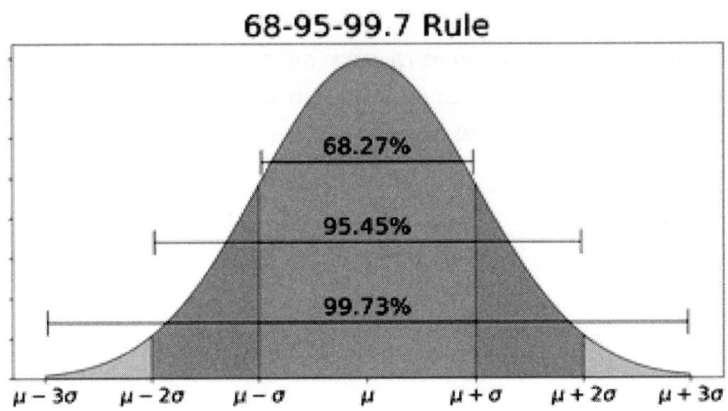

According to the Empirical Rule for Normal Distribution:

- 68.27% of data lies within 1 standard deviation of the mean
- 95.45% of data lies within 2 standard deviations of the mean
- 99.73% of data lies within 3 standard deviations of the mean

Thus, almost all the data lies within 3 standard deviations. This rule enables us to check for Outliers and is very helpful when determining the normality of any distribution.

Normal distribution is a particularly important kind of probability distribution. In statistics, it is the values of our data that are being distributed. Here, the x-axis is the values of our data, and the y-axis is the count of each of these values. Here's the same picture of the normal distribution, but labelled according to a probability and statistical context:

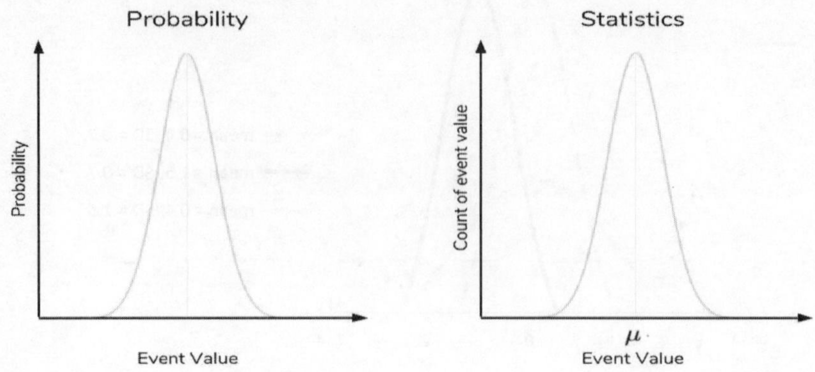

In a probability context, the high point in a normal distribution represents the event with the highest probability of occurring. As you get farther away from this event on either side, the probability drops rapidly, forming that familiar bell-shape. The high point in a statistical context actually represents the mean. As in probability, as you get farther from the mean, you rapidly drop off in frequency. That is to say, extremely high and low deviations from the mean are present but exceedingly rare.

Z Score:

One of the important concept we need to know in Normal distribution is Z-Score. The Z-score is a simple calculation that answers the question, "Given a data point, how many standard deviations is it away from the mean?" The equation below is the Z-score equation.

The data point in question

The mean

The z-score

$$z = \frac{x_i - \mu}{\sigma}$$

The standard deviation

By itself, the Z-score doesn't provide much information. It gains the most value when compared against a Z-table, which tabulates the cumulative probability of a standard normal distribution up until a given Z-score. A standard normal is a normal distribution with a mean of 0 and a standard deviation of 1. The Z-score lets us reference this in the Z-table even if our normal distribution is not standard. The cumulative probability is the sum of the probabilities of all values occurring, up until a given point.

An easy example is the mean itself. The mean is the exact middle of the normal distribution, so we know that the sum of all probabilites of getting values from the left side up until the mean is 50%. The values from the Three Sigma Rule actually come up if you try to calculate the cumulative probability between standard deviations. The picture below provides a visualization of the cumulative probability.

We know that the sum of all probabilities must equal 100%, so we can use the Z-table to calculate probabilities on both sides of the Z-score under the normal distribution.

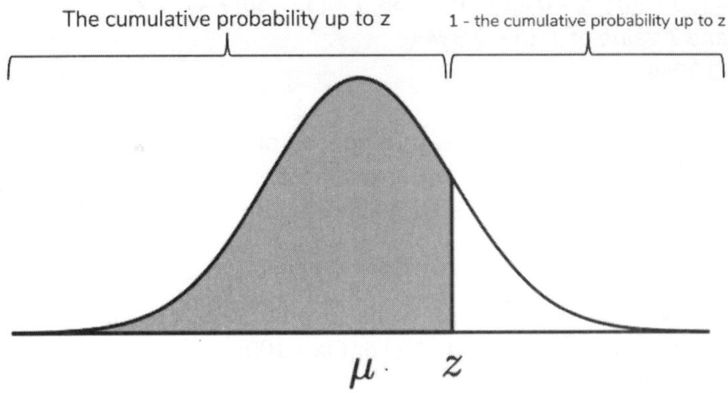

Putting everything together

Let's look at some of the problems in Normal Distribution and how to solve.

Example 1: X is a normally normally distributed variable with mean μ = 30 and standard deviation σ = 4. Find

a. P(x < 40)
b. P(x > 21)
c. P(30 < x < 35)

Solution 1:
Note: What is meant here by area is the area under the standard normal curve.

Z = (Data –Mean)/SD

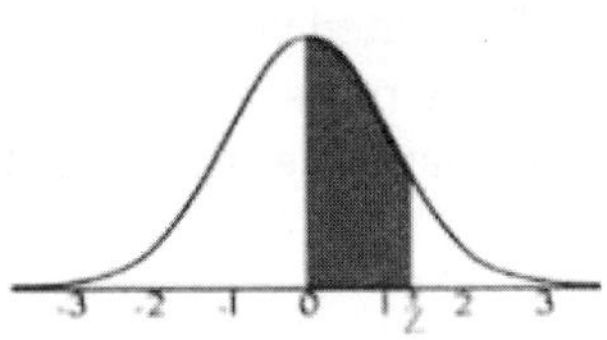

STANDARD NORMAL TABLE (Z)

Entries in the table give the area under the curve between the mean and z standard deviations above the mean. For example, for z = 1.25 the area under the curve between the mean (0) and z is 0.3944.

Note: Z Table gives the area from mean to the value on the left or right (based on the sign)

a) For x = 40, the z-value z = (40 - 30) / 4 = 2.5
Hence P(x < 40) = P(z < 2.5)

z	0.00	0.01	0.02	0.03	0.04	0.05	0.06	0.07	0.08	0.09
2.0	0.4772	0.4778	0.4783	0.4788	0.4793	0.4798	0.4803	0.4808	0.4812	0.4817
2.1	0.4821	0.4826	0.4830	0.4834	0.4838	0.4842	0.4846	0.4850	0.4854	0.4857
2.2	0.4861	0.4864	0.4868	0.4871	0.4875	0.4878	0.4881	0.4884	0.4887	0.4890
2.3	0.4893	0.4896	0.4898	0.4901	0.4904	0.4906	0.4909	0.4911	0.4913	0.4916
2.4	0.4918	0.4920	0.4922	0.4925	0.4927	0.4929	0.4931	0.4932	0.4934	0.4936
2.5	0.4938	0.4940	0.4941	0.4943	0.4945	0.4946	0.4948	0.4949	0.4951	0.4952

Z Value at 2.5 from the table is (i.e. from Zero to 2.5) = 0.4938
Solution = [area to the left of 2.5] = 0.5 + 0.4938 = **0.9938**

b) For x = 21, z = (21 - 30) / 4 = -2.25
Hence P(x > 21) = P(z > -2.25) = Z Value of 2.25 = 0.4878
= 0.5 + 0.4878 = **0.9878**

c) For x = 30 , z = (30 - 30) / 4 = **0** and for x = 35, z = (35 - 30) / 4 = **1.25**
Z Value of 0 = 0 and Z Value of 1.25 = 0.3944
= 0.0 + 0.3944 = **0.3944**

Example 2: A radar unit is used to measure speeds of cars on a motorway. The speeds are normally distributed with a mean of 90 km/hr and a standard deviation of 10 km/hr. What is the probability that a car picked at random is travelling at more than 100 km/hr?

Solution 2:
Let x be the random variable that represents the speed of cars. x has μ = 90 and σ = 10. We have to find the probability that x is higher than 100 or P(x > 100)
For x = 100 , z = (100 - 90) / 10 = 1
P(x > 90) = P(z > 1) = [total area] - [area to the left of z = 1]
= 1 - 0.8413 = 0.1587
The probability that a car selected at a random has a speed greater than 100 km/hr is equal to **0.1587**

Example 3: Entry to a certain University is determined by a national test. The scores on this test are normally distributed with a mean of 500 and a standard deviation of 100. Tom wants to be admitted to this university and he knows that he must score better than at least 70% of the students who took the test. Tom takes the test and scores 585. Will he be admitted to this university?

Solution 3:
Let x be the random variable that represents the scores. x is normally ditsributed with a mean of 500 and a standard deviation of 100. The total area under the normal curve represents the total number of students who took the test. If we multiply the values of the areas under the curve by 100, we obtain percentages.
For x = 585 , z = (585 - 500) / 100 = **0.85**
The proportion P of students who scored below 585 is given by
P = [area to the left of z = 0.85] = 0.8023 = 80.23%
Tom scored better than 80.23% of the students who took the test and he will be admitted to this University.

Example 4: A large group of students took a test in Physics and the final grades have a mean of 70 and a standard deviation of 10. If we can approximate the distribution of these grades by a normal distribution, what percent of the students

a. scored higher than 80?
b. should pass the test (grades≥60)?
c. should fail the test (grades<60)?

Solution 4:
a) For x = 80, z = 1
Area to the right (higher than) z = 1 is equal to 0.1586 = **15.87% scored more that 80.**

b) For x = 60, z = -1
Area to the right of z = -1 is equal to 0.8413 = **84.13% should pass the test.**

c) 100% - 84.13% = **15.87% should fail the test.**

Python Implementation

Let's understand more about Normal distribution using python code. We will solve above 3 problems using Python Code

Solution 1:

```
import numpy as np
import matplotlib.pyplot as plt
from scipy.stats import norm

#Given Values
mu = 30
sd = 4
val=40

#Plotting Values:
x_axis = np.arange(mu-4*sd, mu+4*sd, 0.0001)

#Condition is based on less than or greater than
#X < 40
cond = x_axis<val
#Calculation of Z Value
z = (val - mu)/sd
#Read probability using cdf Table:
import scipy.stats as st
prob = st.norm.cdf(z)
#Note: Z table values are read from Mean
# and cdf reads value from Zero
#Let's round off to 2 decimal places
prob = round(prob,4)
print("a. Probability is: ",prob)
#Plotting: pdf
plt.plot(x_axis, norm.pdf(x_axis,mu,sd))
#Shading X<40
# use the fill_between function
z_plot = x_axis[cond]
plt.fill_between(z_plot, 0, norm.pdf(z_plot, mu, sd))
plt.title("Plot: Prob for < 40")
plt.show()

#b
val=21
```

```
#Condition X > 21
cond = x_axis>val
#Calculation of Z Value
z = (val - mu)/sd
#Read probability using cdf Table:
prob = 1 - st.norm.cdf(z)
#Let's round off to 2 decimal places
prob = round(prob,4)
print("b. Probability is: ",prob)
#Plotting: pdf
plt.plot(x_axis, norm.pdf(x_axis,mu,sd))
#Shading X<40
# use the fill_between function
z_plot = x_axis[cond]
plt.fill_between(z_plot, 0, norm.pdf(z_plot, mu, sd))
plt.title("Plot: Prob for > 21")
plt.show()

#Solving for c: 30 < x < 35
#Approach: P(35)-P(30) is the prob
val1=30
cond1 = x_axis>val1
z1 = (val1 - mu)/sd
prob = st.norm.cdf(z1)
prob1 = round(prob,4)
val2=35
cond2 = x_axis<val2
z2 = (val2 - mu)/sd
prob = st.norm.cdf(z2)
prob2 = round(prob,4)
print("c. Probability is: ",prob2-prob1)
x_axis_shade = np.arange(val1, val2, 0.0001)
y_shade = norm.pdf(x_axis_shade,mu,sd)

y_all = norm.pdf(x_axis,mu,sd)
#Plotting: pdf
plt.plot(x_axis, y_all)
plt.fill_between(x_axis_shade,y_shade,0, alpha=0.3, color='b')
plt.title("Plot: Prob for 30 < X < 35")
plt.show()
```

Output:

a. Probability is: 0.9938

b. Probability is: 0.9878

c. Probability is: 0.3944

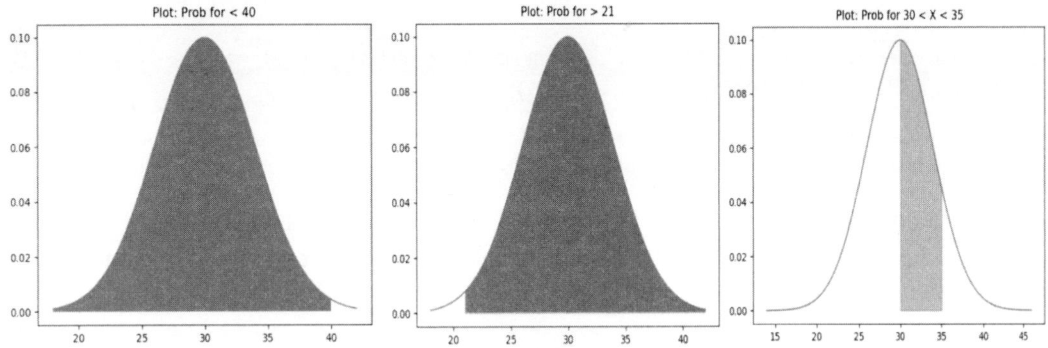

Solution 3:

```
import numpy as np
import matplotlib.pyplot as plt
from scipy.stats import norm
import scipy.stats as st

#Given Values
mu = 500
sd = 100
val=585

#Plotting Values:
x_axis = np.arange(mu-4*sd, mu+4*sd, 0.0001)

#Condition is based on less than or greater than
#X < 585
cond = x_axis<val
#Calculation of Z Value
z = (val - mu)/sd
#Read probability using cdf Table:
prob = st.norm.cdf(z)
prob = round(prob*100,4)
print("Probability is {}%.".format(prob))
check_prob = 70
if prob > check_prob:
    print("Tom scored better than given 70% of the students who
took the test and he will be admitted to this University.")
else:
    print("Tom has scored less than 70% of the students hence
he will not get admitted in the university.")
#Plotting: pdf
plt.plot(x_axis, norm.pdf(x_axis,mu,sd))
#Shading X<40
# use the fill_between function
```

```
z_plot = x_axis[cond]
plt.fill_between(z_plot, 0, norm.pdf(z_plot, mu, sd))
plt.title("Plot: Prob for < 585")
plt.show()
```

Output:
Probability is 80.2337%.
Tom scored better than given 70% of the students who took the test and he will be admitted to this University.

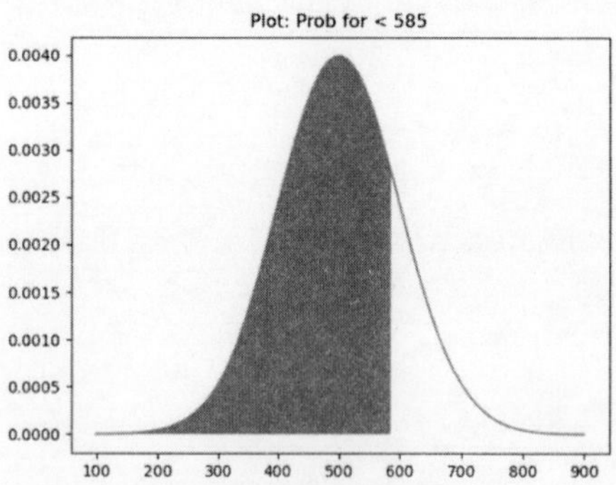

Calculating ppf (perfcentage point function) and rvs
In this case, we are given the probability and we need to find the value X.

```
from scipy.stats import norm

mu=30
sd=4
prob = 0.9989
#Percent point function (inverse of cdf - percentiles).
val = norm.ppf(prob, mu,sd)
print("Value of X: ",round(val,0))
vals = norm.rvs(mu,sd, size = 10)
print("10 randomly selected values from the distribution: ",
vals)
```

Output:
Value of X: 42.0

SImilarly, questsions 2 and 4 can also be solved using above code.

Refer the official documentation from here:
https://docs.scipy.org/doc/scipy/reference/generated/scipy.stats.norm.html

EXPONENTIAL DISTRIBUTION

The exponential distribution is the probability distribution of the time between events in a Poisson point process, i.e., a process in which events occur continuously and independently at a constant average rate. It is a particular case of the gamma distribution. It is the continuous analogue of the geometric distribution, and it has the key property of being memoryless. In addition to being used for the analysis of Poisson point processes it is found in various other contexts.

The exponential distribution is not the same as the class of exponential families of distributions, which is a large class of probability distributions that includes the exponential distribution as one of its members, but also includes the normal distribution, binomial distribution, gamma distribution, Poisson, and many others.

The exponential distribution is one of the widely used continuous distributions. It is often used to model the time elapsed between events.

A continuous random variable X is said to have an *exponential* distribution with parameter $\lambda > 0$, shown as $X \sim Exponential(\lambda)$, if its PDF is given by

$$f_X(x) = \begin{cases} \lambda e^{-\lambda x} & x > 0 \\ 0 & \text{otherwise} \end{cases}$$

The parameter lambda is called rate parameter. Figure below shows the PDF of exponential distribution for several values of λ.

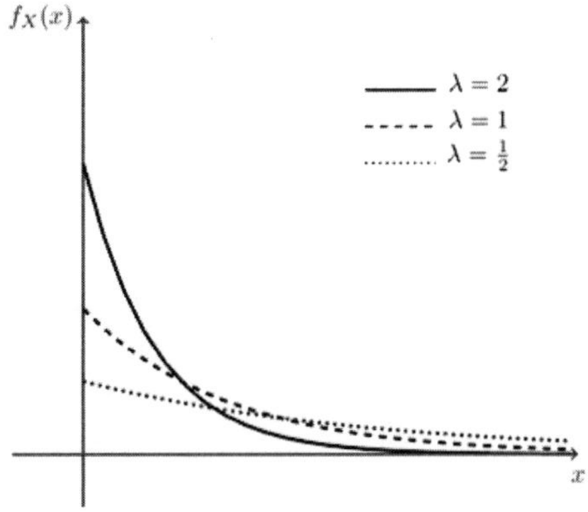

Examples are:

- Length of time beteeen metro arrivals,
- Length of time between arrivals at a gas station
- The life of an Air Conditioner
- Time interval between calls at a call center

Parameters of Exponential Distribution:

1. The expected value of an exponential random variable X is: E(X) = 1/lambda
2. The variance of an exponential random variable X is: Var(X) = 1/(lambda)^2

3. The moment generating function of an exponential random variable X is defined for any t<lambda: M(t) = lambda/(lambda-t)

Example:

Let X = amount of time (in minutes) a postal clerk spends with his or her customer. The time is known to have an exponential distribution with the average amount of time equal to four minutes.

X is a continuous random variable since time is measured. It is given that $\mu = 4$ minutes. To do any calculations, you must know m, the decay parameter.

Parameter $m = 1/\mu = 0.25$

The standard deviation, σ, is the same as the mean. $\mu = \sigma$

The distribution notation is X ~ Exp(m). Therefore, X ~ Exp(0.25).

The probability density function is $f(x) = me^{-mx}$. The number e = 2.71828182846... It is a number that is used often in mathematics. Scientific calculators have the key "ex." If you enter one for x, the calculator will display the value e.

The curve is:

$f(x) = 0.25e^{-0.25x}$ where x is at least zero and m = 0.25.

Implementation using Python

You can generate an exponentially distributed random variable using scipy.stats module's expon.rvs() method which takes shape parameter scale as its argument which is nothing but 1/lambda in the equation. To shift distribution use the loc argument, size decides the number of random variates in the distribution. If you want to maintain reproducibility, include a random_state argument assigned to a number.

```
from scipy.stats import expon
import matplotlib.pyplot as plt

import numpy as np
lam = 0.5
x = np.arange(0,15,0.1)
y = expon.pdf(x)
plt.plot(x,y)
plt.title("Expontential Distribution")
plt.show()
```

Problems and Solutions

At a police station in a large city, calls come in at an average rate of four calls per minute. Assume that the time that elapses from one call to the next has the exponential distribution. Take note that we are concerned only with the rate at which calls come in, and we are ignoring the time spent on the phone. We must also assume that the times spent between calls are independent.

This means that a particularly long delay between two calls does not mean that there will be a shorter waiting period for the next call. We may then deduce that the total number of calls received during a time period has the Poisson distribution.

1. Find the average time between two successive calls.
2. Find the probability that after a call is received, the next call occurs in less than ten seconds.
3. Find the probability that exactly five calls occur within a minute.
4. Find the probability that less than five calls occur within a minute.
5. Find the probability that more than 40 calls occur in an eight-minute period.

Solutions

Solution 1:

On average there are four calls occur per minute, so 15 seconds, or 15/60 = 0.25 minutes occur between successive calls on average.

Solution 2:

Let T = time elapsed between calls.

From part a, μ=0.25 , so m =1/0.25 = 4. Thus, T ~ Exp(4).

The cumulative distribution function is $P(T < t) = 1 - e^{-4t}$. The probability that the next call occurs in less than ten seconds (ten seconds = 1/6 minute) is P(T <1/6)

$= 1 - e^{-4 * 1/6} \approx 0.4866$

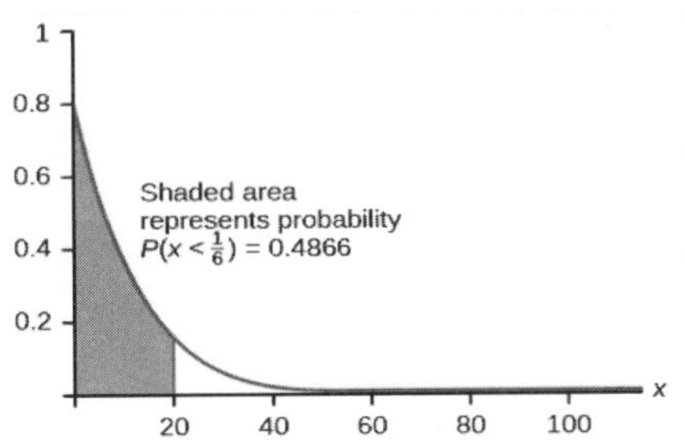

Graph with shaded area representing probability P(x < 1/6) = 0.4866

Solution 3:

Let X = the number of calls per minute. As previously stated, the number of calls per minute has a Poisson distribution, with a mean of four calls per minute. Therefore, X ~ Poisson(4), and so $P(X = 5) = 4^5e^{-4}/5! \approx$ **0.1563** (5! = (5)(4)(3)(2)(1))

Solution 4:

Keep in mind that X must be a whole number, so $P(X < 5) = P(X \le 4)$.

To compute this, we could take P(X = 0) + P(X = 1) + P(X = 2) + P(X = 3) + P(X = 4).

We see that $P(X \le 4)$ = **0.6288**

Solution 5:

Let Y = the number of calls that occur during an eight minute period.

Since there is an average of four calls per minute, there is an average of (8)(4) = 32 calls during each eight minute period.

Hence, Y ~ Poisson(32). Therefore, $P(Y > 40) = 1 - P(Y \le 40) = 1 - 0.9294$ = **0.0707**

Python Implementation

The exponential distribution can be defined using one parameter:

- Scale (Beta): The mean and standard deviation of the distribution.

Sometimes the distribution is defined more formally with a parameter lambda or rate. The beta parameter is defined as the reciprocal of the lambda parameter (beta = 1/lambda)

- Rate (lambda) = Rate of change in the distribution.

Now, let's solve problem 1 from the above:

```
from scipy.stats import expon
import matplotlib.pyplot as plt
import numpy as np
#Number of calls in one minute
call_per_min = 4
lam = 1/4
#1: average time between two successive calls = lambda
theta = lam *60
print("1. Average time between two successive calls is",
round(theta,0))," seconds.")

#2. probability x<10 sec -> cdf
x=10
loc = 0 #default
prob = round(expon.cdf(x,loc,theta),4)
print("2. Probability that the next call occurs in <10 seconds
is ",prob)
x_axis = np.linspace(0.001, theta, 5000)
y = expon.pdf(x_axis)
plt.plot(x_axis,y)
plt.title("Exponential Distribution")
plt.show()
```

Output:

1. Average time between two successive calls is 15.0
2. Probability that the next call occurs in <10 seconds is 0.4866

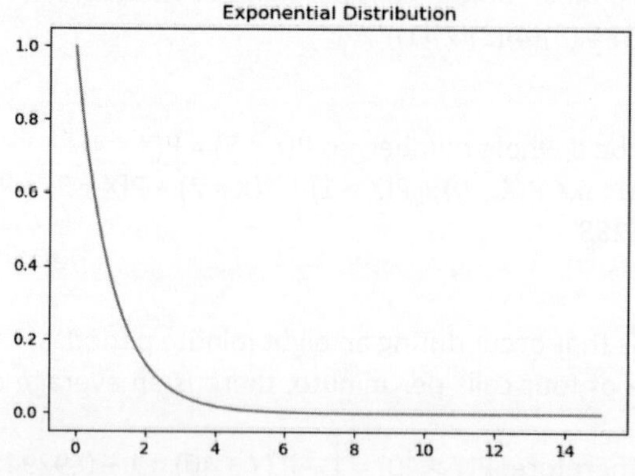

Note: Readers are encouraged to solve using Python other manually solved problems discussed above.

Formula Review

- pdf: $f(x) = me^{-mx}$ where $x \geq 0$ and $m > 0$
- cdf: $P(X \leq x) = 1 - e^{-mx}$
- mean $\mu = \frac{1}{m}$
- standard deviation $\sigma = \mu$
- percentile, k: $k = \frac{ln(\text{AreaToTheLeftOfK})}{-m}$
- Additionally
  - $P(X > x) = e^{(-mx)}$
  - $P(a < X < b) = e^{(-ma)} - e^{(-mb)}$

MORE DISTRIBUTION TO COVER:

Other popular continous distribution which we have not covered here but are recommended for further read:

- Uniform Distribution
- Beta Distribution
- The PERT distribution is a special case of the beta distribution

Application of Probability Distribution

Probability Distributions are prevalent in many sectors, namely, insurance, physics, engineering, computer science and even social science wherein the students of psychology and medical are widely using probability distributions. It has an easy application and widespread use. In this and in last chapter, we have studied some of the important distributions which are observed in day-to-day life. Intention to study these distributions is that you will be able to identify, relate and differentiate among these distributions and solve the problem based on the properties.

Closing Remarks of Distributions

Covering all the distribution and their working is beyond the scope of this book. If you want to master the distributions, we recommend you to refer the statistics books on distribution but for our future journey into Machine Learning, the knowledge of these distributions are enough.

***

UNIT 8: INFERENTIAL STATISTICS

When we talk about inferential statistics, its about Sample and Population. Since its practically not possible to study population, we generally take a random subset from the population, called Sample and based on the sample behavior, we make our assumptions for the population.

For most part, we study two things: differences between groups and relationship between two variables. Statitstics tells us are these differences or relationships Real!

Examples of studying differences between groups:

1. Male versus Female
2. Buy versus no Buy

Examples of relationships between two variables:

1. Study in hours and Marks obtained
2. Height and Weight
3. R&D Spend and Stock Price

Let's understand with an example. Lets take research question where we want to study the relationship between height and weight of people in India. We cant measure the height and weight of entire India's population, instead we take a random sample of the population. We measure the height and the weight of that sample and also collect some additional information like age and gender.

Population

Sample

We take the data and arrange in a spreadsheet in rows and column format as shown below:

	Gender	Age Group	Height (M)	Weight (Kg)
Person 1	Female	Adult	1.4	65
Person 2	Male	Adult	1.6	75
Person 3	Male	Child	1.2	20
Person 4	Male	Elderly	1.5	60
Person 5	Female	Adult	1.4	72
Person 6	Female	Adult	1.5	68
Person 7	Female	Child	1.1	22
Person 8	Male	Adult	1.4	89
Person 9	Male	Elderly	1.4	65
Person 10	Male	Child	1	18

The sample has various attributes which are put as columns. These are also called as variables. We have seen that variables are of two types: Categorical and Numeric. In this example, Gender and Age group are categorical values. The categorical examples can be arranged as a group. Height is a numeric type which can be arranged on a numberline. To understand the data better, we summarize and visualize it. Categorical data can be summarized in a data and visualized as a bar graph. For example, Gender can be summarized in below table and visualized as a bar graph as shown below:

	n	%
Male	6	60%
Female	4	40%

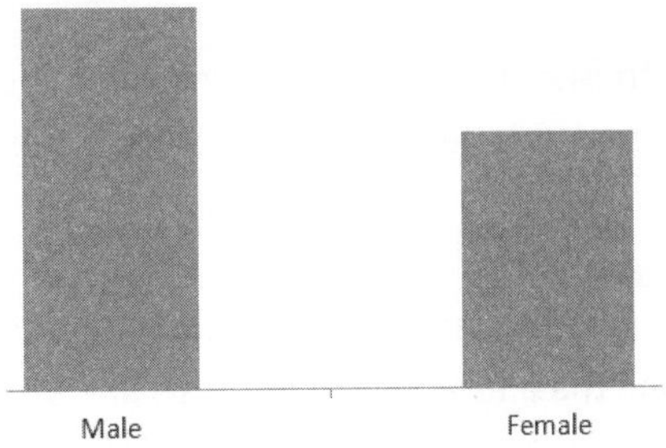

Numeric data can be summarized using following metric: Range, Inter Quartile Range(IQR), Median, Mode, Mean, etc. Data can be visualized in a box plot, histogram plot, etc.

This is a simple dataset with just 2 categorical and 2 numeric dataset. Things start to become interesting when we start to look at the combinations of variables. For example, we can look at a categorical and a numeric variable like Gender and Height. Something like:

	Mean	Range	Median
Male	1.35	1 - 1.6	1.4
Female	1.35	1.1 - 1.4	1.4

This is an example of a combination of Categorical and Numeric variable. You can imagine that there are other possible combinations as well: both numeric combination (Height and Weight), both categorical combination (Age group and Gender). In each case, we might see either the differences between the groups or the relationship between the variables. In each case, we can check if what we see in the sample, has an implication on the population. Can we infer anything about the population based on the sample data. For that reason, we perform various tests. Let's look at the five most important data we have:

	What we observe in the Sample Data	Is it real?
One categorical	e.g. Gender	1 sample proportion test
Two categorical	e.g. Gender and Age group	Chi squared test
One numeric	e.g. Height	t-test or Z-test
One numeric and one categorical	e.g. Gender and Height	t-test or ANOVA
Two numeric	e.g. Height and Weight	Correlation test

How do you perform the analysis?

Its not a good practice to start your analysis blindly. We need to follow a best practice approach. We need to state your objective and a Hypothesis associated with it.

We need to define Null hypothesis and Alternative Hyposthesis. The null hypothesis is the statement subjected to a statistical test in an experiment. It is denoted by H0. For example, consider the following null hypothesis: H0: μi = μj

Here, μi is the population mean for group i, and μj is the population mean for group j. This hypothesis makes the assumption that population means in groups i and j are equal.

Alternative hypothesis: The alternative hypothesis is the hypothesis that is tenable if the null hypothesis is rejected. It is denoted by H1 or Ha. For example, consider the following alternative hypothesis: H1: μi ≠ μj

This hypothesis makes the assumption that population means in groups i and j are not equal. The null hypothesis and the alternative hypothesis are written to be mutually exclusive. If one is true, the other is not. **Experiments rely on sample data to test the null hypothesis. If experimental results, based on sample statistics, are consistent with the null hypothesis, the null hypothesis cannot be rejected; otherwise, the null hypothesis is rejected in favor of the alternative hypothesis which is observed in the sample**.

Finally, analyze the data.

RESEARCH QUESTIONS

1. **One Categorical Value**

   Question: Is there a difference in the number of Male and Female in the population?

   a. State Hypothesis:
      i. H0 (Null Hypothesis): There is no difference
      ii. H1 (Alternative Hyposthesis): There is a difference

   b. Explanation: In the sample, we see that 60% of the data is Male and 40% is Female. Does that mean Population also have similar observation? If yes, then our Hypothesis

H1 is accepted and H0 rejected. So, did we get the answer to our question? No, not yet, because this is just a sample data and we could have selected a sample which shows the difference. If our Null Hypothesis is true, how likely it would be, what is the probability that there is a difference in population also?

c. Alpha Value: is the degree of confidence. Generally taken as 0.05 or 5%
d. P Value: It is the probability of accepting H0 Hypothesis. If this probability is low we can reject the H0. How small this p should be to reject the H0? We must decide this cutoff before we calculate p value. The cut off is the alpha value.
e. Test: We need to perform a test to calculate the P value. Here we perform One Sample Proportion Test.

2. Two Categorical Values

We add Age Group and Gender. One possible research question is: Does the proportion of males and females differ across age groups?

a. State Hypothesis
    i. H0: No it does not depend
    ii. H1: Proportion of males and females is dependent on different age groups. In our sample data, the proportions change over the difference age group. Let's test this idea.
b. Test: Conduct Chi-squared test to get the P value.
c. If P-Value is less than alpha (0.05) we can reject the null Hypothesis.

3. One Numeric Value

When we take into just one numeric value, then we don't have any groups to look for differences between. Also, we don't have any other variable to check any sort of correlation or association to look for. In this case, we might have some theoretical value that we need to compare with. For example, for average height we might have some historical data against which we might want to compare the recent data.

Research Question: Is the current average of height significantly different than the historical height?

a. State Hypothesis:
    i. H0 (Null Hypothesis): There is no difference
    ii. H1 (Alternative Hyposthesis): There is a difference between current height and the previously established height.
b. Test: Conduct t- test to get the P value when the sample is small in size (<32) else perform Z-test.
c. If P-Value is less than alpha (0.05) we can reject the null Hypothesis.

4. One Categorical and One Numeric Value

Research Question: Let's take example of gender and height. Is there a difference between average height of male and female? In our sample, we do observe a difference.

a. State Hypothesis:
    i. H0: There is no difference
    ii. H1: There is a difference between average height of male and female.

b. Test: We conduct t-test and get the P value, if P is less than alpha then reject the null hypothesis.

Note: If we have more than 1 categorical value along with numeric value, like Gender, Age group and Height, then we perform ANOVA (Analysis of Variance).

5. Two Numeric Values

Question: Is there a relationship between Height and Weight?

a. State Hypothesis:
   i. H0: There is no difference
   ii. H1: There is a relationship between height and weight.
b. Test: We conduct correlation test. This gives us correlation coefficient and also P value.
   i. If P Value is less than alpha, we reject the null hypothesis
   ii. Correlation coefficient lies between -1 and +1. Sign indicate the type of relationship between the two numeric values – are they directly or inversely dependent to each other. If the value of value A increases and B also increases then we have +ve correlation and if increasing one leads to decrease in another value then we say they have negatively correlated. The absolute value closer to 1 indicate strong correlation and closer to 0 indicate no correlation. Correlation of A to B and B to A is same.

CALCULATING P VALUE

We have seen the use of p values but hows that calculated? We use table to do that for us but let's undesrstand the concepts using few examples. Please note that p value is related to Probability but they are not same.

Example 1: What is the p value and probability of getting 2 Heads when we toss a coin two times. By now, we are familier with probability.

P(H) = possible outcome / total outcome = ¼ = 0.25

Now let's see the definition of p value: A p value is the probability that random chance generated the data, or something else that is equal or rarer. Here we see, we have 3 parts which makes p value: 1. Random chance generated the data 2. Something else that is equal 3. Something that is rarer.

In the above example:

1. random chance that generated the data = 0.25
2. something that is equal = this is same as getting 2 Tails, which is also = 0.25
3. In this case, there is nothing that is rarer, so = 0

Hence, the probability of getting 2 Heads when we toss the coin 2 times is 0.25 and the p value is 0.5

Example 2: Let's take another discrete value example. This time we toss the coin 5 times then what is the probability of getting 5 Heads?

Let's look at the 3 values:

1. random chance that generated the data = 5 Heads = 1/32 = 0.031 (3.1%)
2. something that is equal = this is same as getting 5 Tails, which is also = 0.031
3. In this case, there is nothing that is rarer, so = 0

The probability of getting 5 Heads when we toss the coin 5 times is 0.031 and the p value is 0.062 (0.031+0.031+0.0)

Example 3: In the experiment 2, let's check for getting 4Heads and 1 Tails.
Solution: Probability of getting 4H and 1 T = 5/32 = 0.156

1. random chance that generated the data = 4 Heads and 1 Tails = 5/32 = 0.156
2. something that is equal = this is same as getting 4 Tails and 1 Heads = 0. 156
3. In this case, we do have rare events, that is getting 5 Heads or 5 tails = 0.031 + 0.031

The probability of getting 4Heads and 1 Tails when we toss the coin 5 times is 0.156 and the p value is 0.375 (0.156 + 0.156 + 0.031+0.031)

Now, lets move to something complex – checking for a continous value. In such cases, we cannot list down all the values. In such cases, we take into account the density.

Example 4: let's took at the below example, where we are looking at the height measurement of Brazilian women in 1996.

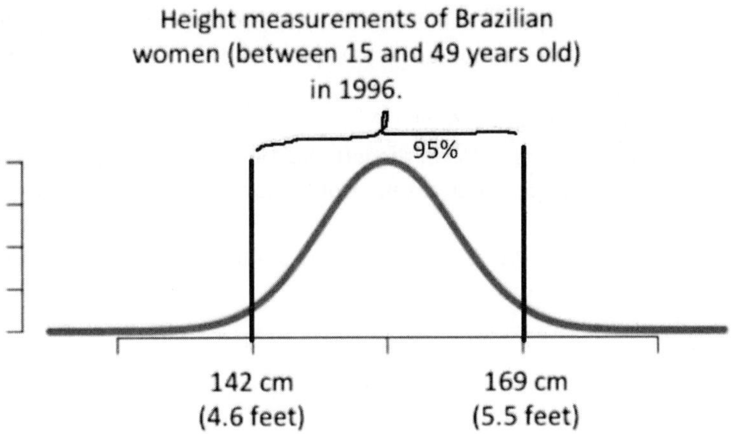

Height of Nations: A Socioeconomic Analysis of Cohort Differences and Patterns among Women in 54 Low- to Middle-Income Countries, Subramanian, Özaltin and Finlay (2011)

The complete area under the curve indicates the probability that a person will have a height within a range of possible values. 95% of the area under the curve is between 142 cm and 169 cm, indicating that the most Brazillian women are between these two values. In other words, there is a 95% probability that each time we measure someone, their height will be between 142 and 169cm.

2.5% of the total area under the curve is greater than 169cm. In other words, there is a 2.5% probability that each time we measure a Brazillian woman, their height will be greater than 169 cm. Also, 2.5% of the total area under the curve is under 142 cm. In other words, there is a 2.5% probability that each time we measure a Brazillian woman, their height will be less than 142 cm. Here too, for p value calculation, we add up the percentages of areas under the curve.

For example, the p-value for someone who is 142 cm tall is:

1. The 2.5% of the area for the people 142 cm or shorter

2. The probability of finding a Brazillian woman greater than 169 cm height is similar to the problem so we need to add this area as well: 2.5%
3. Rarer is included in the first question itself, here its 0

Total p value =0.05 whereas the probability is 0.25%

Example:

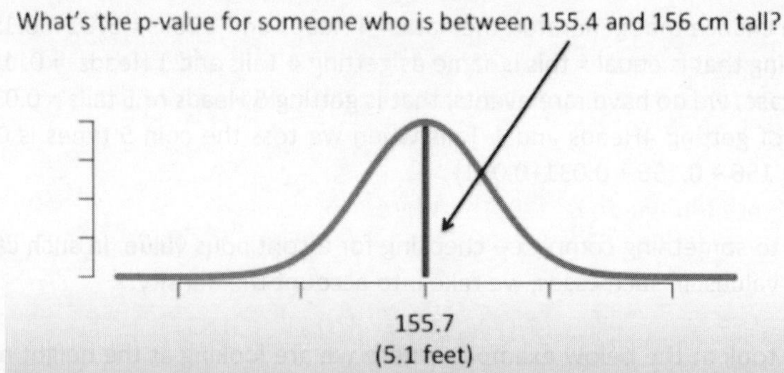

The probability of someone being between 155.4 and 156 cm tall is only 0.04 [refer distribution chapter for the calculations]. The area marked as 0.04 (4%) is very small, almost looks like a line. Now let's calculate the p-value:

1. Its same the probability, which is 0.04
2. The rare even is here 2 parts: 48% on the left and 48% on the right, the p value = 1
   That is, there is nothing special about measuring someone's height which is close to the mean value.

In this example, though the probability is very small, the p-value is huge (=1). Its because there is no importance of measuring mean value.

Z SCORE

The plot on the next page shows the alpha (confidence level), alpha/2, the 95% confidence level which range from -1.96 to +1.96. If the experiement gives a Z score less than -1.96 or greater than +1.96, we put it part of rejection area. Critical values shows the part of rejection region.

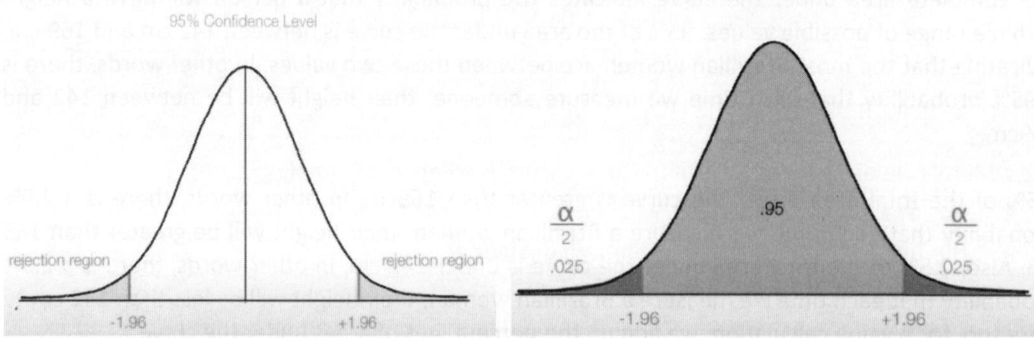

This is just the beginning. We will deep dive into each of the topics in the next few chapters.

***

UNIT 8: SAMPLING AND SAMPLING DISTRIBUTION

Sampling definition: Sampling is a technique of selecting individual members or a subset of the population to make statistical inferences from them and estimate characteristics of the whole population. Different sampling methods are widely used by researchers in market research so that they do not need to research the entire population to collect actionable insights. It is also a time-convenient and a cost-effective method and hence forms the basis of any research design. Sampling techniques can be used in a research survey software for optimum derivation.

For example, if a drug manufacturer would like to research the adverse side effects of a drug on the country's population, it is almost impossible to conduct a research study that involves everyone. In this case, the researcher decides a sample of people from each demographic and then researches them, giving him/her indicative feedback on the drug's behavior.

TYPES OF SAMPLING

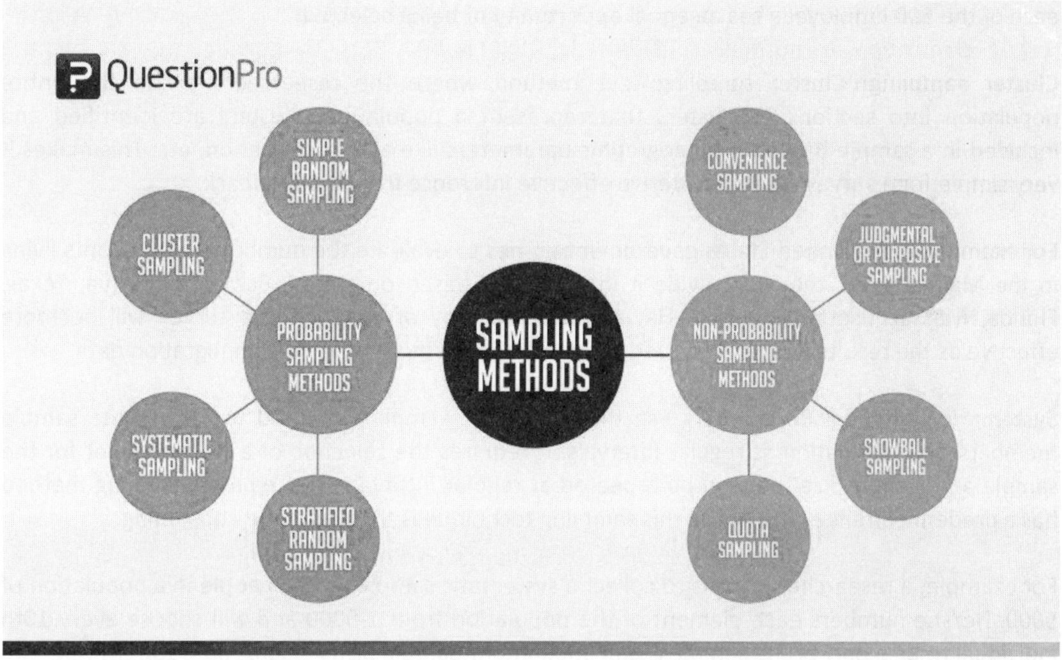

(Source: QuestionPro website)

Sampling in market research is of two types – probability sampling and non-probability sampling. Let's understand these two methods of sampling.

Probability sampling

Probability sampling is a sampling technique where a researcher sets a selection of a few criteria and chooses members of a population randomly. All the members have an equal opportunity to be a part of the sample with this selection parameter.

Types of probability sampling with examples:
Probability sampling is a sampling technique in which researchers choose samples from a larger population using a method based on the theory of probability. This sampling method considers every member of the population and forms samples based on a fixed process. For example, in a population of 1000 members, every member will have a 1/1000 chance of being selected to be a part of a sample. Probability sampling eliminates bias in the population and gives all members a fair chance to be included in the sample.

There are four types of probability sampling techniques:

Simple random sampling: One of the best probability sampling techniques that helps in saving time and resources, is the Simple Random Sampling method. It is a reliable method of obtaining information where every single member of a population is chosen randomly, merely by chance. Each individual has the same probability of being chosen to be a part of a sample.

For example, in an organization of 500 employees, if the HR team decides on conducting team building activities, it is highly likely that they would prefer picking chits out of a bowl. In this case, each of the 500 employees has an equal opportunity of being selected.

Cluster sampling: Cluster sampling is a method where the researchers divide the entire population into sections or clusters that represent a population. Clusters are identified and included in a sample based on demographic parameters like age, sex, location, etc. This makes it very simple for a survey creator to derive effective inference from the feedback.

For example, if the United States government wishes to evaluate the number of immigrants living in the Mainland US, they can divide it into clusters based on states such as California, Texas, Florida, Massachusetts, Colorado, Hawaii, etc. This way of conducting a survey will be more effective as the results will be organized into states and provide insightful immigration data.

Systematic sampling: Researchers use the systematic sampling method to choose the sample members of a population at regular intervals. It requires the selection of a starting point for the sample and sample size that can be repeated at regular intervals. This type of sampling method has a predefined range, and hence this sampling technique is the least time-consuming.

For example, a researcher intends to collect a systematic sample of 500 people in a population of 5000. He/she numbers each element of the population from 1-5000 and will choose every 10th individual to be a part of the sample (Total population/ Sample Size = 5000/500 = 10).

Stratified random sampling: Stratified random sampling is a method in which the researcher divides the population into smaller groups that don't overlap but represent the entire population. While sampling, these groups can be organized and then draw a sample from each group separately.

For example, a researcher looking to analyze the characteristics of people belonging to different annual income divisions will create strata (groups) according to the annual family income. Eg – less than $20,000, $21,000 – $30,000, $31,000 to $40,000, $41,000 to $50,000, etc. By doing this, the researcher concludes the characteristics of people belonging to different income groups.

Marketers can analyze which income groups to target and which ones to eliminate to create a roadmap that would bear fruitful results.

Uses of probability sampling

There are multiple uses of probability sampling. They are:

- Reduce Sample Bias: Using the probability sampling method, the bias in the sample derived from a population is negligible to non-existent. The selection of the sample mainly depicts the understanding and the inference of the researcher. Probability sampling leads to higher quality data collection as the sample appropriately represents the population.
- Diverse Population: When the population is vast and diverse, it is essential to have adequate representation so that the data is not skewed towards one demographic. For example, if Square would like to understand the people that could make their point-of-sale devices, a survey conducted from a sample of people across the US from different industries and socio-economic backgrounds helps.
- Create an Accurate Sample: Probability sampling helps the researchers plan and create an accurate sample. This helps to obtain well-defined data.

Non-probability sampling

In non-probability sampling, the researcher chooses members for research at random. This sampling method is not a fixed or predefined selection process. This makes it difficult for all elements of a population to have equal opportunities to be included in a sample.

The non-probability method is a sampling method that involves a collection of feedback based on a researcher or statistician's sample selection capabilities and not on a fixed selection process. In most situations, the output of a survey conducted with a non-probable sample leads to skewed results, which may not represent the desired target population. But, there are situations such as the preliminary stages of research or cost constraints for conducting research, where non-probability sampling will be much more useful than the other type.

Types of non-probability sampling with examples

Four types of non-probability sampling explain the purpose of this sampling method in a better manner:

Convenience sampling: This method is dependent on the ease of access to subjects such as surveying customers at a mall or passers-by on a busy street. It is usually termed as convenience sampling, because of the researcher's ease of carrying it out and getting in touch with the subjects. Researchers have nearly no authority to select the sample elements, and it's purely done based on proximity and not representativeness. This non-probability sampling method is used when there are time and cost limitations in collecting feedback. In situations where there are resource limitations such as the initial stages of research, convenience sampling is used.
For example, startups and NGOs usually conduct convenience sampling at a mall to distribute leaflets of upcoming events or promotion of a cause – they do that by standing at the mall entrance and giving out pamphlets randomly.

Judgmental or purposive sampling: Judgemental or purposive samples are formed by the discretion of the researcher. Researchers purely consider the purpose of the study, along with the understanding of the target audience. For instance, when researchers want to understand the thought process of people interested in studying for their master's degree. The selection criteria will be: "Are you interested in doing your masters in ...?" and those who respond with a "No" are excluded from the sample.

Snowball sampling: Snowball sampling is a sampling method that researchers apply when the subjects are difficult to trace. For example, it will be extremely challenging to survey shelterless people or illegal immigrants. In such cases, using the snowball theory, researchers can track a few categories to interview and derive results. Researchers also implement this sampling method in situations where the topic is highly sensitive and not openly discussed—for example, surveys to gather information about HIV Aids. Not many victims will readily respond to the questions. Still, researchers can contact people they might know or volunteers associated with the cause to get in touch with the victims and collect information.

Quota sampling: In Quota sampling, the selection of members in this sampling technique happens based on a pre-set standard. In this case, as a sample is formed based on specific attributes, the created sample will have the same qualities found in the total population. It is a rapid method of collecting samples.

Uses of non-probability sampling

Non-probability sampling is used for the following:

- Create a hypothesis: Researchers use the non-probability sampling method to create an assumption when limited to no prior information is available. This method helps with the immediate return of data and builds a base for further research.
- Exploratory research: Researchers use this sampling technique widely when conducting qualitative research, pilot studies, or exploratory research.
- Budget and time constraints: The non-probability method when there are budget and time constraints, and some preliminary data must be collected. Since the survey design is not rigid, it is easier to pick respondents at random and have them take the survey or questionnaire.

How do you decide on the type of sampling to use?

For any research, it is essential to choose a sampling method accurately to meet the goals of your study. The effectiveness of your sampling relies on various factors. Here are some steps expert researchers follow to decide the best sampling method.

- Jot down the research goals. Generally, it must be a combination of cost, precision, or accuracy.
- Identify the effective sampling techniques that might potentially achieve the research goals.
- Test each of these methods and examine whether they help in achieving your goal.
- Select the method that works best for the research.

PROBABILITY SAMPLING USING PYTHON

For the following example, let's obtain samples from a set of 10 products using probability sampling to determine the population mean of a particular measure of interest.

Code: generate 10 products

```
# Import required libraries
import numpy as np
import pandas as pd

# Set random seed
np.random.seed(1)

# Define total number of products
num_products = 10

# Create data dictionary
data = {'product_id':np.arange(1, num_products+1).tolist(),
       'size':np.round(np.random.normal(loc=10, scale=0.5,
size=num_products),3)}
#Normal distrobution: mean = 10, sd = 0.5

# Transform dictionary into a data frame
df = pd.DataFrame(data)

# Store the real mean in a separate variable
real_mean = round(df['size'].mean(),3)

# View data frame
print(df)
```

Output:

```
   product_id    size
0           1  10.812
1           2   9.694
2           3   9.736
3           4   9.464
4           5  10.433
5           6   8.849
6           7  10.872
7           8   9.619
8           9  10.160
9          10   9.875
```

1. Now lets perform Simple Random Sampling

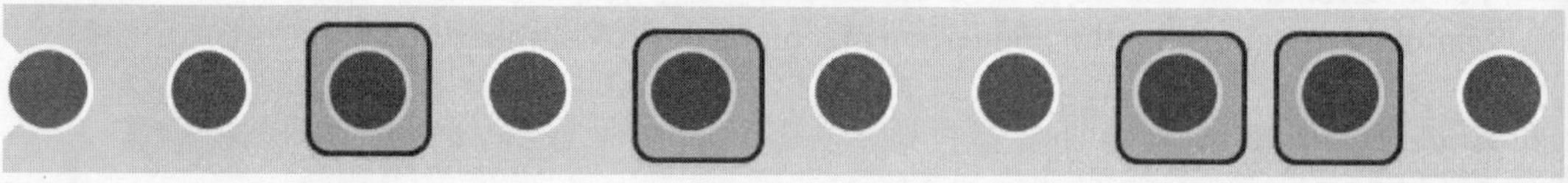

```
#Simple Random sampling
simple_random_sample =
df.sample(n=4).sort_values(by='product_id')

# Save the sample mean in a separate variable
simple_random_mean =
round(simple_random_sample['size'].mean(),3)

# View sampled data frame
print("\nSimple random data: \n",simple_random_sample)
```

Output:

```
Simple random data:
    product_id    size
3            4   9.464
5            6   8.849
8            9  10.160
9           10   9.875
```

2. Systematic Sampling

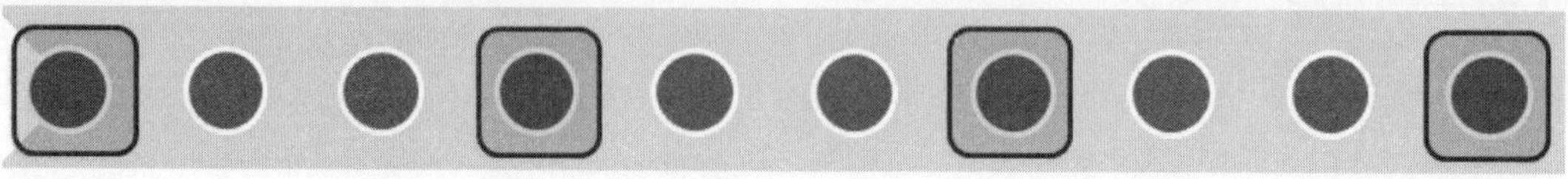

```
# Define systematic sampling function
def systematic_sampling(df, step):
    indexes = np.arange(0, len(df), step=step)
    systematic_sample = df.iloc[indexes]
    return systematic_sample

# Obtain a systematic sample and save it in a new variable
systematic_sample = systematic_sampling(df, 3)

# Save the sample mean in a separate variable
systematic_mean = round(systematic_sample['size'].mean(), 3)

# View sampled data frame
print("\n Systematic Sample Data: \n", systematic_sample)
```

Output

```
 Systematic Sample Data:
    product_id    size
0            1  10.812
3            4   9.464
6            7  10.872
9           10   9.875
```

3. **Cluster Sampling**

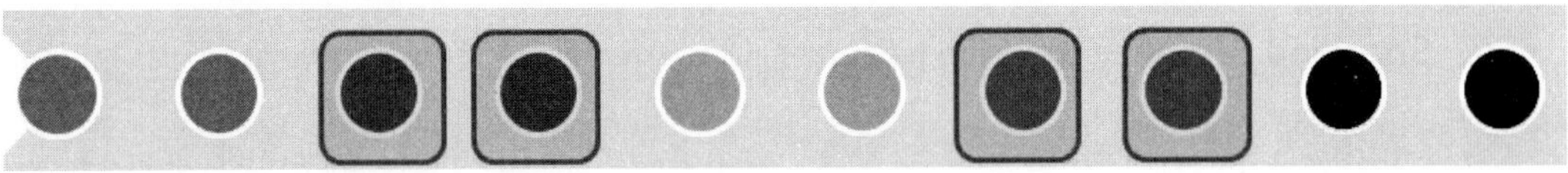

```
#Define clusters
def cluster_sampling(df, number_of_clusters):
    ''' Defining clusters'''
    try:
        # Divide the units into cluster of equal size
        df['cluster_id'] = np.repeat([range(1,
number_of_clusters + 1)], len(df) / number_of_clusters)

        # Create an empty list
        indexes = []

        # Append the indexes from the clusters that meet the
criteria
        # For this formula, clusters id must be an even number
        for i in range(0, len(df)):
            if df['cluster_id'].iloc[i] % 2 == 0:
                indexes.append(i)
        cluster_sample = df.iloc[indexes]
        return (cluster_sample)

    except:
        print("The population cannot be divided into clusters
of equal size!")


# Obtain a cluster sample and save it in a new variable
cluster_sample = cluster_sampling(df, 5)

# Save the sample mean in a separate variable
cluster_mean = round(cluster_sample['size'].mean(), 3)

# View sampled data frame
print("\n Sample data from Clusters Sample: \n",cluster_sample)
```

Output

```
Sample data from Clusters Sample:
   product_id    size  cluster_id
2           3   9.736           2
3           4   9.464           2
6           7  10.872           4
7           8   9.619           4
```

4. **Stratified Sampling**

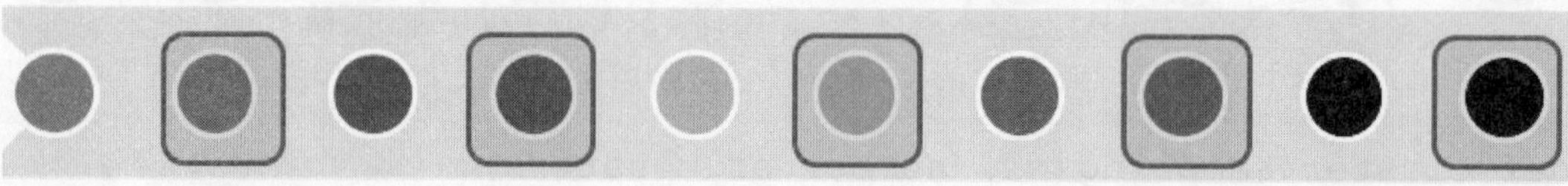

```
### Using Stratified Sampling
# Create data dictionary
data = {'product_id':np.arange(1, num_products+1).tolist(),
       'product_strata':np.repeat([1,2],
num_products/2).tolist(),
       'size':np.round(np.random.normal(loc=10, scale=0.5,
size=num_products),3)}

# Transform dictionary into a data frame
df = pd.DataFrame(data)

# View data frame
print("\n Stratified Sampling: \n",df)

# Import StratifiedShuffleSplit
from sklearn.model_selection import StratifiedShuffleSplit

# Set the split criteria
split = StratifiedShuffleSplit(n_splits=1, test_size=4)

# Perform data frame split
for x, y in split.split(df, df['product_strata']):
    stratified_random_sample =
df.iloc[y].sort_values(by='product_id')

# Obtain the sample mean for each group
stratified_random_sample.groupby('product_strata').mean().drop(
['product_id'],axis=1)

# View sampled data frame
```

```
print("\n Data from Stratified Sampling:
\n",stratified_random_sample)
```

Output

```
 Stratified Sampling:
   product_id  product_strata    size
0           1               1  10.731
1           2               1   8.970
2           3               1   9.839
3           4               1   9.808
4           5               1  10.567
5           6               2   9.450
6           7               2   9.914
7           8               2   9.561
8           9               2  10.021
9          10               2  10.291

 Data from Stratified Sampling:
   product_id  product_strata    size
0           1               1  10.731
4           5               1  10.567
7           8               2   9.561
9          10               2  10.291
```

Measure Mean Comparison per Sampling Method

Once samples have been obtained using each sampling technique, let's compare the samples means with the population mean (which usually is unknown, but not in this case) to determine the sampling technique that leads to the best approximation of the population measure mean.

```
# Create a dictionary with the mean outcomes for each sampling
method and the real mean
outcomes =
{'sample_mean':[simple_random_mean,systematic_mean,cluster_mean
],
            'real_mean':real_mean}

# Transform dictionary into a data frame
outcomes = pd.DataFrame(outcomes, index=['Simple Random
Sampling','Systematic Sampling','Cluster Sampling'])

# Add a value corresponding to the absolute error
outcomes['abs_error'] = abs(outcomes['real_mean'] -
outcomes['sample_mean'])

# Sort data frame by absolute error
outcomes.sort_values(by='abs_error')
```

```
#print all the values:
print("Display Sample, Real Mean and Absolute_Error:")
print(outcomes)
```

Output:

```
Display Sample, Real Mean and Absolute_Error:
                          sample_mean  real_mean  abs_error
Simple Random Sampling          9.587      9.951      0.364
Systematic Sampling            10.256      9.951      0.305
Cluster Sampling                9.923      9.951      0.028
```

According to the Measure Mean Comparison per Sampling Method Table, the measure mean of the sample obtained through the cluster sampling technique was the closest one to the real mean, with an absolute error of 0.028 units.

Sampling represents a useful and effective method for drawing conclusions about a population from a sample. However, analysts and engineers must define sampling techniques with adequate sample sizes capable of reducing sampling bias (e.g. convenience sampling selection bias, systematic sampling bias selection bias, environmental bias, non-response bias) to obtain representative samples of a given population.

SAMPLING DISTRIBUTION

What is a Sampling Distribution?
A sampling distribution is a graph of a statistic for your sample data. While, technically, you could choose any statistic to paint a picture, some common ones you'll come across are:

- Mean
- Mean absolute value of the deviation from the mean
- Range
- Standard deviation of the sample
- Unbiased estimate of variance
- Variance of the sample

In the next chapter, we will learn about how to estimate Population based on sample information.

***

UNIT 9: ESTIMATION IN STATISTICS

In statistics, estimation refers to the process by which one makes inferences about a population, based on information obtained from a sample.

Point Estimate vs. Interval Estimate

Statisticians use sample statistics to estimate population parameters. For example, sample means are used to estimate population means; sample proportions, to estimate population proportions.

An estimate of a population parameter may be expressed in two ways:

- Point estimate. A point estimate of a population parameter is a single value of a statistic. For example, the sample mean x is a point estimate of the population mean μ. Similarly, the sample proportion p is a point estimate of the population proportion P.
- Interval estimate. An interval estimate is defined by two numbers, between which a population parameter is said to lie. For example, a < x < b is an interval estimate of the population mean μ. It indicates that the population mean is greater than a but less than b.

Confidence Intervals

Statisticians use a confidence interval to express the precision and uncertainty associated with a particular sampling method. A confidence interval consists of three parts.

- A confidence level.
- A statistic.
- A margin of error.

The confidence level describes the uncertainty of a sampling method. The statistic and the margin of error define an interval estimate that describes the precision of the method. The interval estimate of a confidence interval is defined by the sample statistic + margin of error.

For example, suppose we compute an interval estimate of a population parameter. We might describe this interval estimate as a 95% confidence interval. This means that if we used the same sampling method to select different samples and compute different interval estimates, the true population parameter would fall within a range defined by the sample statistic + margin of error 95% of the time.

Confidence intervals are preferred to point estimates, because confidence intervals indicate (a) the precision of the estimate and (b) the uncertainty of the estimate.

Confidence Level

The probability part of a confidence interval is called a confidence level. The confidence level describes the likelihood that a particular sampling method will produce a confidence interval that includes the true population parameter.

Here is how to interpret a confidence level. Suppose we collected all possible samples from a given population, and computed confidence intervals for each sample. Some confidence intervals would include the true population parameter; others would not. A 95% confidence level means that 95% of the intervals contain the true population parameter; a 90% confidence level means that 90% of the intervals contain the population parameter; and so on.

Margin of Error

In a confidence interval, the range of values above and below the sample statistic is called the margin of error.

For example, suppose the local newspaper conducts an election survey and reports that the independent candidate will receive 30% of the vote. The newspaper states that the survey had a 5% margin of error and a confidence level of 95%. These findings result in the following confidence interval: We are 95% confident that the independent candidate will receive between 25% and 35% of the vote.

Note: Many public opinion surveys report interval estimates, but not confidence intervals. They provide the margin of error, but not the confidence level. To clearly interpret survey results you need to know both! We are much more likely to accept survey findings if the confidence level is high (say, 95%) than if it is low (say, 50%).

The confidence level is not affected by the margin of error. When the margin of error is small, the confidence level can low or high or anything in between. A confidence interval is a type of interval estimate, not a type of point estimate. A population mean is not an example of a point estimate; a sample mean is an example of a point estimate.

ESTIMATION USING THE Z STATISTIC

In the distribution chapter, we found that it was possible to estimate the probability of getting an element greater than or equal to a particular value (X) in a population with the known parameters, mean (μ) and standard deviation (σ). In these cases the z statistic is calculated to locate the position of X in a standard normal distribution where:

$$z = (X - \mu) / \sigma$$

A similar process can be used when dealing with sample means. If a sufficient number of samples have been taken, and their means plotted, then they begin to take up a normal distribution. It can be shown mathematically that the mean of this distribution (**μ_x**) is the same as the population mean (**μ**). Furthermore, the standard deviation of the distribution is equal to **σ/√n**, where **n** is the number of cases in the sample. This is known as the standard error of the mean (SEM). To estimate the probability of getting a value greater than or equal to a particular sample mean (x), in a population with a known mean (μ) and standard deviation (σ), we again calculate the **z statistic**. However, as we are dealing with the distribution of the means, we use the SEM rather than the population's standard deviation:

$$z = [(x - \mu) / (\sigma / \sqrt{n})]$$

You will have noticed that both of these calculations are dependent upon knowing the population's mean and standard deviation. In clinical and experimental practice this is rarely the case. However, we know that the best single estimate we have for the parameter μ is our sample mean. Unfortunately, the same does not apply to the sample's standard deviation. We get around this problem by using the estimated standard error of the mean.

Estimated standard error of the mean
If we simply replaced the sample's standard deviation for σ to determine the SEM, we would end up with an underestimation of its true value. To overcome this we use an estimation of the population's standard deviation (s) using the following formula:

$$s = \sqrt{[\sum(x - sample\ mean)^2 \ / \ (n-1)]}$$

where: s is the estimate of the population standard deviation based upon the sample data
n is the number in the sample
n−1 is called the degrees of freedom

Example: Consider a hospital Hyderabad Medical Institute. As part of their continuing assessment of staff in the Emergency Department, selects five female night nurses at random and weighs them (50 kg, 60 kg, 60 kg, 60 kg, 70 kg). What is their best estimate of the population mean and standard deviation based upon this sample?

The best estimate of the population mean is the sample mean:

Estimated population mean = (sum of all measures/n) =300/5 = 60.0 kg

The best estimation of the population's standard deviation is s where:

$$s = \sqrt{[\sum(x - 60)^2 \ /4]} = 7.07\text{kg}$$

We use s as a substitute for σ when trying to estimate the chances of getting a particular sample mean in a population with an unknown standard deviation. In these cases, rather than using the SEM:

SEM = σ/√n

we use the estimated SEM:

ESEM = s/√n

Comparing a large sample mean with a population with unknown SD
The ESEM will provide a close approximation of the SEM if the sample size is 100 or greater. It is possible to determine:

- The chance of getting a sample mean greater than or equal to a particular value
- The value of a sample mean with a particular chance of occurring
- The chance of getting a sample mean between two particular values

The chance of getting a sample mean greater than or equal to a particular value

To demonstrate this consider the following example. Hospital wonders whether the female staff in the Emergency Directorate are as unfit as their male counterparts. To test this he measures the weight in 100 randomly selected female medical and nursing staff. The sample mean is 60 kg and s is 20 kg. From actuarial tables he finds that the mean weight for fit females is 55 kg, but the standard deviation is unknown. Hospital therefore wants to know what is the chance of getting a mean weight equal or greater to 60 kg from a sample that is still part of a normal fit female population?

The sample size is large enough to allow the normal probability distribution to be used even though the standard deviation of the population is not known. The z statistic for this weight is therefore: z = (sample mean – population mean)/ESEM

Where the ESEM is = s/√n = 20/√100 = 2

Therefore the z statistic is: (60 – 55)/2 = 2.5

Using the z statistic table, the area between z = 0 and z = 2.5 is 0.4938.

Therefore the probability of getting a z value greater than or equal to 2.5 is: 0.5–0.4938 = 0.0062.

Consequently the chances of a similar sample of fit women having a mean weight greater than or equal to 60 kg is 0.0062 or 0.62%.

The value of a sample mean with a particular chance of occurring
Hospital can also determine what sample mean demarcates the top 2.5% of the population.

Convert the 2.5% to the proportion = 0.025

Determine the proportion of a standard normal distribution curve from the midline to 0.025. This is equal to 0.5–0.025 = 0.475

Convert the proportion 0.475 to a z statistic.

Using the z statistic tables, 0.475 gives a z statistic of 1.96.

Using this value for z, determine the sample mean.

Remembering that: z = (sample mean – population mean)/ESEM
i.e. 1.96 = (sample mean – 55)/2

Therefore the element value is 3.92 + 55 = 59 kg (rounded up). Consequently there is a 2.5% chance that a randomly selected sample of 100 fit women would have a mean weight of 59 kg or greater.

The chance of getting a sample mean between two particular values
Looking at the middle of the population, Hospital then wants to know what range of means from similar samples would demarcate the middle 95% of the population of fit women.

As the upper 2.5% has already been calculated, Hospital calculates the value for the lower 2.5%. Using the same system as shown above he finds the lower 2.5% is:

$$-3.92 + 55 = 51\ kg\ (rounded\ down).$$

Consequently the middle 95% of random samples of 100 fit women would have a mean weight between 51 to 59 kg. This range of values is known as the 95% confidence interval.1 In other words we are 95% confident that a random sample of 100 fit women from this population would have a mean weight between 51 and 59 kg.

Therefore, provided the sample is large enough, the z statistic can be used to calculate confidence intervals when the population's standard deviation is not known. In these cases the confidence interval is equal to the sample mean plus/minus the z statistic appropriate for the level of confidence (zo) multiplied by the ESEM:

$$Confidence\ interval = sample\ mean\ +/-\ (z_o \times ESEM)$$

Estimating a population's probability values from a large sample

We have seen in the above example that it is possible to determine the confidence interval of the estimation of the population's mean when σ is not known. It is also possible to do the same thing with respect to determining the confidence interval for the population's probability (P) using the sample's probability value (p). This is because the binomial probability distribution becomes approximately normal in shape when the sample is large. Consequently the z statistic can again be used to determine confidence intervals.

To demonstrate this: consider the following example. In the midst of his study on emergency staff, Hospital has been asked by one of its consultant to determine the proportion of patients who are covered for tetanus. A team is formed. The team surveys 700 patients at random and finds 550 have adequate immunisation against tetanus infection.

The probability (p) of adequate tetanus immunisation is therefore:

$$p = 550/700 = 0.786$$

This represents the proportion of adequate tetanus immunisation in the sample. Hospital now needs to estimate what the proportion would be in a population of similar patients (P). As with the situation described previously, the best estimate for the population's probability is p—that is, 0.786. What is now needed is the confidence interval of this estimation.

The formula for calculating the confidence interval for P from a large sample is:

$$p \pm [z_o \times \sqrt{(pq/n)}]$$

where:

zo is the z statistic appropriate for the confidence interval p is the probability we are concerned with (that is, tetanus covered)

q is the probability we are not concerned with (that is, not tetanus covered)

This formula assumes that the sample is large and that the smaller of the two groups must have at least 10 cases. As these both apply in this example, Hospital calculates the 95% confidence interval to be:

$$= 0.786 \pm [1.96 \times \sqrt{(0.786 \times 0.214/700)}] = 0.757 \text{ to } 0.815$$

He therefore reports to his consultant that the proportion of patients adequately immunised against tetanus is 0.79 with a 95% confidence interval of 0.76 to 0.82.

Calculate Z0 Value:
Calculate a 95% confidence interval for the true population proportion.

Divide your confidence level by 2: .95/2 = 0.475. Look up the value you calculated in the z-table and find the corresponding z-value. The z-value that has an area of .475 is 1.96.

1.8	0.4641	0.4649	0.4656	0.4664	0.4671	0.4678	0.4686	0.4693	0.4699
1.9	0.4713	0.4719	0.4726	0.4732	0.4738	0.4744	0.4750	0.4756	0.4761
2.0	0.4772	0.4778	0.4783	0.4788	0.4793	0.4798	0.4803	0.4808	0.4812

A Z-score is a numerical measurement that describes a value's relationship to the mean of a group of values. Z-score is measured in terms of standard deviations from the mean. If a Z-score is 0, it indicates that the data point's score is identical to the mean score.

ESTIMATION USING THE T STATISTIC

We commonly deal with a small sample mean with a population with unknown SD. Mostly in our analysis, we have sample sizes smaller than 100 from populations with unknown standard deviations. When dealing with such samples to make inferences about the population it is no longer valid to use the z statistic. To over come these difficulties, W S Gossett derived a replacement known as the t statistic.

Gossett carried out his work while working in the Guinness Brewery in Dublin. It was based upon samples taken from a population made up of the heights of 3000 criminals. At the time the company would not allow employees to publish their own work. He therefore had to have his findings printed under the pseudonym "Student" in 1908. Hence the name "Student's t distribution" and "Student's t test".

THE t STATISTIC

The t statistic is derived in a similar fashion to the z statistic:

t = (sample mean – population mean)/ESEM

Consequently the t statistic is the number of estimated SEM a particular sample mean lies above or below the population mean.

t DISTRIBUTION CURVES

The t statistic tables show the area under the curve between a particular t value and the tip of the tail. Along the horizontal axis is the t value. These are equivalent to the SD seen with the normal distribution plots. Therefore the same principle applies regarding set areas under the curve representing particular probabilities.

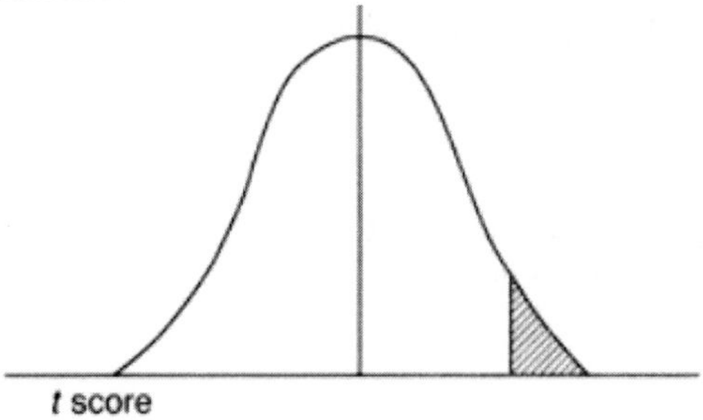

df \ p	0.1	0.05	0.025	0.01	0.005
1	3.078	6.314	12.706	31.821	63.657
2	1.886	2.920	4.303	6.965	9.925
3	1.683	2.353	3.182	4.541	5.841
4	1.533	2.132	2.776	3.747	4.604
5	1.476	2.015	2.571	3.365	4.032
10	1.372	1.812	2.228	2.764	3.169
11	1.363	1.796	2.201	2.718	3.106
12	1.356	1.782	2.160	2.650	3.055
13	1.350	1.771	2.160	2.650	3.012
14	1.345	1.761	2.145	2.624	2.977
15	1.341	1.753	2.131	2.602	2.947
24	1.318	1.711	2.064	2.492	2.797

The curve from which the z statistics were derived remains constant irrespective of the number in the sample. Consequently z values of mean +/- 1.96 will always mark out the middle 95% of the population. In contrast, the t statistics vary with sample size because the shape of the distribution changes. It is always symmetrical but with small sample sizes the curve is flatter and has longer "tails". This is a result of the variation in ESEM as the sample size changes.

With larger samples the t distribution becomes indistinguishable from a normal distribution. Consequently in these cases the z and t statistic values are the same. Therefore, a relevant question at this stage is how small does the sample need to be before the use of the t statistic is necessary. There is no definite answer because it depends upon several factors, including the distribution of the data. For example, when the data are normally distributed the z statistic can be used when there is as little as 30 subjects in the sample. In general however, it is recommended that the t test should be used when dealing with ESEM derived from samples sizes that are less than 100.

USING THE t TABLE

As there is a family of t distribution curves, depending upon the sample size, the t table does not look initially like the z statistic table. However, each line of the table represents the equivalent of a whole z table for a particular sample size. The left column deals with the size of the sample. It is labelled the "degrees of freedom" rather than sample number because, for mathematical reasons, we need to use a value one less than the number in the sample. For example, the t statistics for a sample of 15 would be found along the line whose degree of freedom was 14. Therefore, for this sample size, 2.5% of the total area under the curve lies between a t value of +2.145 to the right tail tip.

As described above, the t statistic allows estimations of the population's standard error of the mean to be made from the sample data. This enables you to determine, in a population with an unknown standard deviation:

- The chance of getting a sample mean greater than or equal to a particular value
- The value of a sample mean with a particular chance of occurring
- The chance of getting a sample mean between two particular values

THE CHANCE OF GETTING A SAMPLE MEAN GREATER THAN OR EQUAL TO A PARTICULAR VALUE

To demonstrate this, consider Hospital's result when they measured the resting heart rate in all the 25 male members of the department. He found the sample mean to be 70/minute with an **s** of 16. The population mean for fit men was found to be 60/minute.

Therefore:

$$ESEM = s/\sqrt{n} = 16/\sqrt{25}$$

Without knowing the population's SEM, Hospital must use the ESEM to determine the chance of getting a resting heart rate equal or greater to 70/minute if the department's men were part of a fit male population.

The t statistic for this resting heart rate is: ***(sample mean – population mean)/ESEM***

Therefore the t statistic is:

$$(70-60)/3.2 = 3.13$$

Using the t statistic table, for a sample size of 25, the area between t = 3.13 and the tip of the tail is less than 0.005. Consequently the chances of a sample having a resting heart rate greater than or equal to 70/minute in a fit male population is less than 0.5%.

THE VALUE OF SAMPLE MEAN WITH A PARTICULAR CHANCE OF OCCURRING

Using the ESEM, Hospital then determines what random, 25 male person sample mean demarcates the top 2.5% of the population of fit men. This is carried out in a similar manner to before, but this time using the t statistic.

Using the t statistic table, the proportion 0.025 is equal to 2.064.

This value for t can then be used to determine the sample mean by remembering that:

t = sample mean – population mean/ESEM

Therefore: 2.064 = (sample mean – 60)/3.2

Consequently the sample mean is 6.6 + 60 = 67/minute (rounded up)

Therefore 2.5% of random samples of 25 fit men would have a mean resting heart rate of 67/minute or greater.

THE CHANCE OF GETTING A SAMPLE MEAN BETWEEN TWO PARTICULAR VALUES

Again with the ESEM, Egbert can determine the value of the sample means demarcating the middle 95% of the population of fit men. Using the same system, the lower 2.5% of the curve is demarcated by the t statistic −2.064 for a sample size of 25.

With this value for t, the sample mean can be determined by: −2.064 = (sample mean – 60)/3.2

Therefore the element value is −6.6 + 60 = 53/minute (rounded).

It follows that the middle 95% of random samples of 25 fit men would have a mean resting heart rate between 53 to 67/minute. This also represents the 95% confidence interval—that is, we are 95% confident that a random sample of 25 men from this population would have a mean resting heart rate between 53 and 67 beats/minute.

The t statistic can therefore be used to calculate confidence intervals. When using data from a sample, the confidence intervals are equal to the sample mean plus/minus the t statistic appropriate for the level of confidence (to) multiplied by the ESEM:

$$Confidence\ interval\ =\ sample\ mean\ +/-\ (\ t_o\ x\ ESEM)$$

Provided the sample size is large enough (that is, n greater than 100), the z statistic can be used to determine the confidence interval estimation of the population mean even when the σ is not known. In these cases the estimation of the standard error of the mean is used. The z statistic is also valid when determining the population's proportion based upon a large sample.
However, when dealing with smaller samples, the z statistic is replaced by the t statistic. This makes it possible to estimate, in a population with an unknown standard deviation:

- The probability of getting a sample mean greater than or equal to a particular value
- The value of a sample mean with a particular probability of occurring
- The probability of getting a sample mean between two particular values

The confidence interval for the estimation of the population mean can also be determined using the t statistic.

Practice Problems

1. A sample of five patients with fractured necks of femurs was studied. The trolley waiting times were: 1, 2, 2, 2, 3 hours respectively. What is the best estimate for the population's mean and estimated standard deviation of the mean?

2. The systolic blood pressure (SBP) is measured in 144 randomly selected, elderly (over 70 years) male patients, presenting to Hospital's Emergency Department. The mean SBP is 140 mm Hg and s = 30 mm Hg. What is the 95% confidence interval for the mean SBP for this population of patients?

3. Hospital asks its staff to determine the proportion of asthmatics who had their inhaler technique assessed before discharge from their emergency departments. After a year's study 160 were appropriately assessed out of a random sample of 200 asthmatics. What is the 99% confidence interval for the proportion assessed in the population?

4. Hospital management is interested in the total cholesterol concentrations of patients presenting with chest pain. He finds the mean concentration is 8.1 mmol/l in a sample of 25 randomly selected patients. s is calculated to be 2.5 mmol/l. Assuming that the population is normally distributed, what is the 95% confidence interval for the population's mean cholesterol level?

Solution1 :

The best estimate of the population mean is the sample mean:

Estimated population mean = ***(sum of all measures/n)*** =10/5 = **2 hours**

The ESEM is s/ n :

where:

$$s = \sqrt{[\sum (x-2)^2 \ /4]} = \sqrt{[2/4]} = 0.707$$

therefore;

ESEM = 0.707/√5 = **0.32 hours** (approximately)

Solution2 :

The best estimate for the population's mean SBP is the sample mean (that is, 140 mm Hg). The SEM of the population is not known but the estimated standard error of the mean can be calculated:

$$ESEM = s/\sqrt{n} = 30/12 = 2.5$$

As the sample is over 100 it is reasonable to assume the z statistic will be valid. Therefore the confidence interval for the estimated mean is:

Sample mean +/− (zo × ESEM)

zo for a 95% confidence interval is 1.96. Therefore:

$$95\%\ CI\ =\ 140\ +/-\ (1.96 \times 2.5)=\ 140\ +/-\ 4.9=\ 135\ to\ 145\ mm\ Hg$$

Solution 3:

Again the best estimation of the population's proportion is the samples proportion. This is:

$$160/200\ =\ 0.8$$

As the smallest group is greater than 10, and the sample is large, it is valid to determine the confidence interval for this estimated proportion by the following formula:

$$p \pm [z_o\ \sqrt{(pq/n)}]$$

For a 99% confidence interval zo is 2.58. Therefore:

$$99\%\ confidence\ intervals\ =\ 0.8\ +/-\ [2.58 \times \sqrt{}\ (0.75 \times 0.25/200)]$$

$$=\ 0.8\ +/-\ 0.07\ =\ 0.73\ to\ 0.87$$

Solution 4:

The best estimation for the population mean is the sample mean—that is, 8.1 mmol/l.

We do not know the standard deviation of the population but it is possible to calculate an estimation of the standard error of the mean:

$$ESEM\ =\ s/\sqrt{n}=\ 2.5/5\ =\ 0.5$$

The sample size is less than a 100 but we know the population is normally distributed. Consequently the confidence intervals should be determined using the t statistic:

$$Confidence\ interval\ =\ sample\ mean\ +/-\ (t_o \times ESEM)$$

In this case we are interested in the 95% confidence intervals. The sample size is 25, which means the degrees of freedom = 24. Using the t table this gives a to of 2.064. Therefore:

$$95\%\ confidence\ interval\ =\ 8.1\ +/-\ (2.064 \times 0.5)$$

$$=\ 8.1\ +/-\ 1.03=\ 7.1\ to\ 9.1\ mmol/l$$

Z-STATISTIC VERSUS T-STATISTIC

The general rule of thumb for when to use a t score is when your sample:

- Has a sample size below 30,
- Has an unknown population standard deviation.

You must know the standard deviation of the population and your sample size should be above 30 in order for you to be able to use the z-score. Otherwise, use the t-score.

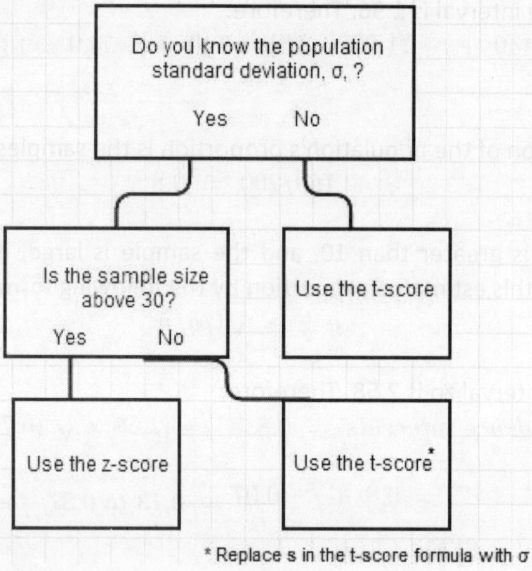

The z-score is calculated using the formula:

$$z = (X-\mu)/\sigma$$

Where:

- σ is the population standard deviation and
- μ is the population mean.

The z-score formula doesn't say anything about sample size; The rule of thumb applies that your sample size should be above 30 to use it.

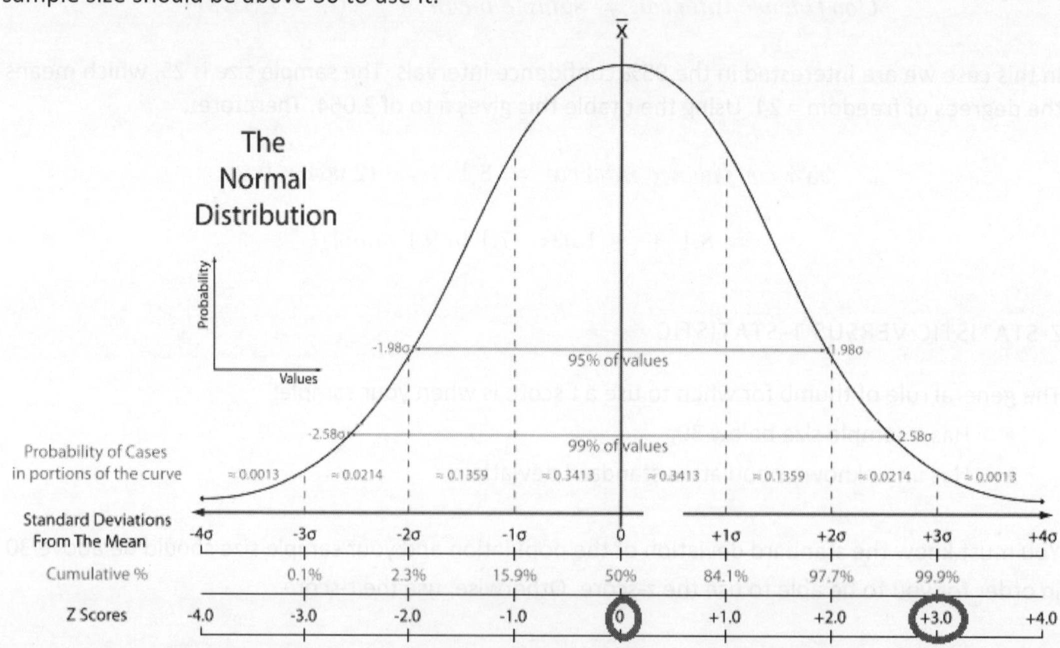

Like z-scores, t-scores are also a conversion of individual scores into a standard form. However, t-scores are used when you don't know the population standard deviation; You make an estimate by using your sample.

$$T = (X - \mu) / [\ s/\sqrt{(n)}\ ].$$

Where:
s is the standard deviation of the sample.
If you have a larger sample (over 30), the t-distribution and z-distribution look pretty much the same. Therefore, you can use either. That said, if you know σ, it doesn't make much sense to use a sample estimate instead of the "real thing", so just substitute σ into the equation in place of s:

$$T = (X - \mu) / [\ \sigma/\sqrt{(n)}\ ].$$

This makes the equation identical to the one for the z-score; the only difference is you're looking up the result in the T table, not the Z-table. For sample sizes over 30, you'll get the same result.

***

UNIT 10: STATISTICAL INFERENCE – ESTIMATION FOR SINGLE POPULATION

In this chapter we will cover topics to understand estimating parameters of single populations, thereby enabling us to:

- Estimate the population mean with a known population standard deviation with the z statistic, correcting for a finite population if necessary.
- Estimate the population mean with an unknown population standard deviation using the t statistic and properties of the t distribution.
- Estimate a population proportion using the z statistic.
- Determine the sample size needed in order to estimate the population mean and population proportion.

INTRODUCTION TO HYPOTHESIS TESTING

Cold Fusion Experiment

In 1989, two electrochemists, Martin Fleischmann and Stanley Pons, reported that their apparatus had produced anomalous heat ("excess heat") of a magnitude they asserted would defy explanation except in terms of nuclear processes. They further reported measuring small amounts of nuclear reaction byproducts, including neutrons and tritium. The small tabletop experiment involved electrolysis of heavy water on the surface of a palladium (Pd) electrode. The reported results received wide media attention and raised hopes of a cheap and abundant source of energy.

Many scientists tried to replicate the experiment with the few details available. Hopes faded due to the large number of negative replications, the withdrawal of many reported positive replications, the discovery of flaws and sources of experimental error in the original experiment, and finally the discovery that Fleischmann and Pons had not actually detected nuclear reaction byproducts. By late 1989, most scientists considered cold fusion claims dead, and cold fusion subsequently gained a reputation as pathological science. Pathological science is an area of research where "people are tricked into false results ... by subjective effects, wishful thinking or threshold interactions." The term was first used by Irving Langmuir, Nobel Prize–winning chemist, during a 1953 colloquium at the Knolls Research Laboratory. Langmuir said a pathological science is an area of research that simply will not "go away"—long after it was given up on as "false" by the majority of scientists in the field. He called pathological science "the science of things that aren't so."

In 1989 the United States Department of Energy (DOE) concluded that the reported results of excess heat did not present convincing evidence of a useful source of energy and decided against allocating funding specifically for cold fusion. A second DOE review in 2004, which looked at new research, reached similar conclusions and did not result in DOE funding of cold fusion.

Why did we discuss Cold Fusion, because the experiement which can not be repeated, will be called fake by the community. The main purpose of statistics is to test a hypothesis. For example, you might run an experiment and find that a certain drug is effective at treating headaches. But if you can't repeat that experiment, no one will take your results seriously.

A hypothesis is an educated guess about something in the world around you. It should be testable, either by experiment or observation. It can really be anything at all as long as you can put it to the test.

What is a Hypothesis Statement?

If you are going to propose a hypothesis, it's customary to write a statement. Your statement will look like this:

"If I...(do this to an independent variable)....then (this will happen to the dependent variable)."

For example:

- If I (decrease the amount of water given to herbs) then (the herbs will increase in size).
- If I (give patients counseling in addition to medication) then (their overall depression scale will decrease).
- If I (give exams at noon instead of 7) then (student test scores will improve).
- If I (look in this certain location) then (I am more likely to find new species).

A good hypothesis statement should:

- Include an "if" and "then" statement (according to the University of California).
- Include both the independent and dependent variables.
- Be testable by experiment, survey or other scientifically sound technique.
- Be based on information in prior research (either yours or someone else's).
- Have design criteria (for engineering or programming projects).

WHAT IS HYPOTHESIS TESTING?

Hypothesis testing in statistics is a way for you to test the results of a survey or experiment to see if you have meaningful results. You're basically testing whether your results are valid by figuring out the odds that your results have happened by chance. If your results may have happened by chance, the experiment won't be repeatable and so has little use.

Hypothesis testing can be one of the most confusing aspects for students, mostly because before you can even perform a test, you have to know what your null hypothesis is. Often, those tricky word problems that you are faced with can be difficult to decipher. But it's easier than you think; all you need to do is:

- Figure out your null hypothesis,
- State your null hypothesis,
- Choose what kind of test you need to perform,
- Either support or reject the null hypothesis.

Figure out your null hypothesis

The null hypothesis, H0 is the commonly accepted fact; it is the opposite of the alternate hypothesis. Researchers work to reject, nullify or disprove the null hypothesis. Researchers come up with an alternate hypothesis, one that they think explains a phenomenon, and then work to reject the null hypothesis.If you trace back the history of science, the null hypothesis is always the accepted fact. Simple examples of null hypotheses that are generally accepted as being true are:

- DNA is shaped like a double helix.
- There are 9 planets in the solar system.
- Taking Vioxx can increase your risk of heart problems (a drug now taken off the market).

Example 1: Null hypothesis, H0: The world is flat.
Alternate hypothesis: The world is round.

Several scientists, including Copernicus, set out to disprove the null hypothesis. This eventually led to the rejection of the null and the acceptance of the alternate

State your null hypothesis
Hypothesis Testing Examples #1: Basic Example
Example Problem: A researcher thinks that if knee surgery patients go to physical therapy twice a week (instead of 3 times), their recovery period will be longer. Average recovery times for knee surgery patients is 8.2 weeks.

Step 1: Figure out the hypothesis from the problem. The hypothesis is usually hidden in a word problem, and is sometimes a statement of what you expect to happen in the experiment. The hypothesis in the above question is "I expect the average recovery period to be greater than 8.2 weeks."

Step 2: Convert the hypothesis to math. Remember that the average is sometimes written as μ.

$$H1: \mu > 8.2$$

Broken down into general words, that's H1 (The hypothesis): μ (the average) > (is greater than) 8.2

Step 3: State what will happen if the hypothesis doesn't come true. If the recovery time isn't greater than 8.2 weeks, there are only two possibilities, that the recovery time is equal to 8.2 weeks or less than 8.2 weeks.

$H0: \mu \leq 8.2$

Broken down again into general workds, that's H0 (The null hypothesis): μ (the average) ≤ (is less than or equal to) 8.2

But what if the researcher doesn't have any idea what will happen?
Sample Problem: A researcher is studying the effects of radical exercise program on knee surgery patients. There is a good chance the therapy will improve recovery time, but there's also the possibility it will make it worse. Average recovery times for knee surgery patients is 8.2 weeks.

Step 1: State what will happen if the experiment doesn't make any difference. That's the null hypothesis–that nothing will happen. In this experiment, if nothing happens, then the recovery time will stay at 8.2 weeks.

$$H0: \mu = 8.2$$

Broken down into English, that's H0 (The null hypothesis): μ (the average) = (is equal to) 8.2

Step 2: Figure out the alternate hypothesis. The alternate hypothesis is the opposite of the null hypothesis. In other words, what happens if our experiment makes a difference?

$$H1: \mu \neq 8.2$$

In general wrod, that's H1 (The alternate hypothesis): μ (the average) ≠ (is not equal to) 8.2

Choose what kind of test you need to perform

- Use One Tailed or Two tailed test and use Z- statistics of t-statistics to test. We are going to cover them in detailed in this chapter.

Either support or reject the null hypothesis

Let's understand this with couple of examples here.

Example 1: A principal at a certain school claims that the students in his school are above average intelligence. A random sample of thirty students IQ scores have a mean score of 112. Is there sufficient evidence to support the principal's claim? The mean population IQ is 100 with a standard deviation of 15.

Solution:

Step 1: State the Null hypothesis. The accepted fact is that the population mean is 100, so:

$$H0: \mu=100$$

Step 2: State the Alternate Hypothesis. The claim is that the students have above average IQ scores, so:

$$H1: \mu > 100$$

The fact that we are looking for scores "greater than" a certain point means that this is a one-tailed test.

Step 3: Draw a picture to help you visualize the problem.

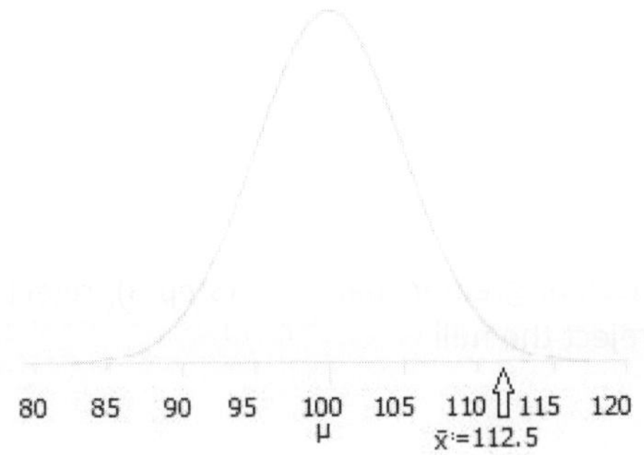

Step 4: State the alpha level. If you aren't given an alpha level, use 5% (0.05).

Step 5: Find the rejection region area (given by your alpha level above) from the z-table. An area of .05 is equal to a z-score of 1.645.

Step 6: Find the test statistic using this formula:

$$Z = \frac{\overline{x} - \mu_0}{\sigma / \sqrt{n}}$$

For this set of data: z= (112.5 – 100) / (15/√30) = 4.56.

Step 6: If Step 6 is greater than Step 5, reject the null hypothesis. If it's less than Step 5, you cannot reject the null hypothesis. In this case, it is greater (4.56 > 1.645), so you can reject the null.

Problem 2:

Blood glucose levels for obese patients have a mean of 100 with a standard deviation of 15. A researcher thinks that a diet high in raw cornstarch will have a positive or negative effect on blood glucose levels. A sample of 30 patients who have tried the raw cornstarch diet have a mean glucose level of 140. Test the hypothesis that the raw cornstarch had an effect.

Step 1: State the null hypothesis: H0:μ=100

Step 2: State the alternate hypothesis: H1:≠100

Step 3: State your alpha level. We'll use 0.05 for this example. As this is a two-tailed test, split the alpha into two.
0.05/2=0.025

Step 4: Find the z-score associated with your alpha level. You're looking for the area in one tail only. A z-score for 0.75 1-0.025=0.975) is 1.96. As this is a two-tailed test, you would also be considering the left tail (z = 1.96)

Step 5: Find the test statistic using this formula:

$$Z = \frac{\overline{x} - \mu_0}{\sigma / \sqrt{n}}$$

z = (140 – 100) / (15/√30) = 14.60.

Step 6: If Step 5 is less than -1.96 or greater than 1.96 (Step 3), reject the null hypothesis. In this case, it is greater, so you can reject the null.

In this chapter, we are going to discuss this concept in detail so stay tuned.

DECISION ERRORS

Hypothesis tests use sample data to make inferences about the properties of a population. You gain tremendous benefits by working with random samples because it is usually impossible to measure the entire population.

However, there are tradeoffs when you use samples. The samples we use are typically a minuscule percentage of the entire population. Consequently, they occasionally misrepresent the population severely enough to cause hypothesis tests to make errors.

Statisticians define two types of errors in hypothesis testing. Creatively, they call these errors Type I and Type II errors. Both types of error relate to incorrect conclusions about the null hypothesis.

Two types of errors can result from a hypothesis test:

- Type I error. A Type I error occurs when the researcher rejects a null hypothesis when it is true. The probability of committing a Type I error is called the significance level. This probability is also called alpha, and is often denoted by α.
- Type II error. A Type II error occurs when the researcher fails to reject a null hypothesis that is false. The probability of committing a Type II error is called Beta, and is often denoted by β. The probability of not committing a Type II error is called the Power of the test.

Truth Based on Entire Population

Conclusion Based on Sample		We Reject Ho	We Fail to Reject Ho
	Ho is TRUE	FALSE POSITIVE Type 1 Error Alpha Error	TRUE POSITIVE (1-Beta)
	Ho is FALSE	TRUE NEGATIVE (1-alpha)	FALSE NEGATIVE Type II Error Beta Error

Type I Errors: False Positives

When you see a p-value that is less than your significance level, you get excited because your results are statistically significant. However, it could be a type I error. The supposed effect might not exist in the population. Again, there is usually no warning when this occurs.

Why do these errors occur? It comes down to sample error. Your random sample has overestimated the effect by chance. It was the luck of the draw. This type of error doesn't indicate that the researchers did anything wrong. The experimental design, data collection, data validity, and statistical analysis can all be correct, and yet this type of error still occurs.

Even though we don't know for sure which studies have false positive results, we do know their rate of occurrence. The rate of occurrence for Type I errors equals the significance level of the hypothesis test, which is also known as alpha (α).

The significance level is an evidentiary standard that you set to determine whether your sample data are strong enough to reject the null hypothesis. Hypothesis tests define that standard using the probability of rejecting a null hypothesis that is actually true. You set this value based on your willingness to risk a false positive.

Using the significance level to set the Type I error rate

When the significance level is 0.05 and the null hypothesis is true, there is a 5% chance that the test will reject the null hypothesis incorrectly. If you set alpha to 0.01, there is a 1% of a false positive. If 5% is good, then 1% seems even better, right? As you'll see, there is a tradeoff between Type I and Type II errors. If you hold everything else constant, as you reduce the chance for a false positive, you increase the opportunity for a false negative.

Type II Errors: False Negatives

When you perform a hypothesis test and your p-value is greater than your significance level, your results are not statistically significant. That's disappointing because your sample provides insufficient evidence for concluding that the effect you're studying exists in the population. However, there is a chance that the effect is present in the population even though the test results don't support it. If that's the case, you've just experienced a Type II error. The probability of making a Type II error is known as beta (β).

What causes Type II errors? Whereas Type I errors are caused by one thing, sample error, there are a host of possible reasons for Type II errors—small effect sizes, small sample sizes, and high data variability. To estimate the Type II error rate, you create a hypothetical probability distribution that represents the properties of a true alternative hypothesis. However, when you're performing a hypothesis test, you typically don't know which hypothesis is true, much less the specific properties of the distribution for the alternative hypothesis. Consequently, the true Type II error rate is usually unknown!

Type II errors and the power of the analysis

The Type II error rate (beta) is the probability of a false negative. Therefore, the inverse of Type II errors is the probability of correctly detecting an effect. Statisticians refer to this concept as the power of a hypothesis test. Consequently, $1 - \beta$ = the statistical power.

Graphing Type I and Type II Errors

The graph below illustrates the two types of errors using two sampling distributions. The critical region line represents the point at which you reject or fail to reject the null hypothesis. Of course, when you perform the hypothesis test, you don't know which hypothesis is correct. And, the properties of the distribution for the alternative hypothesis are usually unknown. However, use this graph to understand the general nature of these errors and how they are related.

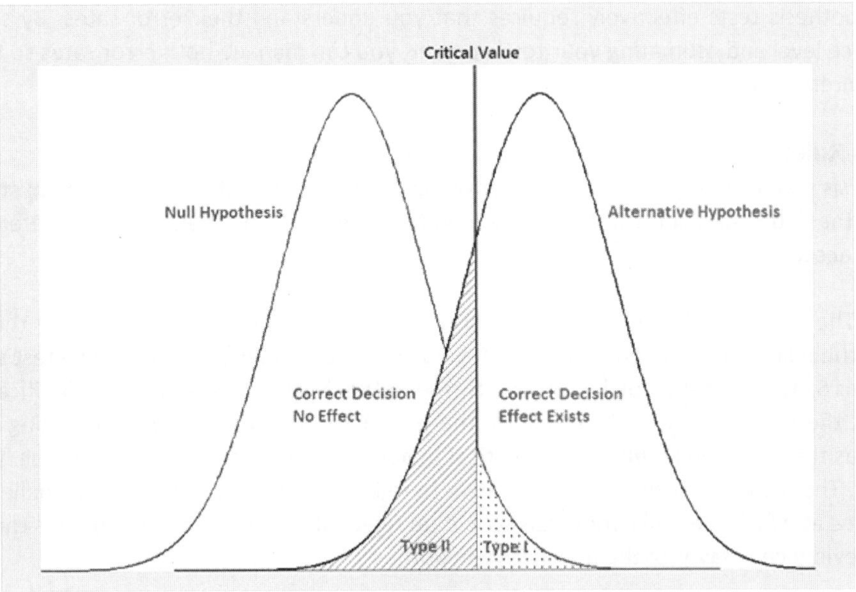

The distribution on the left represents the null hypothesis. If the null hypothesis is true, you only need to worry about Type I errors, which is the shaded portion of the null hypothesis distribution. The rest of the null distribution represents the correct decision of failing to reject the null.

On the other hand, if the alternative hypothesis is true, you need to worry about Type II errors. The shaded region on the alternative hypothesis distribution represents the Type II error rate. The rest of the alternative distribution represents the probability of correctly detecting an effect—power.

Moving the critical value line is equivalent to changing the significance level. If you move the line to the left, you're increasing the significance level (e.g., α 0.05 to 0.10). Holding everything else constant, this adjustment increases the Type I error rate while reducing the Type II error rate. Moving the line to the right reduces the significance level (e.g., α 0.05 to 0.01), which decreases the Type I error rate but increases the type II error rate.

Is One Error Worse Than the Other?

Suppose you are assessing the strength of a new jet engine part that is under consideration. Peoples lives are riding on the part's strength. A false negative in this scenario merely means that the part is strong enough but the test fails to detect it. This situation does not put anyone's life at risk. On the other hand, Type I errors are worse in this situation because they indicate the part is strong enough when it is not.

Now suppose that the jet engine part is already in use but there are concerns about it failing. In this case, you want the test to be more sensitive to detecting problems even at the risk of false positives. Type II errors are worse in this scenario because the test fails to recognize the problem and leave these problematic parts in use for longer.

Using hypothesis tests effectively requires that you understand their error rates. By setting the significance level and estimating your test's power, you can manage both error rates so they meet your requirements.

Decision Rules

The analysis plan includes decision rules for rejecting the null hypothesis. In practice, statisticians describe these decision rules in two ways - with reference to a P-value or with reference to a region of acceptance.

P-value. The strength of evidence in support of a null hypothesis is measured by the P-value. Suppose the test statistic is equal to S. The P-value is the probability of observing a test statistic as extreme as S, assuming the null hypothesis is true. If the P-value is less than the significance level, we reject the null hypothesis. In statistics, the p-value is the probability of obtaining results as extreme as the observed results of a statistical hypothesis test, assuming that the null hypothesis is correct. The p-value is used as an alternative to rejection points to provide the smallest level of significance at which the null hypothesis would be rejected. A smaller p-value means that there is stronger evidence in favor of the alternative hypothesis.

Application Example of P-Value

Assume an investor claims that their investment portfolio's performance is equivalent to that of the Standard & Poor's (S&P) 500 Index. To determine this, the investor conducts a two-tailed test. The null hypothesis states that the portfolio's returns are equivalent to the S&P 500's returns over a specified period, while the alternative hypothesis states that the portfolio's returns and the S&P 500's returns are not equivalent. (If the investor conducted a one-tailed test, the alternative hypothesis would state that the portfolio's returns are either less than or greater than the S&P 500's returns.)

One commonly used significance level is 0.05. If the investor finds that the p-value is less than 0.05, then there is evidence against the null hypothesis. As a result, the investor would reject the null hypothesis and accept the alternative hypothesis. The smaller the p-value, the greater the evidence against the null hypothesis. Thus, if the investor finds that the p-value is 0.001, there is strong evidence against the null hypothesis, and the investor can confidently conclude the portfolio's returns and the S&P 500's returns are not be equivalent.

Conversely, a p-value that is greater than 0.05 indicates that there is (at best) weak evidence against the conjecture, so the investor would fail to reject the null hypothesis. In this case, the differences observed between the investment portfolio data and the S&P 500 data are explainable by chance alone.

Region of acceptance. The region of acceptance is a range of values. If the test statistic falls within the region of acceptance, the null hypothesis is not rejected. The region of acceptance is defined so that the chance of making a Type I error is equal to the significance level.
The set of values outside the region of acceptance is called the region of rejection. If the test statistic falls within the region of rejection, the null hypothesis is rejected. In such cases, we say that the hypothesis has been rejected at the α level of significance.

These approaches are equivalent. Some statistics texts use the P-value approach; others use the region of acceptance approach. On this website, we tend to use the region of acceptance approach.

ONE-TAILED AND TWO-TAILED TESTS

A test of a statistical hypothesis, where the region of rejection is on only one side of the sampling distribution, is called a one-tailed test. For example, suppose the null hypothesis states that the mean is less than or equal to 10. The alternative hypothesis would be that the mean is greater than 10. The region of rejection would consist of a range of numbers located on the right side of sampling distribution; that is, a set of numbers greater than 10.

A test of a statistical hypothesis, where the region of rejection is on both sides of the sampling distribution, is called a two-tailed test. For example, suppose the null hypothesis states that the mean is equal to 10. The alternative hypothesis would be that the mean is less than 10 or greater than 10. The region of rejection would consist of a range of numbers located on both sides of sampling distribution; that is, the region of rejection would consist partly of numbers that were less than 10 and partly of numbers that were greater than 10.

One-Tailed Test

A one-tailed test is a statistical test in which the critical area of a distribution is one-sided so that it is either greater than or less than a certain value, but not both. If the sample being tested falls into the one-sided critical area, the alternative hypothesis will be accepted instead of the null hypothesis. A one-tailed test is also known as a directional hypothesis or directional test.

Hypothesis testing is run to determine whether a claim is true or not, given a population parameter. A test that is conducted to show whether the mean of the sample is significantly greater than and significantly less than the mean of a population is considered a two-tailed test. When the testing is set up to show that the sample mean would be higher or lower than the population mean, it is referred to as a one-tailed test. The one-tailed test gets its name from testing the area under one of the tails (sides) of a normal distribution, although the test can be used in other non-normal distributions as well.

Example of a One-Tailed Test

Let's say an analyst wants to prove that a portfolio manager outperformed the S&P 500 index in a given year by 16.91%. He may set up the null (H0) and alternative (Ha) hypotheses as:

H0: $\mu \leq 16.91$

Ha: μ > 16.91

The null hypothesis is the measurement that the analyst hopes to reject. The alternative hypothesis is the claim made by the analyst that the portfolio manager performed better than the S&P 500. If the outcome of the one-tailed test results in rejecting the null, the alternative hypothesis will be supported. On the other hand, if the outcome of the test fails to reject the null, the analyst may carry out further analysis and investigation into the portfolio manager's performance.

The region of rejection is on only one side of the sampling distribution in a one-tailed test. To determine how the portfolio's return on investment compares to the market index, the analyst must run an upper-tailed significance test in which extreme values fall in the upper tail (right side) of the normal distribution curve. The one-tailed test conducted in the upper or right tail area of the curve will show the analyst how much higher the portfolio return is than the index return and whether the difference is significant.

The most common significance levels (p-values) used in a one-tailed test is 1%, 5% or 10%
Before the one-tailed test can be performed, null and alternative hypotheses have to be established. A null hypothesis is a claim that the researcher hopes to reject. An alternative hypothesis is the claim that is supported by rejecting the null hypothesis.

Determining Significance in a One-Tailed Test
To determine how significant the difference in returns is, a significance level must be specified. The significance level is almost always represented by the letter "p", which stands for probability. The level of significance is the probability of incorrectly concluding that the null hypothesis is false. The significance value used in a one-tailed test is either 1%, 5% or 10%, although any other probability measurement can be used at the discretion of the analyst or statistician. The probability value is calculated with the assumption that the null hypothesis is true. The lower the p-value, the stronger the evidence that the null hypothesis is false.

If the resulting p-value is less than 5%, then the difference between both observations is statistically significant, and the null hypothesis is rejected. Following our example above, if p-value = 0.03, or 3%, then the analyst can be 97% confident that the portfolio returns did not equal or fall below the return of the market for the year. He will, therefore, reject H0 and support the claim that the portfolio manager outperformed the index. The probability calculated in only one tail of a distribution is half the probability of a two-tailed distribution if similar measurements were tested using both hypothesis testing tools.

Two-Tailed Test

In statistics, a two-tailed test is a method in which the critical area of a distribution is two-sided and tests whether a sample is greater than or less than a certain range of values. It is used in null-hypothesis testing and testing for statistical significance. If the sample being tested falls into either of the critical areas, the alternative hypothesis is accepted instead of the null hypothesis. The two-tailed test gets its name from testing the area under both tails of a normal distribution, although the test can be used in other non-normal distributions.

A two-tailed test is designed to examine both sides of a specified data range as designated by the probability distribution involved. A two-tailed test, on the other hand, is designed to examine both sides of a specified data range to test whether a sample is greater than or less than the range of values. The probability distribution should represent the likelihood of a specified outcome based on predetermined standards. This requires the setting of a limit designating the highest (or upper) and lowest (or lower) accepted variable values included within the range. Any data point that exists above the upper limit or below the lower limit is considered out of the acceptance range and in an area referred to as the rejection range.

There is no inherent standard with regard to the number of data points that must exist within the acceptance range. In instances where precision is required, such as in the creation of pharmaceutical drugs, a rejection rate of 0.001% or less may be instituted. In instances where precision is less critical, such as the number of food items in a product bag, a rejection rate of 5% may be appropriate.

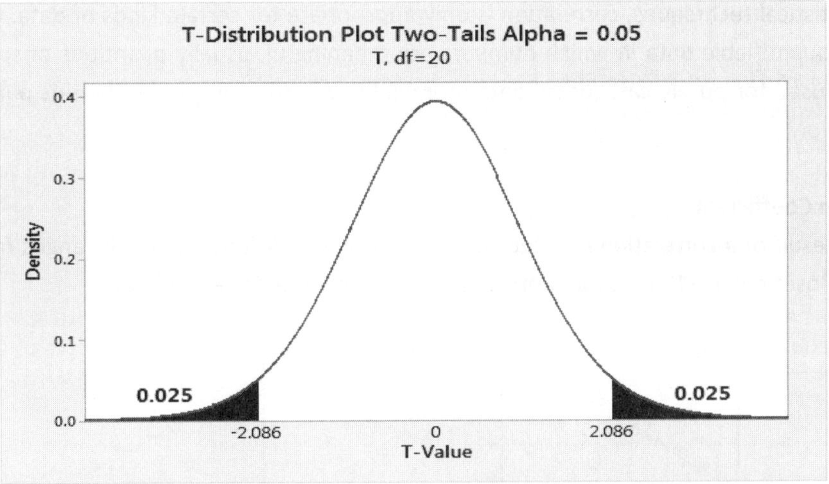

Two-tailed hypothesis tests are also known as nondirectional and two-sided tests because you can test for effects in both directions. When you perform a two-tailed test, you split the significance level percentage between both tails of the distribution. In the example below, I use an alpha of 5% and the distribution has two shaded regions of 2.5% (2 * 2.5% = 5%).

When a test statistic falls in either critical region, your sample data are sufficiently incompatible with the null hypothesis that you can reject it for the population.

In a two-tailed test, the generic null and alternative hypotheses are the following:

- Null: The effect equals zero.
- Alternative: The effect does not equal zero.

The specifics of the hypotheses depend on the type of test you perform because you might be assessing means, proportions, or rates.

CORRELATION

Correlation is a statistical technique that can show whether and how strongly pairs of variables are related. For example, height and weight are related; taller people tend to be heavier than shorter people. The relationship isn't perfect. People of the same height vary in weight, and you can easily think of two people you know where the shorter one is heavier than the taller one. Nonetheless, the average weight of people 5'5'' is less than the average weight of people 5'6'', and their average weight is less than that of people 5'7'', etc. Correlation can tell you just how much of the variation in peoples' weights is related to their heights. Although this correlation is fairly obvious your data may contain unsuspected correlations. You may also suspect there are correlations, but don't know which are the strongest. An intelligent correlation analysis can lead to a greater understanding of your data.

Like all statistical techniques, correlation is only appropriate for certain kinds of data. Correlation works for quantifiable data in which numbers are meaningful, usually quantities of some sort. It cannot be used for purely categorical data (nominal data), such as gender, brands purchased, or favorite color.

Correlation Coefficient

The main result of a correlation is called the correlation coefficient (or "r"). It ranges from -1.0 to +1.0. The closer r is to +1 or -1, the more closely the two variables are related.

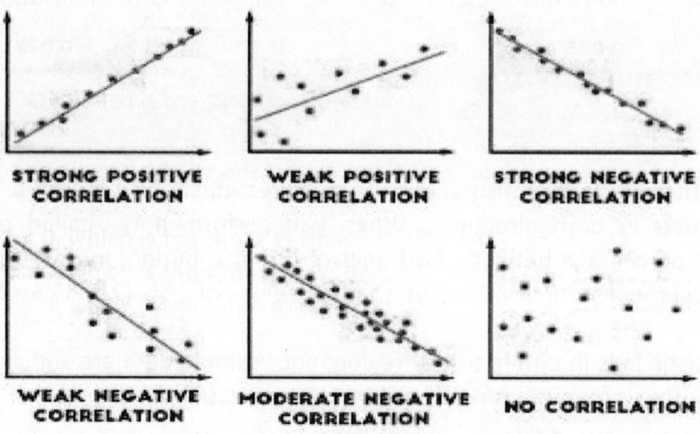

If r is close to 0, it means there is no relationship between the variables. If r is positive, it means that as one variable gets larger the other gets larger. If r is negative it means that as one gets larger, the other gets smaller (often called an "inverse" correlation).

While correlation coefficients are normally reported as r = (a value between -1 and +1), squaring them makes then easier to understand. The square of the coefficient (or r square) is equal to the percent of the variation in one variable that is related to the variation in the other. After squaring r, ignore the decimal point. An r of .5 means 25% of the variation is related (.5 squared =.25). An r value of .7 means 49% of the variance is related (.7 squared = .49).

Let's now look at the below set of formulae:

$$\textbf{VAR(X)} = \frac{1}{n-1}\sum_{i=1}^{n}(x_i - E(X))^2 \tag{1}$$

$$\textbf{COV(X, Y)} = \frac{1}{n-1}\sum_{i=1}^{n}(x_i - E(X))(y_i - E(Y)) \tag{2}$$

$$\textbf{COR(X, Y)} = \frac{\textbf{COV(X, Y)}}{\sqrt{\textbf{VAR(X)VAR(Y)}}} \tag{3}$$

$$\textbf{R}^2 = 1 - \frac{\textbf{VAR(X, Y)}_{FittedLine}}{\textbf{VAR(X, Y)}_{Mean}} \tag{4}$$

Formula (1) calculates variance, which we have already seen before in this chapter.

Formula (2) talks about Covariance. Covariance is a measure used to determine how much two variables change in tandem. The unit of covariance is a product of the units of the two variables. Covariance is affected by a change in scale. The value of covariance lies between -∞ and +∞.

Formula (3) shows how to calculate correlation. It shows it dependent on covariance. In simple words, both the terms- Covariance and Correlation, measure the relationship and the dependency between two variables. "Covariance" indicates the direction of the linear relationship between variables. "Correlation" on the other hand measures both the strength and direction of the linear relationship between two variables. Correlation is a function of the covariance. What sets them apart is the fact that correlation values are standardized whereas, covariance values are not. You can obtain the correlation coefficient of two variables by dividing the covariance of these variables by the product of the standard deviations of the same values. When you divide the covariance values by the standard deviation, it essentially scales the value down to a limited range of -1 to +1. This is precisely the range of the correlation values.

R-squared (shown in Formula 4) is a statistical measure of how close the data are to the fitted regression line. It is also known as the coefficient of determination, or the coefficient of multiple determination for multiple regression. 0% indicates that the model explains none of the variability of the response data around its mean. Here we only introduce the concept; discussion on R-squared is out of scope for this book.

Lets take the previous example of Ice cream sale versus the temperature and calculate the correlation factor:

Calculate Correlation factor using Excel:

Select a blank cell that you will put the calculation result, enter this formula =CORREL(A4:A15,B4:B15), where the cell numbers are where you data is present, and press Enter key to get the correlation coefficient. See screenshot as shown above. The result is 0.89 which means there is a strong positive correlation between the two dataset.

	A	B	C	D	E	F
1	**Temperature v Ice Cream**					
2						
3	Temperature (^{0}C)	Sales (Rs)				
4	25.4	₹ 3,400		=CORREL(A4:A15, B4:B15)		
5	32.8	₹ 4,500		0.890239		
6	36.4	₹ 5,800				
7	21.2	₹ 2,560				
8	28.7	₹ 4,360				
9	26.9	₹ 3,500				
10	35.7	₹ 5,600				
11	36.3	₹ 5,490				
12	37.1	₹ 6,340				
13	36.3	₹ 4,500				
14	34.4	₹ 5,900				
15	35.7	₹ 6,800				

A key thing to remember when working with correlations is never to assume a correlation means that a change in one variable causes a change in another. Sales of personal computers and athletic shoes have both risen strongly over the years and there is a high correlation between them, but you cannot assume that buying computers causes people to buy athletic shoes (or vice versa).

The second caveat is that the Pearson correlation technique works best with linear relationships: as one variable gets larger, the other gets larger (or smaller) in direct proportion. It does not work well with curvilinear relationships (in which the relationship does not follow a straight line). An example of a curvilinear relationship is age and health care. They are related, but the relationship doesn't follow a straight line. Young children and older people both tend to use much more health care than teenagers or young adults. Multiple regression can be used to examine curvilinear relationships, but that is outside the scope of this book.

Python Program to find Correlation coefficient

```
# calculate the covariance between two variables
from numpy import cov
temp_data = [25.4, 32.8, 36.4, 21.2, 28.7, 26.9, 35.7, 36.3, 37.1,
36.3, 34.4, 35.7]
sales_data = [3400, 4500, 5800, 2560, 4360, 3500, 5600, 5490,
6340, 4500, 5900, 6800]
# calculate covariance matrix
covariance = cov(temp_data, sales_data)
```

```
print(covariance)
#print('Covariance: %.2f' % covariance)

from scipy.stats import spearmanr, pearsonr
# calculate spearman's correlation
corr, pvalue = spearmanr(sales_data, temp_data)
print('Spearmans correlation: %.2f' % corr)
# calculate pearson's correlation
corr, pvalue = pearsonr(sales_data, temp_data)
print('Pearsons correlation: %.2f' % corr)
import matplotlib.pyplot as plt
plt.scatter(temp_data, sales_data)
plt.show()
```

Sample Output

```
[[2.84117424e+01 6.17518939e+03]
 [6.17518939e+03 1.69351742e+06]]
Spearmans correlation: 0.78
Pearsons correlation: 0.89
```

The 2x2 array returned by np.cov(a,b) has elements equal to:

```
cov(a,a)  cov(a,b)

cov(a,b)  cov(b,b)
```

- The Pearson Product Moment Correlation tests the linear relationship between two continuous variables. Linear means a relationship when two variables change in the same direction at a constant rate. Excel performs Pearson Correlation.
- Spearman Rank Correlation evaluates the monotonic relationship between the ranked values. In a monotonic relationship, the variables also tend to change together, but not necessarily at a constant rate.

Plot:

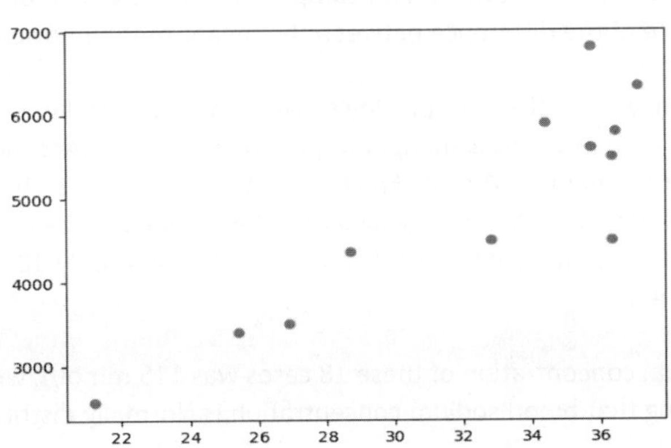

TESTING HYPOTHESIS ABOUT A POPULATION MEAN USING THE Z STATISTIC

Example:

Imagine that a new stockbroker (XYZ) claims that his brokerage fees are lower than that of your current stock broker's (ABC). Data available from an independent research firm indicates that the mean and standard deviation of all ABC broker clients are $18 and $6, respectively.

A sample of 100 clients of ABC is taken, and brokerage charges are calculated with the new rates of XYZ broker. If the mean of the sample is $18.75 and the sample standard deviation is $6, can any inference be made about the difference in the average brokerage bill between ABC and XYZ broker?

- H0: Null Hypothesis: mean = 18
- H1: Alternative Hypothesis: mean <> 18 (This is what we want to prove.)
- Rejection region: Z <= -Z(2.5) and Z >= Z(2.5) (assuming 5% significance level, split 2.5 each on either side).
- Z = (sample mean – mean) / (std-dev / sqrt (no. of samples)) = (18.75 – 18) / (6/(sqrt(100)) = 1.25

This calculated Z value falls between the two limits defined by: - Z(2.5) = -1.96 and Z(2.5) = 1.96.

TESTING HYPOTHESIS ABOUT A POPULATION MEAN USING THE T STATISTIC

The application of the t distribution to the following four types of problem will now be considered.

- The calculation of a confidence interval for a sample mean.
- The mean and standard deviation of a sample are calculated and a value is postulated for the mean of the population. How significantly does the sample mean differ from the postulated population mean?
- The means and standard deviations of two samples are calculated. Could both samples have been taken from the same population?
- Paired observations are made on two samples (or in succession on one sample). What is the significance of the difference between the means of the two sets of observations?

Example: A rare congenital disease, Everley's syndrome, generally causes a reduction in concentration of blood sodium. This is thought to provide a useful diagnostic sign as well as a clue to the efficacy of treatment. Little is known about the subject, but the director of a dermatological department in a London teaching hospital is known to be interested in the disease and has seen more cases than anyone else. Even so, he has seen only 18. The patients were all aged between 20 and 44.

The mean blood sodium concentration of these 18 cases was 115 mmol/l, with standard deviation of 12 mmol/l. Assuming that blood sodium concentration is Normally distributed what is the 95%

confidence interval within which the mean of the total population of such cases may be expected to lie?

The data are set out as follows:

Number of observations	18
Mean blood sodium concentration	115 mmol/l
Standard deviation	12 mmo1/l
Standard error of mean	$SD/\sqrt{n} = 12/\sqrt{18} = 2.83$ mmol/l

To find the 95% confidence interval above and below the mean we now have to find a multiple of the standard error. For small samples we use the table of t. Since the size of the sample influences the value of t, the size of the sample is taken into account in relating the value of t to probabilities in the table. In practice the degrees of freedom amount in these circumstances to one less than the number of observations in the sample. With these data we have 18 - 1 = 17 d.f. This is because only 17 observations plus the total number of observations are needed to specify the sample, the 18th being determined by subtraction.

To find the number by which we must multiply the standard error to give the 95% confidence interval we enter t table at 17 in the left hand column and read across to the column headed 0.05 to discover the number 2.110. The 95% confidence intervals of the mean are now set as follows:

Mean + 2.110 SE to Mean - 2.110 SE

which gives us:

115 - (2.110 x 283) to 115 + 2.110 x 2.83 or 109.03 to 120.97 mmol/l.

We may then say, with a 95% chance of being correct, that the range 109.03 to 120.97 mmol/l includes the population mean.

Likewise from the table 99% confidence interval of the mean is as follows:

Mean + 2.898 SE to Mean - 2.898 SE

which gives:

115 - (2.898 x 2.83) to 115 + (2.898 x 2.83) or 106.80 to 123.20 mmol/l.

Difference of sample mean from population mean (one sample t test)

Estimations of plasma calcium concentration in the 18 patients with Everley's syndrome gave a mean of 3.2 mmol/l, with standard deviation 1.1. Previous experience from a number of investigations and published reports had shown that the mean was commonly close to 2.5 mmol/l in healthy people aged 20-44, the age range of the patients. Is the mean in these patients abnormally high?

We set the figures out as follows:

Mean of general population μ		2.5 mmol/l
Mean of sample $\bar{x}$		3.2 mmol/l
Standard deviation of sample , SD		1.1 mmol/l
Standard error of sample mean,	$SD/\sqrt{n} = 1.1/\sqrt{18}$	0.26 mmo1/l
Difference between means $\mu - \bar{x} = 2.5 - 3.2$		-0.7 mmol/l

t difference between means divided by standard error of sample mean

t difference between means divided by standard error of sample mean. Ignoring the sign of the t value, and entering in t-table at 17 degrees of freedom, we find that 2.69 comes between probability values of 0.02 and 0.01, in other words between 2% and 1% and so It is therefore unlikely that the sample with mean 3.2 came from the population with mean 2.5, and we may conclude that the sample mean is, at least statistically, unusually high. Whether it should be regarded clinically as abnormally high is something that needs to be considered separately by the physician in charge of that case.

$$t = \frac{\mu - \bar{x}}{SD / \sqrt{n}} = \frac{-0.7}{0.26} = -2.69$$

PYTHON IMPLEMENTATION OF COMPARING MEANS: Z AND T TESTS

Suppose that we want to hypothesize that the mean number of TV hours watched per week is 28.5; we'll define this as our null hypothesis, Ho. Let's also assume that we only have access to a subset of household data (i.e. a sample), x,

```
x = [25.7, 38.5, 29.3, 25.1, 30.6, 34.6, 30.0, 39.0, 33.7,
31.6,25.9, 34.4, 26.9, 23.0, 31.1, 29.3, 34.5, 35.1, 31.2,
33.2,30.2, 36.4, 37.5, 27.6, 24.6, 23.9, 27.0, 29.5, 30.1,
29.6,27.3, 31.2, 32.5, 25.7, 30.1, 24.2, 24.1, 26.4, 31.0,
20.7,33.5, 32.2, 34.7, 32.6, 33.5, 32.7, 25.6, 31.1, 32.9,
25.9]
```

from which we can estimate the population mean and the standard error of the sample mean as:

```
import math
import numpy as np

mean_x = np.mean(x)
print("Sample Mean: ",mean_x)
StdErr_x = np.std(x) / math.sqrt(len(x))
print("Standard Error of Sample Mean: ", StdErr_x)
```

The arithmetic mean of x is 30.14 which is slightly different from our hypothesized value of 28.5. This begs the question: is this difference significant, or is it due to chance variation alone?

The null and the alternative hypotheses

The objective of hypothesis testing is to assess whether the observed data are consistent with a well specified (hypothesized) random process, Ho.

The null and alternative hypotheses as follows:
The null hypothesis corresponds to the idea that an observed difference is due to chance. The alternative hypothesis corresponds to the idea that the observed difference is real.
Ho is a statement about the true nature of things. To assess whether our observed data are consistent with our null hypothesis we seek to compare our data with the hypothesized value .

In essence, we compare our observed data (usually as a statistical summary) to the hypothesized distribution using a test statistic from which a test of significance is calculated (this tells us how likely our observed statistic agrees with our hypothesized process).

```
Ho =28.5
```

Test Statistics

A test statistic is a numerical summary of the data that is compared to what would be expected under the null hypothesis. Test statistics can take on many forms such as the z-tests (usually used for large datasets) or t-tests (usually used when datasets are small).

z-tests

The z-statistic is a measure of how much an observed statistic differs from an expected statistic put forward by the null hypothesis. It is computed as:

$$z = \frac{observed - expected}{SE}$$

In computing the z-statistic, the SE used is not the standard error of the observed data, but the standard error for the null. To be more precise, the SE in this formula is computed from the null's SD, if given. However, in many cases (such as in this working example) the null's SD can only be estimated from the observed data's SD.

For example, the z-statistic for our scenario is:

```
z = (mean_x - Ho) / StdErr_x
print("Z Value: ",z)
```

where StdErr_x is the observed sample's standard error. In our working example, z's value of 2.76 indicates that the sample mean is 2.76 SE 's away from the hypothesized value.

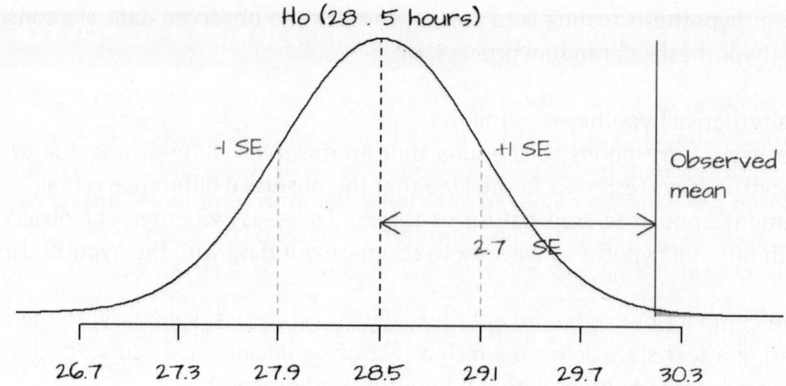

The red line shows where our observed statistic (mean number of TV hours watched) lies on the hypothesized distribution of mean values defined by Ho. The grey dashed lines represent 1 SE to the left and to the right of the hypothesized mean. Each tic mark interval represents a standard deviation. From the graph, it appears that the observed mean value of 30.14 is almost 3 SE's away from the hypothesized mean of 28.5. If we were to draw many samples from the population described by Ho (i.e. a population whose mean number of TV hours watched equals 28.5), only a small fraction of the sample means would produce a z-value more extreme than the one calculated from our dataset. The area shaded in light red highlights the probability of z-values being more extreme than the one computed from our sample. We can quantify this probability P by looking up its value in a Normal distribution table (the old fashion way), or more simply, by passing the z parameter 2.76 to the scipy.stats.norm.cdf.

The cdf function gives us the probability of a z value "greater than" or "less than" the z value computed from our data. In this case, we are interested in knowing the probability of having z values more extreme than the one computed. Since our z value is on the right side of the distribution curve, we will 1-cdf value to ensure that the probability returned is for the right tail-end section of the distribution (the pink area in the next figure).

```
P_Ho = st.norm.cdf(z)
print("P_Ho: ",1-P_Ho)
```

Output:
P_Ho: 0.002851584518680727 6

Here, z is on the right side of the curve and the probability of getting a test statistic more extreme than our z is about 0.00285 or 0.29% . P is called the observed significance level and is sometimes referred to as the P-value. The smaller this probability, the stronger the evidence against Ho meaning that the odds of the mean TV hours watched per household being 28.5 is very small. Careful, P is not the chance of Ho being right.

Sometimes researchers will define a P value for which Ho will be rejected. Such value is usually referred to as the α-value (alpha value). If such a test is requested, we must determine if the test is one-tailed or two-tailed. A test is one-tailed if the alternate hypothesis, Ha, is of the form "greater than" or "less than" (e.g. the mean number of TV hours watched are greater than 28.5).

A test is two-tailed if Ha is not of the form "greater than" or "less than" (e.g. the mean number of TV hours watched differs from 28.5). Here are a few examples:

- If we chose an α value of 0.05 and we wanted to test the hypothesis that our observed mean hours is different than Ho we would define a two-tailed test, meaning that we would have to define rejection regions associated with P values of less than 0.025 and greater than 0.975 (or z values of -1.96 and 1.96 respectively). The reason we choose p values of 0.025/0.975 and not 0.05/0.95 is because we need to split the 0.05 α value across both tails of the curve (remember that we are rejecting the null if our z value falls in either tails of the curve).

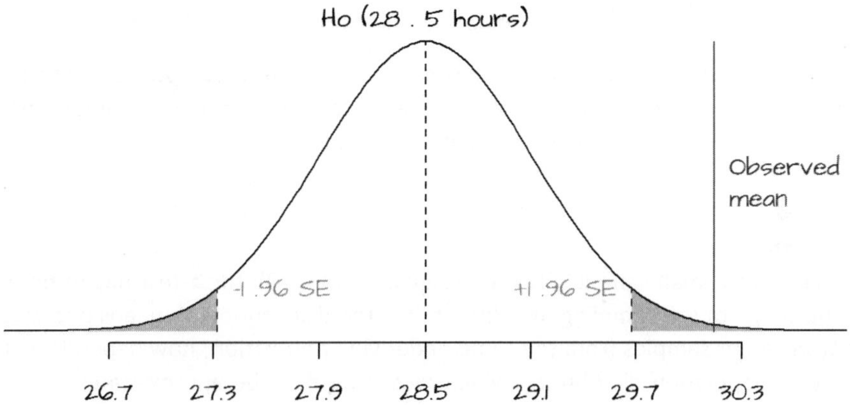

- If we chose an α value of 0.05 and we wanted to test the hypothesis that our observed mean hours is greater than Ho, we would define a one-tailed test, meaning that we would have to define a rejection region associated with a P value greater than 0.95.

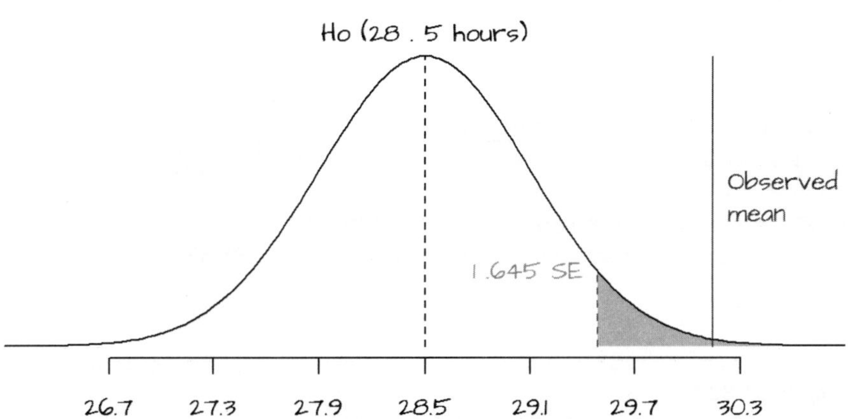

In our working example, if we had chosen a two-tailed test, we would reject the null at a 5% and 1% α value (these would represent rejection regions associated with z values of +/- 1.96 and +/- 2.58 respectively). However, if our α value was set at 0.005 (0.5%), we could not reject the null hypothesis since the z-value associated with a two-tailed test for α=0.005 is 2.81 (greater than our observed z value of 2.76).

The following table highlights popular α values and their associated z values for a one-tailed and two-tailed test:

	$\alpha = 0.1$	$\alpha = 0.05$	$\alpha = 0.01$	$\alpha = 0.005$
1-tailed	-1.28 or 1.28	-1.645 or 1.645	-2.33 or 2.33	-2.58 or 2.58
2-tailed	-1.645 & 1.645	-1.96 & 1.96	-2.58 & 2.58	-2.81 & 2.81

Note that the one-tailed test requires that only one condition be met (only one of the rejection regions is of concern) whereas a two-tailed test requires that two conditions be met (both rejection regions are of concern).

It's important to note that the z-test makes some restrictive assumptions: * the sample size is reasonably large * the normal (Gaussian) distribution can be used to approximate the distribution of the sample statistic (e.g. the mean) being investigated.

t-tests

When working with small sample sizes (typically less than 30), the z-test has to be modified. For starters, the shape of the sampling distribution (i.e. the distribution of means one would compute from many different samples from the same underlying population) now depends on the shape of the underlying population distribution which must therefore be approximately normal in shape. These requirements can be quite restrictive because in most cases we do not know the population's distribution.

Continuing with our working example, let's assume that instead of a sample size of 50 we now have a sample size of 10. Next we compute the mean and standard deviation of the sample.

```
import math
import numpy as np

mean_x2 = np.mean(x2)
print("Sample Mean: ",mean_x2)
sd_x2 = np.std(x2)
#Calculate Standard Error
StdErr_x2 = sd_x2 / math.sqrt(len(x2))
print("Standard Error of Sample Mean: ", StdErr_x2)
```

Output:
Sample Mean: 31.823
Standard Error of Sample Mean: 1.7740000281848924

The next step is to find the P-value. When working with large sample sizes, the normal (Gaussian) distribution curve does a good job in approximating the distribution of a sample statistic (such as the mean). It does not, however, do a good job in approximating the distribution of that same statistic when these are computed from small sample sizes.

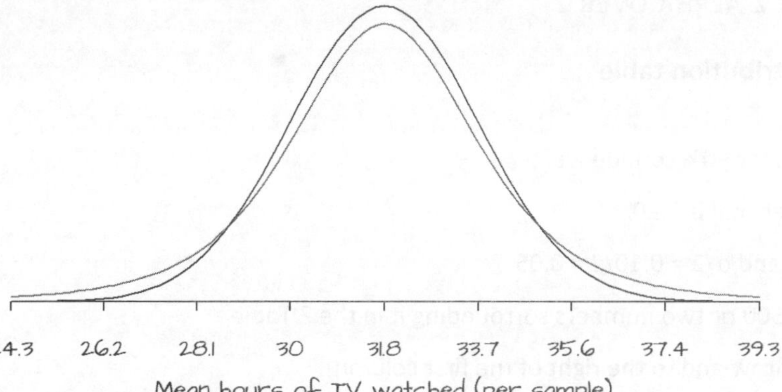

The black line represents the distribution of the mean hours (from many hypothetical samples) of TV watched as approximated by the normal curve. The red line represents the same parameter but represented this time by a student distribution curve with a degree of freedom, df, of 4. The df is computed by subtracting 1 from the total number of data points in the sample.

By convention when computing a test statistic for small sample sizes (and when a student curve is used), we refer to the test statistic as the t statistic (or t value). For our dataset t can be computed as follows:

```
#Compute the P-value.
# 1. Compute P using normal distribution curve
# (which we normally do for a large sample)
P_Ho_norm = st.norm.cdf(t_val)
print("P_Ho_norm: ",1-P_Ho_norm)

# Calculate Student's curve
# (which is recommended for a small sample).
P_Ho_stud=st.t.cdf(t_val, df = len(x2) - 1)
print("P_Ho_stud: ",1-P_Ho_stud)
```

Output:
P_Ho_norm: 0.030522598132406653
P_Ho_stud: 0.04691171485206691

The P-value computed from the normal curve is 0.030 and that computed from Student's curve is 0.047. If an α value of 5% was requested, the normal distribution approximation would suggest that chance variation alone could not explain the discrepancy between our hypothesized mean number of TV hours watched and that computed from our sample. Yet, if Student's approximation of the distribution is used (as it should be with the small sample), we could not reject the null (at least not at the 5% significance level).

STEPS TO CALCULATE Z ALPHA OVER 2

1. Use the normal distribution table

Example: Find Zα/2 for 90% confidence.

90% written as a decimal is 0.90.

1 – 0.90 = 0.10 = α and α/2 = 0.10/2 = 0.05.

Look for 0.05 = 0.0500 or two numbers surrounding it in the Z Table

(i.e. below the first row and to the right of the first column).

The number 0.0500 is not in the table, but it is between 0.0505 and 0.0495, which are in the table.

Next, check the differences between these last two numbers and 0.0500 to see which number is closer to 0.0500. 0.0505 – 0.0500 = 0.0005 and 0.0500 – 0.0495 = 0.0005.

Since the differences are equal, we average the corresponding standard scores.

Because 0.0505 is to the right of -1.6 and under 0.04, its standard score is -1.64.

Because 0.0495 is to the right of -1.6 and under 0.05, its standard score is -1.65.

(-1.64 + (-1.65))/2 = -1.645

Thus Zα/2 = 1.645 for 90% confidence.

2. Use the t-Distribution table

Example: Find Zα/2 for 98% confidence.

98% written as a decimal is 0.98.

1 – 0.98 = 0.02 = a and α/2 = 0.01.

Find 0.01 in the "df" row at the top of page in t table.

Zα/2 is the very last entry in the column under 0.01.

Hence Zα/2 = 2.326 for 98% confidence.

3. Memorize the values of Zα/2.

The only confidence levels we use on tests or assignments are 90%, 95%, 98% and 99%, and the values of Zα/2 corresponding to these confidence levels are always the same.
As a result, memorizing the necessary values of Zα/2 is fairly easy to do.

Confidence (1–α) g 100%	Significance α	Critical Value $Z_{\alpha/2}$
90%	0.10	1.645
95%	0.05	1.960
98%	0.02	2.326
99%	0.01	2.576

4. Use Python

```
from scipy.stats import t, norm

#for the t-statistic
conf_t = 0.98
t_zalphaover2 = t.ppf((1-conf_t)/2, df=999)
print("t_zalphaover2 for for 98% confidence:
",abs(t_zalphaover2))

#for the z-statistic
conf_z = 0.90
z_zalphaover2 = norm.ppf((1-conf_z)/2)
print("z_zalphaover2 for 90% confidence: +/-",
abs(z_zalphaover2))
```

***

UNIT 11: STATISTICAL INFERENCE – ESTIMATION FOR TWO POPULATIONS

PROBLEM STATEMENT

Lets describe an experiment with pseudoscorpions of the species Cordylochernes scorpiodes which live in the tropics. The females typically mate multiple times, even though mating once provides sufficient sperm for fertilization. Researchers conducted an experiment to examine a possible evolutionary explanation for this behavior. If there is genetic incompatibility between some pairs, a female may be more fertile by having multiple partners. In the experiment, females were randomly assigned to one of two treatment groups. In one group, a female was mated with the same male twice; in the other group, two different males were mated to the same female. The response variable is the number of successful broods. This variable is a small integer, ranging from 0 in some cases to a maximum of observed value of 7.

Data

- The data set is small enough that we can display it.
- The mean of the 20 values in the Same treatment group is 2.2.
- The mean of the 16 values in the Different treatment group is 3.6.

Group	Number of Successful Broods
Same	0 0 0 0 1 1 2 2 2 2 2 2 3 3 3 3 4 4 4 6
Different	0 1 2 2 2 3 3 4 4 4 4 4 6 6 6 7

Questions

- Do female pseudoscorpions have more successful broods on average, when they have multiple partners?
- The real biological question of interest involves the pseudoscorpions in their natural environment.
- The experimental setting seeks to explore the question in a controlled setting.
- In the experiment, the sample means are 2.2 and 3.6; what does this imply about the populations?
- Here, there is a single biological population of pseudoscorpions that can be thought of as two statistical populations on the basis of assignment to experimental treatment groups.

A statistical model

- A statistical model for the experiment is that there are two probability distributions for the number of successful broods, one for each treatment group.
- The specific distributions are not specified, but each is summarized my a mean or expected value, say $\mu 1$ for the Same treatment group and $\mu 2$ for the Different treatment group.
- The null hypothesis is $\mu 1 = \mu 2$; the biologically interesting alternative (Alternate Hypothesis) here is $\mu 1 < \mu 2$.
- How can we test this hypothesis? For the sample estimates, $2.2 < 3.6$, but what can we infer about the populations?

The Big Picture

- We have two populations with means μ1 and μ2.
- We have independent samples from each sample means ¯x1 and ¯x2 of sizes n1 and n2 respectively.
- We want to test H0 : μ1 = μ2 versus the alternative HA : μ1 < μ2 with few assumptions about the distributions in the populations.
- The key idea of a randomization test is to consider the null distribution of the difference in sample means for all possible random samples assuming that the randomization is independent of the observed data.

Solution

- In the example, there are 20 females in the Same treatment group and 16 in the Different treatment group.
- The observed difference in sample means is 2.2 – 3.625 = –1.425
- What if the number of successful broods each female pseudoscorpion had was independent of the assignment to treatment group?
- If this were the case, we could compare the observed difference in sample means to the null distribution of differences in sample means for all other possible results of the randomization.
- There are (36C20 - combinations) = 7307872110 possible ways to randomly separate 36 individuals into groups of size 20 and 16.
- Instead of finding exactly how many of these 7 billion+ possible randomization results have differences in sample means at least as extreme as the observed –1.425, we can use the computer to simulate the randomization process and estimate the p-value.

Before beginning, we will examine methods to graph the data

Dot Plot of the Data:

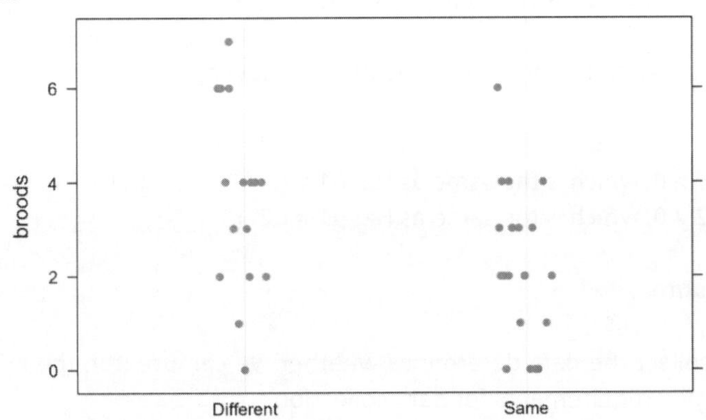

Comments on the Graphics

- There is a lot of overlap between the samples.
- It would be difficult to place an individual in one group or the other on the basis of the number of successful broods.
- But the centers of the distributions appear to be a bit different with generally larger values for the Different group on average.

State Hypotheses

- H0: There would be no difference in the mean number of successful broods for each experimental condition among all female pseudoscorpions in the population.
- H1: The experimental condition with different partners produces a larger mean number of successful broods than the experimental condition with the same partner mating twice.

In symbols, letting μ1 and μ2 represent the mean number of successful broods in the population for the Same and Different groups, respectively, the hypotheses are:
H0 : $\mu1 = \mu2$
H1 : $\mu1 < \mu2$
One could also test the alternative hypotheses HA : μ1 6= μ2 or HA : $\mu1 > \mu2$ if appropriate for the setting.

SOLUTION FORMATION

The Hypothesis Test for a Difference in Two Population Means
The general steps of this hypothesis test are the same as always. As expected, the details of the conditions for use of the test and the test statistic are unique to this test (but similar in many ways to what we have seen before.)

Step 1: Determine the hypotheses.

The hypotheses for a difference in two population means are similar to those for a difference in two population proportions. The null hypothesis, H0, is again a statement of "no effect" or "no difference."

H0: $\mu1 - \mu2 = 0$, which is the same as H0: $\mu1 = \mu2$

The alternative hypothesis, Ha, can be any one of the following.

Ha: $\mu1 - \mu2 < 0$, which is the same as Ha: $\mu1 < \mu2$
Ha: $\mu1 - \mu2 > 0$, which is the same as Ha: $\mu1 > \mu2$
Ha: $\mu1 - \mu2 \neq 0$, which is the same as Ha: $\mu1 \neq \mu2$

Step 2: Collect the data.

As usual, how we collect the data determines whether we can use it in the inference procedure. We have our usual two requirements for data collection.

- Samples must be random to remove or minimize bias.
- Samples must be representative of the populations in question.

We use this hypothesis test when the data meets the following conditions.

- The two random samples are independent.
- The variable is normally distributed in both populations. If this variable is not known, samples of more than 30 will have a difference in sample means that can be modeled

adequately by the t-distribution. As we discussed in "Hypothesis Test for a Population Mean," t-procedures are robust even when the variable is not normally distributed in the population. If checking normality in the populations is impossible, then we look at the distribution in the samples. If a histogram or dotplot of the data does not show extreme skew or outliers, we take it as a sign that the variable is not heavily skewed in the populations, and we use the inference procedure. (Note: This is the same condition we used for the one-sample t-test in "Hypothesis Test for a Population Mean.")

Step 3: Assess the evidence.

If the conditions are met, then we calculate the t-test statistic. The t-test statistic has a familiar form.

$$T = \frac{\text{(Observeddifferenceinsamplemeans)} - \text{(Hypothesizeddifferenceinpopulationmeans)}}{\text{Standarderror}}$$

$$T = \frac{(\bar{x}_1 - \bar{x}_2) - (\mu_1 - \mu_2)}{\sqrt{\frac{{s_1}^2}{n_1} + \frac{{s_2}^2}{n_2}}}$$

Since the null hypothesis assumes there is no difference in the population means, the expression (μ1 – μ2) is always zero.

The t-distribution depends on the degrees of freedom (df). In the one-sample and matched-pair cases df = n – 1. For the two-sample t-test, determining the correct df is based on a formula. We can use Python code to find the df. With the t-test statistic and the degrees of freedom, we can use the appropriate t-model to find the P-value, just as we did in the previous chapter.

Step 4: State a conclusion.

To state a conclusion, we follow what we have done with other hypothesis tests. We compare our P-value to a stated level of significance.

- *If the P-value ≤ α, we reject the null hypothesis in favor of the alternative hypothesis.*
- If the P-value > α, we fail to reject the null hypothesis. We do not have enough evidence to support the alternative hypothesis.

EXAMPLE

Problem Statement: *Do women purchase fewer calories when they eat with men compared to when they eat with women?*

Step 1: Stating the hypotheses

Here the two populations are "women eating with women" (population 1) and "women eating with men" (population 2). The variable is the calories in the meal. We test the following hypotheses at the 5% level of significance.

The null hypothesis is always H0: μ1 – μ2 = 0, which is the same as H0: μ1 = μ2.

The alternative hypothesis Ha: μ1 – μ2 > 0, which is the same as Ha: μ1 > μ2.

Here μ1 represents the mean number of calories ordered by women when they were eating with other women, and μ2 represents the mean number of calories ordered by women when they were eating with men.

Note: It does not matter which population we label as 1 or 2, but once we decide, we have to stay consistent throughout the hypothesis test. Since we expect the number of calories to be greater for the women eating with other women, the difference is positive if "women eating with women" is population 1. If you prefer to work with positive numbers, choose the group with the larger expected mean as population 1.

Step 2: Collect Data.

As usual, there are two major things to keep in mind when considering the collection of data.

- Samples need to be representative of the population in question.
- Samples need to be random in order to remove or minimize bias.

Representative Samples?

The researchers state their hypothesis in terms of "women." We did the same. But the researchers gathered data by watching people eat at the HUB Rock Café II on the campus of Indiana University of Pennsylvania during the Spring semester of 2006. Almost all of the women in the data set were white undergraduates between the ages of 18 and 24, so there are some definite limitations on the scope of this study. These limitations will affect our conclusion (and the specific definition of the population means in our hypotheses.)

Random Samples?

The observations were collected on February 13, 2006, through February 22, 2006, between 11 a.m. and 7 p.m. We can see that the researchers included both lunch and dinner. They also made observations on all days of the week to ensure that weekly customer patterns did not confound their findings. The authors state that "since the time period for observations and the place where [they] observed students were limited, the sample was a convenience sample." Despite these limitations, the researchers conducted inference procedures with the data, and the results were published in a reputable journal. We will also conduct inference with this data, but we also include a discussion of the limitations of the study with our conclusion. The authors did this, also.

Do the data met the conditions for use of a t-test?

The researchers reported the following sample statistics.

- In a sample of 45 women dining with other women, the average number of calories ordered was 850, and the standard deviation was 252.
- In a sample of 27 women dining with men, the average number of calories ordered was 719, and the standard deviation was 322.

One of the samples has fewer than 30 women. We need to make sure the distribution of calories in this sample is not heavily skewed and has no outliers, but we do not have access to a spreadsheet of the actual data. Since the researchers conducted a t-test with this data, we will assume that the conditions are met. This includes the assumption that the samples are independent.

Step 3: Assess the evidence.
As noted previously, the researchers reported the following sample statistics.

- In a sample of 45 women dining with other women, the average number of calories ordered was 850, and the standard deviation was 252.
- In a sample of 27 women dining with men, the average number of calories ordered was 719, and the standard deviation was 322.

To compute the t-test statistic, make sure sample 1 corresponds to population 1. Here our population 1 is "women eating with other women." So x1 = 850, s1 = 252, n1 =45, and so on.

$$T = \frac{(\bar{x}_1-\bar{x}_2)-(\mu_1-\mu_2)}{\sqrt{\frac{s_1^2}{n_1}+\frac{s_2^2}{n_2}}} \approx 131/72.47 \approx 1.81$$

The degrees of freedom are about 45 for this data. Using Python code, let's calculate the P-value.

```
print("Cjecking")
from scipy.stats import t
## Compare with the critical t-value
#Degrees of freedom
df = 45
t_stat = 1.81
#p-value after comparison with the t
p = 1 - t.cdf(t_stat,df=df)
print("P-Value : ",p)
```

Output:

```
P-Value :  0.03848845591310346
```

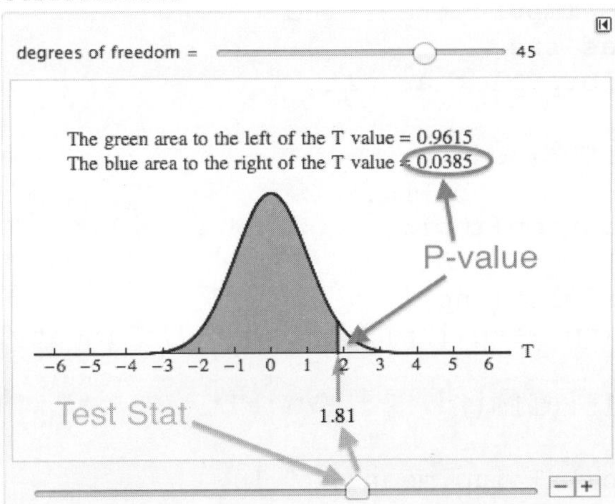

Since the alternative hypothesis is a "greater than" statement, we look for the area to the right of T = 1.81. The P-value is 0.0385.

Step 4: State a conclusion.

The hypotheses for this test are H0: μ1 – μ2 = 0 and Ha: μ1 – μ2 > 0. Since the P-value is less than the significance level (0.0385 < 0.05), we reject H0 and accept Ha.
So we conclude that, At Indiana University of Pennsylvania, the mean number of calories ordered by undergraduate women eating with other women is greater than the mean number of calories ordered by undergraduate women eating with men (P-value = 0.0385).

SOLVING USING PYTHON PROGRAM

When dating someone, what matters more to you: looks or personality? This question was the focus of a community college student's class project for an introductory statistics course. She devised a 25-point scale. An answer of 1 means "personality matters most and looks don't matter at all." A score of 25 means "looks matter most and personality does not matter at all." Her hypothesis is that the mean scores for males and females will differ, but she does not have an opinion about which population will have a higher mean score.

The data is entered in the below Python Code.

Here are her hypotheses.

H0: μ1 – μ2 = 0
Ha: μ1 – μ2 ≠ 0

We can also write the hypotheses as follows.

H0: μ1 = μ2
Ha: μ1 ≠ μ2

```
import numpy as np
from scipy.stats import ttest_ind
import seaborn as sns
import matplotlib.pyplot as plt

# to draw distribution

def plot_distribution(inp):
    plt.figure()
    ax = sns.distplot(inp)
    plt.axvline(np.mean(inp), color="k", linestyle="dashed",
linewidth=5)
    _, max_ = plt.ylim()
    plt.text(
        inp.mean() + inp.mean() / 10,
```

```
        max_ - max_ / 10,
        "Mean: {:.2f}".format(inp.mean()),
    )
    return plt.figure

#Population 1 - Boys
boys_d = np.array([5,25,1,15,18,22,19,13,12,23,12])
plot_distribution(boys_d)
plt.show()

mean_1 = np.mean(boys_d)
#Population 2 - Girls
girls_d =
np.array([5,2,11,5,18,16,19,21,15,9,8,13,7,8,8,13,12,23,12])
plot_distribution(girls_d)
plt.show()
mean_2 = np.mean(girls_d)

#Putting the distributions together
ax1 = sns.distplot(girls_d)
ax2 = sns.distplot(boys_d)
plt.axvline(np.mean(girls_d), color='b', linestyle='dashed',
linewidth=5)
plt.axvline(np.mean(boys_d), color='orange',
linestyle='dashed', linewidth=5)
plt.show()
#Set Sample size
ssize = 10
#Randomly select ssize data from both
boy_sampled =np.random.choice(boys_d, ssize)
girl_samples = np.random.choice(girls_d, ssize)
stat,p = ttest_ind(boys_d, girls_d)
print("T-Statistics: ", stat)
print("P-Value: ", p)
alpha = 0.05
if p>alpha:
    print("Fail to reject H0: Two populations are similar")
else:
    print("Reject H0: Two populations are not similar")
```

Output:

```
T-Statistics:  1.3002920356055028
P-Value:  0.2041026229571062
Fail to reject H0: Two populations are similar
```

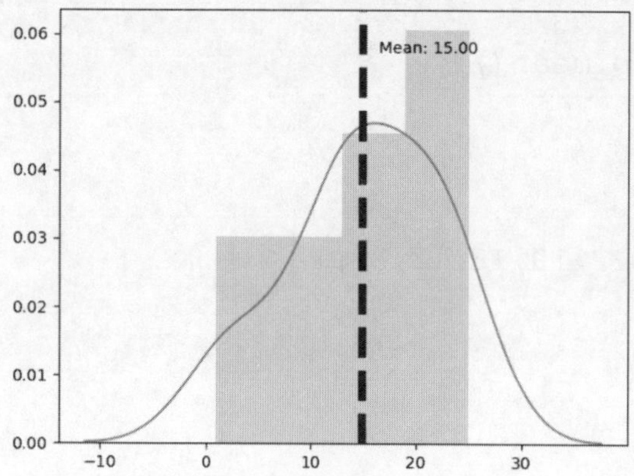

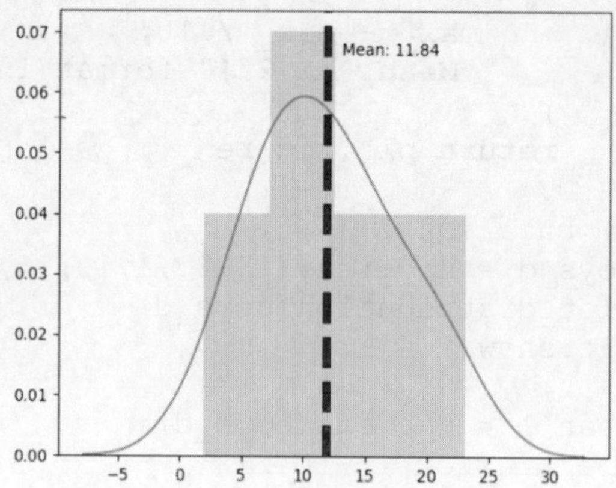

Putting both graphs together:

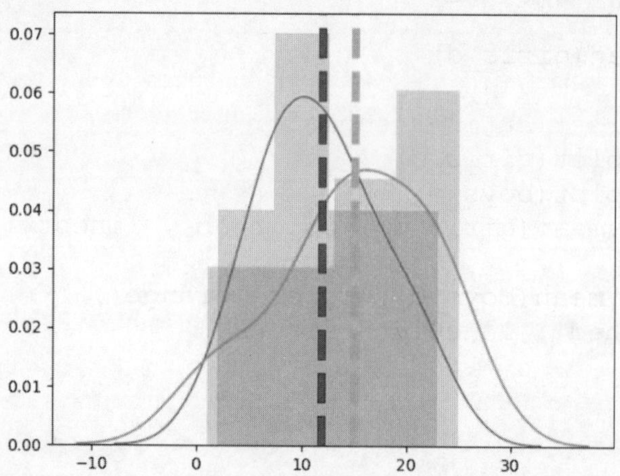

HOW TO FIND A CONFIDENCE INTERVAL FOR TWO POPULATIONS (PROPORTIONS)

Look at the daunting formula:

$$(\hat{p}_1 - \hat{p}_2) - z_{\alpha/2}\sqrt{\frac{\hat{p}_1\hat{q}_1}{n_1} + \frac{\hat{p}_2\hat{q}_2}{n_2}} < p_1 - p_2 < (\hat{p}_1 - \hat{p}_2) + z_{\alpha/2}\sqrt{\frac{\hat{p}_1\hat{q}_1}{n_1} + \frac{\hat{p}_2\hat{q}_2}{n_2}}$$

It looks a lot worse than it is, because the right side of the equation is actually a repeat of the left! Finding confidence intervals for two populations can be broken down to an easy three steps. Let's understand this with an example:

Example question: A study revealed that 65% of men surveyed supported the war in Afghanistan and 33% of women supported the war. If 100 men and 75 women were surveyed, find the 90% confidence interval for the data's true difference in proportions.

Step 1: Find the following variables from the information given in the question:

n1 (population 1)=100
Phat1 (population 1, positive response): 65% or 0.65
Qhat1 (population 1, negative response): 35% or 0.35
n2(population 2)=75
Phat2 (population 2, positive response): 33% or 0.33
Qhat2 (population 2, negative response): 67% or 0.67

Step 2: Find Zα/2

Zα/2=0.13

Step 3: Enter your data into the following formula and solve:

$$(\hat{p}_1 - \hat{p}_2) - z_{\alpha/2}\sqrt{\frac{\hat{p}_1\hat{q}_1}{n_1} + \frac{\hat{p}_2\hat{q}_2}{n_2}} < p_1 - p_2 < (\hat{p}_1 - \hat{p}_2) + z_{\alpha/2}\sqrt{\frac{\hat{p}_1\hat{q}_1}{n_1} + \frac{\hat{p}_2\hat{q}_2}{n_2}}$$

- multiply phat1 and qhat1 together (.65 x .35 = .2275)
- divide your answer to (1) by n1. Set this number aside. (.2275 x 100=.00275)
- multiply phat2 and qhat2 together (.33 x .67=.2211).
- divide your answer to (3) by n2 (.2211/75=.002948).
- Add (3) and (4) together (.00275 + .002948=.005698)
- Take the square root of (5): (sqrt.005698=.075485)
- Multiply (6) by zα/2 found in Step 2. (.075485 x 0.13=.0098). Set this number aside.
- Subtract phat2 from phat1 (.65-.33=.32).
- Subtract (8) from (7) to get the left limit (.32-0.0098 = **31.9902**)
- Add (7) to (8) to get the right limit (.32+.0.0098=**32.0098**)

***

UNIT 12: ANALYSIS OF VARIANCE AND DESIGN OF EXPERIMENTS (ANOVA)

Analysis of variance (ANOVA) is a collection of statistical models and their associated estimation procedures (such as the "variation" among and between groups) used to analyze the differences among group means in a sample. ANOVA was developed by the statistician Ronald Fisher. The ANOVA is based on the law of total variance, where the observed variance in a particular variable is partitioned into components attributable to different sources of variation. In its simplest form, ANOVA provides a statistical test of whether two or more population means are equal, and therefore generalizes the t-test beyond two means. An Analysis of Variance Test, or ANOVA, can be thought of as a generalization of the t-tests for more than 2 groups. The independent t-test is used to compare the means of a condition between two groups. ANOVA is used when we want to compare the means of a condition between more than two groups.

What is ANOVA (ANalysis Of VAriance)

- used to compare the means of more than 2 groups (t-test can be used to compare 2 groups)
- groups mean differences inferred by analyzing variances
- Main types: One-way (one factor) and two-way (two factors) ANOVA (factor is an independent variable)

Note: In ANOVA, group, factors, and independent variables are similar terms

ANOVA Hypotheses

- Null hypotheses: Groups means are equal (no variation in means of groups)
- Alternative hypotheses: At least, one group mean is different from other groups

ANOVA Assumptions

- Residuals (experimental error) are normally distributed (Shapiro-Wilks Test)
- Homogeneity of variances (variances are equal between treatment groups) (Levene or Bartlett Test)
- Observations are sampled independently from each other

How ANOVA works?

- Check sample sizes: equal number of observation in each group
- Calculate Mean Square for each group (MS) (SS of group/level-1); level-1 is a degree of freedom (df) for a group
- Calculate Mean Square error (MSE) (SS error/df of residuals)
- Calculate F-value (MS of group/MSE)

Types of ANOVA Tests

- One-Way ANOVA: A one-way ANOVA has just one independent variable
    - For example, differences in Corona cases can be assessed by Country, and a Country can have 2, 20, or more different categories to compare
- Two-Way ANOVA: A two-way ANOVA (also called factorial ANOVA) refers to an ANOVA using two independent variables

  - Expanding the example above, a two-way ANOVA can examine differences in Corona cases (the dependent variable) by Age group (independent variable 1) and Gender (independent variable 2). Two-way ANOVA can be used to examine the interaction between the two independent variables. Interactions indicate that differences are not uniform across all categories of the independent variables
  - For example, Old Age Group may have higher Corona cases overall compared to the Young Age group, but this difference could be greater (or less) in Asian countries compared to European countries
- N-Way ANOVA: A researcher can also use more than two independent variables, and this is an n-way ANOVA (with n being the number of independent variables you have), aka MANOVA Test.
  - For example, potential differences in Corona cases can be examined by Country, Gender, Age group, Ethnicity, etc, simultaneously
  - An ANOVA will give you a single (univariate) f-value while a MANOVA will give you a multivariate F-value

With Replication vs. Without Replication

You may hear with Replication and without Replication with regards to ANOVA test frequently. Let's understand what these are:

- Two-way ANOVA with replication: Two groups and the members of those groups are doing more than one thing
  - For example, let's say a vaccine has not been developed for COVID-19, and doctors are trying two different treatments to cure two groups of COVID-19 infected patients
- Two-way ANOVA without replication: It's used when you only have one group and you're double-testing that same group
  - For example, let's say a vaccine has been developed for COVID-19, and researchers are testing one set of volunteers before and after they've been vaccinated to see if it works or not

ONE-WAY (ONE FACTOR) ANOVA

The formula for one-way ANOVA test can be written like this:

$$F = \frac{\text{Explained Variance}}{\text{Unexplained variance}} \; or \; \frac{\text{Variance between groups}}{\text{Variance within groups}} = \frac{\text{Sum of squares between groups}}{\text{Sum of squares for error}}$$

$$= \frac{MST}{MSE} = \frac{Mean\ squared\ error\ treatments}{Mean\ squared\ error} = \frac{SS_B/_{Df_T}}{SS_W/_{Df_E}} = \frac{SS_B/_{(k-1)}}{SS_W/_{(N-k)}}$$

Where,

$$SS_B = \sum_i n_i\,(\bar{y}_i - \bar{y})^2$$

$$SS_w = \sum_{ij} (y_{ij} - \bar{y}_i\ )^2$$

Where,

y_i $-$ *sample mean in the* i^{th} *group*
n_i $-$ *number of observation in the* i^{th} *group*
$\bar{y}$ $-$ *total mean of the data*
k $-$ *total number of the groups*

y_{ij} $-$ j^{th} *observation in the out of k groups*
N $-$ *Overall sample size*

Basically, ANOVA is performed by comparing two types of variation, the variation between the sample means, as well as the variation within each of the samples. The below-mentioned formula represents one-way Anova test statistics.

The result of the ANOVA formula, the F statistic (also called the F-ratio), allows for the analysis of multiple groups of data to determine the variability between samples and within samples.

When we plot the ANOVA table, all the above components can be seen in it as below:

Source of Variation	Sums of Squares (SS)	Degrees of Freedom (df)	Mean Squares (MS)	F
Between Treatments	SSB	k-1	$MST = {SS_B}/{(k-1)}$	$F = \frac{MST}{MSE}$
Error (or Residual)	SSE	N-k	$MSE = {SS_W}/{(N-k)}$	
Total	SST= SSB+SSE	N-1	T	

In general, if the p-value associated with the F is smaller than 0.05, then the null hypothesis is rejected and the alternative hypothesis is supported. If the null hypothesis is rejected, we can conclude that the means of all the groups are not equal.

Note: If no real difference exists between the tested groups, which is called the null hypothesis, the result of the ANOVA's F-ratio statistic will be close to 1.

Example:

Consider a scenario where doctors have four medical treatments to apply to cure the patients. Once we have the test results, one approach is to assume that the treatment which took the least time to cure the patients is the best among them. But what if some of these patients had already been partially cured, or if any other medication was already working on them? In order to make a confident and reliable decision, we will need evidence to support our approach. This is where the concept of ANOVA comes into play.

A	B	C	D
25	45	30	54
30	55	29	60
28	29	33	51
36	56	37	62
29	40	27	73

Here, there are four treatments (A, B, C, and D), which are groups for ANOVA analysis. Treatments are independent variable and termed as factor. As there are four types of treatments, treatment factor has four levels.

For this experimental design, there is only factor (treatments) or independent variable to evaluate, and therefore, one-way ANOVA method is suitable for analysis.

```
import pandas as pd
import matplotlib.pyplot as plt
# load data file
d =
pd.read_csv("https://raw.githubusercontent.com/swapnilsaurav/Da
taset/master/onewayAnova_data.csv")
# generate a boxplot to see the data distribution by
treatments. Using boxplot, we can easily detect the differences
# between different treatments
d.boxplot(column=['A', 'B', 'C', 'D'], grid=False)
plt.show()
import scipy.stats as stats
# stats f_oneway functions takes the groups as input and
returns F and P-value
fvalue, pvalue = stats.f_oneway(d['A'], d['B'], d['C'], d['D'])
print("F-Value : ",fvalue)
print("p-Value : ",pvalue)

#Get detailed Output
import statsmodels.api as sm
from statsmodels.formula.api import ols
# reshape the d dataframe suitable for statsmodels package
d_melt = pd.melt(d.reset_index(), id_vars=['index'],
value_vars=['A', 'B', 'C', 'D'])
# replace column names
d_melt.columns = ['index', 'treatments', 'value']
# Ordinary Least Squares (OLS) model
model = ols('value ~ C(treatments)', data=d_melt).fit()
anova_table = sm.stats.anova_lm(model, typ=2)
print("Anova Table: \n",anova_table)
```

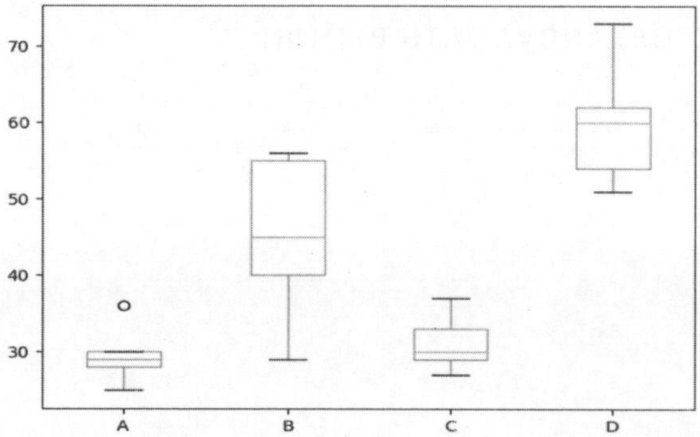

```
F-Value :  17.492810457516338
p-Value :  2.639241146210922e-05
Anova Table:
                  sum_sq    df          F    PR(>F)
C(treatments)  3010.95   3.0  17.49281  0.000026
Residual        918.00  16.0       NaN       NaN
```

Interpretation: The P-value obtained from ANOVA analysis is significant (P<0.05) hence we reject the Null Hypothesis, and therefore, we conclude that there are significant differences among treatments.

From ANOVA analysis, we know that treatment differences are statistically significant, but ANOVA does not tell which treatments are significantly different from each other. To know the pairs of significant different treatments, we will perform multiple pairwise comparison (Post-hoc comparison) analysis using Tukey HSD test.

```
#analysis using Tukey HSD test
# load packages
from pingouin import pairwise_tukey
# perform multiple pairwise comparison (Tukey HSD)
# for unbalanced (unequal sample size) data, pairwise_tukey
uses Tukey-Kramer test
m_comp = pairwise_tukey(data=d_melt, dv='value',
between='treatments')
print(m_comp)
```

Output:

```
   A  B  mean(A)  mean(B)  diff        se         T   p-tukey    hedges
0  A  B     29.6     45.0 -15.4  4.790616 -3.214618  0.010718 -1.836351
1  A  C     29.6     31.2  -1.6  4.790616 -0.333986  0.900000 -0.190790
2  A  D     29.6     60.0 -30.4  4.790616 -6.345739  0.001000 -3.625005
3  B  C     45.0     31.2  13.8  4.790616  2.880632  0.027410  1.645561
4  B  D     45.0     60.0 -15.0  4.790616 -3.131121  0.013679 -1.788654
5  C  D     31.2     60.0 -28.8  4.790616 -6.011753  0.001000 -3.434215
```

Above results from Tukey HSD suggests that except A-C, all other pairwise comparisons for treatments rejects null hypothesis (P-tukey<0.05) and indicates statistical significant differences.

TWO-WAY (TWO FACTOR) ANOVA WITH PYTHON

Genotype	1_year	2_year	3_year
A	1.53	4.08	6.69
A	1.83	3.84	5.97
A	1.38	3.96	6.33
B	3.6	5.7	8.55
B	2.94	5.07	7.95
B	4.02	7.2	8.94

From dataset, there are two factors (independent variables) viz. genotypes and yield in years. Genotypes and years has five and three levels respectively. For this experimental design, there are two factors to evaluate, and therefore, two-way ANOVA method is suitable for analysis. Here, using two-way ANOVA, we can simultaneously evaluate how type of genotype and years affects the yields of plants. If you apply one-way ANOVA here, you can able to evaluate only one factor at a time.

From two-way ANOVA, we can tests three hypotheses

- effect of genotype on yield
- effect of time (years) on yield, and
- effect of genotype and time (years) interactions on yield

```
import pandas as pd
import seaborn as sns
import matplotlib.pyplot as plt

# load data file
d =
pd.read_csv("https://raw.githubusercontent.com/swapnilsaurav/Da
taset/master/twowayAnova_data.csv")
# reshape the d dataframe suitable for statsmodels package
# you do not need to reshape if your data is already in stacked
format.
d_melt = pd.melt(d, id_vars=['Genotype'], value_vars=['1_year',
'2_year', '3_year'])
# replace column names
d_melt.columns = ['Genotype', 'years', 'value']
# generate a boxplot to see the data distribution by genotypes
and years.
sns.boxplot(x="Genotype", y="value", hue="years", data=d_melt,
palette="Set3")
plt.show()
import statsmodels.api as sm
from statsmodels.formula.api import ols
# Ordinary Least Squares (OLS) model
# C(Genotype):C(years) represent interaction term
model = ols('value ~ C(Genotype) + C(years) +
C(Genotype):C(years)', data=d_melt).fit()
anova_table = sm.stats.anova_lm(model, typ=2)
print("Anova Table: \n",anova_table)
```

```
Anova Table:
                           sum_sq    df           F        PR(>F)
C(Genotype)             58.551733   5.0   32.748581  1.931655e-12
C(years)               278.925633   2.0  390.014868  4.006243e-25
C(Genotype):C(years)    17.122967  10.0    4.788525  2.230094e-04
Residual                12.873000  36.0         NaN           NaN
```

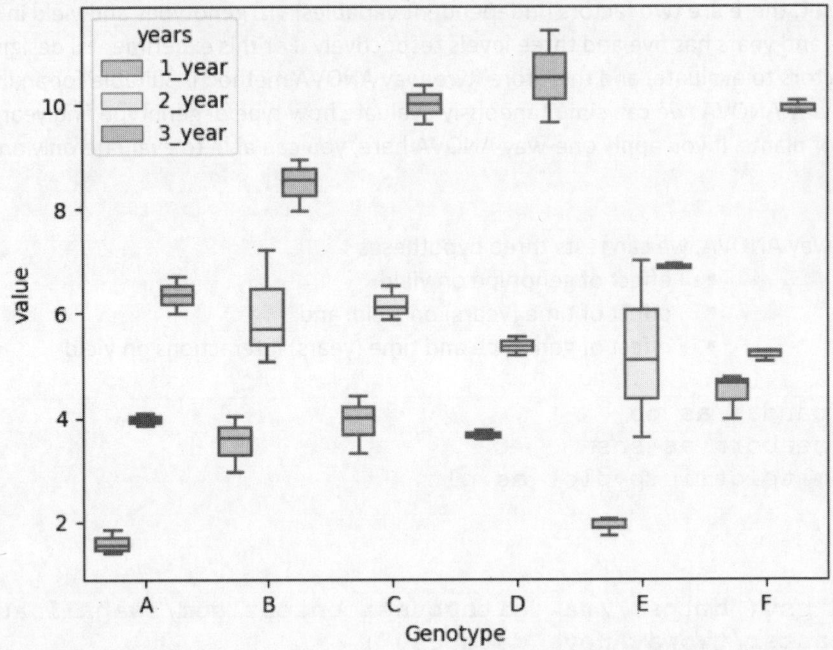

Interpretation: The P-value obtained from ANOVA analysis for genotype, years, and interaction are statistically significant (P<0.05). We reject the Null Hypothesis here. We conclude that type of genotype significantly affects the yield outcome, time (years) significantly affects the yield outcome, and interaction of both genotype and time (years) significantly affects the yield outcome.

Now, we know that genotype and time (years) differences are statistically significant, but ANOVA does not tell which genotype and time (years) are significantly different from each other. To know the pairs of significant different genotype and time (years), perform multiple pairwise comparison (Post-hoc comparison) analysis using Tukey HSD test.

Note: Three factor designs can be analyzed in a similar way to two-way ANOVA

***

UNIT 13: ANALYSIS OF CATEGORICAL DATA

Categorical data is also known as nominal data, meaning that one uses labels as opposed to numbers; for example, race and gender are categorical variables. The central tendency of categorical variables is given by its mode, since median and mean can only be computed on numerical data. Therefore, it does not follow a normal bell-curve distribution, and cannot be analyzed with tests that rely on a normal distribution such as the t-test or ANOVA. The Chi Square test is a statistical hypothesis test in which the sampling distribution of the test statistic is a chi-square distribution when the null hypothesis is true. A common usage of the Chi-square test is the Pearson's chi-square test, also known as the chi-square goodness-of-fit test or chi-square test for independence. The Chi square test is used to compare a group with a value, or to compare two or more groups, always using categorical data.

Chi-squared test for nominal (categorical) data

The c2 test is used to determine whether an association (or relationship) between 2 categorical variables in a sample is likely to reflect a real association between these 2 variables in the population.

Note: In the case of 2 variables being compared, the test can also be interpreted as determining if there is a difference between the two variables.

The sample data is used to calculate a single number (or test statistic), the size of which reflects the probability (p-value) that the observed association between the 2 variables has occurred by chance, ie due to sampling error.

Example

A group of students were classified in terms of personality (introvert or extrovert) and in terms of colour preference (red, yellow, green or blue) with the purpose of seeing whether there is an association (relationship) between personality and colour preference. Data was collected from 400 students and presented in the 2 (rows) x 4 (cols) contingency table below:

The Contingency Table :

A Contingency table (also called crosstab) is used in statistics to summarise the relationship between several categorical variables.

(Observed counts)	Colours				
	Red	Yellow	Green	Blue	Totals
Introvert personality	20	6	30	44	100
Extrovert personality	180	34	50	36	300
Totals	200	40	80	80	400

Suitable null and alternative hypotheses might be:

- H0: Colour preference is not associated with personality, and
- H1: Colour preference is associated with personality

To perform a chi-squared test, the number of students expected in each cell of the table if the null hypothesis is true, is calculated.

Calculation:
The expected numbers (under the null hypothesis) in each cell are equal to:

$$\frac{\text{row total x column total}}{\text{grand total}}$$

Thus for the introvert/red cell the expected number is:

$$\frac{100 \times 200}{400} = 50$$

(Expected counts)	Colours				
	Red	Yellow	Green	Blue	Totals
Introvert personality	50	10	20	20	100
Extrovert personality	150	30	60	60	300
Totals	200	40	80	80	400

To calculate the chi-squared (c2) statistic:

$$\frac{(\text{observed frequency} - \text{expected frequency})^2}{\text{expected frequency}}$$

The value of needs to be calculated for each cell in the table. For the introvert/red cell this is

$$\frac{(20 - 50)^2}{50} = 18.00$$

Chi Squared Test	Colours				
	Red	Yellow	Green	Blue	Totals
Introvert personality	18.0	1.6	5.0	28.8	53.4
Extrovert personality	6.0	0.5	1.7	9.6	17.8
Totals	24.0	2.1	6.7	38.4	71.2

Test Statistics:
The chi-square statistic is calculated to be total of these values, which is **71.2**
Degree of Freedom = (nrows-1) * (ncol-1) = 1 * 3 = **3**

P-Value

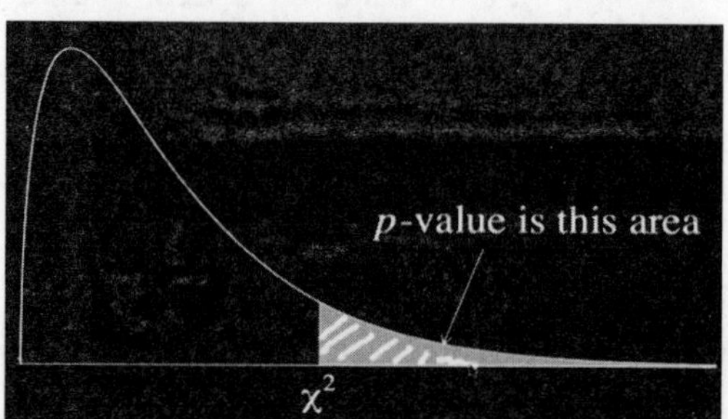

Let's check from the table:

df	$\chi^2_{0.9995}$	$\chi^2_{0.999}$	$\chi^2_{0.995}$	$\chi^2_{0.990}$	$\chi^2_{0.975}$	$\chi^2_{0.95}$	$\chi^2_{0.90}$	$\chi^2_{0.85}$	$\chi^2_{0.80}$
1	0.000	0.000	0.000	0.000	0.001	0.004	0.016	0.036	0.064
2	0.001	0.002	0.010	0.020	0.051	0.103	0.211	0.325	0.446
3	0.015	0.024	0.072	0.115	0.216	0.352	0.584	0.798	1.005

Our of test value of 71.2 is difficult to get from the table we have here, so we will find the exact value from the Python program. However, we ca estimate the p-value to be really really small here, close to zero.

The chi-squared test statistic is 71.20 with an associated $p < 0.001$.
Note: 0.000 should not be interpreted as exactly zero.

Let's verify with Python Code:

```
from scipy.stats import chi2_contingency

# defining the table
data = [[20,6,30,44], [180,34,50,36]]
stat, p, dof, expected = chi2_contingency(data)

# interpret p-value
alpha = 0.05
print("p value is " + str(p))
if p <= alpha:
    print('Dependent (reject H0)')
else:
    print('Independent (H0 holds true)')
```

Output:
p value is 2.3619600509176005e-15
Dependent (reject H0)

The null hypothesis is rejected, since $p < 0.001$, and a conclusion is made that colour preference is associated with personality. Examining the pattern of numbers it is noted that more introverts prefer blue than expected and less preferred red. The extroverts tend to favour red more than blue.

Example:
We have collected the data that shows the number of men and women buying different types of pets. The aim of the test is to conclude whether the two variables (gender and choice of pet) are related to each other.

The Contingency Table :

(Observed counts)	Pets			
	Dog	Cat	Bird	Totals
Men	207	282	241	730
Women	234	242	232	708
Totals	441	524	473	1438

The aim of the test is to conclude whether the two variables(gender and choice of pet) are related to each other.

Null hypothesis (H0) : There is no relation between the variables.
An alternate hypothesis (H1): There is a significant relation between the two.

Expected Values Table :

$$\frac{\text{row total x column total}}{\text{grand total}}$$

(Expected counts)	Pets			
	Dog	Cat	Bird	Totals
Men	223.9	266.0	240.1	730.0
Women	217.1	258.0	232.9	708.0
Totals	441.0	524.0	473.0	1438.0

To calculate the chi-squared (c2) statistic:

$$\frac{(\text{observed frequency} - \text{expected frequency})^2}{\text{expected frequency}}$$

The value of needs to be calculated for each cell in the table:

Chi Squared Test	Pets			
	Dog	Cat	Bird	Totals
Men	1.3	1.0	0.0	2.2
Women	1.3	1.0	0.0	2.3
Totals	2.6	2.0	0.0	4.5

Test Statistics:
The chi-square statistic is calculated to be total of these values, which is **4.5**
Degree of Freedom = (nrows-1) * (ncol-1) = 1 * 2 = **2**

Critical value of Chi-square (P-Value):
Calculate using Python program:

```
from scipy.stats import chi2_contingency

# defining the table
data = [[207, 282, 241], [234, 242, 232]]
stat, p, dof, expected = chi2_contingency(data)

# interpret p-value
alpha = 0.05
print("p value is " + str(p))
if p <= alpha:
   print('Dependent (reject H0)')
else:
   print('Independent (H0 holds true)')
```

Output:

p value is 0.1031971404730939
Independent (H0 holds true)

Therefore, we accept H0, that is, the variables do not have a significant relation.

***

UNIT 14: SUMMARY OF STATISTICS

EXPERIMENTAL DESIGN

There is a close relationship between experimental design and statistical analysis. The way that an experiment is designed determines the types of analyses that can be appropriately conducted. In this lesson, we review aspects of experimental design that a researcher must understand in order to properly interpret experimental data with analysis of variance.

What Is an Experiment?

An experiment is a procedure carried out to investigate cause-and-effect relationships. For example, the experimenter may manipulate one or more variables (independent variables) to assess the effect on another variable (the dependent variable).

Conclusions are reached on the basis of data. If the dependent variable is unaffected by changes in independent variables, we conclude that there is no causal relationship between the dependent variable and the independent variables. On the other hand, if the dependent variable is affected, we conclude that a causal relationship exists.

What Is Experimental Design?

The term experimental design refers to a plan for conducting the experiment in such a way that research results will be valid and easy to interpret. This plan includes three interrelated activities:

- Write statistical hypotheses.
- Collect data.
- Analyze data.

Let's look in a little more detail at these three activities.

Statistical Hypotheses

A statistical hypothesis is an assumption about the value of a population parameter. There are two types of statistical hypotheses:

Null hypothesis: The null hypothesis is the statement subjected to a statistical test in an experiment. It is denoted by H0. For example, consider the following null hypothesis:

$$H0: \mu i = \mu j$$

Here, μi is the population mean for group i, and μj is the population mean for group j. This hypothesis makes the assumption that population means in groups i and j are equal.

Alternative hypothesis: The alternative hypothesis is the hypothesis that is tenable if the null hypothesis is rejected. It is denoted by H1 or Ha. For example, consider the following alternative hypothesis:

$$H1: \mu i \neq \mu j$$

This hypothesis makes the assumption that population means in groups i and j are not equal.

The null hypothesis and the alternative hypothesis are written to be mutually exclusive. If one is true, the other is not.

Experiments rely on sample data to test the null hypothesis. If experimental results, based on sample statistics, are consistent with the null hypothesis, the null hypothesis cannot be rejected; otherwise, the null hypothesis is rejected in favor of the alternative hypothesis.

Data Collection

The data collection phase of experimental design is all about methodology - how to run the experiment to produce valid, relevant statistics that can be used to test a null hypothesis.

Identify Variables

Every experiment exists to examine a cause-and-effect relationship. With respect to the relationship under investigation, an experimental design needs to account for three types of variables:

- Dependent variable. The dependent variable is the outcome being measured, the effect in a cause-and-effect relationship.
- Independent variables. An independent variable is a variable that is explicitly included in an experiment, because the experimenter believes it is a potential cause in a cause-and-effect relationship.
- Extraneous variables. An extraneous variable is any other variable that could affect the dependent variable, but is not explicitly included in the experiment.

Note: The independent variables that are explicitly included in an experiment are also called factors.

Define Treatment Groups

In an experiment, treatment groups are built around factors, each group defined by a unique combination of factor levels.

For example, suppose that a drug company wants to test a new cholesterol medication. The dependent variable is total cholesterol level. One independent variable is dosage. And, since some drugs affect men and women differently, the researchers include a second independent variable - gender.

This experiment has two factors - dosage and gender. The dosage factor has three levels (0 mg, 50 mg, and 100 mg), and the gender factor has two levels (male and female). Given this combination of factors and levels we can define six unique treatment groups, as shown below:

Observation	Dose		
	0 mg	50 mg	100 mg
Men	Group 1	Group 3	Group 5
Women	Group 2	Group 4	Group 6

Select Factor Levels

A factor in an experiment can be described by the way in which factor levels are chosen for inclusion in the experiment:

- Fixed factor. The experiment includes all factor levels about which inferences are to be made.
- Random factor. The experiment includes a random sample of levels from a much bigger population of factor levels.

Experiments can be described by the presence or absence of fixed or random factors:

- Fixed-effects model. All of the factors in the experiment are fixed.
- Random-effects model. All of the factors in the experiment are random.
- Mixed model. At least one factor in the experiment is fixed, and at least one factor is random

The use of fixed factors versus random factors has implications for how experimental results are interpreted. With a fixed factor, results apply only to factor levels that are explicitly included in the experiment. With a random factor, results apply to every factor level from the population.

For example, consider the blood pressure experiment described above. Suppose the experimenter only wanted to test the effect of three particular dosage levels - 0 mg, 50 mg, and 100 mg. He would include those dosage levels in the experiment, and any research conclusions would apply to only those particular dosage levels. This would be an example of a fixed-effects model.

On the other hand, suppose the experimenter wanted to test the effect of any dosage level. Since it is not practical to test every dosage level, the experimenter might choose three dosage levels at random from the population of possible dosage levels. Any research conclusions would apply not only to the selected dosage levels, but also to other dosage levels that were not included explicitly in the experiment. This would be an example of a random-effects model.

Select Experimental Units

The experimental unit is the entity that provides values for the dependent variable. Depending on the needs of the study, an experimental unit may be a person, animal, plant, product - anything. For example, in the cholesterol study described above, researchers measured cholesterol level (the dependent variable) of people; so the experimental units were people.

Note: When the experimental units are people, they are often referred to as subjects. Some researchers prefer the term participant, because subject has a connotation that the person is subservient.

If time and money were no object, you would include the entire population of experimental units in your experiment. In the real world, where there is never enough time or money, you will usually select a sample of experimental units from the population.

Ultimately, you want to use sample data to make inferences about population parameters. With that in mind, it is best practice to draw a random sample of experimental units from the population. This provides a defensible, statistical basis for generalizing from sample findings to the larger population.

Finally, it is important to consider sample size. The larger the sample, the greater the statistical power; and the more confidence you can have in your results.

Assign Experimental Units to Treatments

Having selected a sample of experimental units, we need to assign each unit to one or more treatment groups. Here are two ways that you might assign experimental units to groups:

- Independent groups design. Each experimental unit is randomly assigned to one, and only one, treatment group. This is also known as a between-subjects design.
- Repeated measures design. Experimental units are assigned to more than one treatment group. This is also known as a within-subjects design.

Control for Extraneous Variables

Extraneous variables can mask effects of independent variables. Therefore, a good experimental design controls potential effects of extraneous variables. Here are a few strategies for controlling extraneous variables:

- Randomization Assign subjects randomly to treatment groups. This tends to distribute effects of extraneous variables evenly across groups.

- Repeated measures design. To control for individual differences between subjects (age, attitude, religion, etc.), assign each subject to multiple treatments. This strategy is called using subjects as their own control.
- Counterbalancing. In repeated measures designs, randomize or reverse the order of treatments among subjects to control for order effects (e.g., fatigue, practice).

As we describe specific experimental designs in upcoming lessons, we will point out the strategies that are used with each design to control the confounding effects of extraneous variables.

Data Analysis

Researchers follow a formal process to determine whether to reject a null hypothesis, based on sample data. This process, called hypothesis testing, consists of five steps:

1. Formulate hypotheses. This involves stating the null and alternative hypotheses. Because the hypotheses are mutually exclusive, if one is true, the other must be false.
2. Choose the test statistic. This involves specifying the statistic that will be used to assess the validity of the null hypothesis. Typically, in analysis of variance studies, researchers compute a F ratio to test hypotheses. For, analysis of categprical values, we use Chi-square test.
3. Compute a P-value, based on sample data. Suppose the observed test statistic is equal to S. The P-value is the probability that the experiment would yield a test statistic as extreme as S, assuming the null hypothesis is true.
4. Choose a significance level. The significance level, denoted by α, is the probability of rejecting the null hypothesis when it is really true. Researchers often choose a significance level of 0.05 or 0.01.
5. Test the null hypothesis. If the P-value is smaller than the significance level, we reject the null hypothesis; if it is larger, we fail to reject.

A good experimental design includes a precise plan for data analysis. Before the first data point is collected, a researcher should know how experimental data will be processed to accept or reject the null hypotheses.

***

UNIT 15: INTRODUCTION TO MACHINE LEARNING

It is no doubt that machine learning is increasingly gaining popularity and has become the hottest trend in the tech industry. Machine learning is incredibly powerful to make predictions or calculated suggestions based on large amounts of data. So, what is a machine learning?

Machine learning is an application of artificial intelligence (AI) that provides systems the ability to automatically learn and improve from experience without being explicitly programmed. Machine learning focuses on the development of computer programs that can access data and use it learn for themselves. How does a system learn?

A Computer program is said to learn from Experience "E" with respect to some task "T" and some performance measure "P", if its performance on "T", as measured by "P", improves with "E".

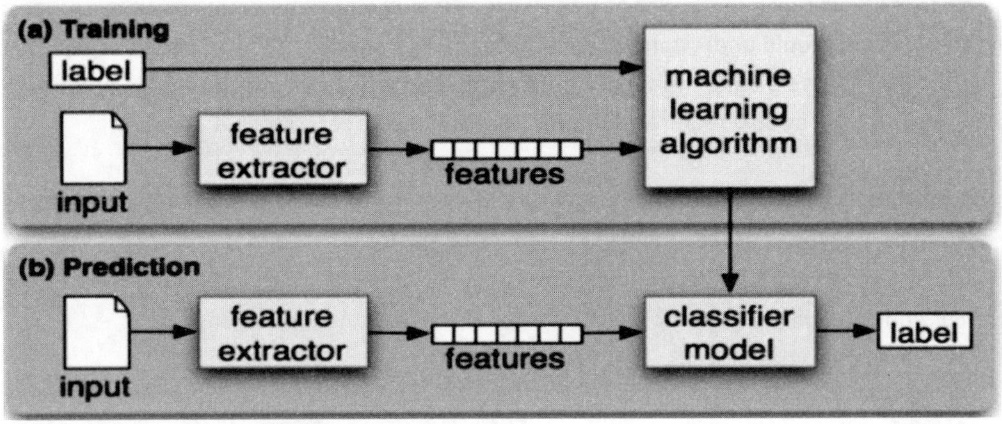

Figure 1: Machine Learning Workflow

The process of learning begins with observations or data (Training Data), such as examples, direct experience, or instruction, in order to look for patterns in data and make better decisions in the future based on the examples that we provide. The primary aim is to allow the computers learn automatically without human intervention or assistance and adjust actions accordingly.

Machine learning algorithms are often categorized as ***supervised*** or ***unsupervised***.

<u>**Supervised machine learning algorithms**</u> can apply what has been learned in the past to new data using labeled examples to predict future events. Starting from the analysis of a known training dataset, the learning algorithm produces an inferred function to make predictions about the output values. The system is able to provide targets for any new input after sufficient training. The learning algorithm can also compare its output with the correct, intended output and find errors in order to modify the model accordingly.

<u>**Unsupervised machine learning algorithms**</u> are used when the information used to train is neither classified nor labeled. Unsupervised learning studies how systems can infer a function to describe a hidden structure from unlabeled data. The system doesn't figure out the right output, but it explores the data and can draw inferences from datasets to describe hidden structures from unlabeled data.

Semi-supervised machine learning algorithms fall somewhere in between supervised and unsupervised learning, since they use both labeled and unlabeled data for training – typically a small amount of labeled data and a large amount of unlabeled data. The systems that use this method are able to considerably improve learning accuracy. Usually, semi-supervised learning is chosen when the acquired labeled data requires skilled and relevant resources in order to train it / learn from it.

Reinforcement machine learning algorithms is a learning method that interacts with its environment by producing actions and discovers errors or rewards. Trial and error search and delayed reward are the most relevant characteristics of reinforcement learning. Simple reward feedback is required for the agent to learn which action is best; this is known as the reinforcement signal.

Still no cleared about these methods? Not to worry. We will learn and practice in the chapters to come. One thing we should understand is Machine learning enables analysis of massive quantities of data and generally delivers faster, more accurate results in order to identify profitable opportunities or dangerous risks, it may also require additional time and resources to train it properly.

Let's undertstand them with an example:

- Suppose you had a basket and filled it with different kinds of fruits.
- Your task is to arrange them into groups.
- For understanding let me explain the names of the fruits in our basket.
- We have four types of fruits. They are

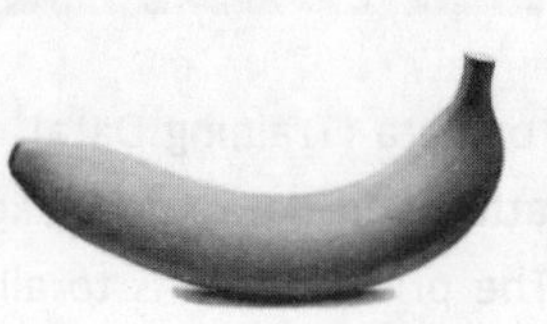

Please note Reinforcement Learning is out of scope for this book and we haven't covered this in detail. We will come out with another book where we will focus on Reinforcement learning.

Supervised Learning:

- You already learn from your previous work about the physical characters of fruits So arranging the same type of fruits at one place is easy now
- In data mining terminology the earlier work is called as training the data
- You already learn the things from your train data. This is because of response variable
- Response variable means just a decision variable
- You can observe response variable below (FRUIT NAME)
- Suppose you have taken a new fruit from the basket then you will see the size, color, and shape of that particular fruit.

- If size is Big, color is Red, the shape is rounded shape with a depression at the top, you will confirm the fruit name as apple and you will put in apple group.
- Likewise for other fruits also.
- The job of grouping fruits was done and the happy ending.
- You can observe in the table that a column was labeled as "FRUIT NAME". This is called as a response variable.
- If you learn the thing before from training data and then applying that knowledge to the test data(for new fruit), This type of learning is called as Supervised Learning.

No.	SIZE	COLOR	SHAPE	FRUIT NAME
1	Big	Red	Rounded shape with depression at the top	Apple
2	Small	Red	Heart-shaped to nearly globular	Cherry
3	Big	Green	Long curving cylinder	Banana
4	Small	Green	Round to oval,Bunch shape Cylindrical	Grape

Unsupervised Learning

Suppose you have a basket and it is filled with some different types of fruits and your task is to arrange them as groups.

- This time, you don't know anything about the fruits, honestly saying this is the first time you have seen them. You have no clue about those.
- So, how will you arrange them?
- What will you do first???
- You will take a fruit and you will arrange them by considering the physical character of that particular fruit.
- Suppose you have considered color.
- Then you will arrange them on considering base condition as color.
- Then the groups will be something like this.
  - RED COLOR GROUP: apples & cherry fruits.
  - GREEN COLOR GROUP: bananas & grapes.
- So now you will take another physical character such as size.
  - RED COLOR AND BIG SIZE: apple.
  - RED COLOR AND SMALL SIZE: cherry fruits.
  - GREEN COLOR AND BIG SIZE: bananas.
  - GREEN COLOR AND SMALL SIZE: grapes.
- The job has done, the happy ending.
- Here you did not learn anything before, means no train data and no response variable.

The Purpose of Train/Test Sets

Why do we use train and test sets?

Creating a train and test split of your dataset is one method to quickly evaluate the performance of an algorithm on your problem. The training dataset is used to prepare a model, to train it.

We pretend the test dataset is new data where the output values are withheld from the algorithm. We gather predictions from the trained model on the inputs from the test dataset and compare them to the withheld output values of the test set.

Comparing the predictions and withheld outputs on the test dataset allows us to compute a performance measure for the model on the test dataset. This is an estimate of the skill of the algorithm trained on the problem when making predictions on unseen data. You will be able to understand by now that test and train set analysis is done for Supervised algorightms and not for unsupervised algorithms.

Different Models

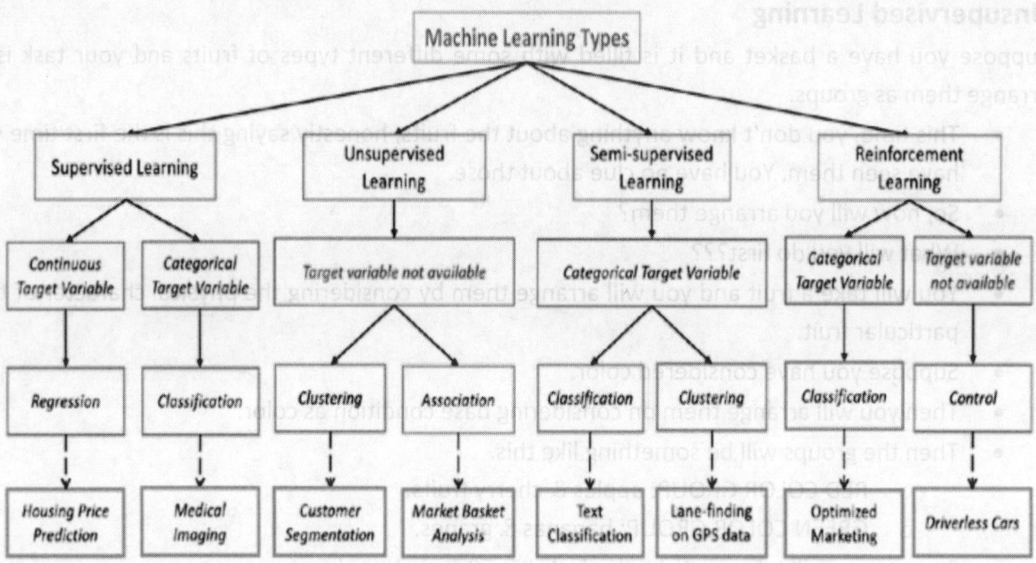

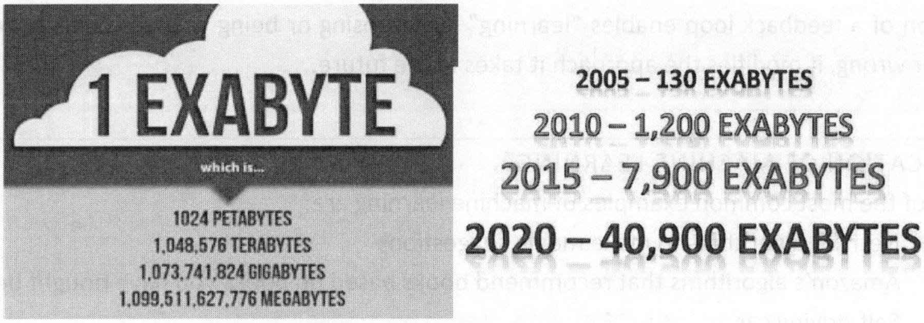

Figure 2: Exabyte and growth of data. (Source: IDC)

We live in 21st century and the data is everywhere. Every second tons of data are produced, if could be the text messages you are sending or posting a pic on Instagram. Since the dawn of time until 2005, humans had created 130 Exabytes of data. By 2020, its expected to reach 40,900 Exabytes. To understand this, we know that one letter takes about 1 byte of space. This is a phenomenal growth of the data we create. This is the reality of the world we live in. Our capacity to process this data is very less and even though machine can process much more data but still it will not be possible to process all these data. Machine learning provides us with that opportunity. Machine Learning algorithm can help us to step us to analyze all these data and help us to create value out of it.

DIFFERENCE BETWEEN ARTIFICIAL INTELLIGENCE AND MACHINE LEARNING

Artificial Intelligence (AI) and Machine Learning (ML) are two very hot buzzwords, and are often seem to be used interchangeably. They are not quite the same thing. Let's understand the difference between the two:

- Artificial Intelligence is the broader concept of machines being able to carry out tasks in a way that we would consider “smart”.
- Machine Learning is a current application of AI based around the idea that we should really just be able to give machines access to data and let them learn for themselves.

Artificial Intelligences – devices designed to act intelligently – are often classified into one of two fundamental groups – applied or general. Applied AI is far more common – systems designed to intelligently trade stocks and shares, or maneuver an autonomous vehicle would fall into this category.

Engineers and Scientists have realized that rather than teaching computers and machines how to do everything, it would be far more efficient to code them to think like human beings, and then plug them into the internet to give them access to all of the information in the world. This is machine learning. A Neural Network is a computer system designed to work by classifying information in the same way a human brain does. It can be taught to recognize, for example, images, and classify them according to elements they contain. Essentially it works on a system of probability – based on data fed to it, it is able to make statements, decisions or predictions with a degree of certainty. The addition of a feedback loop enables "learning" – by sensing or being told whether its decisions are right or wrong, it modifies the approach it takes in the future.

APPLICATION OF MACHINE LEARNING

Some of the most common examples of machine learning are:

1. Netflix's algorithms to make movie suggestions
2. Amazon's algorithms that recommend books based on books you have bought before.
3. Self-driving car
4. Knowing what customers are saying about you on Twitter?
5. Fraud detection? One of the more obvious, important uses in our world today.
6. Speech recognition, Natural language processing and Computer vision
7. Computational biology and Medical outcomes analysis
8. Virtual Reality (VR) games, etc

Readers can add more such applications to the list.

SCIKIT-LEARN

Scikit-learn is a free machine learning library for Python. It features various algorithms like support vector machine, random forests, and k-neighbours, and it also supports Python numerical and scientific libraries like NumPy and SciPy. In this chapter we will learn to code python and apply Machine Learning with the help of the scikit-learn library, which was created to make doing machine learning in Python easier and more robust.

We will import the data set using pandas, explore the data using pandas methods like head(), tail(), dtypes(), and then try our hand at using plotting techniques to visualize our data.

Then we'll dive into scikit-learn and use preprocessing.LabelEncoder() in scikit-learn to process the data, and train_test_split() to split the data set into test and train samples. We have already seen the different types of Machine Learning algorithm which we will use a cheat sheet to help us decide which algorithms to use for the data set. We will compare their performance using methods like accuracy_score() provided by the scikit-learn library. We will also visualize the performance score of different models.

If you have not read pandas fundamentals and Seaborn and matplotlib basics, its advised to read them before reading this chapter. You refer to the book "Learn and Practice Data Visualization using Python by Swapnil Saurav", available online and in stores.

Scikit-learn was initially developed by David Cournapeau as a Google summer of code project in 2007. Later Matthieu Brucher joined the project and started to use it as apart of his thesis work. In 2010 INRIA got involved and the first public release (v0.1 beta) was published in late January

2010. The project now has more than 30 active contributors and has had paid sponsorship from INRIA, Google, Tinyclues and the Python Software Foundation.

scikit-learn provides a library of transformers, which may clean (Preprocessing data), reduce (Unsupervised dimensionality reduction), expand (Kernel Approximation) or generate (Feature extraction) feature representations. Like other estimators, these are represented by classes with a fit method, which learns model parameters (e.g. mean and standard deviation for normalization) from a training set, and a transform method which applies this transformation model to unseen data. fit_transform may be more convenient and efficient for modelling and transforming the training data simultaneously.

HOW TO USE JUPYTER NOTEBOOK

Jupyter Notebook is an open-source web application that allows you to create and share documents that contain live code, equations, visualizations, and narrative text. Uses include data cleaning and transformation, numerical simulation, statistical modeling, data visualization, machine learning, and much more.

Jupyter has support for over 40 different programming languages and Python is one of them. Python is a requirement for installing the Jupyter Notebook itself.

Jupyter Notebook can be installed by using either of the two ways described below:

Using Anaconda:
Install Python and Jupyter using the Anaconda Distribution, which includes Python, the Jupyter Notebook, and other commonly used packages for scientific computing and data science. To install Anaconda, go through How to install Anaconda on windows? and follow the instructions provided at this location: https://test-jupyter.readthedocs.io/en/latest/install.html

Using PIP:
Install Jupyter using the PIP package manager used to install and manage software packages/libraries written in Python. To install pip, go through How to install PIP on Windows? and follow the instructions provided.

PIP is a package management system used to install and manage software packages/libraries written in Python. These files are stored in a large "on-line repository" termed as Python Package Index (PyPI).
pip uses PyPI as the default source for packages and their dependencies.

1. To install Jupyter using pip, we need to first check if pip is updated in our system. Use the following command to update pip:

python -m pip install --upgrade pip

2. After updating the pip version, follow the instructions provided below to install Jupyter:

Command to install Jupyter:

python -m pip install jupyter

3. Launching Jupyter:

Use the following command to launch Jupyter using command-line:

jupyter notebook

Server is now started.

Jupyter Notebook will be launched in browser and would look like this:

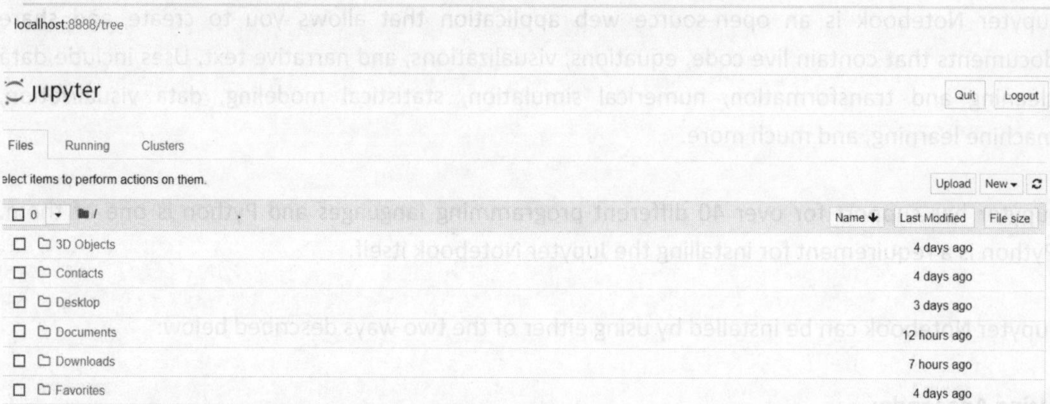

Let's create a folder now, create on New -> Folder:

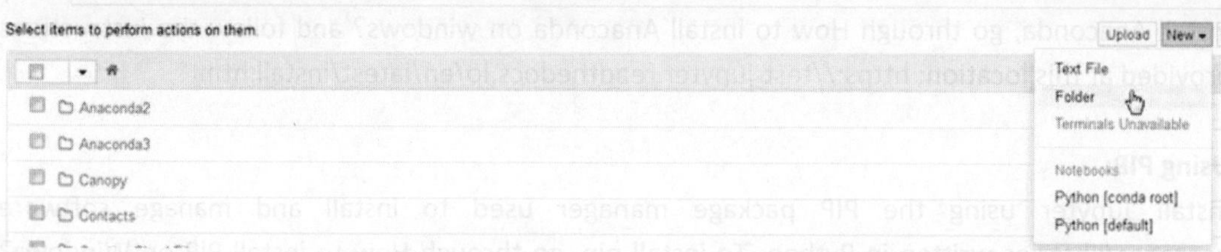

Rename it the way you want to by selecting the checkbox next to folder. Then go into this folder and create new text file.

Write your program in this and rename the file to your program name and **.py**

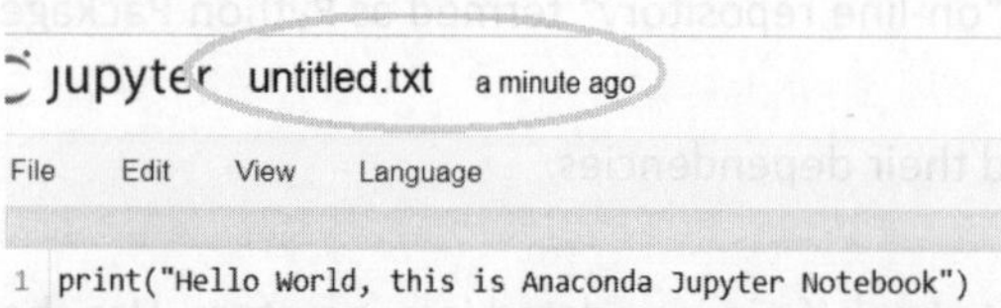

Save this file, it will not auto save your file.

Now switch to the Tab where the folder is create and this time, select New -> Python file. This will open a file as shown below:

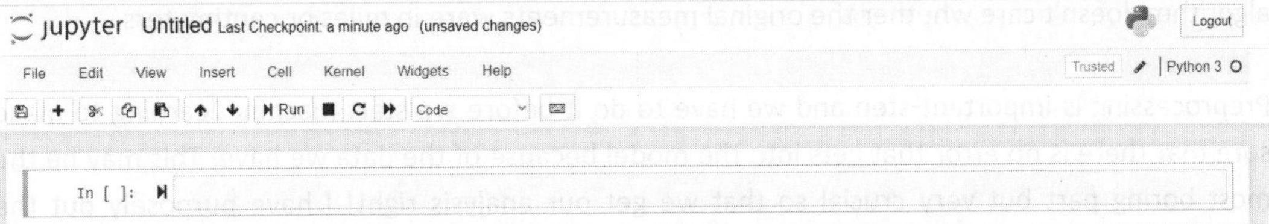

Let's try to plot something:

```
In [4]:  import matplotlib.pyplot as plt
         x = [5, 2, 9, 4, 7]
         y = [10, 5, 8, 4, 2]
         plt.plot(x, y)

Out[4]: [<matplotlib.lines.Line2D at 0xad80418>]
```

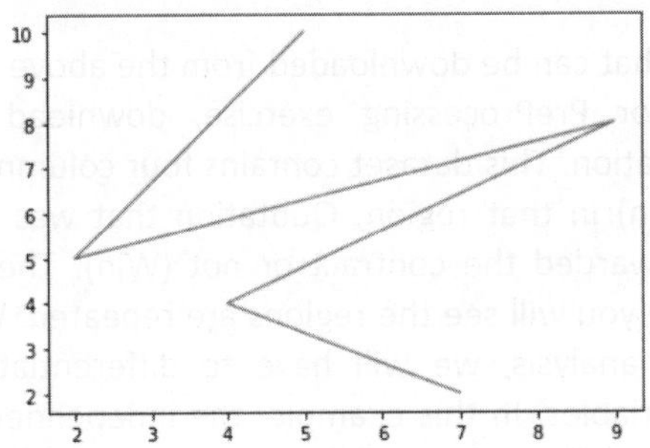

```
In [5]:  plt.bar(x, y)

Out[5]: <BarContainer object of 5 artists>
```

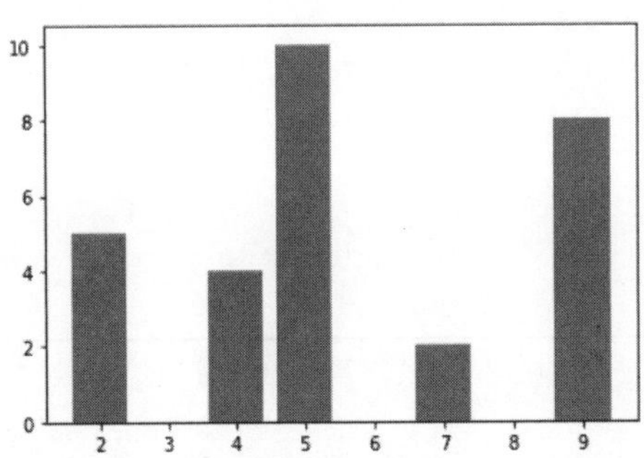

GETTING STARTED: DATA PROCESSING

Data cleaning and preprocessing is the first step toward building a working machine learning model. It's critical! If your data hasn't been cleaned and preprocessed, your model does not work.

Data preprocessing is an umbrella term that covers an array of operations data scientists will use to get their data into a form more appropriate for what they want to do with it. For example, before performing sentiment analysis of twitter data, you may want to strip out any html tags, white spaces, expand abbreviations and split the tweets into lists of the words they contain. When analyzing spatial data, you may scale it so that it is unit-independent, that is, so that your algorithm doesn't care whether the original measurements were in miles or centimeters.

Preprocessing is important step and we have to do it before we start machine learning to make sure that there is no error that gets into the model because of the data we have. This may be the most boring part but very crucial so that we get our analysis right! I have purposely put the headers as a separate section because we will have to repeat them every time we work on performing analysis. Let's get started.

GET THE DATASET

Step 1 is to get the dataset to work on the analysis. The dataset to be worked with this book has been placed on the Github location:
https://github.com/swapnilsaurav/MachineLearning

We will mention the filename of the dataset that can be downloaded from the above location for each of the exercise as we go along. For PreProcessing exercise, download the file - 1_Data_PreProcessing.csv from the above location. This dataset contains four columns – Regions (Region), number of Salesperson (Salesperson) in that region, Quotation that was given for a contract (Quotation) and if the team was awarded the contract or not (Win). The data from multiple contract is presented together hence you will see the regions are repeated. We have 14 observations. Before we proceed with the analysis, we will have to differentiate between dependent variables and the independent variables. In this example, the independent variables are the first 3 columns – Region, Salesperson and Quotation and dependent variable is Win. In our learning of the machine learning, we will use the independent variable to predict the dependent variable. We will use Region, Salesperson and Quotation column to predict if the contract can be won or not.

Region	Salesperson	Quotation	Win
North	44	72000	No
South	27	48000	Yes
East	30	54000	No

Figure 3: Dataset snapshot

IMPORT THE LIBRARY

The sklearn.preprocessing package provides several common utility functions and transformer classes to change raw feature vectors into a representation that is more suitable for the data analysis.

STANDARDIZATION, OR MEAN REMOVAL AND VARIANCE SCALING (FEATURE SCALING)

Looking at the dataset, the Salesperson independent variable value varies from 27 to 48 and the Quotation value varies from 40000 to 90000. In scenarios like these, owing to mere greater numeric range, the impact on response variables by the feature having greater numeric range could be more than the one having less numeric range, and this could, in turn, impact prediction accuracy. The objective is to improve predictive accuracy and not allow a particular feature impact the prediction due to large numeric value range. Thus, we may need to normalize or scale values before proceeding under different features such that they fall under common range.

There is couple of ways to scale the value:

- Min-Max Normalization: Data frame could be normalized using Min-Max normalization technique which specify following formula to be applied on each value of features to be normalized: (X - min(X))/(max(X) - min(X))
- Z-Score Normalization: The disadvantage with min-max normalization technique is that it tends to bring data towards the mean. If there is a need for outliers to get weighted more than the other values, z-score standardization technique suits better.
  Formula is: (X - mean(X))/(Std. Dev.(X))

The function scale provides a quick and easy way to perform this operation on a single array-like dataset but before install the sklearn package using: **Python37-32\Scripts>pip install sklearn** on command prompt.

```
from sklearn import preprocessing
#import sklearn as sk
import numpy as np
X_train = np.array([[ 0, -35,  25],
                    [ 200,  0,  20],
                    [ 30,  10, 0]])
X_scaled = preprocessing.scale(X_train)
print(X_scaled)

#Calculate Mean of the Scaled values
print(X_scaled.mean(axis=0))
#Calculate Standard Deviation of the Scaled values
print(X_scaled.std(axis=0))
```

Output:

```
[[-0.87056284 -1.38218948  0.9258201 ]
 [ 1.40047065  0.43193421  0.46291005]
 [-0.52990781  0.95025527 -1.38873015]]
```

Scaled data has zero mean and unit variance.

FEATURE SCALING

What is feature scaling? Why do we need it?

Look at our data. Since you will be handling lot of features (columns), you might see columns with varying size of numerical data. For example, there can be a column with ages from 20 - 65 and we can have their salary ranges from $40,000-$800,000. Not only is the salary column made up of much higher numbers than the age column, but the variables also cover a much wider range of data. That means that the Euclidean distance will be dominated by worth and will wind up dominating the age data.

What if Euclidean distance doesn't play a part in your specific machine learning model? Scaling the features will still make the model much faster, so you might want to include this step when you're preprocessing your data.

There are many ways to do feature scaling. They all mean that we're putting all of our features into the same scale so that none are dominated by another.

Scaling Feature to a range

An alternative standardization is scaling features to lie between a given minimum and maximum value, often between zero and one, or so that the maximum absolute value of each feature is scaled to unit size. This can be achieved using MinMaxScaler or MaxAbsScaler, respectively.

Here is an example to scale a data matrix to the [0, 1] range:

```
from sklearn import preprocessing
#import sklearn as sk
import numpy as np
X_train = np.array([[ 0, -35,  25],
                     [ 200,  0,  20],
                     [ 30,  10,  0]])
min_max_scaler = preprocessing.MinMaxScaler()
X_train_minmax = min_max_scaler.fit_transform(X_train)
print(X_train_minmax)
```

Output:

```
[[0.    0.    1.    ]
 [1.    0.77777778 0.8    ]
 [0.15   1.    0.    ]]
```

If MinMaxScaler is given an explicit feature_range=(min, max) the full formula is:

X_std = (X - X.min(axis=0)) / (X.max(axis=0) - X.min(axis=0))

X_scaled = X_std * (max - min) + min

MaxAbsScaler works in a very similar fashion, but scales in a way that the training data lies within the range [-1, 1] by dividing through the largest maximum value in each feature. It is meant for data that is already centered at zero or sparse data.

```
from sklearn import preprocessing
#import sklearn as sk
import numpy as np
X_train = np.array([[ 0, -35,  25],
                     [ 200,  0,  20],
                     [ 30,  10,  0]])
```

```
max_abs_scaler = preprocessing.MaxAbsScaler()
X_train_maxabs = max_abs_scaler.fit_transform(X_train)
print(X_train_maxabs)
```

Example using StandardScaler:

```
from sklearn.preprocessing import StandardScaler
data = [[0, 0], [0, 0], [1, 1], [1, 1]]
scaler = StandardScaler()
print(scaler.fit(data))
# StandardScaler(copy=True, with_mean=True, with_std=True)
#Get the transformed data
print(scaler.transform(data))
print(scaler.mean_)
print(scaler.transform([[2, 2]]))
```

MISSING DATA AND SPARSE MATRICES

For various reasons, many real world datasets contain missing values, often encoded as blanks, NaNs or other placeholders. Such datasets however are incompatible with scikit-learn estimators which assume that all values in an array are numerical, and that all have and hold meaning. This happens very frequently while working with the real time dataset hence you need to learn the trick to handle missing data and make it look good so that machine learning algorithm can run correctly. As you can see in the current dataset, we have 2 missing data – one under Quotation and other under Salesperson.

One option is to remove the missing data altogether from the analysis but that's not the right approach because this comes at the price of losing data which may be valuable (even though incomplete). Another option which is the most common option is to be replace the missing data with the mean of all the other value. Let's understand how sklearn package handles it.
A better strategy is to impute the missing values, i.e., to infer them from the known part of the data. The SimpleImputer class provides basic strategies for imputing missing values. Missing values can be imputed with a provided constant value, or using the statistics (mean, median or most frequent) of each column in which the missing values are located. This class also allows for different missing values encodings.

The following snippet demonstrates how to replace missing values, encoded as np.nan, using the mean value of the columns (axis 0) that contain the missing values:

```
import numpy as np
from sklearn.impute import SimpleImputer
imp = SimpleImputer(missing_values=np.nan, strategy='mean')
print(imp.fit([[1, 2], [np.nan, 3], [7, 6]]))

#SimpleImputer(copy=True, fill_value=None, missing_values=nan,
strategy='mean', verbose=0)
X = [[np.nan, 2], [6, np.nan], [7, 6]]
```

```
print(imp.transform(X))
```

Output:

SimpleImputer(copy=True, fill_value=None, missing_values=nan, strategy='mean',
verbose=0)

[[4. 2.]
[6. 3.66666667]
[7. 6.]] Note: 4 is because of mean(1,NaN,7) and mean of (2,3,6) of fit model

Sparse matrices are dataset with zero or not usable values like negatives. The SimpleImputer class also supports sparse matrices:

```
import scipy.sparse as sp
from sklearn.impute import SimpleImputer
X = sp.csc_matrix([[1, 2], [0, -1], [8, 4]])
imp = SimpleImputer(missing_values=-1, strategy='mean')
imp.fit(X)
#SimpleImputer(copy=True, fill_value=None, missing_values=-1,
strategy='mean', verbose=0)
X_test = sp.csc_matrix([[-1, 2], [6, -1], [7, 6]])
print(imp.transform(X_test).toarray())
```

Output:
[[3. 2.]
[6. 3.]
[7. 6.]]

HANDLING OUTLIERS

In Data Science, an Outlier is an observation point that is distant from other observations. An Outlier may be due to variability in the measurement or it may indicate experimental error. Outliers, being the most extreme observations, may include the sample maximum or sample minimum, or both, depending on whether they are extremely high or low. However, the sample maximum and minimum are not always outliers because they may not be unusually far from other observations. Let's look at an example of below:

***Example 1*: Let's look at the total score of Opening Batsmen at a Cricket World cup:**

Player	Total Score
Player 1	450
Player 2	350
Player 3	400
Player 4	500
Player 5	475
Player 6	25
Player 7	1900
Player 8	350
Player 9	425
Player 10	550

As you can see from the above collected data that most of the players have scored between 350 and 550. There is also one score of 25 which looks very low and other 1900 which looks very high. These figures can be just a typing mistake or it is showing the variance in your data and indicating that Player6 is performing very bad and Player 7 is performing very well.
Now that we know outliers can either be a mistake or just variance, how would you decide if they are important or not. Well, it is pretty simple if they are the result of a mistake, then we can ignore them, but if it is just a variance in the data we would need think a bit further.
The outliers can be a result of a mistake during data collection or it can be just an indication of variance in your data. In either case, Outliers in data can distort predictions and affect the accuracy, if you don't detect and handle them. Before we try to understand whether to ignore the outliers or not, we need to know the ways to identify them.

For this section, we will be using Boston House Pricing Dataset which is included in the sklearn dataset API. We will load the dataset and separate out the features and targets.

Reading the dataset:

```
from sklearn.datasets import load_boston
import pandas as pd

boston = load_boston()
x = boston.data
y = boston.target
columns = boston.feature_names
#create the dataframe
boston_df = pd.DataFrame(boston.data)
boston_df.columns = columns
print(boston_df.head())
```

Discover outliers with visualization tools

Box plot

We have seen BoxPlot in Data Visualization chapter. In Box Plot, outliers may be plotted as individual points. Let's try with above dataset and see:

```
import seaborn as sns
from matplotlib import pyplot as plt
sns.boxplot(x=boston_df['DIS'])
plt.show()
```

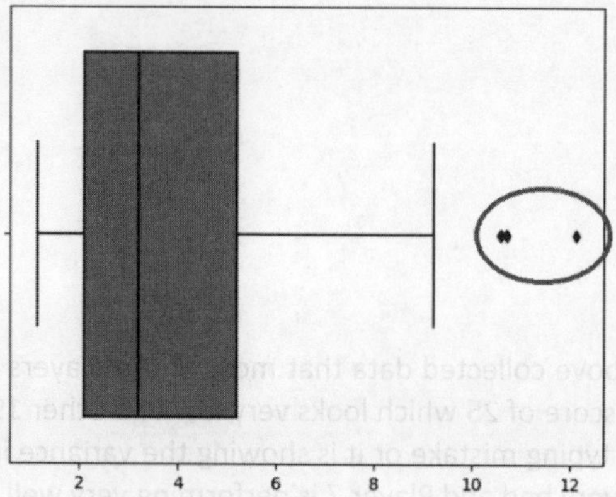

Above plot shows three points between 10 to 12, these are outliers as there are not included in the box of other observation i.e no where near the quartiles. Here we analysed Uni-variate outlier i.e. we used DIS column only to check the outlier. But we can do multivariate outlier analysis too. We can do the multivariate analysis with Box plot, if we have a categorical values that can be used with any continuous variable and do multivariate outlier analysis. As we do not have categorical value in our Boston Housing dataset, we can not do multivariate outlier analysis using box plot.

Scatter Plot

The scatter plot is the collection of points that shows values for two variables. We can try and draw scatter plot for two variables from our housing dataset.

```
fig, ax = plt.subplots(figsize=(16,8))
ax.scatter(boston_df['INDUS'], boston_df['TAX'])
ax.set_xlabel('Proportion of non-retail business acres per town')
ax.set_ylabel('Full-value property-tax rate per $10,000')
plt.show()
```

We can see that most of data points are lying bottom left side but there are points which are far from the population like top right corner which can be considered as outliers.

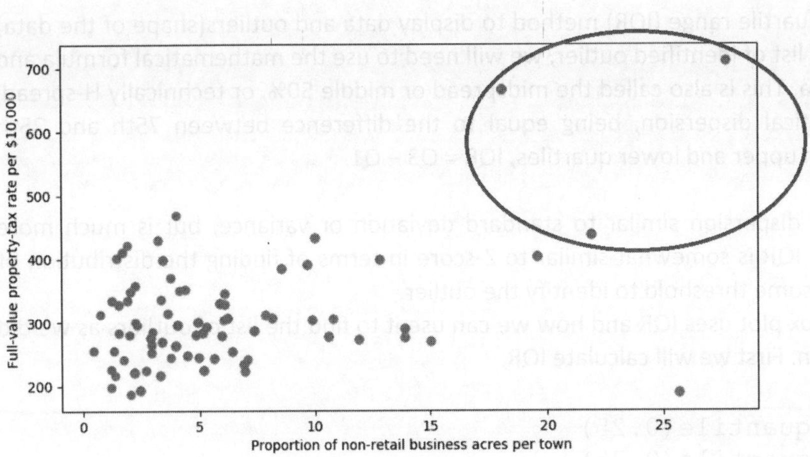

Discover outliers with mathematical function

Z-Score

The Z-score is the signed number of standard deviations by which the value of an observation or data point is above the mean value of what is being observed or measured. While calculating the Z-score we re-scale and center the data and look for data points which are too far from zero. These data points which are way too far from zero will be treated as the outliers. In most of the cases a threshold of 3 or -3 is used i.e if the Z-score value is greater than or less than 3 or -3 respectively, that data point will be identified as outliers.

We will use Z-score function defined in scipy library to detect the outliers.

```
from scipy import stats
import numpy as np
z = np.abs(stats.zscore(boston_df))
print(z)
# From above output, it is difficult to say which data point is
an outlier.
# Let's define a threshold to identify an outlier.
threshold = 3
print(np.where(z > 3))
```

Second print function will give data points where z-score is greater than 3. In the output, the first array contains the list of row numbers and second array respective column numbers, which mean z[55][1] have a Z-score higher than 3.

You can test by:

```
print(z[55][1])
Output: 3.3750387635l7309
```

IQR score

Box plot use the interquartile range (IQR) method to display data and outliers(shape of the data) but in order to be get a list of identified outlier, we will need to use the mathematical formula and retrieve the outlier data. This is also called the midspread or middle 50%, or technically H-spread, is a measure of statistical dispersion, being equal to the difference between 75th and 25th percentiles, or between upper and lower quartiles, IQR = Q3 – Q1.

It is a measure of the dispersion similar to standard deviation or variance, but is much more robust against outliers. IQR is somewhat similar to Z-score in terms of finding the distribution of data and then keeping some threshold to identify the outlier.
Let's find out we can box plot uses IQR and how we can use it to find the list of outliers as we did using Z-score calculation. First we will calculate IQR,

```
Q1 = boston_df.quantile(0.25)
Q3 = boston_df.quantile(0.75)
IQR = Q3 - Q1
print(IQR)
```

Here we will get IQR for each column. The below code will give an output with some true and false values. The data point where we have False that means these values are valid whereas True indicates presence of an outlier.

```
print(boston_df < (Q1 - 1.5 * IQR)) or (boston_df > (Q3 + 1.5 * IQR))
```

Working with Outliers: Correcting, Removing
During data analysis when you detect the outlier one of most difficult decision could be how one should deal with the outlier. Should they remove them or correct them? Before we talk about this, we will have a look at few methods of removing the outliers.

Z-Score
In the previous section, we saw how one can detect the outlier using Z-score but now we want to remove or filter the outliers and get the clean data. This can be done with just one line code as we have already calculated the Z-score.

```
boston_df_o = boston_df[(z < 3).all(axis=1)]
```

So, above code removed around 90+ rows from the dataset i.e. outliers have been removed.

IQR Score
Just like Z-score we can use previously calculated IQR score to filter out the outliers by keeping only valid values.

```
boston_df_out = boston_df[~((boston_df < (Q1 - 1.5 * IQR))
|(boston_df > (Q3 + 1.5 * IQR))).any(axis=1)]
boston_df_out.shape
```

The above code will remove the outliers from the dataset. There are multiple ways to detect and remove the outliers but the methods, we have used for this exercise, are widely used. Whether an outlier should be removed or not. Every data analyst/data scientist might get these thoughts once in every problem they are working on and its best left to them to take a call. There can be multiple reasons you want to understand and correct the outliers.

CATEGORICAL DATA

Categorical variables represent types of data which may be divided into groups. In the current dataset we have 2 such variables – Region (categories are: North, South, East, West) and Win (categories are: Yes, No). That system of labeling implies a hierarchical value to the data that could affect your model. 3 has a higher value than 0, but the categorical values doesnt work that way. Its important to convey to the machine learning algorithms about categorical values so that it doesn't treat them as regular values. The SimpleImputer class also supports categorical data represented as string values or pandas categoricals when using the 'most_frequent' or 'constant' strategy:

```
import pandas as pd
import numpy as np
from sklearn.impute import SimpleImputer
df = pd.DataFrame([["a", "x"],
                    [np.nan, "y"],
                    ["a", np.nan],
                    ["b", "y"]], dtype="category")
imp = SimpleImputer(strategy="most_frequent")
print(imp.fit_transform(df))
```

We need to create dummy variables to avoid algorithm reading the data as a heirarchical. Dummy variables are an awesome option for data cleaning and preprocessing. We can create one column each for the categorical values. Then we'll fill the columns in with 1s and 0s (think 1=yes and 0=no.) That means that if you had North in your original column, now you'd have a 0 in the South, a 0 in the East column, a 0 in the West column, and a 1 in the North column. We achieve this using OneHotEncoder. In the later examples, we will be using OneHotEncoder to specify that the given column has a categorical value and do not treat at values.

Marking imputed values

The MissingIndicator transformer is useful to transform a dataset into corresponding binary matrix indicating the presence of missing values in the dataset. This transformation is useful in conjunction with imputation. When using imputation, preserving the information about which values had been missing can be informative. NaN is usually used as the placeholder for missing values. However, it enforces the data type to be float. The parameter missing_values allows to specify other placeholder such as integer. In the following example, we will use -1 as missing values:

```
import numpy as np
from sklearn.impute import MissingIndicator
```

```
X = np.array([[-1, -1, 1, 3],
              [4, -1, 0, -1],
              [8, -1, 1, 0]])
indicator = MissingIndicator(missing_values=-1)
mask_missing_values_only = indicator.fit_transform(X)
print(mask_missing_values_only)
```

Output:

```
[[ True True False]
 [False True True]
 [False True False]]
```

Now we create a FeatureUnion. All features will be imputed using SimpleImputer, in order to enable classifiers to work with this data. Additionally, it adds the indicator variables from MissingIndicator.

```
from sklearn.impute import SimpleImputer, MissingIndicator
from sklearn.pipeline import FeatureUnion
transformer = FeatureUnion(
     transformer_list=[
          ('features', SimpleImputer(strategy='mean')),
          ('indicators', MissingIndicator())])
transformer = transformer.fit(X_train, y_train)
results = transformer.transform(X_test)
print(results)
print(results.shape)
```

We will learn about X_train and y_train in the next section where we talk about training set and test set.

TRAINING SET AND TEST SET

We need to split our dataset into training set and test set for machine learning algorithm. We need to split the dataset because we want the machine to learn the algorithm and make prediction. We are going to build our machine learning algorithm on the training dataset and test it on the test set to know how well it has "learnt" the correlation.

Next question that is asked is how much of the data should be Training set and Test set. Best practice is to choose 80% of the data as Training set and 20% as Test set. Below is the example of splitting in train set and test set. In the examples running the models, we will see the application and understand better about it.

Always separate your data into training and testing sets and never use your testing data for training! You need to avoid overfitting. (You can think of overfitting like memorizing super specific details before a test without understanding the information of you are given lot of cotent to read. When you memorize details, you'll do a great job with your flashcards at home. You'll fail any real test, though, where you're presented with new information.)

Right now, we have a machine that needs to learn something. It needs to train on data and see how well it understands what it's learned on separate data. Memorizing the training set is not the same thing as learning! The better your model learns on the training set, the better it will be at predicting the results for the testing set. You never want to overfit your model. You really want it to learn!

```
# Splitting the dataset into the Training set and Test set
from sklearn.cross_validation import train_test_split
X_train, X_test, y_train, y_test = train_test_split(X, y,
test_size = 0.2, random_state = 0)
```

EXAMPLE USING 1_DATA_PREPROCESSING.CSV FILE

That was the last step in Data Preprocessing and now our data is ready to be used by Machine Learning algorithm. We have learnt all the basic steps in data preprocessing. We are not going to use all these steps always. It depends on the given dataset. Lets use all the pre-processing steps on our dataset.

```
# Data Preprocessing
# Importing the libraries
import numpy as np
import matplotlib.pyplot as plt
import pandas as pd

# Importing the dataset
dataset =
pd.read_csv('https://raw.githubusercontent.com/swapnilsaurav/MachineL
earning/master/1_Data_PreProcessing.csv')
X = dataset.iloc[:, :-1].values
y = dataset.iloc[:, 3].values

# Taking care of missing data
from sklearn.impute import SimpleImputer
imputer = SimpleImputer(missing_values = np.nan, strategy = 'mean')
imputer = imputer.fit(X[:, 1:3])
X[:, 1:3] = imputer.transform(X[:, 1:3])

#Encoding Categorical data into 0, 1,...
from sklearn.preprocessing import LabelEncoder, OneHotEncoder
from sklearn.compose import ColumnTransformer
labelencoder_X = LabelEncoder()
X[:, 0] = labelencoder_X.fit_transform(X[:, 0])
transformer = ColumnTransformer([('one_hot_encoder', OneHotEncoder(),
[0])],remainder='passthrough')
X = np.array(transformer.fit_transform(X), dtype=np.float)
labelencoder_Y = LabelEncoder()
Y = labelencoder_Y.fit_transform(y)

# Splitting the dataset into the Training set and Test set
```

```
from sklearn.model_selection import train_test_split
X_train, X_test, y_train, y_test = train_test_split(X, y, test_size =
0.2, random_state = 0)
print("X_train: \n",X_train)
print("X_test: \n",X_test)
print("y_train: \n",y_train)
print("y_test: \n",y_test)
```

Example 2:

master ▾ Dataset / **pet_animal_data.csv**

	Animal	Age	Worth	Friendly
1	Animal	Age	Worth	Friendly
2	Cat	4	72000	No
3	Dog	17	48000	Yes
4	Moose	6	54000	No
5	Dog	8	61000	No
6	Moose	4		Yes
7	Cat	15	58000	Yes
8	Dog		52000	No
9	Cat	12	79000	Yes
10	Moose	5	83000	No
11	Cat	7	67000	Yes

Preprocessing is very important step. Let's take another very similar example; we will only manipulate the coloumn headers to get a new dataset as shown in the previous page.

Python Code:

```
### Example 2: Preprocessing a dataset using sklearn
#Step 1: import libraries
import numpy as np
import matplotlib.pyplot as plt
import pandas as pd
#Step 2: Get the dataset
data_df =
pd.read_csv('https://raw.githubusercontent.com/swapnilsaurav/Da
taset/master/pet_animal_data.csv')
#Step 3: create the matrix of dependent variables
#All but the last column (Friendly, index 3)
#Select all the rows
X = data_df.iloc[:, :-1].values
#Step 4: dependent variable Y
#Any dataset you will have just one dependent variable
```

```
y = data_df.iloc[:, 3].values

#Step 5: Handle missing data
#Mean is the default strategy, so we don't
# actually need to specify that
from sklearn.impute import SimpleImputer
imputer = SimpleImputer(missing_values = np.nan, strategy =
'mean')
#Now to fit this imputer
#We only want to fit the imputer to
# the columns where data are missing
imputer = imputer.fit(X[:, 1:3])
#method that will actually replace the missing data
X[:, 1:3] = imputer.transform(X[:, 1:3])

#Step 6: Handle categorical data
#encode the categorical values as numbers
from sklearn.preprocessing import LabelEncoder, OneHotEncoder
labelencoder_X = LabelEncoder()
#Only first column need to be transformed
X[:, 0] = labelencoder_X.fit_transform(X[:, 0])

#create dummy variables
from sklearn.compose import ColumnTransformer
transformer = ColumnTransformer([('one_hot_encoder',
OneHotEncoder(), [0])],remainder='passthrough')
#Now a little fit and transform
X = np.array(transformer.fit_transform(X), dtype=np.float)

#single column has been replaced by one column for
# each of the categorical variables
#use label encoder for our y column if we have "yes" /"no."
labelencoder_Y = LabelEncoder()
Y = labelencoder_Y.fit_transform(y)

#Step 7: Train test split
#never use your testing data for training to avoid overfitting
from sklearn.model_selection import train_test_split
X_train, X_test, y_train, y_test = train_test_split(X, y,
test_size = 0.2, random_state = 0)
#capital Y in the below code will replace Y values to 0 & 1
X_train, X_test, y_train, y_test = train_test_split(X, Y,
test_size = 0.2, random_state = 0)

#Step 8: Feature Scaling
from sklearn.preprocessing import StandardScaler
#create an object that we'll scale and call the standard scaler
sc_X = StandardScaler()
```

```
#directly fit and transform our dataset
X_train = sc_X.fit_transform(X_train)
X_test = sc_X.transform(X_test)
#don't need scale Y as we have only Yes and No - 2 options
#sc_y = StandardScaler()
#print("y_train: \n",y_train)
#y_train = sc_y.fit_transform(y_train)

##Print values
print("X_train: \n",X_train)
print("X_test: \n",X_test)
print("y_train: \n",y_train)
print("y_test: \n",y_test)
```

What about the dummy variables? Do you need to scale them?

I dont prefer to scale them. It's a question of how much you want to hang on to your interpretation. It is good to have all of our data at the same scale. But if we scale our data, we lose our ability to easily interpret which observations belong to which variable.

What about Y values?

What about y? If you have a dependent variable like 0 and 1, you really don't need to apply feature scaling. It's a classification problem with a categorically dependent value. But if you have a large range of feature values, then yes! You do want to apply the scaler!

OUTLIER DETECTION EXAMPLE USING SKLEARN.DATASETS.LOAD_BOSTON

This example illustrates the need for robust covariance estimation on a real data set. It is useful both for outlier detection and for a better understanding of the data structure. We selected two sets of two variables from the Boston housing data set as an illustration of what kind of analysis can be done with several outlier detection tools. For the purpose of visualization, we are working with two-dimensional examples, but one should be aware that things are not so trivial in high-dimension, as it will be pointed out.

In both examples below, the main result is that the empirical covariance estimate, as a non-robust one, is highly influenced by the heterogeneous structure of the observations. Although the robust covariance estimate is able to focus on the main mode of the data distribution, it sticks to the assumption that the data should be Gaussian distributed, yielding some biased estimation of the data structure, but yet accurate to some extent. The One-Class SVM does not assume any parametric form of the data distribution and can therefore model the complex shape of the data much better.

```
import numpy as np
from sklearn.covariance import EllipticEnvelope
from sklearn.svm import OneClassSVM
import matplotlib.pyplot as plt
import matplotlib.font_manager
```

```
from sklearn.datasets import load_boston

# Get data
X1 = load_boston()['data'][:, [8, 10]]  # two clusters
X2 = load_boston()['data'][:, [5, 12]]  # "banana"-shaped

# Define "classifiers" to be used
classifiers = {
    "Empirical Covariance":
EllipticEnvelope(support_fraction=1.,

contamination=0.261),
    "Robust Covariance (Minimum Covariance Determinant)":
    EllipticEnvelope(contamination=0.261),
    "OCSVM": OneClassSVM(nu=0.261, gamma=0.05)}
colors = ['m', 'g', 'b']
legend1 = {}
legend2 = {}

# Learn a frontier for outlier detection with several
classifiers
xx1, yy1 = np.meshgrid(np.linspace(-8, 28, 500), np.linspace(3,
40, 500))
xx2, yy2 = np.meshgrid(np.linspace(3, 10, 500), np.linspace(-5,
45, 500))
for i, (clf_name, clf) in enumerate(classifiers.items()):
    plt.figure(1)
    clf.fit(X1)
    Z1 = clf.decision_function(np.c_[xx1.ravel(), yy1.ravel()])
    Z1 = Z1.reshape(xx1.shape)
    legend1[clf_name] = plt.contour(
        xx1, yy1, Z1, levels=[0], linewidths=2,
colors=colors[i])
    plt.figure(2)
    clf.fit(X2)
    Z2 = clf.decision_function(np.c_[xx2.ravel(), yy2.ravel()])
    Z2 = Z2.reshape(xx2.shape)
    legend2[clf_name] = plt.contour(
        xx2, yy2, Z2, levels=[0], linewidths=2,
colors=colors[i])

legend1_values_list = list(legend1.values())
legend1_keys_list = list(legend1.keys())

# Plot the results (= shape of the data points cloud)
plt.figure(1)  # two clusters
plt.title("Outlier detection on a real data set (boston
housing)")
```

```
plt.scatter(X1[:, 0], X1[:, 1], color='black')
bbox_args = dict(boxstyle="round", fc="0.8")
arrow_args = dict(arrowstyle="->")
plt.annotate("several confounded points", xy=(24, 19),
             xycoords="data", textcoords="data",
             xytext=(13, 10), bbox=bbox_args,
arrowprops=arrow_args)
plt.xlim((xx1.min(), xx1.max()))
plt.ylim((yy1.min(), yy1.max()))
plt.legend((legend1_values_list[0].collections[0],
            legend1_values_list[1].collections[0],
            legend1_values_list[2].collections[0]),
           (legend1_keys_list[0], legend1_keys_list[1],
legend1_keys_list[2]),
           loc="upper center",

prop=matplotlib.font_manager.FontProperties(size=12))
plt.ylabel("accessibility to radial highways")
plt.xlabel("pupil-teacher ratio by town")

legend2_values_list = list(legend2.values())
legend2_keys_list = list(legend2.keys())

plt.figure(2)  # "banana" shape
plt.title("Outlier detection on a real data set (boston
housing)")
plt.scatter(X2[:, 0], X2[:, 1], color='black')
plt.xlim((xx2.min(), xx2.max()))
plt.ylim((yy2.min(), yy2.max()))
plt.legend((legend2_values_list[0].collections[0],
            legend2_values_list[1].collections[0],
            legend2_values_list[2].collections[0]),
           (legend2_keys_list[0], legend2_keys_list[1],
legend2_keys_list[2]),
           loc="upper center",

prop=matplotlib.font_manager.FontProperties(size=12))
plt.ylabel("% lower status of the population")
plt.xlabel("average number of rooms per dwelling")
plt.show()
```

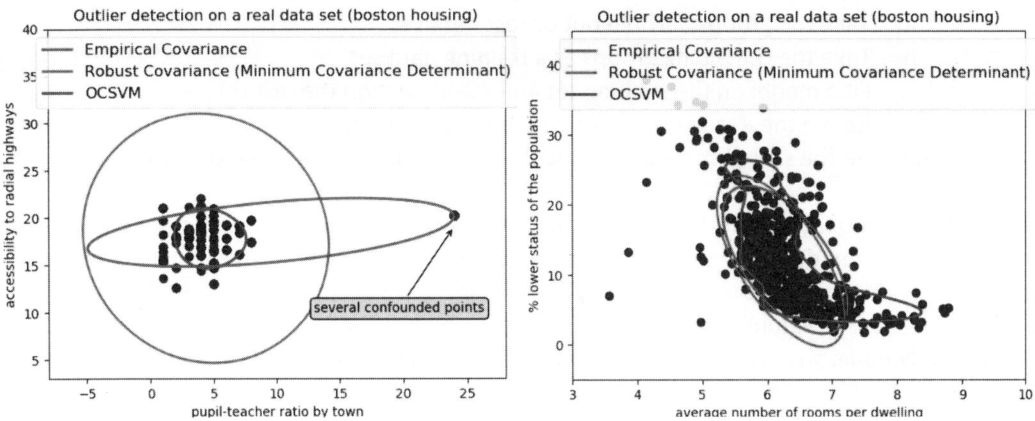

Covariance is a measure of the joint variability of two random variables. If the greater values of one variable mainly correspond with the greater values of the other variable, and the same holds for the lesser values, (i.e., the variables tend to show similar behavior), the covariance is positive. In the opposite case, when the greater values of one variable mainly correspond to the lesser values of the other, (i.e., the variables tend to show opposite behavior), the covariance is negative. The sign of the covariance therefore shows the tendency in the linear relationship between the variables. The magnitude of the covariance is not easy to interpret because it is not normalized and hence depends on the magnitudes of the variables. The normalized version of the covariance, the correlation coefficient, however, shows by its magnitude the strength of the linear relation.

In this example, we are using a one-class SVM for novelty detection. One-class SVM is an unsupervised algorithm that learns a decision function for novelty detection: classifying new data as similar or different to the training set.

K-FOLD CROSS-VALIDATION

Cross-validation is a resampling procedure used to evaluate machine learning models on a limited data sample. The procedure has a single parameter called k that refers to the number of groups that a given data sample is to be split into. As such, the procedure is often called k-fold cross-validation. When a specific value for k is chosen, it may be used in place of k in the reference to the model, such as k=10 becoming 10-fold cross-validation.

Cross-validation is primarily used in applied machine learning to estimate the skill of a machine learning model on unseen data. That is, to use a limited sample in order to estimate how the model is expected to perform in general when used to make predictions on data not used during the training of the model. It is a popular method because it is simple to understand and because it generally results in a less biased or less optimistic estimate of the model skill than other methods, such as a simple train/test split.

The general procedure is as follows:

1. Shuffle the dataset randomly.
2. Split the dataset into k groups
3. For each unique group:

  a. Take the group as a hold out or test data set
  b. Take the remaining groups as a training data set
  c. Fit a model on the training set and evaluate it on the test set
  d. Retain the evaluation score and discard the model
4. Summarize the skill of the model using the sample of model evaluation scores

Importantly, each observation in the data sample is assigned to an individual group and stays in that group for the duration of the procedure. This means that each sample is given the opportunity to be used in the hold out set 1 time and used to train the model k-1 times. This approach involves randomly dividing the set of observations into k groups, or folds, of approximately equal size. The first fold is treated as a validation set, and the method is fit on the remaining k – 1 folds.

Configuration of k

The k value must be chosen carefully for your data sample. A poorly chosen value for k may result in a mis-representative idea of the skill of the model, such as a score with a high variance (that may change a lot based on the data used to fit the model), or a high bias, (such as an overestimate of the skill of the model).

Three common tactics for choosing a value for k are as follows:

- **Representative**: The value for k is chosen such that each train/test group of data samples is large enough to be statistically representative of the broader dataset.
- **k=10:** The value for k is fixed to 10, a value that has been found through experimentation to generally result in a model skill estimate with low bias a modest variance.
- **k=n**: The value for k is fixed to n, where n is the size of the dataset to give each test sample an opportunity to be used in the hold out dataset. This approach is called leave-one-out cross-validation.

The choice of k is usually 5 or 10, but there is no formal rule. As k gets larger, the difference in size between the training set and the resampling subsets gets smaller. As this difference decreases, the bias of the technique becomes smaller.

Example: Imagine we have a data sample with 10 observations. The first step is to pick a value for k in order to determine the number of folds used to split the data. Here, we will use a value of k=5. That means we will shuffle the data and then split the data into 5 groups. Because we have 10 observations, each group will have an equal number of 2 observations.

For example, dataset:

0.20	0.40	0.60	0.10	0.30	0.70	0.50	0.80	0.45	0.90

Groups:

Fold 1: [0.2, 0.4]
Fold 2: [0.6, 0.1]
Fold 3: [0.3, 0.7]
Fold 4: [0.5, 0.8]
Fold 5: [0.45, 0.90]

Five models are trained and evaluated with each fold given a chance to be the held out test set.
For example:

- Model1: Trained on Fold1 + Fold2, Tested on Fold3
- Model2: Trained on Fold2 + Fold3, Tested on Fold4
- Model3: Trained on Fold3 + Fold4, Tested on Fold5
- Model4: Trained on Fold4 + Fold5, Tested on Fold1
- Model5: Trained on Fold5 + Fold1, Tested on Fold2

The models are then discarded after they are evaluated as they have served their purpose. The skill scores are collected for each model and summarized for use.

Cross Validation Implementation using Python

The KFold() scikit-learn class can be used. It takes as arguments the number of splits, whether or not to shuffle the sample, and the seed for the pseudorandom number generator used prior to the shuffle.

The split() function can then be called on the class where the data sample is provided as an argument. Called repeatedly, the split will return each group of train and test sets. Specifically, arrays are returned containing the indexes into the original data sample of observations to use for train and test sets on each iteration.

Let's implement the above example using Python:

```
# scikit-learn k-fold cross-validation
from numpy import array
from sklearn.model_selection import KFold
# data sample
data = array([0.20, 0.40, 0.60, 0.10, 0.30, 0.70, 0.50, 0.80,
0.45, 0.90])
# prepare cross validation
kfold = KFold(n_splits=5,shuffle=False)
# enumerate splits
for train, test in kfold.split(data):
   print('train: %s, test: %s' % (data[train], data[test]))
```

Output:

```
train: [0.6  0.1  0.3  0.7  0.5  0.8  0.45 0.9 ], test: [0.2 0.4]
train: [0.2  0.4  0.3  0.7  0.5  0.8  0.45 0.9 ], test: [0.6 0.1]
train: [0.2  0.4  0.6  0.1  0.5  0.8  0.45 0.9 ], test: [0.3 0.7]
train: [0.2  0.4  0.6  0.1  0.3  0.7  0.45 0.9 ], test: [0.5 0.8]
train: [0.2 0.4 0.6 0.1 0.3 0.7 0.5 0.8], test: [0.45 0.9 ]
```

Variations on Cross-Validation

There are a number of variations on the k-fold cross validation procedure.

- Train/Test Split: Taken to one extreme, k may be set to 2 (not 1) such that a single train/test split is created to evaluate the model.

- LOOCV: Taken to another extreme, k may be set to the total number of observations in the dataset such that each observation is given a chance to be the held out of the dataset. This is called leave-one-out cross-validation, or LOOCV for short.
- Stratified: The splitting of data into folds may be governed by criteria such as ensuring that each fold has the same proportion of observations with a given categorical value, such as the class outcome value. This is called stratified cross-validation.
- Repeated: This is where the k-fold cross-validation procedure is repeated n times, where importantly, the data sample is shuffled prior to each repetition, which results in a different split of the sample.
- Nested: This is where k-fold cross-validation is performed within each fold of cross-validation, often to perform hyperparameter tuning during model evaluation. This is called nested cross-validation or double cross-validation.

***

UNIT 16: REGRESSION ALGORITHM

The following are a set of methods intended for regression in which the target value is expected to be a linear combination of the input variables. In mathematical notion, if y^ is the predicted value.

$$\hat{y}(w,x)=w_0+w_1x_1+...+w_px_p$$

Across the module, we designate the vector $w=(w_1,...,w_p)$ as `coef_` and w_0 as `intercept_`.

Regression models (both linear and non-linear) are used for predicting a real value, like salary for example. If your independent variable is time, then you are forecasting future values, otherwise your model is predicting present but unknown values. Regression techniques vary from Linear Regression to SVR and Random Forests Regression.

In this part, you will understand and learn how to implement the following Machine Learning Regression models using SciKit Learn package:

- Simple Linear Regression
- Multiple Linear Regression
- Polynomial Regression
- Support Vector for Regression (SVR)
- Decision Tree Classification
- Random Forest Classification
- Non Linear Regression
- Regression Methods
- Ridge & Lasso Regression
- Supprt Vector Machine regression

SIMPLE LINEAR REGRESSION

Linear Regression is a machine learning algorithm based on supervised learning. It performs a regression task. Regression models a target prediction value based on independent variables. It is mostly used for finding out the relationship between variables and forecasting. Different regression models differ based on – the kind of relationship between dependent and independent variables, they are considering and the number of independent variables being used.

Simple linear regression is a statistical method that allows us to summarize and study relationships between two continuous (quantitative) variables:

- One variable, x, is regarded as the predictor, explanatory, or independent variable.
- The other, denoted y, is regarded as the response, outcome, or dependent variable.

Simple linear regression gets its adjective "simple," because it concerns the study of only one predictor variable. In contrast, multiple linear regression, which we study in the next section, gets its adjective "multiple," because it concerns the study of two or more predictor variables.

We will use Student_marks dataset for this exercise. Dataset contains number of hour students have studied per week and the marks obtained in the final examination. Problem statement is to find the correlation between the number of hour and the marks obtained and then we will be able to predict the marks student can get if we know the number of hours he or she spend studying.

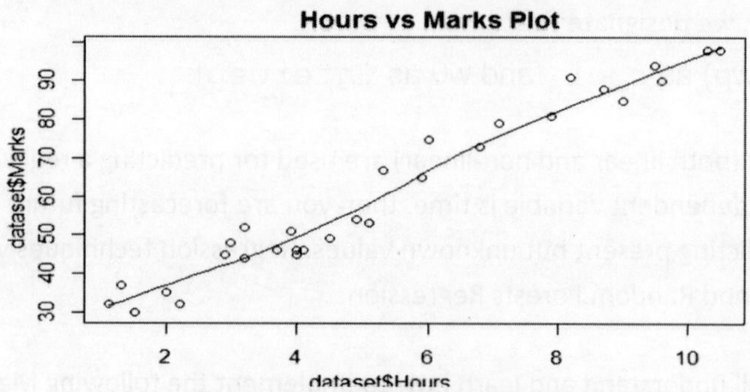

Figure: Scatter Plot (Hours v Marks)

Linear regression consists of finding the best-fitting straight line through the points. The best-fitting line is called a regression line. Scatter Plot which represents the relationship between two variables can be drawn between the X and Y variable to see the relationship using the function ***reg.fit()***.

The diagonal line in the scatter plot is the regression line and consists of the predicted score on Y for each possible value of X. The points located away from the regression line represent the errors of prediction. A line that fits the data "best" will be one for which the n prediction errors — one for each observed data point — are as small as possible in some overall sense. One way to achieve this goal is to invoke the "least squares criterion," which says to "minimize the sum of the squared prediction errors." That is:

- The equation of the best fitting line is: y=b0+b1xi
- b0 is the intercept and b1 represents the slope of the line
- We just need to find the values b0 and b1 that make the sum of the squared prediction errors the smallest it can be.

Let's now see how we can solve it using Python. Complete code with explanation given in the comment section is given below:

Step 1: Getting the data ready to begin the analysis

```
import pandas as pd
import matplotlib.pyplot as plt

slr_df =
pd.read_csv("https://raw.githubusercontent.com/swapnilsaurav/Da
taset/master/student_scores.csv")
print("Columns in the dataset: \n",slr_df.columns)
```

```
#Display first 5 records
slr_df.head()
#Size of the dataset
slr_df.shape
#Get the statistics
slr_df.describe()
#Scatter plot for complete dataset
plt.scatter(slr_df['Hours'], slr_df['Scores'])
plt.show()
```

Output:

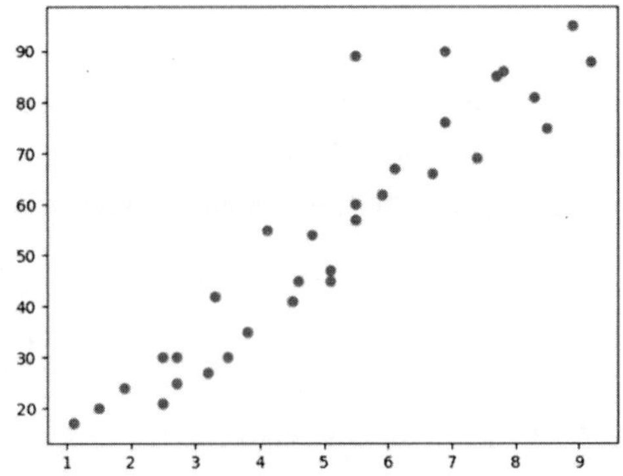

Step 2: Preparing the data

Now we will divide the data into "attributes" and "labels". Attributes are the independent variables while labels are dependent variables whose values are to be predicted. In this example of simple linear regression, we will have only one attribute - "Hours" column, and the label will be the "Score" column. The attributes are stored in the X variable. We specified "-1" as the range for columns since we wanted our attribute set to contain all the columns except the last one, which is "Scores". Similarly the y variable contains the labels. We specified 1 for the label column since the index for "Scores" column is 1. Remember, the column indexes start with 0, with 1 being the second column.

After identifying out X and y columns, we will now split this data into training and test sets. We'll do this by using Scikit-Learn's built-in train_test_split() method. There is generally no specific rule around how much data you choose for training set and test set, I generally follow 80-20 or 75-25 rule. In this case, we will split 80% of the data to training set while 20% of the data to test set.

Once identified the train and test test, we will now training the algorithm on train set.
Next step, execute Scikit-Learn's linear regression model. It is a straight forward implementation - we just need to do import the LinearRegression class, instantiate it, and call the fit() method along with our training data.

```
#Getting X and Y values
X = slr_df.iloc[:, :1].values
y = slr_df.iloc[:, 1].values
#Split into training and test set
from sklearn.model_selection import train_test_split
X_train, X_test, y_train, y_test = train_test_split(X, y,
test_size=0.2, random_state=0)

#Train the Algorithm
from sklearn.linear_model import LinearRegression
regressor = LinearRegression()
regressor.fit(X_train, y_train)
```

Linear regression model basically finds the best value for the intercept and slope, which results in a line that best fits the data. To see the value of the intercept and slop calculated by the linear regression algorithm for our dataset, execute the following code:

```
#intercept value: c
print("Intercept value: ",regressor.intercept_)
#coef as m
print("Coefficient value: ",regressor.coef_)
```

Output:

```
Intercept value:   4.32299207978879
Coefficient value:  [9.61660311]
```

The coefficient is returned as a list, as the number of coefficient values can be more than one (same as the number of attributes).

The Simple Linear Regression, equation is written as:

y = mx + c

Coefficient "m" is 9.6 and intercept "c" is 4.3

The above equation can be now written as:

y = 9.6x + 4.3

We an easily substitute the value of number of hours studied in the above equation to get the marks that can be expected. This means that for every one unit of change in hours studied, the change in the score is about 9.6%. Or in simpler words, if a student studies one hour more than they previously studied for an exam, they can expect to achieve an increase of 9.91% in the score achieved by the student previously.

Step 3: Making Prediction

Next step is to predict the values for the dataset we already know the result (test set) so that we can evaluate the performance of the model in the next step.

```
y_pred = regressor.predict(X_test)
#The y_pred is a numpy array that contains all the predicted
values
#compare the actual output values for X_test with the predicted
values
output_df = pd.DataFrame({'Actual': y_test, 'Predicted':
y_pred})
print("Actual v Predicted: \n",output_df)
```

Output:

```
Actual v Predicted:
   Actual  Predicted
0      45  53.367668
1      95  89.910760
2      89  57.214309
3      27  35.096122
4      25  30.287820
5      60  57.214309
6      54  50.482687
```

Note: The values in the columns above may be different each time you run as the split into training and test sets happen randomly.

Step 4: Plotting graphs

```
#Plot train data output
plt.scatter(X_test, y_test,  color='black')
plt.plot(X_test, y_pred, color='blue', linewidth=3)
plt.xticks(())
plt.yticks(())
plt.show()
```

Output:

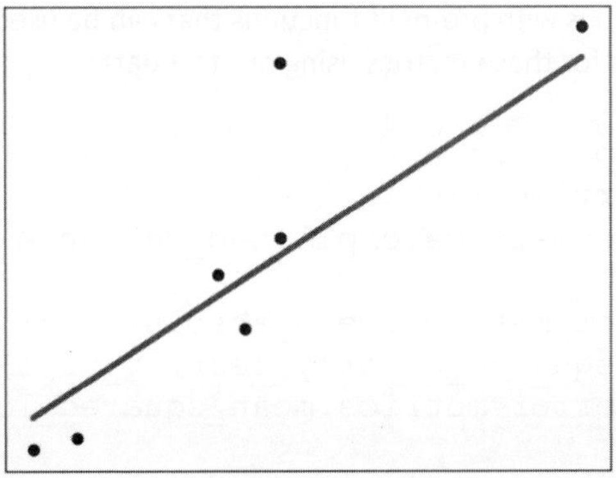

We see that, except one point, all the other points are close to the regression line.

Step 5: Evaluating the model

For regression algorithms, three evaluation metrics are commonly used:

1. Mean Absolute Error (MAE) measures how close the predictions are to the actual outcomes; thus, a lower score is better. It is the mean of the absolute value of the errors. It is calculated as:

$$\frac{1}{n}\sum_{i=1}^{n}|Actual - Predicted|$$

2. Mean Squared Error (MSE) is the mean of the squared errors and is calculated as:

$$\frac{1}{n}\sum_{i=1}^{n}|Actual - Predicted|^2$$

3. Root Mean Squared Error (RMSE) is the square root of the mean of the squared errors. creates a single value that summarizes the error in the model. By squaring the difference, the metric disregards the difference between over-prediction and under-prediction. Formula:

$$\sqrt{\frac{1}{n}\sum_{i=1}^{n}|Actual - Predicted|^2}$$

5. Relative absolute error (RAE) is the relative absolute difference between expected and actual values; relative because the mean difference is divided by the arithmetic mean.
6. Relative squared error (RSE) similarly normalizes the total squared error of the predicted values by dividing by the total squared error of the actual values.
7. Mean Zero One Error (MZOE) indicates whether the prediction was correct or not. In other words: ZeroOneLoss(x,y) = 1 when x!=y; otherwise 0.
8. Coecient of determination, often referred to as R2, represents the predictive power of the model as a value between 0 and 1. Zero means the model is random (explains nothing); 1 means there is a perfect t. However, caution should be used in interpreting R2 values, as low values can be entirely normal and high values can be suspect.

The Scikit-Learn library comes with pre-built functions that can be used to find out these values for us. Let's find the values for these metrics using our test data:

```
import numpy as np
from sklearn import metrics
explained_variance=metrics.explained_variance_score(y_test,
y_pred)
mean_absolute_error=metrics.mean_absolute_error(y_test, y_pred)
mse=metrics.mean_squared_error(y_test, y_pred)
mean_squared_log_error=metrics.mean_squared_log_error(y_test,
y_pred)
median_absolute_error=metrics.median_absolute_error(y_test,
y_pred)
r2=metrics.r2_score(y_test, y_pred)
```

```
print('Explained_variance: ', round(explained_variance,2))
print('Mean_Squared_Log_Error: ',
round(mean_squared_log_error,2))
print('R-squared: ', round(r2,4))
print('Mean Absolute Error(MAE): ',
round(mean_absolute_error,2))
print('Mean Squared Error (MSE): ', round(mse,2))
print('Root Mean Squared Error (RMSE): ',
round(np.sqrt(mse),2))
```

Output:

```
Explained_variance:  0.75
Mean_Squared_Log_Error:  0.05
R-squared:  0.732
Mean Absolute Error(MAE):  9.28
Mean Squared Error (MSE):  174.27
Root Mean Squared Error (RMSE):  13.2
```

Root mean squared error is also known as the inverse of Accuracy for Regression. Root mean squared error and R-squared values are compared to check the accuracy of regression models.

Step 6: Statistical Analysis

In this section, we will focus on more metric other than those discussed in the previous step. statsmodels package gives a quiet decent summary.

Linear regression, also called Ordinary Least-Squares (OLS) Regression. Ordinary Least Squares is the simplest and most common estimator in which the two (beta)s are chosen to minimize the square of the distance between the predicted values and the actual values. Even though this model is quite rigid and often does not reflect the true relationship, this still remains a popular approach for several reasons. For one, it is computationally cheap to calculate the coefficients. It is also easier to interpret than more sophisticated models, and in situations where the goal is understanding a simple model in detail, rather than estimating the response well, they can provide insight into what the model captures. Finally, in situations where there is a lot of noise, it may be hard to find the true functional form, so a constrained model can perform quite well compared to a complex model which is more affected by noise.

```
from statsmodels.api import OLS
import statsmodels.api as sm
#In our model, y will be dependent on 2 values: coefficienct
# and constant, so we need to add additional column in X for
#constant value
X = sm.add_constant(X)
summ = OLS(y, X).fit().summary()
print("Summary of the dataset: \n",summ)
```

Outut:

```
Summary of the dataset:
                            OLS Regression Results
==============================================================================
Dep. Variable:                      y   R-squared:                       0.874
Model:                            OLS   Adj. R-squared:                  0.869
Method:                 Least Squares   F-statistic:                     207.5
Date:                Sat, 22 Aug 2020   Prob (F-statistic):           5.12e-15
Time:                        12:15:09   Log-Likelihood:                -113.92
No. Observations:                  32   AIC:                             231.8
Df Residuals:                      30   BIC:                             234.8
Df Model:                           1
Covariance Type:            nonrobust
==============================================================================
                 coef    std err          t      P>|t|      [0.025      0.975]
------------------------------------------------------------------------------
const          3.0859      3.873      0.797      0.432      -4.824      10.996
x1             9.9893      0.694     14.404      0.000       8.573      11.406
==============================================================================
Omnibus:                       20.325   Durbin-Watson:                   1.588
Prob(Omnibus):                  0.000   Jarque-Bera (JB):               30.252
Skew:                           1.574   Prob(JB):                     2.70e-07
Kurtosis:                       6.576   Cond. No.                         14.3
==============================================================================

Warnings:
[1] Standard Errors assume that the covariance matrix of the errors is correctly specified.
```

Interpretation

- The regression line with equation [Y = 3.0859+ (9.9893*X1)], is helpful to predict the value of the Y variable from the given value of the X1 variable.
- The slope (9.9893) represents the change in the Y per unit change in the X1 variable. It means that the value Y increases by 9.9893 with each unit increase in X1
- The intercept (3. 0859) represents the value of Y at X1 = 0. Here need to be cautious to interpret intercept as sometimes the value (X1=0) does not make any sense (e.g. speed of car or height of the person). In such cases, the values within the range of X1 should be considered to interpret the intercept
- The coefficient of determination (r-squared) is 0.874 (87.4%), which suggests that 87.4% of the variance in Y can be explained by X1 alone. Adjusted r-squared is useful where there are multiple X variables in the model (multiple linear regression)
- The correlation coefficient (r) is 0.935 (square root of r-squared), which suggests that there is a positive relationship between X and Y variables. As X1 increases, Y also increases

- From Regression Coefficients, the P-value obtained for X1 independent variable is significant (<0.05), it suggests that X1 significantly influence the response variable Y (there is a significant relationship between X1 and Y)
- From ANOVA, the P-value is significant (<0.05), which suggests that there is a significant relationship between X1 and Y. The X1 variable can reliably predict the Y variable.

Exaplanation:

This summary provides quite a lot of information about the fit. The parts of the table we think are the most important are **bolded** in the description below.

The left part of the first table provides basic information about the model fit:

Element	Description
Dep. Variable	Which variable is the response in the model (dependent variable)
Model	What model you are using in the fit
Method	How the parameters of the model were calculated
No. Observations	The number of observations
DF Residuals	Degrees of freedom of the residuals. Number of observations – number of parameters
DF Model	Number of parameters in the model (not including the constant term if present)

The right part of the first table shows the goodness of fit

Element	Description
R-squared	**The coefficient of determination. A statistical measure of how well the regression line approximates the real data points.**
Adj. R-squared	**The above value adjusted based on the number of observations and the degrees-of-freedom of the residuals**
F-statistic	A measure how significant the fit is. The mean squared error of the model divided by the mean squared error of the residuals
Prob (F-statistic)	The probability that you would get the above statistic, given the null hypothesis that they are unrelated
Log-likelihood	The log of the likelihood function.
AIC	The Akaike Information Criterion. Adjusts the log-likelihood based on the number of observations and the complexity of the model.
BIC	The Bayesian Information Criterion. Similar to the AIC, but has a higher penalty for models with more parameters.

The second table reports for each of the coefficients

Metric	Description
coef	The estimated value of the coefficient
std err	The basic standard error of the estimate of the coefficient. More sophisticated errors are also available.

Metric	Description
t	t-statistic value. This is a measure of how statistically significant the coefficient is.
P > |t|	P-value that the null-hypothesis that the coefficient = 0 is true. If it is less than the confidence level, often 0.05, it indicates that there is a statistically significant relationship between the term and the response.
[95.0% Conf. Interval]	The lower and upper values of the 95% confidence interval

Finally, there are several statistical tests to assess the distribution of the residuals

Element	Description
Skewness	A measure of the symmetry of the data about the mean. Normally-distributed errors should be symmetrically distributed about the mean (equal amounts above and below the line).
Kurtosis	A measure of the shape of the distribution. Compares the amount of data close to the mean with those far away from the mean (in the tails).
Omnibus	D'Angostino's test. It provides a combined statistical test for the presence of skewness and kurtosis.
Prob(Omnibus)	The above statistic turned into a probability
Jarque-Bera	A different test of the skewness and kurtosis
Prob (JB)	The above statistic turned into a probability
Durbin-Watson	A test for the presence of autocorrelation (that the errors are not independent.) Often important in time-series analysis
Cond. No	A test for multicollinearity (if in a fit with multiple parameters, the parameters are related with each other).

<u>Detailed explanation:</u>

Residuals: Residuals are essentially the difference between the actual observed response values (Marks) and the response values that the model predicted. When assessing how well the model fit the data, you should look for a symmetrical distribution across these points on the mean value zero (0).

Coefficients: Theoretically, in simple linear regression, the coefficients are two unknown constants that represent the intercept and slope terms in the linear model. If we wanted to predict the Marks obtained given the hours of study, we would get a training set and produce estimates of the coefficients to then use it in the model formula.

Coefficient - Estimate: Without studying, one can score on average 20.7583 marks - that's Intercept. The second row in the Coefficients is the slope, saying that for every 1-hour increase in the study, the marks goes up by 7.5675.

Coefficient - Standard Error: The coefficient Standard Error measures the average amount that the coefficient estimates vary from the actual average value of our response variable. We'd ideally want a lower number relative to its coefficients. In our example, we've previously determined that 1-hour increase in the study, the marks goes up by 7.5675. The Standard Error can be used to compute an estimate of the expected difference in case we ran the model again and again. In other words, we can say that the Marks obtained can vary by 0.3009. The Standard Errors can also be used to compute confidence intervals and to statistically test the hypothesis of the existence of a relationship between Hours of study and marks obtained.

Coefficient - t value: The coefficient t-value is a measure of how many standard deviations our coefficient estimate is far away from 0. We want it to be far away from zero as this would indicate we could reject the null hypothesis - that is, we could declare a relationship between Hours and Marks exist. In our example, the t-statistic values are relatively far away from zero and are large relative to the standard error, which could indicate a relationship exists. In general, t-values are also used to compute p-values.

Coefficient - Pr(>t): The Pr(>t) acronym found in the model output relates to the probability of observing any value equal or larger than t. A small p-value indicates that it is unlikely we will observe a relationship between the predictor (Hours) and response (Marks) variables due to chance. Typically, a p-value of 5% or less is a good cut-off point. In our model example, the p-values are very close to zero. Note the 'signif. Codes' associated to each estimate. Three stars (or asterisks) represent a highly significant p-value. Consequently, a small p-value for the intercept and the slope indicates that we can reject the null hypothesis which allows us to conclude that there is a relationship between speed and distance.

Residual Standard Error: Residual Standard Error is measure of the quality of a linear regression fit. Theoretically, every linear model is assumed to contain an error term E. Due to the presence of this error term, we are not capable of perfectly predicting our response variable (Marks) from the predictor (Hours) one. The Residual Standard Error is the average amount that the response (Marks) will deviate from the true regression line. In our example, the actual distance required to stop can deviate from the true regression line by approximately 4.599, on average. Simplistically, degrees of freedom are the number of data points that went into the estimation of the parameters used after taking into account these parameters (restriction). *Degree of Freedom* is given by the difference between the number of observations in the sample and the number of variables in the model.

Multiple R-squared, Adjusted R-squared: The R-squared (R2R2) statistic provides a measure of how well the model is fitting the actual data. It takes the form of a proportion of variance. R2R2 is a measure of the linear relationship between our predictor variable (Hours) and our response / target variable (Marks). It always lies between 0 and 1 (i.e.: a number near 0 represents a regression that does not explain the variance in the response variable well and a number close to 1 does explain the observed variance in the response variable). In our example, the R2R2 we get is 0.9576. Or roughly 95% of the variance found in the response variable (Marks) can be explained by the predictor variable (Hours). It's hard to define what level of R2R2 is appropriate to claim the model fits well. Essentially, it will vary with the application and the domain studied.
A side note: In multiple regression settings, the R2R2 will always increase as more variables are included in the model. That's why the adjusted R2R2 is the preferred measure as it adjusts for the number of variables considered.

F-Statistic: F-statistic is a good indicator of whether there is a relationship between our predictor and the response variables. The further the F-statistic is from 1 the better it is. However, how much larger the F-statistic needs to be depends on both the number of data points and the number of predictors. Generally, when the number of data points is large, an F-statistic that is only a little bit larger than 1 is already sufficient to reject the null hypothesis (H0 : There is no relationship between Hours and Marks). The reverse is true as if the number of data points is small, a large F-statistic is required to be able to ascertain that there may be a relationship between predictor and response variables. In our example the F-statistic is 632.4 which is relatively larger than 1 given the size of our data.

Example 2: Practice Example

Using in-built dataset: Diabetes

```
import matplotlib.pyplot as plt
import numpy as np
from sklearn import datasets, linear_model
from sklearn.metrics import mean_squared_error, r2_score

# Load the diabetes dataset
diabetes = datasets.load_diabetes()
# Use only one feature
diabetes_X = diabetes.data[:, np.newaxis, 2]

# Split the data into training/testing sets
diabetes_X_train = diabetes_X[:-20]
diabetes_X_test = diabetes_X[-20:]

# Split the targets into training/testing sets
diabetes_y_train = diabetes.target[:-20]
diabetes_y_test = diabetes.target[-20:]

# Create linear regression object
regr = linear_model.LinearRegression()
# Train the model using the training sets
regr.fit(diabetes_X_train, diabetes_y_train)
# Make predictions using the testing set
diabetes_y_pred = regr.predict(diabetes_X_test)

# The coefficients
print('Coefficients: \n', regr.coef_)
# The Intercepts
print('Intercept: \n', regr.intercept_)

# The mean squared error
print("Mean squared error: %.2f"
      % mean_squared_error(diabetes_y_test, diabetes_y_pred))
# Explained variance score: 1 is perfect prediction
```

```
print('Variance score: %.2f' % r2_score(diabetes_y_test,
diabetes_y_pred))

# Plot outputs
plt.scatter(diabetes_X_test, diabetes_y_test,  color='black')
plt.plot(diabetes_X_test, diabetes_y_pred, color='blue',
linewidth=3)
plt.xticks(())
plt.yticks(())
plt.show()
```

Output:

```
Coefficients:
 [938.23786125]
Intercept:
 152.91886182616167
Mean squared error: 2548.07
Variance score: 0.47
```

MULTIPLE LINEAR REGRESSION

Multiple linear regression (MLR) is a statistical technique that uses several explanatory variables to predict the outcome of a response variable. A linear regression model that contains more than one predictor variable is called a multiple linear regression model. The goal of multiple linear regression (MLR) is to model the relationship between the explanatory and response variables. The model for MLR, given n observations, is:

$y_i = B_0 + B_1x_{i1} + B_2x_{i2} + ... + B_px_{ip} + E$ where $i = 1,2, ..., n$

Let's take an example:

R&D Spend	Administration	Marketing Spend	State	Profit
165349.2	136897.8	471784.1	New York	192261.83
162597.7	151377.59	443898.53	California	191792.06
153441.51	101145.55	407934.54	Florida	191050.39
144372.41	118671.85	383199.62	New York	182901.99

The dataset has 5 columns which contains extract from the Profit and Loss statement of 50 start up companies. This tells about the companies R&D, Admin and Marketing spend, the state in which these companies are based and also profit that the companies realized in that year. A venture capitalist (VC) would be interested in such a data and would to see if factors like R&D Spend, Admin expenses, Marketing spend and State has any role to play on the profitability of a startup. This analysis would help VC to make investment decisions in future.
Profit is the dependent variable and other variables are independent variables.

Dummy Variables

Let's look at the dataset we have for this example:

R&D Spend	Administration	Marketing Spend	State	Profit
165349.2	136897.8	471784.1	New York	192261.83
162597.7	151377.59	443898.53	California	191792.06
153441.51	101145.55	407934.54	Florida	191050.39
144372.41	118671.85	383199.62	New York	182901.99

One challenge we would face while building the linear model is on handling the State variable. State column has a categorical value and can not be treated as like any other numeric value. We need to add dummy variables for each categorical value like below:

State		New York	California	Florida
New York		1	0	0
California		0	1	0
Florida		0	0	1
New York		1	0	0
Florida		0	0	1
New York		1	0	0
California		0	1	0

Add 3 columns for each categorical value of state. Add 1 to the column where row value of state matches to the column header. Row containing New York will have 1 against the column header New York and rest of the values in that column will be zero. Similarly, we need to modify California and Florida columns too. Three additional columns that we added are called dummy variables and these will be used in our model building. State column can be ignored. We can also ignore New York column from analysis because row which has zero under California and Florida implicitly implies New York will have a value of 1. We always use 1 less dummy variable compared to total factors to avoid dummy variable trap.

Python code:

```
import pandas as pd
import matplotlib.pyplot as plt
import numpy as np
#Dataset
data_df =
pd.read_csv("https://raw.githubusercontent.com/swapnilsaurav/Ma
chineLearning/master/3_Startups.csv")
#Getting X and Y values
X = data_df.iloc[:, :-1].values
y = data_df.iloc[:, -1].values

#Encoding the categorical variables:
from sklearn.preprocessing import LabelEncoder, OneHotEncoder
labelencoder_X = LabelEncoder()
#Change the text into numbers 0,1,2 - 4th column
X[: ,3]= labelencoder_X.fit_transform(X[: ,3])
#create dummy variables
from sklearn.compose import ColumnTransformer
transformer = ColumnTransformer([('one_hot_encoder',
```

```
OneHotEncoder(), [3])],remainder='passthrough')
#Now a little fit and transform
X = np.array(transformer.fit_transform(X), dtype=np.float)
#4 Avoid the dummy variables trap
#Delete the first column represent the New York
X= X[:, 1:]

#Split into training and test set
from sklearn.model_selection import train_test_split
X_train, X_test, y_train, y_test = train_test_split(X, y,
test_size=0.2, random_state=0)

#Train the Algorithm
from sklearn.linear_model import LinearRegression
regressor = LinearRegression()
regressor.fit(X_train, y_train)
y_pred = regressor.predict(X_test)
#The y_pred is a numpy array that contains all predicted values
#compare actual output values for X_test with predicted values
output_df = pd.DataFrame({'Actual': y_test, 'Predicted':
y_pred})
print("Actual v Predicted: \n",output_df)
####
import numpy as np
from sklearn import metrics
explained_variance=metrics.explained_variance_score(y_test,
y_pred)
mean_absolute_error=metrics.mean_absolute_error(y_test, y_pred)
mse=metrics.mean_squared_error(y_test, y_pred)
mean_squared_log_error=metrics.mean_squared_log_error(y_test,
y_pred)
median_absolute_error=metrics.median_absolute_error(y_test,
y_pred)
r2=metrics.r2_score(y_test, y_pred)
print('Explained_variance: ', round(explained_variance,2))
print('Mean_Squared_Log_Error: ',
round(mean_squared_log_error,2))
print('R-squared: ', round(r2,4))
print('Mean Absolute Error(MAE): ',
round(mean_absolute_error,2))
print('Mean Squared Error (MSE): ', round(mse,2))
print('Root Mean Squared Error (RMSE): ',
round(np.sqrt(mse),2))
from statsmodels.api import OLS
import statsmodels.api as sm
#In our model, y will be dependent on 2 values: coefficienct
# and constant, so we need to add additional column in X for
#constant value
```

```
X = sm.add_constant(X)
summ = OLS(y, X).fit().summary()
print("Summary of the dataset: \n",summ)
```

Output:

```
Actual v Predicted:
       Actual      Predicted
0  103282.38  103015.201598
1  144259.40  132582.277608
2  146121.95  132447.738452
3   77798.83   71976.098513
4  191050.39  178537.482211
5  105008.31  116161.242302
6   81229.06   67851.692097
7   97483.56   98791.733747
8  110352.25  113969.435330
9  166187.94  167921.065695
Explained_variance:  0.95
Mean_Squared_Log_Error:  0.01
R-squared:  0.9347
Mean Absolute Error(MAE):  7514.29
Mean Squared Error (MSE):  83502864.03
Root Mean Squared Error (RMSE):  9137.99

Summary of the dataset:
                            OLS Regression Results
==============================================================================
Dep. Variable:                      y   R-squared:                       0.951
Model:                            OLS   Adj. R-squared:                  0.945
Method:                 Least Squares   F-statistic:                     169.9
Date:                Sun, 23 Aug 2020   Prob (F-statistic):           1.34e-27
Time:                        02:17:20   Log-Likelihood:                -525.38
No. Observations:                  50   AIC:                             1063.
Df Residuals:                      44   BIC:                             1074.
Df Model:                           5
Covariance Type:            nonrobust
==============================================================================
                 coef    std err          t      P>|t|      [0.025      0.975]
------------------------------------------------------------------------------
const       5.013e+04   6884.820      7.281      0.000    3.62e+04     6.4e+04
x1           198.7888   3371.007      0.059      0.953   -6595.030    6992.607
x2           -41.8870   3256.039     -0.013      0.990   -6604.003    6520.229
x3             0.8060      0.046     17.369      0.000       0.712       0.900
x4            -0.0270      0.052     -0.517      0.608      -0.132       0.078
x5             0.0270      0.017      1.574      0.123      -0.008       0.062
==============================================================================
Omnibus:                       14.782   Durbin-Watson:                   1.283
Prob(Omnibus):                  0.001   Jarque-Bera (JB):               21.266
Skew:                          -0.948   Prob(JB):                     2.41e-05
Kurtosis:                       5.572   Cond. No.                     1.45e+06
==============================================================================
```

In above table, x1 and x2 are the dummy variables for state, x3 is R&D, x4 is Administration, x5 is the marketing spends.

How many independent variables to consider?

We need to be careful to choose which ones we need to keep for input variables. We do not want to include all the variables for mainly 2 reasons:

1. GIGO: If we feed garbage to our model we will get garbage out so we need to feed in right set of data
2. Justifying the input: Can we justify the inclusion of all the data, if no, then we should not include them.

There are 4 methods to build a multiple linear model:

1. Select all in
2. Backward Elimination
3. Forward Selection
4. Bidirectional Elimination

Select-all-in: We select all the independent variables because we know that all variables impact the result or you have to because business leaders want you to include them.

Backward Elimination:

1. Select a significance level to stay in the model (e..g. SL =0.05, higher P value to be removed)
2. Fit the full model with all possible predictors.
3. Consider the predictor with the highest P-value. If P>SL, go to step 4 otherwise goto 5
4. Remove the predictor and refit the model and Go to step 3
5. Your model is ready!

Forward Selection:

1. Select a significance level to stay in the model (e..g. SL =0.05, lower P value to be kept)
2. Fit all the simple regression models, Select the one with the lowest P-value.
3. Keep this variable and fit all possible models with one extra predictor added to the ones you already have. Now Run with 2 variable linear regressions.
4. Consider the predictor with the lowest P-value. If P<SL, go to Step 3, otherwise go to next step.
5. Keep the previous model!

Bi-directional Selection: It is a combination of Forward selection and backward elimination:

1. Select a significant level to enter and stay in the model (SLE = SLS = 0.05)
2. Perform the next step of Forward selection (new variables must have P<SLE)

3. Perform all the step of Backward elimination (old variables must have P<SLS)
4. Iterate between 2 & 3 till no new variables can enter and no old variables can exit.

In the multiple regression example since we have already executed with all the attributes, let's implement backward elimination method here and remoe out the attributes that are not useful for us. Let' have a relook at the stats summary:

```
==============================================================================
                 coef    std err          t      P>|t|      [0.025      0.975]
------------------------------------------------------------------------------
const       5.013e+04   6884.820      7.281      0.000    3.62e+04     6.4e+04
x1           198.7888   3371.007      0.059      0.953   -6595.030    6992.607
x2           -41.8870   3256.039     -0.013      0.990   -6604.003    6520.229
x3             0.8060      0.046     17.369      0.000       0.712       0.900
x4            -0.0270      0.052     -0.517      0.608      -0.132       0.078
x5             0.0270      0.017      1.574      0.123      -0.008       0.062
==============================================================================
```

Look at the highest p-values and remove it. In this condition x2 (second dummy variable has the highest one (0,990). Now, we will remove this variable from the X and re-run the model.

```
X_opt= X[:, [0,1,3,4,5]]
regressor_OLS=sm.OLS(endog = y, exog = X_opt).fit()
summ =regressor_OLS.summary()
print("Summary of the dataset after elimination 1: \n",summ)
```

Output Snapshot:

```
==============================================================================
                 coef    std err          t      P>|t|      [0.025      0.975]
------------------------------------------------------------------------------
const       5.011e+04   6647.870      7.537      0.000    3.67e+04    6.35e+04
x1           220.1585   2900.536      0.076      0.940   -5621.821    6062.138
x2             0.8060      0.046     17.606      0.000       0.714       0.898
x3            -0.0270      0.052     -0.523      0.604      -0.131       0.077
x4             0.0270      0.017      1.592      0.118      -0.007       0.061
==============================================================================
```

Look at the highest p-value again. #First dummy variable, x1's p-value is 0.940. Remove this one. Even though this appeared as high number in the previous step also, but as per the algorithm we need to remove only 1 value at a time. Since, removing an attribute can have impact on other attributes also. Re-run the code again:

```
X_opt= X[:, [0,3,4,5]]
regressor_OLS=sm.OLS(endog = y, exog = X_opt).fit()
summ = regressor_OLS.summary()
print("Summary of the dataset after elimination 2: \n",summ)
```

```
==============================================================================
                 coef    std err          t      P>|t|      [0.025      0.975]
------------------------------------------------------------------------------
const       5.012e+04   6572.353      7.626      0.000    3.69e+04    6.34e+04
x1             0.8057      0.045     17.846      0.000       0.715       0.897
x2            -0.0268      0.051     -0.526      0.602      -0.130       0.076
x3             0.0272      0.016      1.655      0.105      -0.006       0.060
==============================================================================
```

Admin spends (x2) has the highest p-value (0.602). Remove this as well.

```
X_opt= X[:, [0,3,5]]
regressor_OLS=sm.OLS(endog = y, exog = X_opt).fit()
summ = regressor_OLS.summary()
print("Summary of the dataset after elimination 3: \n",summ)
```

```
==============================================================================
                 coef    std err          t      P>|t|      [0.025      0.975]
------------------------------------------------------------------------------
const       4.698e+04   2689.933     17.464      0.000    4.16e+04    5.24e+04
x1             0.7966      0.041     19.266      0.000       0.713       0.880
x2             0.0299      0.016      1.927      0.060      -0.001       0.061
==============================================================================
```

Admin spends (x2) has the highest p-value (0.06). This value is low but since we have selected the significance level (SL) as 0.05, we need to remove this as well.

```
X_opt= X[:, [0,3]]
regressor_OLS=sm.OLS(endog = y, exog = X_opt).fit()
summ =regressor_OLS.summary()
print("Summary of the dataset after elimination 3: \n",summ)
```

```
==============================================================================
                 coef    std err          t      P>|t|      [0.025      0.975]
------------------------------------------------------------------------------
const       4.903e+04   2537.897     19.320      0.000    4.39e+04    5.41e+04
x1             0.8543      0.029     29.151      0.000       0.795       0.913
==============================================================================
```

Finally, we see that only one factor has the significant impact on the profit. The highest impact variable is R&D spendings on profit of these startups. The accuracy of the model has also increased. When we included all the attributes, the R squared value was 0.9347 and now its at 0.947.

The word "linear" in "multiple linear regression" refers to the fact that the model meets all the criteria discussed in the next section.

TEST FOR LINEARITY

The next question we need to understand is when can we perform or not perform Linear Regression. In this section, let's understand the assumptions of linear regression in detail. One of the most essential steps to take before applying linear regression and depending solely on accuracy scores is to check for these assumptions and only when a dataset meet these assumptions, we say that dataset can be used for linear regression model.

For the analysis, we will take the same dataset, we used for Multiple Linear Regression Analysis in the previous section.

```
import pandas as pd
#Dataset
data_df =
pd.read_csv("https://raw.githubusercontent.com/swapnilsaurav/MachineLearning/master/3_Startups.csv")
```

Before we apply regression on all these attributes, we need to understand if we need to really take all of these attributes into consideration. There are two things we need to consider:

First step is to test the dataset if its fits into the linearity definition, which we will perform different tests in this section. Remember, we only test for numerical columns as the categorical columns are not taken into account. As we know that the categorical values are converted into dummy variables of values 0 and 1, dummy variables meet the assumption of linearity by definition, because they creat two data points, and two points define a straight line. There is no such thing as a non-linear relationship for a single variable with only two values.

Code for Prediction: Let's rewrite the code

```
import numpy as np
X = data_df.iloc[:,:-1].values # [[]], [[],[],[]]  #[[]]
y = data_df.iloc[:,-1].values

#handling categorical data
from sklearn.preprocessing import LabelEncoder, OneHotEncoder
le_x = LabelEncoder()
X[:,3] = le_x.fit_transform(X[:,3])
from sklearn.compose import ColumnTransformer
tranformer = ColumnTransformer([('one_hot_encoder',
OneHotEncoder(),[3])], remainder='passthrough')
X = np.array(tranformer.fit_transform(X), dtype=np.float)
X=X[:,1:]

from sklearn.model_selection import train_test_split
X_train, X_test, y_train, y_test =
train_test_split(X,y,test_size=0.2, random_state=0)
from sklearn.linear_model import LinearRegression
regressor = LinearRegression()
regressor.fit(X_train , y_train)
y_pred = regressor.predict(X_test)
```

```
output_df = pd.DataFrame({"Actual":y_test, "Predicted":
y_pred})
```

Let's perform the tests now:

1. Linearity

Linear regression needs the relationship between the independent and dependent variables to be linear. Let's use a pair plot to check the relation of independent variables with the profit variable.

Output:

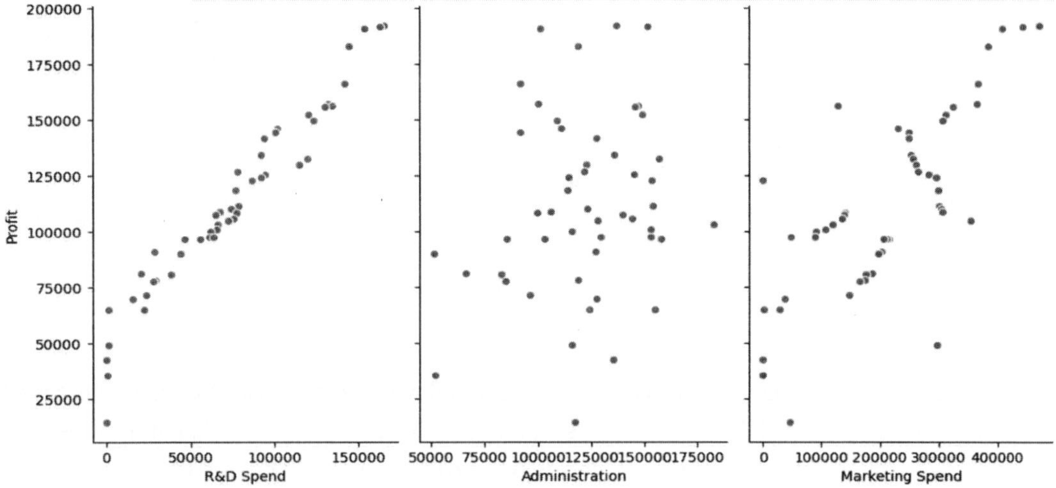

Code:

```
import seaborn as sns
import matplotlib.pyplot as plt

# visualize the relationship between the features and the
response using scatterplots
p = sns.pairplot(data_df, x_vars=['R&D
Spend','Administration','Marketing Spend'], y_vars='Profit',
height=5, aspect=0.7)
plt.show()
```

By looking at the plots we can see that with the R&D Spend form an accurately linear shape and Marketing Spend is somewhat in the linear shape but Administration Spend is all over the graph but still shows increasing trend as Profit value increases on Y-Axis. Here we can use Linear Regression models.

2. Variables follow a Normal Distribution

The variables (X) follow a normal distribution. In order words, we want to make sure that for each x value, y is a random variable following a normal distribution and its mean lies on the regression line. One of the ways to visually test for this assumption is through the use of the Q-Q-Plot. Q-Q stands for Quantile-Quantile plot and is a technique to compare two probability distributions in a visual manner. To generate this Q-Q plot we will be using scipy's probplot function where we compare a variable of our chosen to a normal probability.

```
import scipy.stats as stats
stats.probplot(X[:,3], dist="norm", plot=plt)
plt.show()
```

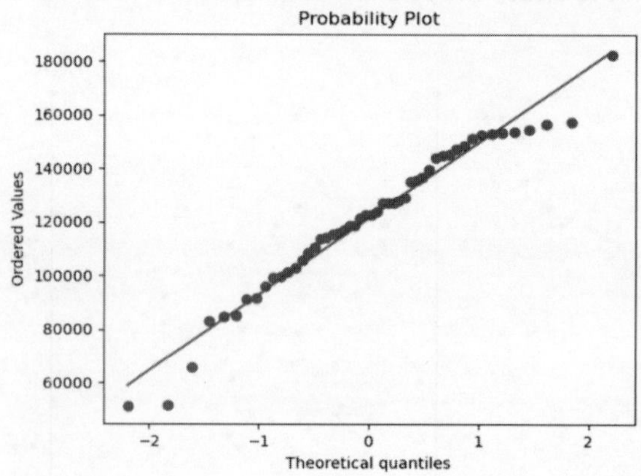

The points must lie on this red line to conclude that it follows a normal distribution. In this case of selecting 3rd column which is R&D Spend, yes it does! A couple of points outside of the line is due to our small sample size. In practice, you decide how strict you want to be as it is a visual test.

3. There is no or little multicollinearity

Multicollinearity means that the independent variables are highly correlated with each other. X's are called independent variables for a reason. If multicollinearity exists between them, they are no longer independent and this generates issues when modeling linear regressions.

To visually test for multicollinearity we can use the power of Pandas. We will use Pandas corr function to compute the pairwise correlation of our columns. If you find any values in which the absolute value of their correlation is >=0.8, the multicollinearity assumption is being broken.

```
#convert to a pandas dataframe
import pandas as pd
df = pd.DataFrame(X)
df.columns = ['x1','x2','x3','x4','x5']
#generate correlation matrix
corr = df.corr()
#Plot HeatMap
p=sns.heatmap(df.corr(), annot=True,cmap='RdYlGn',square=True)
print("Corelation Matrix:\n",corr)
```

```
Corelation Matrix:
          x1        x2        x3        x4        x5
x1  1.000000 -0.492366  0.105711  0.010493  0.205685
x2 -0.492366  1.000000  0.039068  0.005145 -0.033670
x3  0.105711  0.039068  1.000000  0.241955  0.724248
x4  0.010493  0.005145  0.241955  1.000000 -0.032154
x5  0.205685 -0.033670  0.724248 -0.032154  1.000000
```

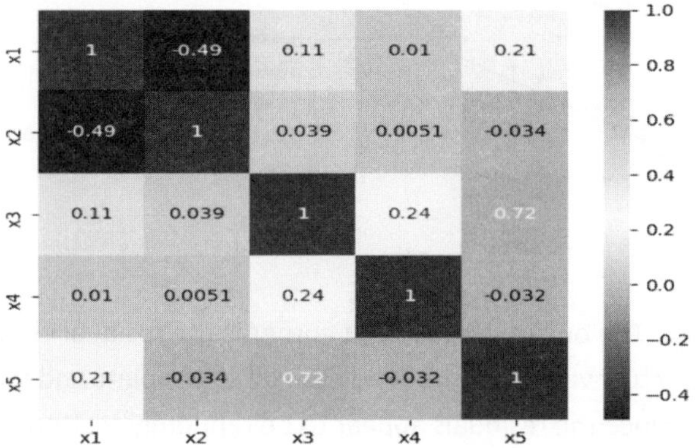

4. Check for Homoscedasticity: The data are needs to be homoscedastic (meaning the residuals are equal across the regression line). Homoscedasticity means that the residuals have equal or almost equal variance across the regression line. By plotting the error terms with predicted terms we can check that there should not be any pattern in the error terms.

```
#produce regression plots
from statsmodels.api import OLS
import statsmodels.api as sm
X = sm.add_constant(X)
model = OLS(y, X).fit()
summ = model.summary()
print("Summary of the dataset: \n",summ)
fig = plt.figure(figsize=(12,8))
#Checking for x3 (R&D Spend)
fig = sm.graphics.plot_regress_exog(model, 'x3', fig=fig)
plt.show()
```

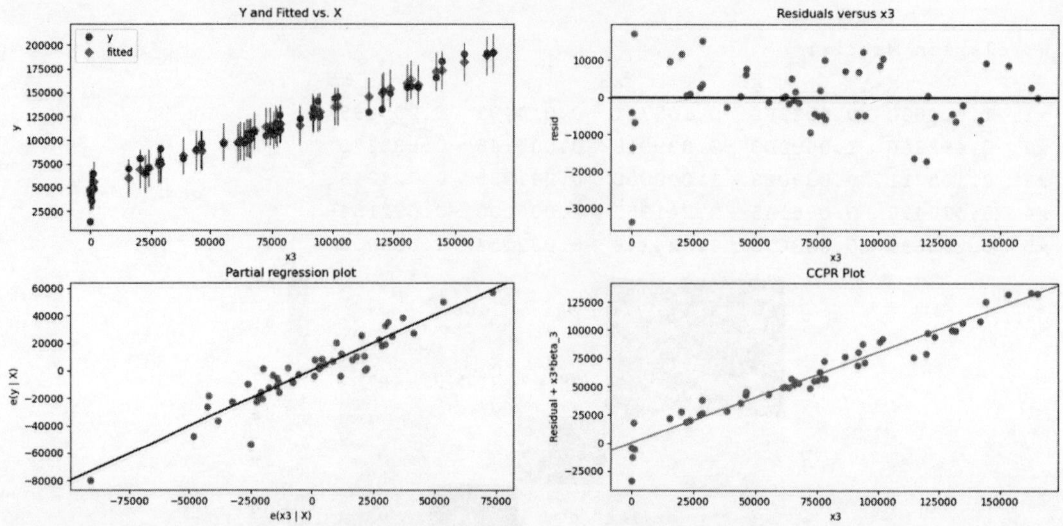

Four plots are produced. The one in the top right corner is the residual vs. fitted plot. The x-axis on this plot shows the actual values for the predictor variable points and the y-axis shows the residual for that value. Since the residuals appear to be randomly scattered around zero, this is an indication that heteroscedasticity is not a problem with the predictor variable x3 (R&D Spend). Multiple Regression, we need to create this plot for each of the predictor variable.

5. Mean of Residuals

Residuals as we know are the differences between the true value and the predicted value. One of the assumptions of linear regression is that the mean of the residuals should be zero. So let's find out.

```
residuals = y_test-y_pred
mean_residuals = np.mean(residuals)
print("Mean of Residuals {}".format(mean_residuals))
```

Output:

Mean of Residuals 3952.010244810798

6. Check for Normality of error terms/residuals

```
p = sns.distplot(residuals,kde=True)
p = plt.title('Normality of error terms/residuals')
plt.show()
```

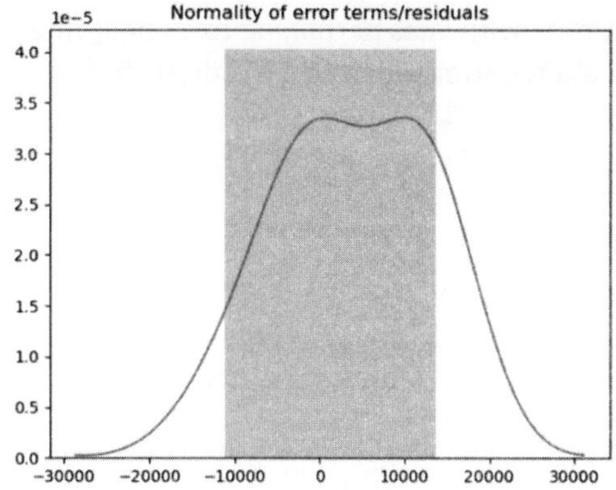

The residual terms are pretty much normally distributed for the number of test points we took.

NON LINEAR REGRESSION REGRESSION METHODS

A model is linear when each term is either a constant or the product of a parameter and a predictor variable. A linear equation is constructed by adding the results for each term. This constrains the equation to just one basic form:

*Response = constant + parameter * predictor + ... + parameter * predictor*

In statistics, a regression equation (or function) is linear when it is linear in the parameters. Where as you can transform the predictor variables in ways that produce curvature.

$y = \beta_0 + \beta_1 x + \beta_2 x^2 + \varepsilon$. This model is still linear in the parameters even though the predictor variable is squared. You can also use log and inverse functional forms that are linear in the parameters to produce different types of curves.

While a linear equation has one basic form, nonlinear equations can take many different forms. The easiest way to determine whether an equation is nonlinear is to find that it's not linear. If the equation doesn't meet the criteria for a linear equation, it's nonlinear. That covers many different forms, which is why nonlinear regression provides the most flexible curve-fitting functionality. Examples of non-linear:

- *Weibull growth*: Theta1 + (Theta2 - Theta1) * exp(-Theta3 * X^Theta4)
- *Fourier*: Theta1 * cos(X + Theta4) + (Theta2 * cos(2*X + Theta4) + Theta3

In statistics, polynomial regression is a form of regression analysis in which the relationship between the independent variable x and the dependent variable y is modelled as an nth degree polynomial in x. We will see this in the program below.

Although polynomial regression is technically a special case of multiple linear regression, the interpretation of a fitted polynomial regression model requires a somewhat different perspective. It is often difficult to interpret the individual coefficients in a polynomial regression fit, since the underlying monomials can be highly correlated. For example, x and x^2 (square) have correlation around 0.97 when x is uniformly distributed on the interval (0, 1).

A data set contains measurements of yield from an experiment done at five different temperature levels. The variables are y = yield and x = temperature in degrees Fahrenheit. The figures below give a scatterplot of the raw data with lines pertaining to a linear fit and a quadratic fit overlayed. Obviously the trend of this data is better suited to a quadratic fit.

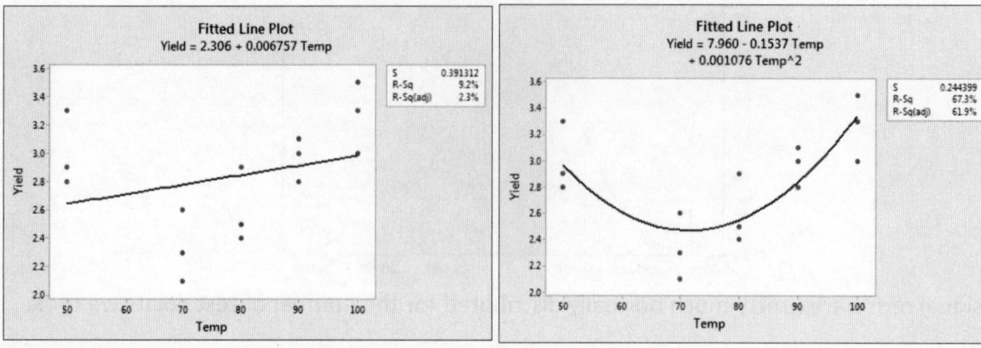

Figure 4: Example of Polynomial Regression

Nonlinear regression is a regression in which the dependent or criterion variables are modeled as a non-linear function of model parameters and one or more independent variables. There are several common models, such as Asymptotic Regression/Growth Model, which is given by:

```
b1 + b2 * exp(b3 * x)
```

Logistic Population Growth Model, which is given by:

```
b1 / (1 + exp(b2 + b3 * x))
```

Asymptotic Regression/Decay Model, which is given by:

```
b1 - (b2 * (b3 * x))
```

The reason that these models are called nonlinear regression is because the relationships between the dependent and independent parameters are not linear.

Let's take the next example, which is of type Non-Lienar type:

```
import numpy, scipy, matplotlib
import matplotlib.pyplot as plt
from scipy.optimize import curve_fit
from scipy.optimize import differential_evolution
import warnings

xData = numpy.array([19.1647, 18.0189, 16.9550, 15.7683,
14.7044, 13.6269, 12.6040, 11.4309, 10.2987, 9.23465, 8.18440,
7.89789, 7.62498, 7.36571, 7.01106, 6.71094, 6.46548, 6.27436,
6.16543, 6.05569, 5.91904, 5.78247, 5.53661, 4.85425, 4.29468,
3.74888, 3.16206, 2.58882, 1.93371, 1.52426, 1.14211, 0.719035,
0.377708, 0.0226971, -0.223181, -0.537231, -0.878491, -1.27484,
-1.45266, -1.57583, -1.61717])
yData = numpy.array([0.644557, 0.641059, 0.637555, 0.634059,
0.634135, 0.631825, 0.631899, 0.627209, 0.622516, 0.617818,
0.616103, 0.613736, 0.610175, 0.606613, 0.605445, 0.603676,
```

```
0.604887, 0.600127, 0.604909, 0.588207, 0.581056, 0.576292,
0.566761, 0.555472, 0.545367, 0.538842, 0.529336, 0.518635,
0.506747, 0.499018, 0.491885, 0.484754, 0.475230, 0.464514,
0.454387, 0.444861, 0.437128, 0.415076, 0.401363, 0.390034,
0.378698])

def func(x, a, b, Offset): # Sigmoid A With Offset from
zunzun.com
    return  1.0 / (1.0 + numpy.exp(-a * (x-b))) + Offset

# function for genetic algorithm to minimize (sum of squared
error)
def sumOfSquaredError(parameterTuple):
    warnings.filterwarnings("ignore") # do not print warnings
by genetic algorithm
    val = func(xData, *parameterTuple)
    return numpy.sum((yData - val) ** 2.0)

def generate_Initial_Parameters():
    # min and max used for bounds
    maxX = max(xData)
    minX = min(xData)
    maxY = max(yData)
    minY = min(yData)

    parameterBounds = []
    parameterBounds.append([minX, maxX]) # search bounds for a
    parameterBounds.append([minX, maxX]) # search bounds for b
    parameterBounds.append([0.0, maxY]) # Offset search bounds

    # "seed" for repeatable random number generator
    result = differential_evolution(sumOfSquaredError,
parameterBounds, seed=3)
    return result.x

# generate initial parameter values
geneticParameters = generate_Initial_Parameters()

# curve fit the test data
fittedParameters, pcov = curve_fit(func, xData, yData,
geneticParameters)

print('Parameters', fittedParameters)

modelPredictions = func(xData, *fittedParameters)

absError = modelPredictions - yData
```

```
SE = numpy.square(absError) # squared errors
MSE = numpy.mean(SE) # mean squared errors
RMSE = numpy.sqrt(MSE) # Root Mean Squared Error, RMSE
Rsquared = 1.0 - (numpy.var(absError) / numpy.var(yData))
print('RMSE:', RMSE)
print('R-squared:', Rsquared)

# graphics output section
def ModelAndScatterPlot(graphWidth, graphHeight):
    f = plt.figure(figsize=(graphWidth/100.0,
graphHeight/100.0), dpi=100)
    axes = f.add_subplot(111)

    # first the raw data as a scatter plot
    axes.plot(xData, yData,  'D')
    # create data for the fitted equation plot
    xModel = numpy.linspace(min(xData), max(xData))
    yModel = func(xModel, *fittedParameters)

    # now the model as a line plot
    axes.plot(xModel, yModel)
    axes.set_xlabel('X Data') # X axis data label
    axes.set_ylabel('Y Data') # Y axis data label
    plt.show()
    plt.close('all') # clean up after using pyplot

graphWidth = 800
graphHeight = 600
ModelAndScatterPlot(graphWidth, graphHeight)
```

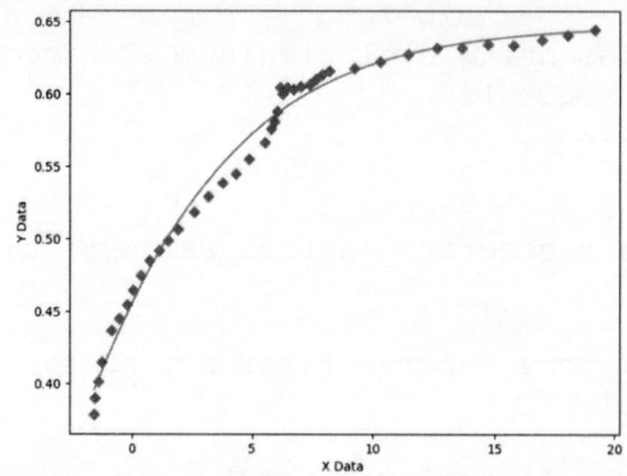

Parameters [0.21540307 -6.67449145 -0.35241296]

RMSE: 0.008428738373450245

R-squared: 0.9886222631484061

The scipy implementation of Differential Evolution uses the Latin Hypercube algorithm to ensure a thorough search of parameter space, and this requires bounds within which to search - in this example code, these bounds are based on the maximum and minimum data values. With creating the model, we are trying to find a mathematical equation that best fits the data we have.

POLYNOMIAL REGRESSION

Polynomial regression is a special case of linear regression where we fit a polynomial equation on the data with a curvilinear relationship between the target variable and the independent variables. In a curvilinear relationship, the value of the target variable changes in a non-uniform manner with respect to the predictor (s). A polynomial regression, we have a polynomial equation of degree n represented as:

$$Y = \theta_0 + \theta_1 x + \theta_2 x^2 + \theta_3 x^3 + \ldots + \theta_n x^n$$

Here:

$\theta 0$ is the bias,

$\theta 1, \theta 2, \ldots, \theta n$ are the weights in the equation of the polynomial regression,

and *n* is the degree of the polynomial

The number of higher-order terms increases with the increasing value of *n,* and hence the equation becomes more complicated.

Dataset 1: *4_Position_Salaries.csv*

Position	Level	Salary
Business Analyst	1	45000
Junior Consultant	2	50000
Senior Consultant	3	60000
Manager	4	80000
Country Manager	5	110000
Region Manager	6	150000
Partner	7	200000
Senior Partner	8	300000
C-level	9	500000
CEO	10	1000000

We have got a dataset of employees' job level/position and the respective salary at that position. We will then predict the salary of a person belonging to certain position. Let's say that the person is at position 5 for last 2 years. If we know that it takes 4 years to get promoted from Position 5 to 6 then we can assume the current position of the person to be 5.5 and predict the salary for this position. Let's analyze the data.

```
import pandas as pd
import matplotlib.pyplot as plt
import numpy as np
#Dataset
```

```
data_df =
pd.read_csv("https://raw.githubusercontent.com/swapnilsaurav/MachineLearning/master/4_Position_Salaries.csv")
x = data_df["Level"]
y = data_df["Salary"]
# plotting dataset
plt.figure(figsize=(10,5))
plt.scatter(x,y,s=15)
plt.xlabel('Predictor',fontsize=16)
plt.ylabel('Target',fontsize=16)
plt.show()
```

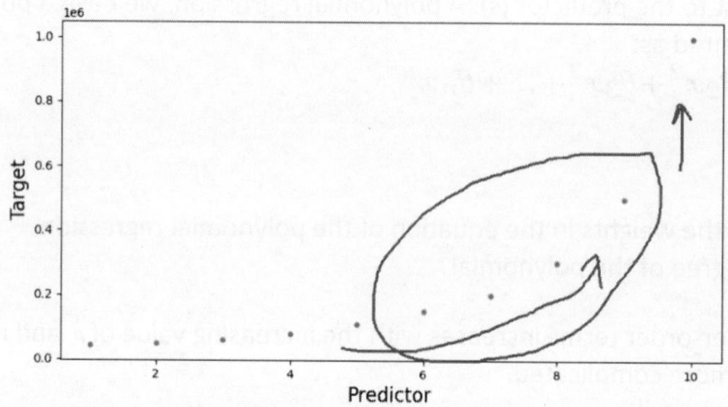

The data from the csv has been plotted as above and we see the area which has been marked in red, increases in a curvilinear manner, indicating that we will need to use Polynmial analysis on it and the linear analysis will not be able to match to the shape of the graph. For our understanding purpose we will perform both Linear and Polynomila Regression to see the difference.

Solve using Linear Regression:

```
#Perform Linear Regression
#Reshaping the dataset into array
x = pd.DataFrame(data_df, columns=['Level'])
#Y is expected to be one column so no need to reshape y
#Train the Algorithm
from sklearn.linear_model import LinearRegression
regressor = LinearRegression()
regressor.fit(x, y)
y_pred=regressor.predict(x)

from sklearn.metrics import mean_squared_error
print('RMSE for Linear
Regression=>',np.sqrt(mean_squared_error(y,y_pred)))

#Plot the actual data
plt.scatter(x, y,  color='black')
#Plot the prediction line
plt.plot(x, y_pred, color='blue', linewidth=3)
```

```
plt.xlabel("Predictor",fontsize=10)
plt.ylabel('Target',fontsize=10)
plt.show()
```

Output:

RMSE for Linear Regression=> 163388.73519272613

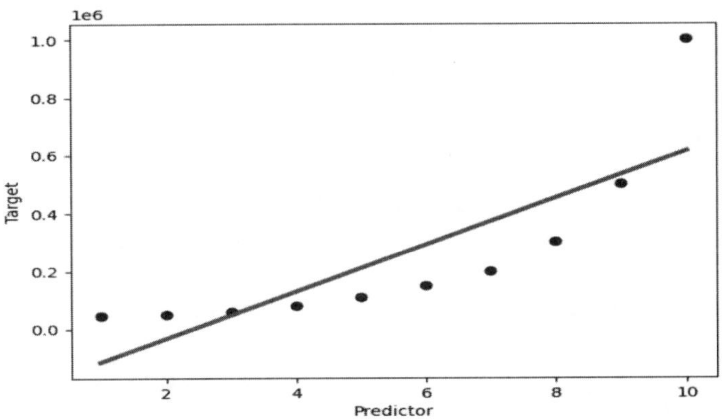

Solve using Polynomial Regression

The implementation of polynomial regression is a two-step process. First, we transform our data into a polynomial using the PolynomialFeatures function from sklearn and then use linear regression to fit the parameters. In the below example, we will take degree of 2,3 and 4 and compare the RMSE value to see which has the lowest error. We can choose the degree of polynomial based on the relationship between target and predictor. The 1-degree polynomial is a simple linear regression; therefore, the value of degree must be greater than 1, for it be called Polynomial regression.

Let's code now:

```
#Polynomial analysis
# importing libraries for polynomial transform
from sklearn.preprocessing import PolynomialFeatures
# for creating pipeline
from sklearn.pipeline import Pipeline
# creating pipeline and fitting it on data
Input=[('polynomial',PolynomialFeatures(degree=2)),('modal',Lin
earRegression())]
pipe=Pipeline(Input)
pipe.fit(x,y)
poly_pred2=pipe.predict(x)

from sklearn.metrics import mean_squared_error
print('RMSE for Polynomial Degree 2
Regression=>',np.sqrt(mean_squared_error(y,poly_pred2)))
#Degree = 3
Input=[('polynomial',PolynomialFeatures(degree=3)),('modal',Lin
```

```
earRegression())]
pipe=Pipeline(Input)
pipe.fit(x,y)
poly_pred3=pipe.predict(x)

from sklearn.metrics import mean_squared_error
print('RMSE for Polynomial Degree 3
Regression=>',np.sqrt(mean_squared_error(y,poly_pred3)))

#plotting predictions
plt.figure(figsize=(10,6))
plt.scatter(x,y,s=15)
plt.plot(x,y_pred,color='red',label='Linear Regression')
plt.plot(x,poly_pred2,color='blue',label='Polynomial Regression
Degree 2')
plt.plot(x,poly_pred3,color='green',label='Polynomial
Regression Degree 3')

plt.xlabel('Predictor',fontsize=10)
plt.ylabel('Target',fontsize=10)
plt.legend()
plt.show()
```

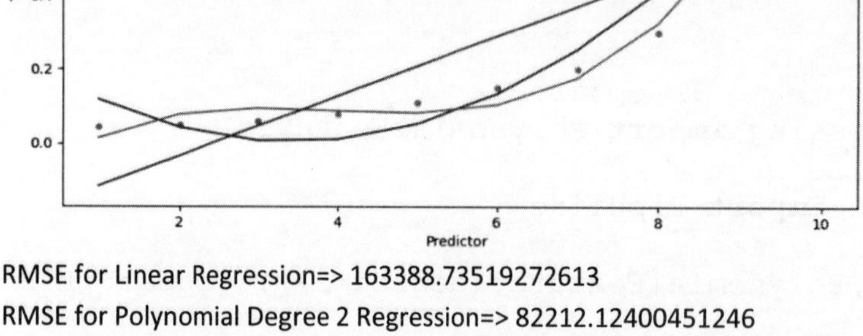

RMSE for Linear Regression=> 163388.73519272613
RMSE for Polynomial Degree 2 Regression=> 82212.12400451246
RMSE for Polynomial Degree 3 Regression=> 38931.50401232923

Note: We see that the RMSE value is lowest for Polynomial with degree 3. If you continue to increase the degree, you will see that the accuracy also increases but we have to be careful of overfitting. On plot, when you see that the regression curve is changing its course and tries to take the shape to cover most of the points, that's a sign of overfitting. Even though this model passes through most of the data, it will fail to generalize on unseen data. We have discussed this in detail towards the end of this chapter.

Next question is, how we choose the degree. We need to go back to our school statistics to understand the degree of a polynomial.

How to calculate degree of a polynomial:

A polynomial's degree is the highest or the greatest power of a variable in a polynomial equation. The degree indicates the highest exponential power in the polynomial (ignoring the coefficients).

For example: $6x^4 + 2x^3 + 3$ is a polynomial. Here $6x^4$, $2x^3$, 3 are the terms where $6x^4$ is a leading term and 3 is a constant term. The coefficients of the polynomial are 6 and 2. The highest power of the polynomial is the degree, so The degree of the polynomial $6x^4 + 2x^3 + 3$ is 4.

To find the degree of the polynomial, add up the exponents of each term and select the highest sum.

$12x^2y^3$: 2 + 3 = 5

$6xy^4z$: 1 + 4 + 1 = 6

2xz: 1 + 1 = 2

The degree is therefore 6.

Let's look at another, before we move to next topic:

```
import numpy as np
import matplotlib.pyplot as plt

#Generate a random set of data
np.random.seed(0)
x_data = 2 - 3 * np.random.normal(0, 1, 20)
#Polynomiall relationship
y_data = x_data - 2 * (x_data ** 4) + 0.5 * (x_data ** 5) +
np.random.normal(-3, 3, 20)
plt.scatter(x_data,y_data, s=10)
plt.show()

#First solve using Linear regression
# transforming the data to include another axis
x = x_data[:, np.newaxis]
y = y_data[:, np.newaxis]

from sklearn.linear_model import LinearRegression
model = LinearRegression()
model.fit(x, y)
y_pred = model.predict(x)

from sklearn.metrics import mean_squared_error, r2_score
print('RMSE for Linear
Regression=>',np.sqrt(mean_squared_error(y,y_pred)))
```

```
r2=r2_score(y, y_pred)
print('R-squared (Linear Regression): ', round(r2,4))
plt.scatter(x, y, s=10)
plt.plot(x, y_pred, color='r')
plt.show()

#We can see that the straight line is unable to
# capture the patterns in the data.
# This is an example of under-fitting.
#To overcome under-fitting, we need to
# increase the complexity of the model.
#degree of Polynomial is 5
from sklearn.preprocessing import PolynomialFeatures
polynomial_features= PolynomialFeatures(degree=5)
x_poly = polynomial_features.fit_transform(x)

model = LinearRegression()
model.fit(x_poly, y)
y_poly_pred = model.predict(x_poly)

rmse = np.sqrt(mean_squared_error(y,y_poly_pred))
r2 = r2_score(y,y_poly_pred)
print('RMSE for Polynomial Regression degree 5=>',rmse)
print('R-squared (Polynomial Regression, degree =5): ',r2)

plt.scatter(x, y, s=10)
# sort the values of x before line plot
import operator
sort_axis = operator.itemgetter(0)
sorted_zip = sorted(zip(x['Level'],y_poly_pred), key=sort_axis)
x, y_poly_pred = zip(*sorted_zip)
plt.plot(x, y_poly_pred, color='m')
plt.show()
```

Output:

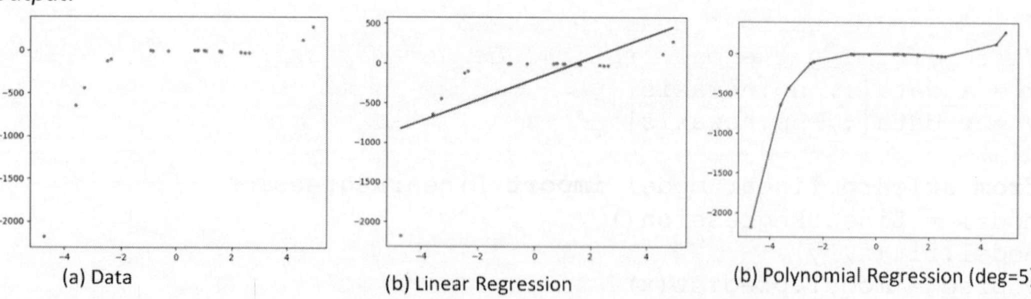

(a) Data (b) Linear Regression (b) Polynomial Regression (deg=5)

RMSE for Linear Regression=> 365.7415878642789
R-squared (Linear Regression): 0.4601

RMSE for Polynomial Regression degree 5=> 3.293351887947396
R-squared (Polynomial Regression, degree =5): 0.9999562217317468

SUPPORT VECTOR MACHINE FOR REGRESSION (SVR)

Support Vector Machine" (SVM) is a supervised machine learning algorithm which can be used for both classification or regression challenges. However, it is mostly used in classification problems. In this example we will see how it can be used in regression models.

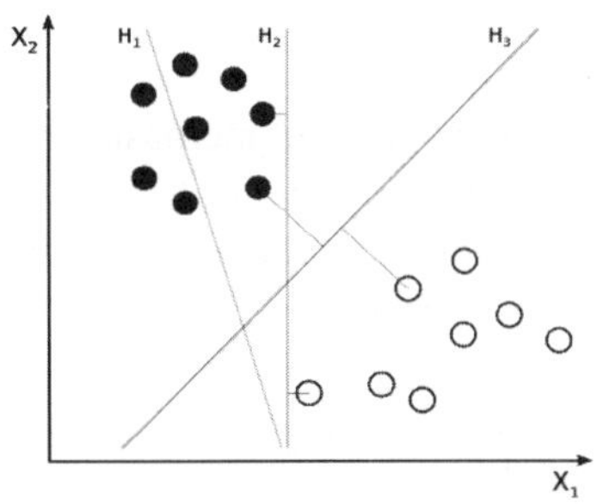

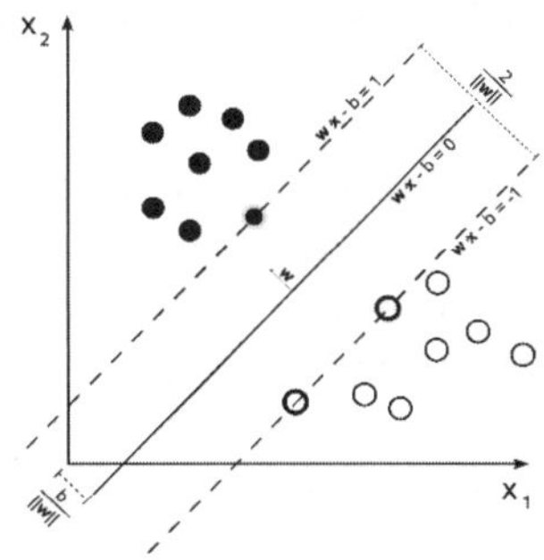

A support vector machine constructs a hyperplane or set of hyperplanes in a high- or infinite-dimensional space, which can be used for classification, regression, or other tasks like outlier detection. Intuitively, a good separation is achieved by the hyperplane that has the largest distance to the nearest training-data point of any class (so-called functional margin), since in general the larger the margin the lower the generalization error of the classifier.

In SVR, you want to find a function such that all points are within a certain distance from this function. Again, if points are outside this distance ["**ε** -tube"], there is a penalty or loss. The linear **ε**-insensitive loss function ignores errors that are within **ε** distance of the observed value by treating them as equal to zero. The loss is measured based on the distance between observed value y and the **ε** boundary. This is formally described by:

$$L_\varepsilon = \begin{cases} 0 & \text{if } |y - f(x)| \le \varepsilon \\ |y - f(x)| - \varepsilon & \text{otherwise} \end{cases}$$

Our goal is to is to find a function f(x) that has at most ε deviation from actually obtained target yi, for all the training data, and at the same time is as flat as possible. In other words, the data points lie in between the two borders of the margin which is maximized under suitable conditions will avoid outlier inclusion.

The line fairly separates the classes. This is what SVM essentially does – simple class separation. Now, what is the data was like that was shown on the left side in the below image? Here, we don't have a simple line separating these two classes. So we'll extend our dimension and introduce a new dimension along the z-axis. We can now separate these two classes:

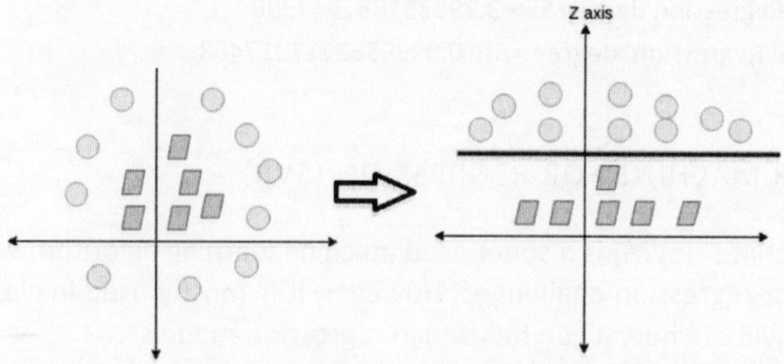

There are a few important parameters of SVM that you should be aware of before proceeding further:

Kernel: A kernel helps us find a hyperplane in the higher dimensional space without increasing the computational cost. Usually, the computational cost will increase if the dimension of the data increases. This increase in dimension is required when we are unable to find a separating hyperplane in a given dimension and are required to move in a higher dimension:

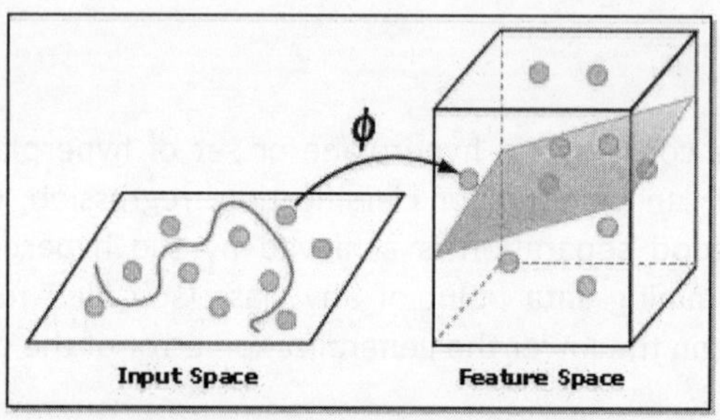

Hyperplane: This is basically a separating line between two data classes in SVM. But in Support Vector Regression, this is the line that will be used to predict the continuous output

Decision Boundary: A decision boundary can be thought of as a demarcation line (for simplification) on one side of which lie positive examples and on the other side lie the negative examples. On this very line, the examples may be classified as either positive or negative. This same concept of SVM, we will apply in the Regression next.

Modeling and Solving SVR Regression

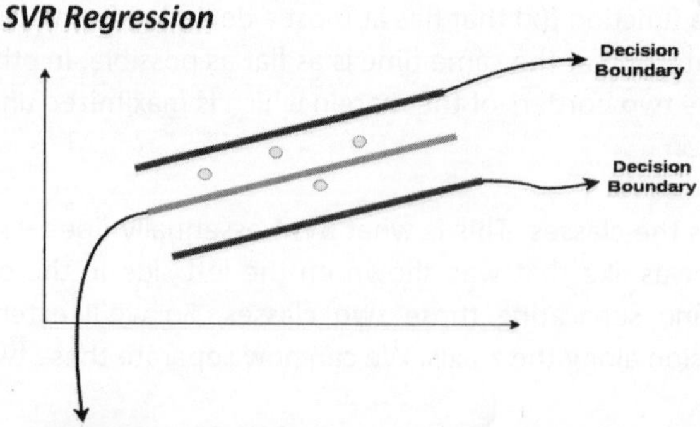

Our objective, when we are moving on with SVR, is to basically consider the points that are within the decision boundary line. Our best fit line is the hyperplane that has a maximum number of points.

The first thing that we'll understand is what is the decision boundary. Consider these lines as being at any distance, say 'a', from the hyperplane. So, these are the lines that we draw at distance '+a' and '-a' from the hyperplane. This 'a' in the text is basically referred to as epsilon.

Assuming that the equation of the hyperplane is as follows:
Y = wx+b (equation of hyperplane)

Then the equations of decision boundary become:
$wx+b= +a$
$wx+b= -a$

Thus, any hyperplane that satisfies our SVR should satisfy:

$-a < Y- wx+b < +a$

Our main aim here is to decide a decision boundary at 'a' distance from the original hyperplane such that data points closest to the hyperplane or the support vectors are within that boundary line. Hence, we are going to take only those points that are within the decision boundary and have the least error rate, or are within the Margin of Tolerance. This gives us a better fitting model.

Let's run the example. Please read through the comments in the code to understand the steps involved.

```
import pandas as pd
import matplotlib.pyplot as plt
import numpy as np
#Dataset
data_df =
pd.read_csv("https://raw.githubusercontent.com/swapnilsaurav/Ma
chineLearning/master/3_Startups.csv")
#Getting X and Y values
X = data_df.iloc[:, :-1].values
y = data_df.iloc[:, -1].values

#Encoding the categorical variables:
from sklearn.preprocessing import LabelEncoder, OneHotEncoder
labelencoder_X = LabelEncoder()
#Change the text into numbers 0,1,2 - 4th column
X[: ,3]= labelencoder_X.fit_transform(X[: ,3])
#create dummy variables
from sklearn.compose import ColumnTransformer
transformer = ColumnTransformer([('one_hot_encoder',
OneHotEncoder(), [3])],remainder='passthrough')
```

```
#Now a little fit and transform
X = np.array(transformer.fit_transform(X), dtype=np.float)
#4 Avoid the dummy variables trap
#Delete the first column represent the New York
X= X[:, 1:]

#Split into training and test set
from sklearn.model_selection import train_test_split
X_train, X_test, y_train, y_test = train_test_split(X, y,
test_size=0.2, random_state=0)

#Train the Algorithm
from sklearn.svm import SVR
# Fit regression model
svr_rbf = SVR(kernel='rbf', C=1e3, gamma=0.1)
y_rbf = svr_rbf.fit(X_train, y_train).predict(X_test)
svr_lin = SVR(kernel='linear')
y_lin = svr_lin.fit(X_train, y_train).predict(X_test)
svr_poly = SVR(kernel='poly', C=1e3, degree=2)
y_poly = svr_poly.fit(X_train, y_train).predict(X_test)

plt.scatter(X_test[:,4], y_test, color='darkorange',
label='data')
plt.plot(X_test[:,4], y_rbf, color='navy', label='RBF model')
plt.plot(X_test[:,4], y_lin, color='c',  label='Linear model')
plt.plot(X_test[:,4], y_poly, color='cornflowerblue',
label='Polynomial model')
plt.xlabel('data')
plt.ylabel('target')
plt.title('Support Vector Regression')
plt.legend()
plt.show()

import numpy as np
from sklearn import metrics
# Linear Model
mae = metrics.mean_absolute_error(y_test, y_lin)
mse = metrics.mean_squared_error(y_test, y_lin)
rmse = np.sqrt(mse)
print("RMSE of Linear Model = ",rmse)
r2 = metrics.r2_score(y_test, y_lin)
print("R Square of Linear Model = ",r2)

# RBF Model
mae = metrics.mean_absolute_error(y_test, y_rbf)
mse = metrics.mean_squared_error(y_test, y_rbf)
rmse = np.sqrt(mse)
print("RMSE of RBF Model = ",rmse)
```

```
r2 = metrics.r2_score(y_test, y_rbf)
print("R Square of RBF Model = ",r2)

# Polynomial Model
mae = metrics.mean_absolute_error(y_test, y_poly)
mse = metrics.mean_squared_error(y_test, y_poly)
rmse = np.sqrt(mse)
print("RMSE of Polynomial Model = ",rmse)
r2 = metrics.r2_score(y_test, y_poly)
print("R Square of Polynomial Model = ",r2)
```

Since, we have run this model on a small dataset and have included all the columns for X, result may not be great. Readers are encouraged to perform this SVR Model on Iris dataset to view the result.

SVM Kernels Examples:

Linear SVM Model: Linear Kernel is used when the data is Linearly separable, that is, it can be separated using a single Line. It is one of the most common kernels to be used. It is mostly used when there are a Large number of Features in a particular Data Set. One of the examples where there are a lot of features, is Text Classification, as each alphabet is a new feature. So we mostly use Linear Kernel in Text Classification.

Radial Basis Function (RBF) SVM Model: RBF kernel is used in SVM because it helps the SVM to become non linear rather than linear. Apart from the classic linear kernel which assumes that the different classes are separated by a straight line, a RBF (radial basis function) kernel is used when the boundaries are hypothesized to be curve-shaped.

Polynomial SVM Model: For degree-d polynomials, the polynomial kernel is defined as:

$$K(x, y) = (x^{\mathsf{T}} y + c)^d$$

Polynomial kernel is quite popular in natural language processing (NLP).

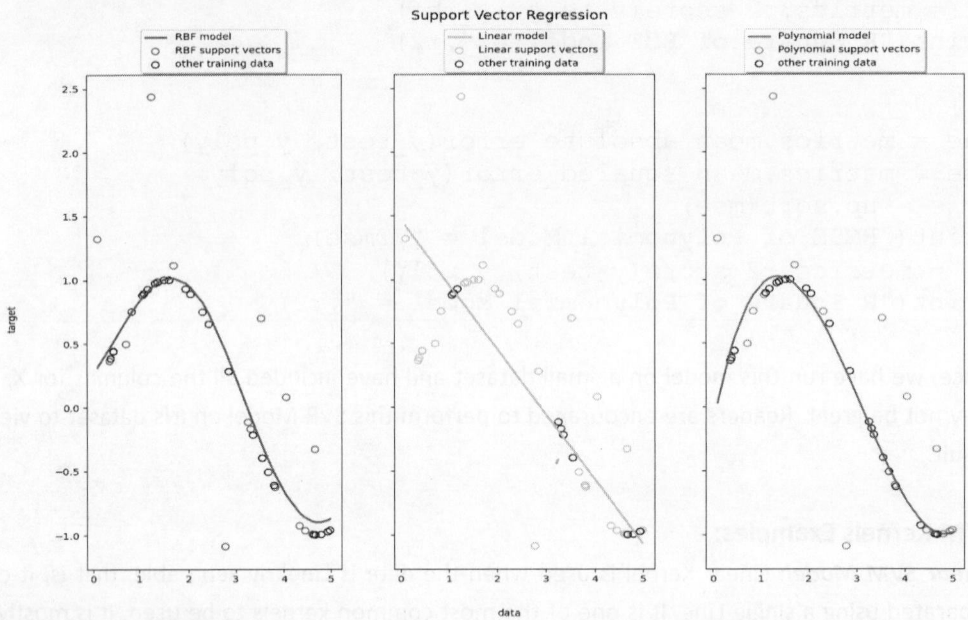

How to select SVM kernels

Given an arbitrary dataset, you typically don't know which kernel may work best. I recommend starting with the simplest hypothesis space first – given that you don't know much about your data – and work your way up towards the more complex hypothesis spaces. So, the linear kernel works fine if your dataset if linearly separable; however, if your dataset isn't linearly separable, a linear kernel isn't going to work.

Let's take an example where both linear and RBF kernel SVM would work equally well on this dataset. So, why prefer the simpler, linear hypothesis? The complexity of the RBF kernel grows with the size of the training set. Not only is it more expensive to train an RBF kernel SVM, but you also have to keep the kernel matrix around, and the projection into this "infinite" higher dimensional space where the data becomes linearly separable is more expensive as well during prediction. Furthermore, you have more hyperparameters to tune, so model selection is more expensive as well! And finally, it's much easier to overfit a complex model!

At the sametime, if your data is not linearly separable, it doesn't make sense to use a linear classifier. Let's take the below dataset:

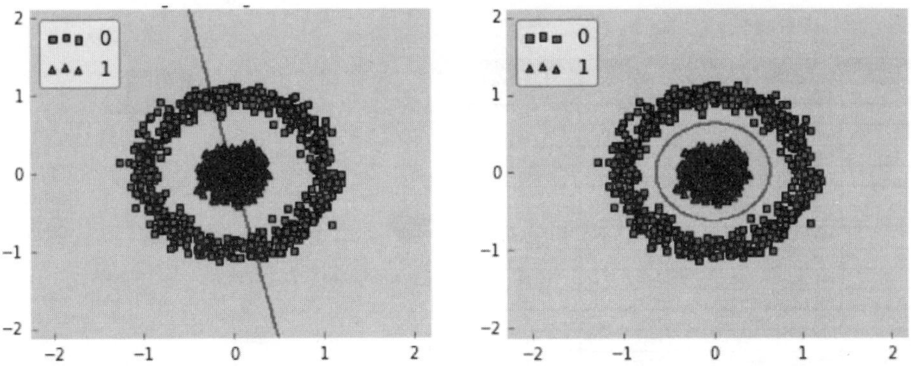

In the above case, a RBF kernel would make so much more sense.

In practice, polynomial kernel is less useful for efficiency (computational as well as predictive) performance reasons. So, the rule of thumb is: use linear SVMs (or logistic regression) for linear problems, and nonlinear kernels such as the Radial Basis Function kernel for non-linear problems.

DECISION TREE CLASSIFICATION

Decision tree builds regression or classification models in the form of a tree structure. It breaks down a dataset into smaller and smaller subsets while at the same time an associated decision tree is incrementally developed. The final result is a tree with decision nodes and leaf nodes. A decision node (e.g., Outlook) has two or more branches (e.g., Sunny, Overcast and Rainy), each representing values for the attribute tested. Leaf node (e.g., Hours Played) represents a decision on the numerical target. The topmost decision node in a tree which corresponds to the best predictor called root node. Decision trees can handle both categorical and numerical data.

Dataset:

Predictors				Target
Outlook	**Temp**	**Humidity**	**Windy**	**Hours Played**
Rainy	Hot	High	False	26
Rainy	Hot	High	True	30
Overcast	Hot	High	False	48
Sunny	Mild	High	False	46
Sunny	Cool	Normal	False	62
Sunny	Cool	Normal	True	23
Overcast	Cool	Normal	True	43
Rainy	Mild	High	False	36
Rainy	Cool	Normal	False	38
Sunny	Mild	Normal	False	48
Rainy	Mild	Normal	True	48
Overcast	Mild	High	True	62
Overcast	Hot	Normal	False	44
Sunny	Mild	High	True	30

Outlook	Temp.	Humidity	Windy	Hours Played
Rainy	Hot	High	False	25
Rainy	Hot	High	True	30
Overcast	Hot	High	False	46
Sunny	Mild	High	False	45
Sunny	Cool	Normal	False	52
Sunny	Cool	Normal	True	23
Overcast	Cool	Normal	True	43
Rainy	Mild	High	False	35
Rainy	Cool	Normal	False	38
Sunny	Mild	Normal	False	46
Rainy	Mild	Normal	True	48
Overcast	Mild	High	True	52
Overcast	Hot	Normal	False	44
Sunny	Mild	High	True	30

(Predictors: Outlook, Temp., Humidity, Windy; Target: Hours Played)

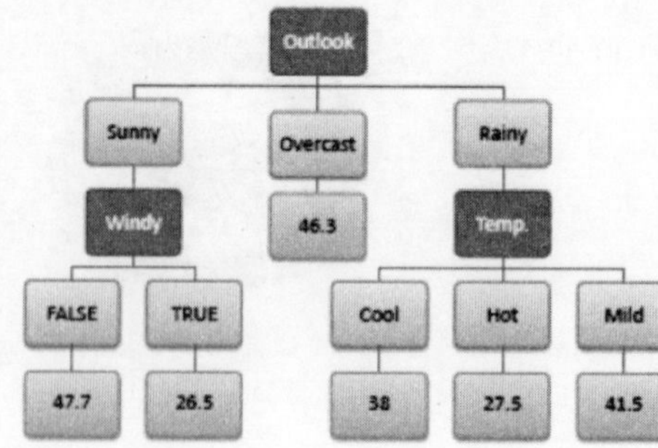

Figure 5: Decision tree example

The goal of the Decision Tree is to create a model that predicts the value of a target variable based on several input variables. An example is shown in the diagram above. Each interior node corresponds to one of the input variables; there are edges to children for each of the possible values of that input variable. Each leaf represents a value of the target variable given the values of the input variables represented by the path from the root to the leaf.

The term Classification And Regression Tree (CART) analysis is an umbrella term used to refer to both Decision Tree Regression and Decision Tree Classification procedures. Trees used for regression and trees used for classification have some similarities - but also some differences, such as the procedure used to determine where to split.

Regression versus Classification

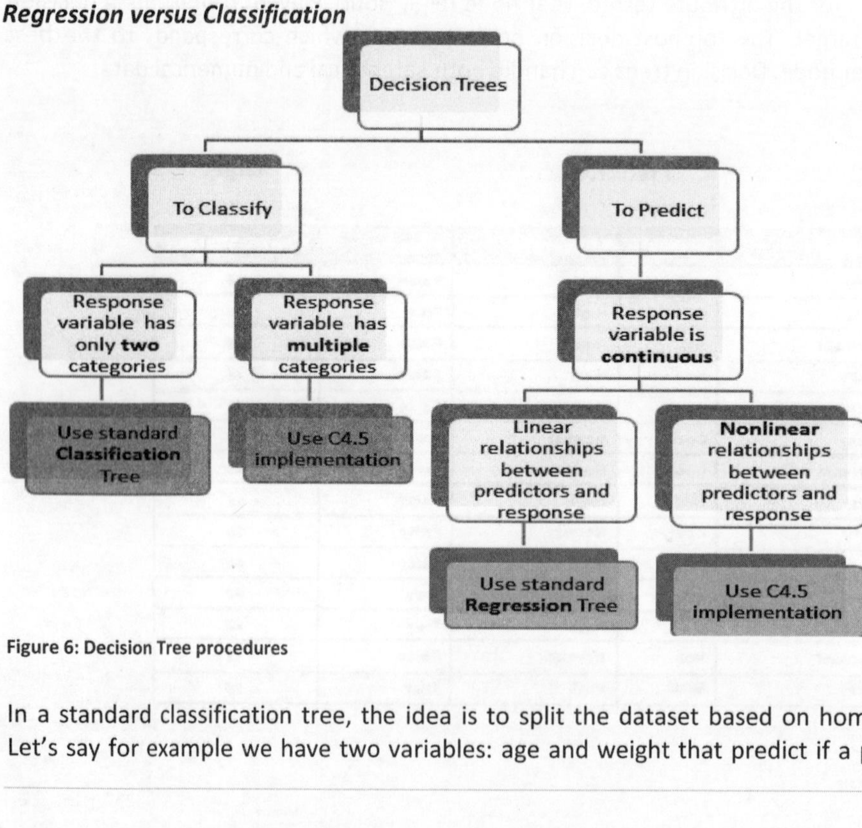

Figure 6: Decision Tree procedures

In a standard classification tree, the idea is to split the dataset based on homogeneity of data. Let's say for example we have two variables: age and weight that predict if a person is going to sign up for a gym membership or not. In our training data if it showed that 90% of the people who are older than 40 signed up, we split the data here and age becomes a top node in the tree. We can almost say that this split has made the data "90% pure".

In a regression tree the idea is this: since the target variable does not have classes, we fit a regression model to the target variable using each of the independent variables. Then for each independent variable, the data is split at several split points. At each split point, the "error" between the predicted value and the actual values is squared to get a "Sum of Squared Errors (SSE)". The split point errors across the variables are compared and the variable/point yielding the lowest SSE is chosen as the root node/split point. This process is recursively continued.

When to use classification vs. regression tree

Classification trees, as the name implies are used to separate the dataset into classes belonging to the response variable. Usually the response variable has two classes: Yes or No (1 or 0). If the target variable has more than 2 categories, then a variant of the algorithm, called C4.5, is used. For binary splits however, the standard CART procedure is used. Thus classification trees are used when the response or target variable is categorical in nature.

Regression trees are needed when the response variable is numeric or continuous. For example, the predicted price of a consumer good. Thus regression trees are applicable for prediction type of problems as opposed to classification. Keep in mind that in either case, the predictors or independent variables may be categorical or numeric. It is the target variable that determines the type of decision tree needed.

Let's see how a decision tree algorithm works for regression.

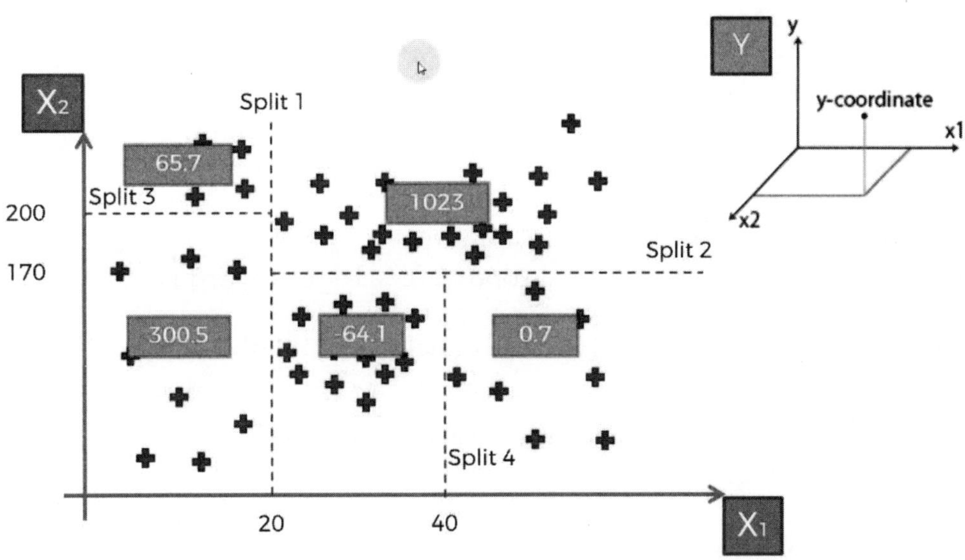

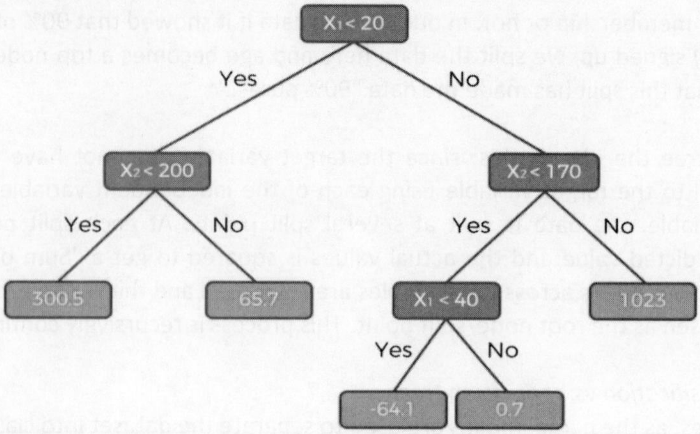

Let's look at an example:

```
#1 Importing the libraries
import numpy as np
import matplotlib.pyplot as plt
import pandas as pd
#2 Importing the dataset
slr_df =
pd.read_csv("https://raw.githubusercontent.com/swapnilsaurav/Ma
chineLearning/master/3_Startups.csv")

#Take only R&D Spend for analysis for this example.
#Algorithm can take multiple columns as well
X = slr_df.iloc[:,:1].values
#Profit last column as Y
y = slr_df.iloc[:,-1].values
#To save effort we are not performing any preprocessing steps
here but like our previous steps, we need to cleanse the data
before running the models

#Split into test and train
from sklearn.model_selection import train_test_split
X_train, X_test, y_train, y_test =
train_test_split(X,y,test_size=0.2, random_state=0)

# Create the Decision Tree regressor object here
from sklearn.tree import DecisionTreeRegressor
regressor = DecisionTreeRegressor(random_state=0)
#Fit the regressor object to the dataset.
regressor.fit(X_train,y_train)
#Predict
y_pred = regressor.predict(X_test)

#Visualising the Decision Tree Regression results
```

```
plt.scatter(X, y, color = 'red')
plt.plot(X, regressor.predict(X), color = 'blue')
plt.title('Check It (Regression Model)')
plt.xlabel('R&D Spend')
plt.ylabel('Profit')
plt.show()

#Analyze
import numpy as np
from sklearn import metrics
mae = metrics.mean_absolute_error(y_test, y_pred)
#RMSE & R2
mse = metrics.mean_squared_error(y_test, y_pred)
rmse = np.sqrt(mse)
print("RMSE = ",rmse)
r2 = metrics.r2_score(y_test, y_pred)
print("R Square = ",r2)
```

Output:

```
RMSE =  12608.806371690385
R Square =  0.8756876665789475
```

RANDOM FOREST CLASSIFICATION

Random forest is a flexible, easy to use machine learning algorithm that produces, even without hyper-parameter tuning, a great result most of the time. It is also one of the most used algorithms, because of its simplicity and diversity (it can be used for both classification and regression tasks). Random forest is a supervised learning algorithm. The "forest" it builds, is an ensemble of decision trees, usually trained with the "bagging" method. The general idea of the bagging method is that a combination of learning models increases the overall result.

In simple terms, random forest builds multiple decision trees and merges them together to get a more accurate and stable prediction.

Random forest adds additional randomness to the model, while growing the trees. Instead of searching for the most important feature while splitting a node, it searches for the best feature among a random subset of features. This results in a wide diversity that generally results in a better model.

Therefore, in random forest, only a random subset of the features is taken into consideration by the algorithm for splitting a node. You can even make trees more random by additionally using random thresholds for each feature rather than searching for the best possible thresholds (like a normal decision tree does).

Python Implementation

The following are the basic steps involved in performing the random forest algorithm:

1. Pick N random records from the dataset.
2. Build a decision tree based on these N records.
3. Choose the number of trees you want in your algorithm and repeat steps 1 and 2.
4. In case of a regression problem, for a new record, each tree in the forest predicts a value for Y (output). The final value can be calculated by taking the average of all the values predicted by all the trees in forest.

Let's see the below program:

Problem Definition: The problem here is to predict the gas consumption (in millions of gallons) in 48 of the US states based on petrol tax (in cents), per capita income (dollars), paved highways (in miles) and the proportion of population with the driving license.

```
#Import Libraries
import pandas as pd
import numpy as np
import matplotlib.pyplot as plt
reg_df =
pd.read_csv("https://raw.githubusercontent.com/swapnilsaurav/Da
taset/master/gasoline_consumption.csv")
#To get a high-level view of what the dataset looks like
reg_df.head()
#divides data into attributes and labels:
X = reg_df.iloc[:, 0:4].values
y = reg_df.iloc[:, 4].values
#Preparing Data For Training
from sklearn.model_selection import train_test_split
X_train, X_test, y_train, y_test = train_test_split(X, y,
test_size=0.2, random_state=0)

#Feature Scaling
#Average_Income field has values in the range of thousands
while Petrol_tax has values in range of tens. Therefore, it
would be beneficial to scale our data
#Although, this step isn't as important for the random forests
algorithm
from sklearn.preprocessing import StandardScaler
sc = StandardScaler()
X_train = sc.fit_transform(X_train)
X_test = sc.transform(X_test)
#Training the Algorithm and Predicting
```

```
from sklearn.ensemble import RandomForestRegressor
regressor = RandomForestRegressor(n_estimators=20,
random_state=0)
regressor.fit(X_train, y_train)
y_pred = regressor.predict(X_test)

#Evaluating the Algorithm
from sklearn import metrics
print('Mean Absolute Error for 20 estimators:',
metrics.mean_absolute_error(y_test, y_pred))
print('Mean Squared Error for 20 estimators:',
metrics.mean_squared_error(y_test, y_pred))
print('Root Mean Squared Error for 20 estimators:',
np.sqrt(metrics.mean_squared_error(y_test, y_pred)))
```

Output:

```
Mean Absolute Error for 20 estimators: 51.765000000000001
Mean Squared Error for 20 estimators: 4216.166749999999
Root Mean Squared Error for 20 estimators: 64.93201637097064
```

Now, run the same model with `n_estimators=200`

Output:

```
Mean Absolute Error for 200 estimators: 48.33899999999999
Mean Squared Error for 200 estimators: 3494.2330150000003
Root Mean Squared Error for 200 estimators: 59.112037818028234
```

With 20 trees, the root mean squared error is 64.93 and for 200 trees, the root mean squared is 59.11. The data clearly shows that as we increase the number of trees, the accuracy also increases.

Important Parameters in Random Forest

The hyperparameters in random forest are either used to increase the predictive power of the model or to make the model faster. Let's look at the hyperparameters of sklearns built-in random forest function.

1. Increasing the predictive power: Firstly, there is the n_estimators hyperparameter, which is just the number of trees the algorithm builds before taking the maximum voting or taking the averages of predictions. In general, a higher number of trees increases the performance and makes the predictions more stable, but it also slows down the computation.

Another important hyperparameter is max_features, which is the maximum number of features random forest considers to split a node. Sklearn provides several options, all described in the documentation. The last important hyperparameter is min_sample_leaf. This determines the minimum number of leafs required to split an internal node.

2. Increasing the model's speed: The n_jobs hyperparameter tells the engine how many processors it is allowed to use. If it has a value of one, it can only use one processor. A value of "-1" means that there is no limit.

The random_state hyperparameter makes the model's output replicable. The model will always produce the same results when it has a definite value of random_state and if it has been given the same hyperparameters and the same training data.

Lastly, there is the oob_score (also called oob sampling), which is a random forest cross-validation method. In this sampling, about one-third of the data is not used to train the model and can be used to evaluate its performance. These samples are called the out-of-bag samples. It's very similar to the leave-one-out-cross-validation method, but almost no additional computational burden goes along with it.

RIDGE, LASSO AND ELASTICNET REGRESSIONS

What are we solving here

We have seen that in the Linear models we are looking to find the best fit line which will pass through the given points such that the line as close as possible to all points, and a similar number of points above and below the line. The distance between the points and the lines, which is calculated as Least Square, is minimum possible. This also means that the residual error is low. The best fit line is given as:

$$Y = mx + c$$

The line has two parameters – y intercept and the slope. We have seen before how to calculate the equation and predict the value of y when a new x is entered. When we have large datapoints we can be confident that the best fit line is infact the best possible solution. But what if we have few training datasets? Look at the example below:

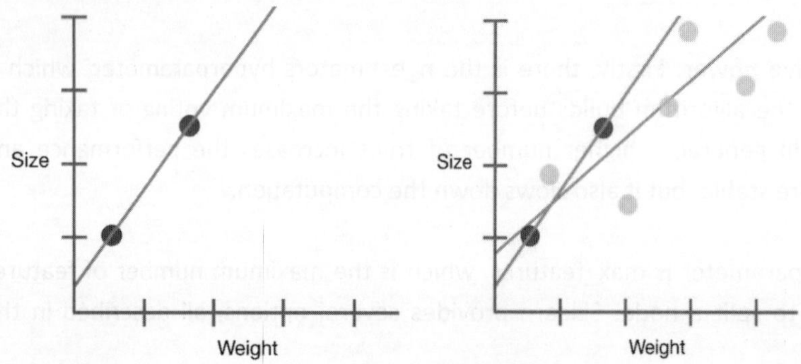

Image A ***Image B***

In the image A, on the left, we have only 2 points and the best fit line will pass trough both the points. The R-squared will be perfect 1, the mean errors will be zero and the sum of squared residuals will also be zero. Let's assume these are 2 training data points. The image B has test dataset as well along with the training data. Since the best fit line will be based on the training data, the training accuracy is 100% but the accuracy of the test data will be very low. The sum of residual of image B will be high. The variance of the test data is high.

To handle such problems with llinear models, we have regularized models which creates a penalty to the training model so it doesn't fit the model so well in training but in test scenario, it does well.

Ridge Regression:

The main idea behind the Ridge regression is to find a new line that doesn't fit the training data well but the accuracy increases in the test data.

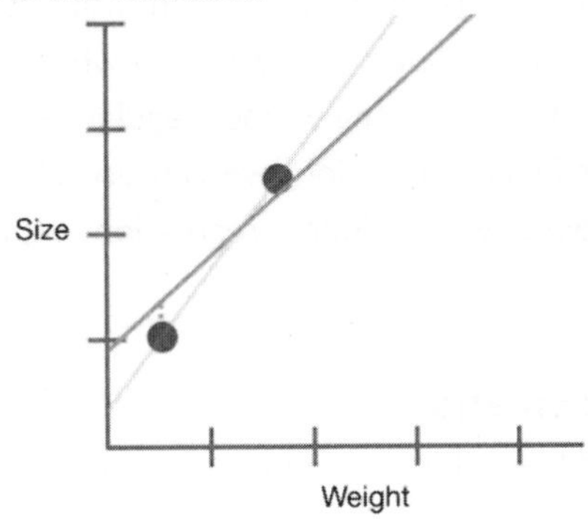

In other words, we introduce small bias into how the new line (Ridge regression line) is fit to the data, resulting in low variance. So by starting with worse fit, Ridge regression can provide a better long term predictions.

Ridge Regression determines the values for the parameters using the below equation:

Y =mx + c + lambda * m square

We are adding a penalty using lambda. Since the lambda is multipled with square of slope.

Lasso Regression

Lasso and Ridge regressions are very similar in the way why we need Lasso Regression. There is one small but very important difference. This can be seen from the below formula:

Y =mx + c + lambda * m

The lambda is multiplied with slope in this case (and not slope square). Lasso and Ridge do similar things (make linear regression prediction less sensitive) and can be applied in same context.

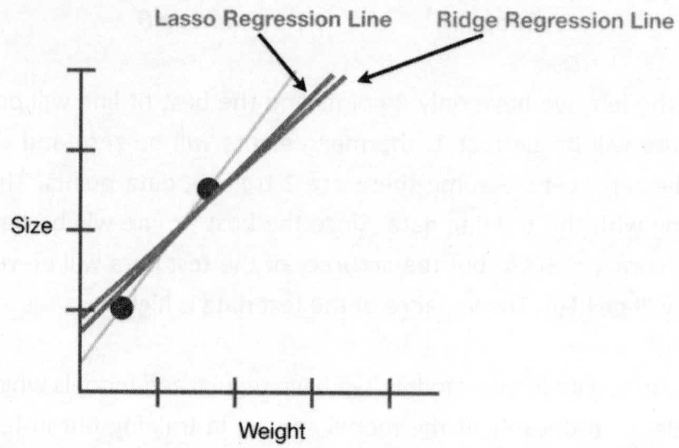

Regularized Regression (Ridge, Lasso & ElasticNet)

As discussed above, linear regression works by selecting coefficients for each independent variable that minimizes a loss function. However, if the coefficients are too large, it can lead to model over-fitting on the training dataset. Such a model will not generalize well on the unseen data. To overcome this shortcoming, we do regularization which penalizes large coefficients. The following sections of the guide will discuss the various regularization algorithms. When we are not sure whether to use Lasso or Ridge regression, we can use Elastic Net regression . Elastic net combines Lasso regression penalty and Ridge regression penalty to the Linear Regression equation.

Linear Regression Implementation

Before we jump into Ridge and Lasso, let's run and see the Linear Regression result.

Problem Statement

A school wants to research the impact of study, playing and watching TV on the total marks obtained in the board exam. In these examples, we will try to build regression algorithms for predicting marks of a student given the number of hours per week a student spend in studying at home, playing outdoor games and watching TV or Mobile inside home.

The data used in this project is randomly generated and has 32 rows and 4 columns, as described below:

- StudyHrs - number of hours per week, a student studies at home apart from school time
- PlayHrs - number of hours per week, a student play outdoor games
- WatchTVHrs - number of hours per week, a student watches TV
- Scores - Total percentage of marks obtained in the board exam (dependent variable).

Data Snapshot (available at Github)

StudyHrs	PlayHrs	WatchTVHrs	Scores
2.5	5	12.2	21
5.1	8.9	9.7	47
3.2	7.4	11.7	27
8.5	18	5.6	75
3.5	6	12.2	30
4.6	9.9	10	45
5.5	13	7.9	57

Evaluation Metrics

We will evaluate the performance of the models using two metrics - R-squared value and Root Mean Squared Error (RMSE). Ideally, lower RMSE and higher R-squared values are indicative of a good model.

Let's run the Regression algorithm

Based on our discussion, to show large Bias and low variance, only 10% of the dataset will be marked at Training test. We are doing this just to show you a large difference in the values.

```
#Step 1: Loading the Required Libraries and Modules
import pandas as pd
import numpy as np
from sklearn import model_selection
from sklearn.linear_model import LinearRegression
from sklearn.linear_model import Ridge
from sklearn.linear_model import Lasso
from sklearn.linear_model import ElasticNet
from sklearn.metrics import r2_score
from sklearn.model_selection import train_test_split
from sklearn.metrics import mean_squared_error
from math import sqrt

#Step 2: Reading the Data and Performing Basic Data Checks
data =
pd.read_csv('https://raw.githubusercontent.com/swapnilsaurav/Da
taset/master/student_scores_multi.csv')
print(data.shape)
print(data.describe())

#Feature Scaling and Categorical Value are not required
#If we had to do it, it would have been same as the we been
doing with
```

```
#other dataset so far in this chapter

#Step 3: divides data into attributes and labels:
X = data.iloc[:, 0:3].values
y = data.iloc[:, 3].values
#Step 4: Preparing Data For Training
from sklearn.model_selection import train_test_split
X_train, X_test, y_train, y_test = train_test_split(X, y,
test_size=0.90, random_state=0)

#Step 5: Build, Predict and Evaluate the Regression Model
#In order to fit the linear regression model, the first step
# is to instantiate the algorithm that is done in the
# first line of code below. The second line
# fits the model on the training set.
lr = LinearRegression()
#Step 6:
lr.fit(X_train, y_train)
pred_train_lr= lr.predict(X_train)
print("Linear Regression - Training Set MSE:
",np.sqrt(mean_squared_error(y_train,pred_train_lr)))
print("Linear Regression - Training Set R-Squared:
",r2_score(y_train, pred_train_lr))

pred_test_lr= lr.predict(X_test)
print("Linear Regression - Test Set MSE:
",np.sqrt(mean_squared_error(y_test,pred_test_lr)))
print("Linear Regression - Test Set R-Squared:
",r2_score(y_test, pred_test_lr))

print("Linear Regression - Difference in R-Squared:
",r2_score(y_train, pred_train_lr) - r2_score(y_test,
pred_test_lr))
```

Output:

```
(32, 4)

       StudyHrs    PlayHrs  WatchTVHrs     Scores
count 32.000000  32.000000   32.000000  32.000000
mean   5.115625  10.731250    8.931250  54.187500
std    2.275977   4.345442    3.258679  24.323674
min    1.100000   5.000000    0.200000  17.000000
25%    3.275000   6.925000    7.000000  30.000000
50%    5.100000   9.950000    9.750000  54.500000
75%    6.900000  14.250000   11.700000  75.250000
max    9.200000  18.100000   13.400000  95.000000
Linear Regression - Training Set MSE:  1.7404671430534633e-14
Linear Regression - Training Set R-Squared:  1.0
Linear Regression - Test Set MSE:  12.94676998863744
Linear Regression - Test Set R-Squared:  0.6759756178810061
Linear Regression - Difference in R-Squared:  0.32402438211899387
```

The R-squared value for training set is very high. It is 92%. Comparatively the Test Set R-squared value is low, which is 71.4%

Ridge Regression

Ridge regression is an extension of linear regression where the loss function is modified to minimize the complexity of the model. This modification is done by adding a penalty parameter that is equivalent to the square of the magnitude of the coefficients.

Loss function = OLS + alpha * summation (squared coefficient values)

In the above loss function, alpha is the parameter we need to select. A low alpha value can lead to over-fitting, whereas a high alpha value can lead to under-fitting.

Let's see the implementation using Python

```
#In scikit-learn, a ridge regression model is constructed by
using the Ridge class.
rr = Ridge(alpha=0.5)
rr.fit(X_train, y_train)
pred_train_rr= rr.predict(X_train)
print("Ridge Regression - Training Set MSE:
",np.sqrt(mean_squared_error(y_train,pred_train_rr)))
print("Ridge Regression - Training Set R-Squared:
",r2_score(y_train, pred_train_rr))
pred_test_rr= rr.predict(X_test)
print("Ridge Regression - Test Set MSE:
",np.sqrt(mean_squared_error(y_test,pred_test_rr)))
print("Ridge Regression - Test Set R-Squared:
",r2_score(y_test, pred_test_rr))
print("Ridge Regression - Difference in R-Squared:
",r2_score(y_train, pred_train_rr) - r2_score(y_test,
pred_test_rr))
```

Output:

```
Ridge Regression - Training Set MSE:  0.9698148189065298
Ridge Regression - Training Set R-Squared:  0.998918366081429
Ridge Regression - Test Set MSE:  11.530578872808876
Ridge Regression - Test Set R-Squared:  0.7429858418568864
Ridge Regression - Difference in R-Squared:  0.2559325242245426
```

Lasso Regression

Lasso regression, or the Least Absolute Shrinkage and Selection Operator, is also a modification of linear regression. In Lasso, the loss function is modified to minimize the complexity of the model by limiting the sum of the absolute values of the model coefficients (also called the l1-norm).

The loss function for Lasso Regression can be expressed as below:

Loss function = OLS + alpha * summation (absolute values of the magnitude of the coefficients)

In the above loss function, alpha is the penalty parameter we need to select. Using an l1 norm constraint forces some weight values to zero to allow other coefficients to take non-zero values.

Lets see the implementation using Python

```
#Lasso Regression
model_lasso = Lasso(alpha=0.1)
model_lasso.fit(X_train, y_train)
pred_train_lasso= model_lasso.predict(X_train)
print("Lasso Regression - Training Set MSE: ",np.sqrt(mean_squared_error(y_train,pred_train_lasso)))
print("Lasso Regression - Training Set R-Squared: ",r2_score(y_train, pred_train_lasso))
pred_test_lasso= model_lasso.predict(X_test)
print("Lasso Regression - Test Set MSE: ",np.sqrt(mean_squared_error(y_test,pred_test_lasso)))
print("Lasso Regression - Test Set R-Squared: ",r2_score(y_test, pred_test_lasso))
print("Lasso Regression - Difference in R-Squared: ",r2_score(y_train, pred_train_lasso) - r2_score(y_test, pred_test_lasso))
```

Output:

```
Lasso Regression - Training Set MSE:  0.06166071375982767
Lasso Regression - Training Set R-Squared:  0.9999956276012533
Lasso Regression - Test Set MSE:  9.39515564989084
Lasso Regression - Test Set R-Squared:  0.8293670947710772
Lasso Regression - Difference in R-Squared:  0.1706285328301761
```

ElasticNet Regression

ElasticNet combines the properties of both Ridge and Lasso regression. It works by penalizing the model using both the l2-norm and the l1-norm.

In scikit-learn, an ElasticNet regression model is constructed by using the ElasticNet class. The first line of code below instantiates the ElasticNet Regression with an alpha value of 0.1.

Lets see the implementation using Python

```
#Elastic Net
model_enet = ElasticNet(alpha = 0.1)
model_enet.fit(X_train, y_train)
```

```
pred_train_enet= model_enet.predict(X_train)
print("ElasticNet Regression - Training Set MSE:
",np.sqrt(mean_squared_error(y_train,pred_train_enet)))
print("ElasticNet Regression - Training Set R-Squared:
",r2_score(y_train, pred_train_enet))
pred_test_enet= model_enet.predict(X_test)
print("ElasticNet Regression - Test Set MSE:
",np.sqrt(mean_squared_error(y_test,pred_test_enet)))
print("ElasticNet Regression - Test Set R-Squared:
",r2_score(y_test, pred_test_enet))
print("ElasticNet Regression - Difference in R-Squared:
",r2_score(y_train, pred_train_enet) - r2_score(y_test,
pred_test_enet))
```

Output:

```
ElasticNet Regression - Training Set MSE:  0.44108457670976436
ElasticNet Regression - Training Set R-Squared:  0.9997762585696012
ElasticNet Regression - Test Set MSE:  11.475596620894839
ElasticNet Regression - Test Set R-Squared:  0.745431083469517
ElasticNet Regression - Difference in R-Squared:  0.25434517510008414
```

Discussion

Compare the values:

Models	R-Squared Train	R-Squared Test	Difference
Linear Regression	100%	67.6%	32.4%
Ridge Regression	99.9%	74.3%	25.6%
Lasso Regression	99.99%	82.9%	17.1%
ElasticNet Regression	99.98%	74.5%	25.4%

What do you think about the result? R-Squared of Training dataset decreases in Regularized regressions compared to Linear Regression however the Test results are better than linear result. How to find the best value for lambda? Use cross validation on different combinations of lambda to find the best values.

UNDERFITTING VERSUS OVERFITTING VERSUS BEST FITTING

Underfitting in Machine Learning

When a model fails to capture important distinctions and patterns in the data, so it performs poorly even in training data, that is called underfitting. Underfitting refers to a model that can neither model the training data nor generalize to new data. An underfit machine learning model is not a suitable model and will be obvious as it will have poor performance on the training data.

Taking an example of human learning, when a student is given less amount of training or say complete syllabus is not taught in the class and students dont make an attempt to learn the remaining portion, they are not going to do well in the tests. Similarly, models when not given enough amount of right data to learn, it will fail to capture relevant patterns, leading to less accurate predictions.

Overfitting in Machine Learning

Overfitting refers to a model that models the training data too well. Overfitting happens when a model learns the detail and noise in the training data to the extent that it negatively impacts the performance of the model on new data. This means that the noise or random fluctuations in the training data is picked up and learned as concepts by the model. The problem is that these concepts do not apply to new data and negatively impact the models ability to generalize.

Consider an example, if you provide a student with too many books to read and to get trained on, it is more likely that student will learn so well that in the examination student will not apply her/his mind to solve the problem but write exactly the same content from one of the book. Samething happens with machine learning. Our model matches the training data almost perfectly, so in the test, model can score very high accuracy but will perform poorly in validation and other new data.

Overfitting is more likely with nonparametric and nonlinear models that have more flexibility when learning a target function. As such, many nonparametric machine learning algorithms also include parameters or techniques to limit and constrain how much detail the model learns. For example, decision trees are a nonparametric machine learning algorithm that is very flexible and is subject to overfitting training data. This problem can be addressed by pruning a tree after it has learned in order to remove some of the detail it has picked up.

Out models can suffer from overfitting as they can capture spurious patterns that won't recur in the future (noise), leading to less accurate predictions.

The Bias vs Variance trade-off

The inability of machine learning models to capture the true relationship (while training the model) is called bias. Now when we move to test set. Same model which captures dataset perfectly in training, fails in testing. The error is high in the test dataset, we say the variance is high.

Bias refers to the error due to the model's simplistic assumptions in fitting the data. A high bias means that the model is unable to capture the patterns in the data and this results in under-fitting. Variance refers to the error due to the complex model trying to fit the data. High variance means the model passes through most of the data points and it results in over-fitting the data.

A Good Fit in Machine Learning

Ideally, you want to select a model at the sweet spot between underfitting and overfitting. This is the goal, but is very difficult to do in practice.

To understand this goal, we can look at the performance of a machine learning algorithm over time as it is learning a training data. We can plot both the skill on the training data and the skill on a test dataset we have held back from the training process.

Over time, as the algorithm learns, the error for the model on the training data goes down and so does the error on the test dataset. If we train for too long, the performance on the training dataset may continue to decrease because the model is overfitting and learning the irrelevant detail and noise in the training dataset. At the same time the error for the test set starts to rise again as the model's ability to generalize decreases.

The sweet spot is the point just before the error on the test dataset starts to increase where the model has good skill on both the training dataset and the unseen test dataset.

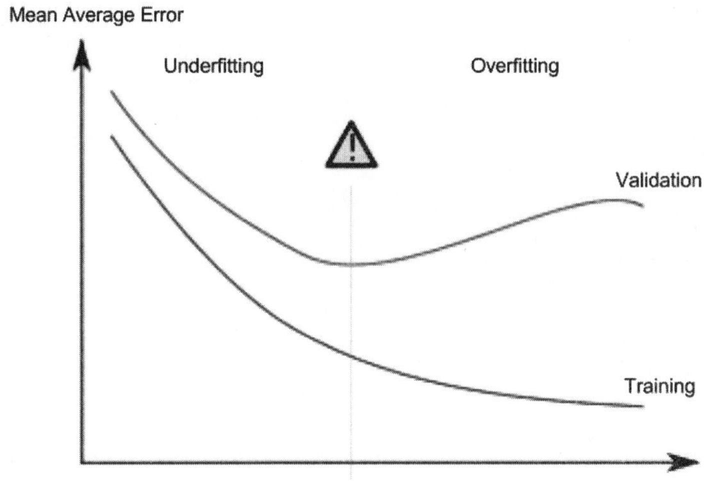

There are two techniques you can use to help find the sweet spot in practice: resampling methods and a validation dataset.

Resampling method: The most popular resampling technique is k-fold cross validation. It allows you to train and test your model k-times on different subsets of training data and build up an estimate of the performance of a machine learning model on unseen data.

Validation dataset: A validation dataset is simply a subset of your training data that you hold back from your machine learning algorithms until the very end of your project. After you have selected and tuned your machine learning algorithms on your training dataset you can evaluate the learned models on the validation dataset to get a final objective idea of how the models might perform on unseen data.

CHOOSING THE RIGHT REGRESSION MODEL

INTERPRETING COEFFICIENT OF REGRESSION

Coefficient of Correlation: Correlation coefficients are used in statistics to measure how strong a relationship is between two variables. There are several types of correlation coefficient: Pearson's correlation (also called Pearson's R) is a correlation coefficient commonly used in linear regression. When anyone refers to the correlation coefficient, they are usually talking about Pearson's.

$$r = \frac{n(\Sigma xy) - (\Sigma x)(\Sigma y)}{\sqrt{[n\Sigma x^2 - (\Sigma x)^2][n\Sigma y^2 - (\Sigma y)^2]}}$$

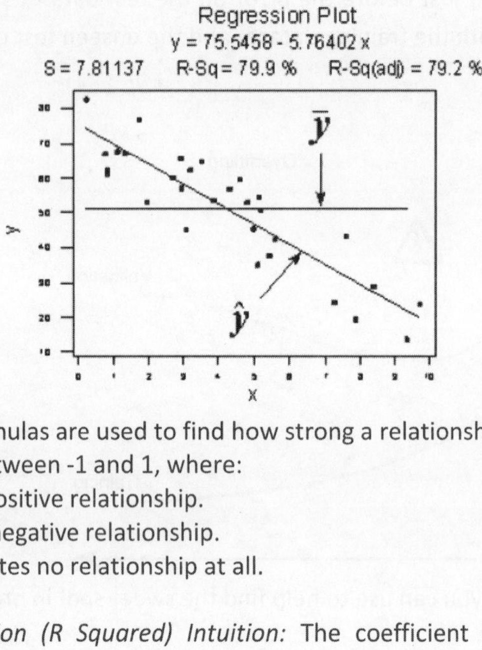

Correlation coefficient formulas are used to find how strong a relationship is between data. The formulas return a value between -1 and 1, where:

- 1 indicates a strong positive relationship.
- -1 indicates a strong negative relationship.
- A result of zero indicates no relationship at all.

Coefficient of Determination (R Squared) Intuition: The coefficient of determination can be thought of as a percent. It gives you an idea of how many data points fall within the results of the line formed by the regression equation. The higher the coefficient, the higher percentage of points the line passes through when the data points and line are plotted. If the coefficient is 0.80, then 80% of the points should fall within the regression line. Values of 1 or 0 would indicate the regression line represents all or none of the data, respectively. A higher coefficient is an indicator of a better goodness of fit for the observations.

$$SS_{res} = SUM\ (y_i - \hat{y}_i)^2$$
$$SS_{tot} = SUM\ (y_i - y_{avg})^2$$

$$R^2 = 1 - \frac{SS_{res}}{SS_{tot}}$$

Two trend lines, one represented by Average (horizontal line) of all the data set and the regression line (slope line) are compared and R squared is calculated as:

1- (Sum of the errors on regression line / Sum of the errors on average line).
2- Can R square be negative? Answer is yes, that's when Average value fits the trend better than regression line.

The usefulness of R2 is its ability to find the likelihood of future events falling within the predicted outcomes. The idea is that if more samples are added, the coefficient would show the probability of a new point falling on the line. Even if there is a strong connection between the two variables, determination does not prove causality.

The Adjusted Coefficient of Determination (Adjusted R-squared) is an adjustment for the Coefficient of Determination that takes into account the number of variables in a data set. It also penalizes you for points that don't fit the model. You might be aware that few values in a data set (a too-small sample size) can lead to misleading statistics, but you may not be aware that too many data points can also lead to problems. Every time you add a data point in regression analysis, R^2 will increase. R^2 never decreases. Therefore, the more points you add, the better the regression will seem to "fit" your data. If your data doesn't quite fit a line, it can be tempting to keep on adding data until you have a better fit. Some of the points you add will be significant (fit the model) and others will not. R^2 doesn't care about the insignificant points. The more you add, the higher the coefficient of determination.

Formula to calculate Adjusted R^2

$$\text{Adj } R^2 = 1 - (1 - R^2)\frac{n-1}{n-p-1}$$

p - number of regressors
n - sample size

The adjusted R^2 can be used to include a more appropriate number of variables, thwarting your temptation to keep on adding variables to your data set. The adjusted R^2 will increase only if a new data point improves the regression more than you would expect by chance. R^2 doesn't include all data points, is always lower than R^2 and can be negative (although it's usually positive). Negative values will likely happen if R^2 is close to zero — after the adjustment, the value will dip below zero a little.

EVALUATING REGRESSION MODELS SPECIFICATION

Model specification is the process of determining which independent variables to include and exclude from a regression equation. How do you choose the best regression model? The world is complicated, and trying to explain it with a small sample doesn't help. Often, the variable selection process is a mixture of statistics, theory, and practical knowledge.

Statistical Methods for Model Specification

We have already discussed about Adjusted R-squared and Predicted R-squared. Typically, we want to select models that have larger adjusted and predicted R-squared values.

P-values for the independent variables: In regression, p-values less than the significance level indicate that the term is statistically significant.

Residual Plots: During the specification process, check the residual plots.

Ultimately, statistical measures can't tell you which regression equation is best. They just don't understand the fundamentals of the subject-area. Your expertise is always a vital part of the model specification process! Choosing the correct regression model is one issue, while choosing the right type of regression analysis for your data is an entirely different matter.

SUMMARY OF TYPES OF REGRESSION MODELS

Regression analysis mathematically describes the relationship between a set of independent variables and a dependent variable. There are numerous types of regression models we have seen but there are more advanced variants. Some of these variants are mentioned here for your knowledge. Choosing the right model often depends on the kind of data you have for the dependent variable and the type of model that provides the best fit. Lets do some revision:

Regression Analysis with Continuous Dependent Variables: Continuous variables are a measurement on a continuous scale, such as weight, time, and length. Some of the examples are:

- Linear regression: Linear regression, also known as ordinary least squares (OLS) and linear least squares, is the real workhorse of the regression world.
- Advanced types of linear regression: OLS has several weaknesses, including a sensitivity to both outliers and multi-collinearity, and it is prone to overfitting. To address these problems, statisticians have developed several advanced variants:
  - Ridge regression allows you to analyze data even when severe multi-collinearity is present and helps prevent overfitting. This type of model reduces the large, problematic variance that multi-collinearity causes by introducing a slight bias in the estimates. The procedure trades away much of the variance in exchange for a little bias, which produces more useful coefficient estimates when multi-collinearity is present.
  - Lasso regression (least absolute shrinkage and selection operator) performs variable selection that aims to increase prediction accuracy by identifying a simpler model. It is similar to Ridge regression but with variable selection.
  - Partial least squares (PLS) regression is useful when you have very few observations compared to the number of independent variables or when your independent variables are highly correlated. PLS decreases the independent variables down to a smaller number of uncorrelated components, similar to Principal Components Analysis. Then, the procedure performs linear regression on these components rather the original data. PLS emphasizes developing predictive models and is not used for screening variables. Unlike OLS, you can include multiple continuous dependent variables. PLS uses the correlation structure to identify smaller effects and model multivariate patterns in the dependent variables.
- Nonlinear regression: Nonlinear regression also requires a continuous dependent variable, but it provides a greater flexibility to fit curves than linear regression.

Regression Analysis with Categorical Dependent Variables: A categorical variable has values that you can put into a countable number of distinct groups based on a characteristic. Logistic regression transforms the dependent variable and then uses Maximum Likelihood Estimation, rather than least squares, to estimate the parameters.

- Binary Logistic Regression: Use binary logistic regression to understand how changes in the independent variables are associated with changes in the probability of an event occurring. This type of model requires a binary dependent variable. A binary variable has only two possible values, such as pass and fail.

- Ordinal Logistic Regression: Ordinal logistic regression models the relationship between a set of predictors and an ordinal response variable. An ordinal response has at least three groups which have a natural order, such as hot, medium, and cold.
- Nominal Logistic Regression: Nominal logistic regression models the relationship between a set of independent variables and a nominal dependent variable. A nominal variable has at least three groups which do not have a natural order, such as scratch, dent, and tear.

Regression Analysis with Count Dependent Variables: If your dependent variable is a count of items, events, results, or activities, you might need to use a different type of regression model. Counts are nonnegative integers.

- Poisson regression: Count data frequently follow the Poisson distribution, which makes Poisson Regression a good possibility. Poisson variables are a count of something over a constant amount of time, area, or another consistent length of observation. With a Poisson variable, you can calculate and assess a rate of occurrence. A classic example of a Poisson dataset is provided by Ladislaus Bortkiewicz, a Russian economist, who analyzed annual deaths caused by horse kicks in the Prussian Army from 1875-1984.
- Alternatives to Poisson regression for count data: Not all count data follow the Poisson distribution because this distribution has some stringent restrictions. Fortunately, there are alternative analyses you can perform when you have count data.
    - Negative binomial regression: Poisson regression assumes that the variance equals the mean. When the variance is greater than the mean, your model has overdispersion. A negative binomial model, also known as NB2, can be more appropriate when overdispersion is present.
    - Zero-inflated models: Your count data might have too many zeros to follow the Poisson distribution. In other words, there are more zeros than the Poisson regression predicts. Zero-inflated models assume that two separate processes work together to produce the excessive zeros. One process determines whether there are zero events or more than zero events. The other is the Poisson process that determines how many events occur, some of which some can be zero.

The knowledge of the regressions we have covered are enough to start performing Machine Learning Regression, as these are the most widely used models. Readers also encouraged to read about other types of regressions to further improve your knowledge about Regression models.

MODEL SELECTION IN REGRESSION

Model specification is the process of determining which independent variables to include and exclude from a regression equation. Often, the variable selection process is a mixture of statistics, theory, and practical knowledge.

The need for model selection often begins when a researcher wants to mathematically define the relationship between independent variables and the dependent variable. Typically, investigators measure many variables but include only some in the model. Analysts try to exclude independent variables that are not related and include only those that have an actual relationship with the dependent variable. During the specification process, the analysts typically try different combinations of variables and various forms of the model. For example, they can try different terms that explain interactions between variables and curvature in the data.

The analysts need to reach a Goldilocks balance by including the correct number of independent variables in the regression equation.

- Too few: Underspecified models tend to be biased.
- Too many: Overspecified models tend to be less precise.
- Just right: Models with the correct terms are not biased and are the most precise.

To avoid biased results, your regression equation should contain any independent variables that you are specifically testing as part of the study plus other variables that affect the dependent variable.

Statistical Methods for Model Specification

You can use statistical assessments during the model specification process. Various metrics and algorithms can help you determine which independent variables to include in your regression equation.

Adjusted R-squared and Predicted R-squared: Typically, you want to select models that have larger adjusted and predicted R-squared values. These statistics can help you avoid the fundamental problem with regular R-squared—it always increases when you add an independent variable. This property tempts you into specifying a model that is too complex, which can produce misleading results.

Adjusted R-squared increases only when a new variable improves the model by more than chance. Low-quality variables can cause it to decrease.

Predicted R-squared is a cross-validation method that can also decrease. Cross-validation partitions your data to determine whether the model is generalizable outside of your dataset.

P-values for the independent variables: In regression, p-values less than the significance level indicate that the term is statistically significant. "Reducing the model" is the process of including all candidate variables in the model, and then repeatedly removing the single term with the highest non-significant p-value until your model contains only significant terms.

Stepwise regression and Best subsets regression: These two automated model selection procedures are algorithms that pick the variables to include in your regression equation. These automated methods can be helpful when you have many independent variables, and you need some help in the investigative stages of the variable selection process.

Real World Complications in the Model Specification Process

- Your best model is only as good as the data you collect. Specification of the correct model depends on you measuring the proper variables. In fact, when you omit important variables from the model, the estimates for the variables that you include can be biased. This condition is known as omitted variable bias.

- The sample you collect can be unusual, either by luck or methodology. False discoveries and false negatives are inevitable when you work with samples.
- Multicollinearity occurs when independent variables in a regression equation are correlated. When multicollinearity is present, small changes in the equation can produce dramatic changes in coefficients and p-values. It can also reduce statistical significance in variables that are relevant. For these reasons, multicollinearity makes model selection challenging.
- If you fit many models during the model selection process, you will find variables that appear to be statistically significant, but they are correlated only by chance. This problem occurs because all hypothesis tests have a false discovery rate. This type of data mining can make even random data appear to have significant relationships!
- P-values, adjusted R-squared, predicted R-squared, and Mallows' Cp can point to different regression equations. Sometimes there is not a clear answer.
- Stepwise regression and best subsets regression can help in the early stages of model specification. However, studies show that these tools can get close to the right answer but they usually don't specify the correct model.

Note to Remember

We evaluate the performance of the model using two metrics - R-squared value and Root Mean Squared Error (RMSE).

R-squared values range from 0 to 1 and are commonly stated as percentages. It is a statistical measure that represents the proportion of the variance for a target variable that is explained by the independent variables. The other commonly used metric for regression problems is RMSE, that measures the average magnitude of the residuals or error. We will be using both these metrics to evaluate the model performance.

Ideally, lower RMSE and higher R-squared values are indicative of a good model.

Packages we have used are:

```
import pandas as pd
import numpy as np
from sklearn import model_selection
from sklearn.linear_model import LinearRegression
from sklearn.linear_model import Ridge
from sklearn.linear_model import Lasso
from sklearn.linear_model import ElasticNet
from sklearn.neighbors import KNeighborsRegressor
from sklearn.tree import DecisionTreeRegressor
from sklearn.svm import SVR
from sklearn.ensemble import RandomForestRegressor
from sklearn.metrics import r2_score
from sklearn.model_selection import train_test_split
from sklearn.metrics import mean_squared_error
```

We end our Regression discussion here and in the next chapter we will see Classification models.

***

UNIT 17: CLASSIFICATION ALGORITHMS

INTRODUCTION

Classification is a process of categorizing a given set of data into classes, It can be performed on both structured or unstructured data. The process starts with predicting the class of given data points. The classes are often referred to as target, label or categories.

The classification predictive modeling is the task of approximating the mapping function from input variables to discrete output variables. The main goal is to identify which class/category the new data will fall into.

Let us try to understand this with a simple example. Heart disease detection can be identified as a classification problem, this is a binary classification since there can be only two classes i.e has heart disease or does not have heart disease. The classifier, in this case, needs training data to understand how the given input variables are related to the class. And once the classifier is trained accurately, it can be used to detect whether heart disease is there or not for a particular patient.

We use the training dataset to get better boundary conditions that could be used to determine each target class. Once the boundary conditions are determined, the next task is to predict the target class. The whole process is known as classification.

Target Class Examples:

- Analysis of the customer data to predict whether he will buy computer accessories (Target class: Yes or No)
- Classifying fruits from features like color, taste, size, weight (Target classes: Apple, Orange, Cherry, Banana)
- Gender classification from hair length (Target classes: Male or Female)

Since classification is a type of supervised learning, even the targets are also provided with the input data. Let us get familiar with the classification in machine learning terminologies.

Classification Terminologies In Machine Learning

- Classifier – It is an algorithm that is used to map the input data to a specific category.
- Classification Model – The model predicts or draws a conclusion to the input data given for training, it will predict the class or category for the data.
- Feature – A feature is an individual measurable property of the phenomenon being observed.
- Binary Classification – It is a type of classification with two outcomes, for eg – either true or false.

- Multi-Class Classification – The classification with more than two classes, in multi-class classification each sample is assigned to one and only one label or target.
- Multi-label Classification – This is a type of classification where each sample is assigned to a set of labels or targets.
- Initialize – It is to assign the classifier to be used for the
- Train the Classifier – Each classifier in sci-kit learn uses the fit(X, y) method to fit the model for training the train X and train label y.
- Predict the Target – For an unlabeled observation X, the predict(X) method returns predicted label y.
- Evaluate – This basically means the evaluation of the model i.e classification report, accuracy score, etc.

Types Of Learners In Classification

Lazy Learners – Lazy learners simply store the training data and wait until a testing data appears. The classification is done using the most related data in the stored training data. They have more predicting time compared to eager learners. Eg – k-nearest neighbor, case-based reasoning.

Eager Learners – Eager learners construct a classification model based on the given training data before getting data for predictions. It must be able to commit to a single hypothesis that will work for the entire space. Due to this, they take a lot of time in training and less time for a prediction. Eg – Decision Tree, Naive Bayes, Artificial Neural Networks.

Python implementation of Classification problems

Let's create a template which can be used by the different algorithms. We will be use a same dataset for different algorithms so that at the end we can compare the accuracy of each of the models.

Steps are explained within the program:

```
# Classification template
# Importing the libraries
import numpy as np
import matplotlib.pyplot as plt
import pandas as pd
# Importing the dataset
dataset =
pd.read_csv('https://raw.githubusercontent.com/swapnilsaurav/Ma
chineLearning/master/5_Ads_Success.csv')
X = dataset.iloc[:, [2, 3]].values
y = dataset.iloc[:, 4].values

# Splitting the dataset into the Training set and Test set
from sklearn.model_selection import train_test_split
```

```
X_train, X_test, y_train, y_test = train_test_split(X, y,
test_size = 0.25, random_state = 0)
# Feature Scaling
from sklearn.preprocessing import StandardScaler
sc = StandardScaler()
X_train = sc.fit_transform(X_train)
X_test = sc.transform(X_test)

# Fitting classifier to the Training set
# Create your classifier here
#classifier = classification model to be built
# Predicting the Test set results
y_pred = classifier.predict(X_test)

# Making the Confusion Matrix
from sklearn.metrics import classification_report,
confusion_matrix, accuracy_score
cm = confusion_matrix(y_test, y_pred)
print("Confusion Matrix: \n",cm)
cr = classification_report(y_test,y_pred)
print("Classification Report: \n",cr)
acc_score = accuracy_score(y_test, y_pred)
print("Accuracy Score: ",acc_score)

# Visualising the Training set results
from matplotlib.colors import ListedColormap
X_set, y_set = X_train, y_train
X1, X2 = np.meshgrid(np.arange(start = X_set[:, 0].min() - 1,
stop = X_set[:, 0].max() + 1, step = 0.01),
                     np.arange(start = X_set[:, 1].min() - 1,
stop = X_set[:, 1].max() + 1, step = 0.01))

plt.contourf(X1, X2, classifier.predict(np.array([X1.ravel(),
X2.ravel()]).T).reshape(X1.shape),
             alpha = 0.75, cmap = ListedColormap(('red',
'green')))

plt.xlim(X1.min(), X1.max())
plt.ylim(X2.min(), X2.max())

for i, j in enumerate(np.unique(y_set)):
    plt.scatter(X_set[y_set == j, 0], X_set[y_set == j, 1],
                color = ListedColormap(('red', 'green'))(i),
label = j)

plt.title('Classifier (Training set)')
plt.xlabel('Age')
plt.ylabel('Estimated Salary')
```

```
plt.legend()
plt.show()

# Visualising the Test set results
from matplotlib.colors import ListedColormap
X_set, y_set = X_test, y_test
X1, X2 = np.meshgrid(np.arange(start = X_set[:, 0].min() - 1,
stop = X_set[:, 0].max() + 1, step = 0.01),
                     np.arange(start = X_set[:, 1].min() - 1,
stop = X_set[:, 1].max() + 1, step = 0.01))
plt.contourf(X1, X2, classifier.predict(np.array([X1.ravel(),
X2.ravel()]).T).reshape(X1.shape),
             alpha = 0.75, cmap = ListedColormap(('red',
'green')))
plt.xlim(X1.min(), X1.max())
plt.ylim(X2.min(), X2.max())
for i, j in enumerate(np.unique(y_set)):
    plt.scatter(X_set[y_set == j, 0], X_set[y_set == j, 1],
                c = ListedColormap(('red', 'green'))(i),
label = j)
plt.title('Classifier (Test set)')
plt.xlabel('Age')
plt.ylabel('Estimated Salary')
plt.legend()
plt.show()
```

SUPPRT VECTOR MACHINE CLASSIFIER

In this algorithm, we plot each data item as a point in n-dimensional space (where n is a number of features you have) with the value of each feature being the value of a particular coordinate. For example, if we only had two features like Height and Hair length of an individual, we'd first plot these two variables in two-dimensional space where each point has two coordinates (these coordinates are known as Support Vectors). Now, we will find some line that splits the data between the two differently classified groups of data. This will be the line such that the distances from the closest point in each of the two groups will be farthest away.

In the example shown on the next page, the line which splits the data into two differently classified groups is the middle line, since the two closest points are the farthest apart from the line. This line is our classifier. Then, depending on where the testing data lands on either side of the line, that's what class we can classify the new data as.

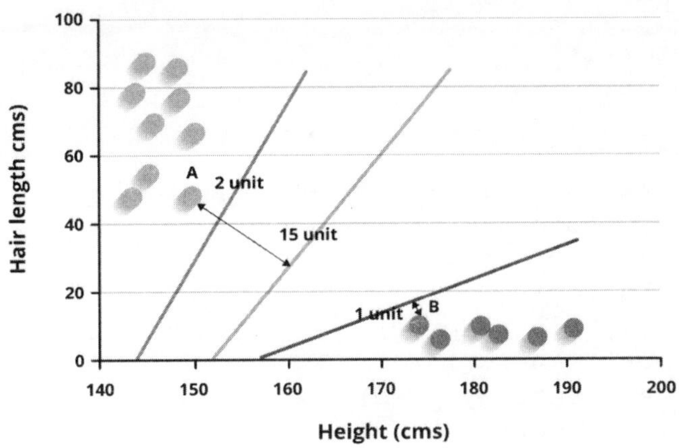

The most basic way to use a SVC is with a linear kernel, which means the decision boundary is a straight line (or hyperplane in higher dimensions). Linear kernels are rarely used in practice, however since it is the most basic version of SVC, let's check this.

Using Linear Kernel Values:

```
# Support Vector Machine (SVM)

# Importing the libraries
import numpy as np
import matplotlib.pyplot as plt
import pandas as pd

# Importing the dataset
dataset = 
pd.read_csv('https://raw.githubusercontent.com/swapnilsaurav/Ma
chineLearning/master/5_Ads_Success.csv ')
X = dataset.iloc[:, [2, 3]].values
y = dataset.iloc[:, 4].values

# Splitting the dataset into the Training set and Test set
from sklearn.model_selection import train_test_split
X_train, X_test, y_train, y_test = train_test_split(X, y, 
test_size = 0.25, random_state = 0)

# Feature Scaling
from sklearn.preprocessing import StandardScaler
sc = StandardScaler()
X_train = sc.fit_transform(X_train)
X_test = sc.transform(X_test)

# Fitting SVM to the Training set
from sklearn.svm import SVC
classifier = SVC(kernel = 'linear', random_state = 0)
```

```
classifier.fit(X_train, y_train)

# Predicting the Test set results
y_pred = classifier.predict(X_test)

# Making the Confusion Matrix
from sklearn.metrics import classification_report,
confusion_matrix, accuracy_score
cm = confusion_matrix(y_test, y_pred)
print("Confusion Matrix: \n",cm)
cr = classification_report(y_test,y_pred)
print("Classification Report: \n",cr)
acc_score = accuracy_score(y_test, y_pred)
print("Accuracy Score: ",acc_score)

# Visualising the Training set results
from matplotlib.colors import ListedColormap
X_set, y_set = X_train, y_train
X1, X2 = np.meshgrid(np.arange(start = X_set[:, 0].min() - 1,
stop = X_set[:, 0].max() + 1, step = 0.01),
                     np.arange(start = X_set[:, 1].min() - 1,
stop = X_set[:, 1].max() + 1, step = 0.01))
plt.contourf(X1, X2, classifier.predict(np.array([X1.ravel(),
X2.ravel()]).T).reshape(X1.shape),
             alpha = 0.75, cmap = ListedColormap(('red',
'green')))
plt.xlim(X1.min(), X1.max())
plt.ylim(X2.min(), X2.max())
for i, j in enumerate(np.unique(y_set)):
    plt.scatter(X_set[y_set == j, 0], X_set[y_set == j, 1],
                c = ListedColormap(('red', 'green'))(i),
label = j)
plt.title('SVM (Training set)')
plt.xlabel('Age')
plt.ylabel('Estimated Salary')
plt.legend()
plt.show()

# Visualising the Test set results
from matplotlib.colors import ListedColormap
X_set, y_set = X_test, y_test
X1, X2 = np.meshgrid(np.arange(start = X_set[:, 0].min() - 1,
stop = X_set[:, 0].max() + 1, step = 0.01),
                     np.arange(start = X_set[:, 1].min() - 1,
stop = X_set[:, 1].max() + 1, step = 0.01))
plt.contourf(X1, X2, classifier.predict(np.array([X1.ravel(),
X2.ravel()]).T).reshape(X1.shape),
             alpha = 0.75, cmap = ListedColormap(('red',
```

```
'green')))
plt.xlim(X1.min(), X1.max())
plt.ylim(X2.min(), X2.max())
for i, j in enumerate(np.unique(y_set)):
    plt.scatter(X_set[y_set == j, 0], X_set[y_set == j, 1],
                color = ListedColormap(('red', 'green'))(i),
label = j)
plt.title('SVM (Test set)')
plt.xlabel('Age')
plt.ylabel('Estimated Salary')
plt.legend()
plt.show()
```

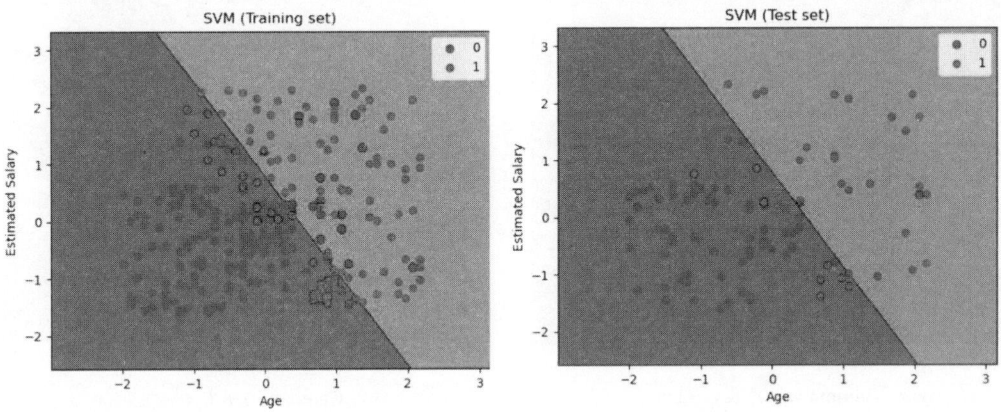


```
Confusion Matrix:
 [[66  2]
 [ 8 24]]
```

Using RBF

Radial Basis Function is a commonly used kernel in SVC:

$$K(\mathbf{x}, \mathbf{x}') = \exp\left(-\frac{||\mathbf{x} - \mathbf{x}'||^2}{2\sigma^2}\right)$$

Let's look at the Python Implementation: Change just the classifier declaration line from the linear SVM model as:

```
from sklearn.svm import SVC
#classifier = SVC(kernel = 'linear', random_state = 0)
classifier = SVC(kernel='rbf', random_state=0, gamma=0.01, C=1)
```

There are two important values in the formula: gamma and c

Gamma

gamma is a parameter of the RBF kernel and can be thought of as the 'spread' of the kernel and therefore the decision region. When gamma is low, the 'curve' of the decision boundary is very low and thus the decision region is very broad. When gamma is high, the 'curve' of the decision boundary is high, which creates islands of decision-boundaries around data points. We will see this very clearly below.

C

C is a parameter of the SVC learner and is the penalty for misclassifying a data point. When C is small, the classifier is okay with misclassified data points (high bias, low variance). When C is large, the classifier is heavily penalized for misclassified data and therefore bends over backwards avoid any misclassified data points (low bias, high variance).

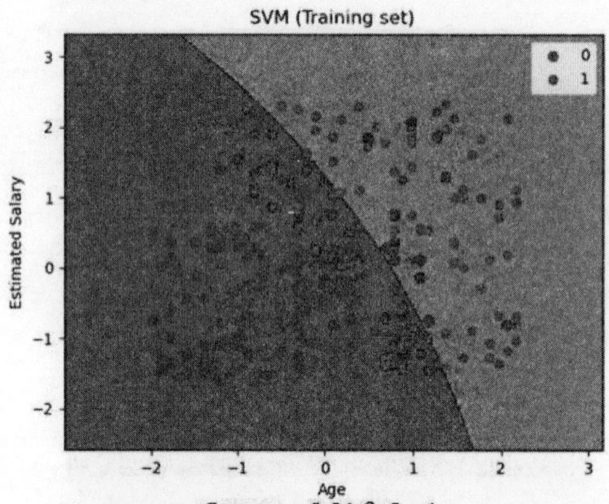

Gamma = 0.01 & C = 1

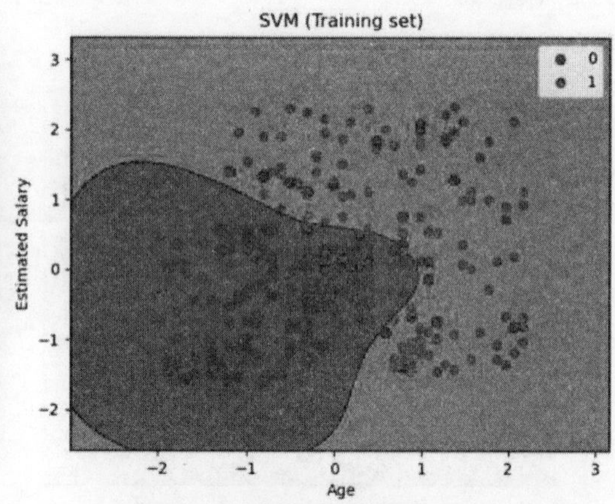

Gamma = 1 & C = 1

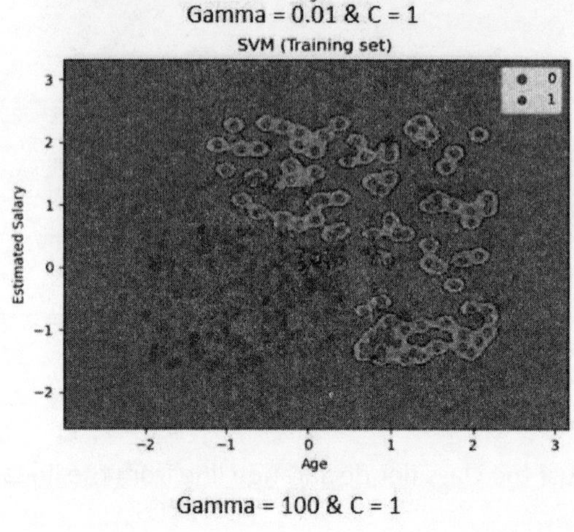

Gamma = 100 & C = 1

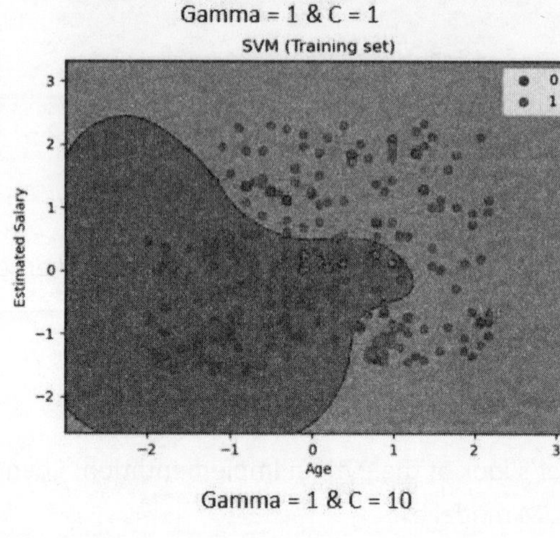

Gamma = 1 & C = 10

Look at the above plots. When we increase the gamma value from 0.01 to 1, keeping the c constsant, we can see a big difference - the decision boundary is starting to better cover the spread of the data. At gamma = 10 the spread of the kernel is less pronounced. The decision boundary starts to be highly effected by individual data points (i.e. variance). With high gamma, the decision boundary is almost entirely dependent on individual data points, creating "islands". This data is clearly overfitted.

Now repeat the same process for C: we will use the same classifier, same data, and hold gamma constant. The only thing we will change is the C, the penalty for misclassification. With C = 1, the classifier is clearly tolerant of misclassified data point. At C = 10, the classifier is less tolerant to misclassified data points and therefore the decision boundary is more severe. When C = 1000, the classifier starts to become very intolerant to misclassified data points and thus the decision boundary becomes less biased and has more variance (i.e. more dependent on the individual data points). At C = 10000, the classifier "works really hard" to not misclassify data points and we see signs of overfitting.

LOGISTIC REGRESSION

Logistic Regression is a classification not a regression algorithm. It is used to estimate discrete values (Binary values like 0/1, yes/no, true/false) based on given set of independent variable(s). In simple words, it predicts the probability of occurrence of an event by fitting data to a logit function. Hence, it is also known as logit regression. Since, it predicts the probability, its output values lie between 0 and 1.

Understanding Logistic Regression

We will be using 5_Ads_Success.csv dataset to work on Logistic Classification. For understanding Logistic Regression, we will look at only one independent variable i.e. Age in this explanation. For the implementation we will take 2 variables – Age and Salary to predict. Plotting Age on x-axis and Purchased on y-axis, we might get a graph as shown below, which indicate that the younger people are more likely not purchase the product but older age group people tend to buy the product.

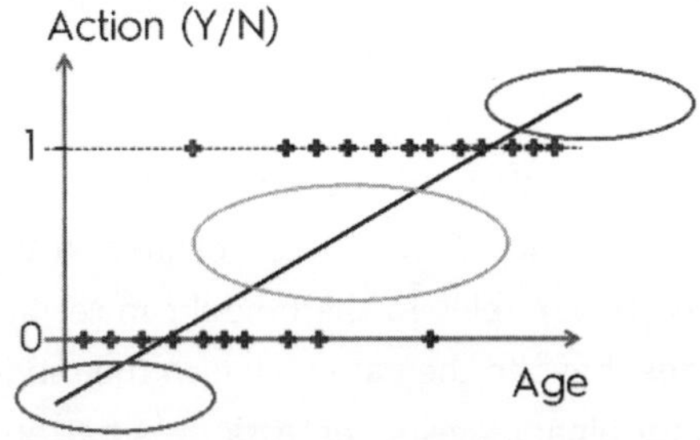

We can draw a regression line as shown above which will divide the data into two sets. However, there are some issues with the regression line. We have only two values possible – Yes/No or probability 1/0. The regression line, we see, extends beyond the limit 0 and 1 which is not possible. To avoid this, we use Sigmoid function as shown in the figure below. A sigmoid function is a mathematical function having a characteristic "S"-shaped curve or sigmoid curve. A sigmoid function is a bounded differentiable real function that is defined for all real input values and has a non-negative derivative at each point.

Another issue with the linear plot is that we will have to find a way to interpret the points of the line between 0 and 1 as the output probability can range from 0 to 1 but the output has to be either 0 or 1. To handle this, we can define our own reference value above which the output will be 1 and below it would be 0. In our example we have use 0.5 as the reference value but remember you can define your own based on the business requirements.

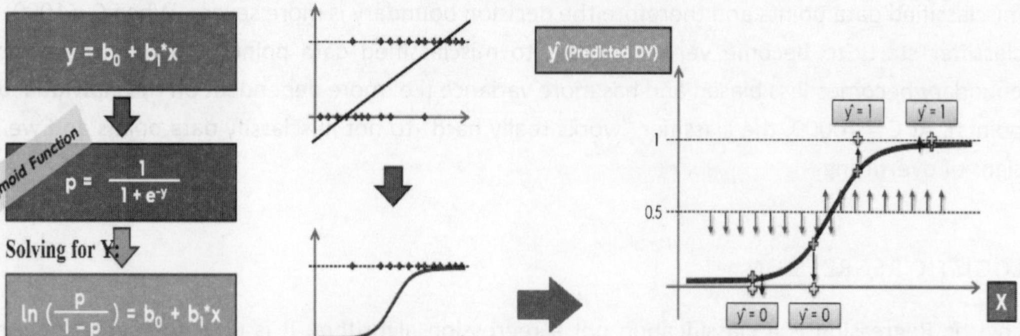

Binary logistic regression major assumptions

- The dependent variable should be dichotomous in nature (e.g., presence vs. absent).
- There should be no outliers in the data, which can be assessed by converting the continuous predictors to standardized scores, and removing values below -3.29 or greater than 3.29.
- There should be no high correlations (multicollinearity) among the predictors. This can be assessed by a correlation matrix among the predictors. Tabachnick and Fidell (2013) suggest that as long correlation coefficients among independent variables are less than 0.90 the assumption is met.
- At the center of the logistic regression analysis is the task estimating the log odds of an event. Mathematically, logistic regression estimates a multiple linear regression function defined as:

Overfitting: Just like multiple regression, adding independent variables to a logistic regression model will always increase the amount of variance explained in the log odds (expressed as R^2). However, adding more and more variables to the model can result in overfitting, which reduces the generalizability of the model beyond the data on which the model is fit. Numerous pseudo- R^2 values have been developed for binary logistic regression. A better approach is to present any of the goodness of fit tests available: Hosmer-Lemeshow is a commonly used measure of goodness of fit based on the Chi-square test.

Implementing the Logistic Regression

Change the classifier declarion part

```
# Fitting Logistic Regression to the Training set
from sklearn.linear_model import LogisticRegression
classifier = LogisticRegression(random_state = 0)
classifier.fit(X_train, y_train)
```

```
# Predicting the Test set results
y_pred = classifier.predict(X_test)
```

Output:

```
Confusion Matrix:
 [[65  3]
 [ 8 24]]
```

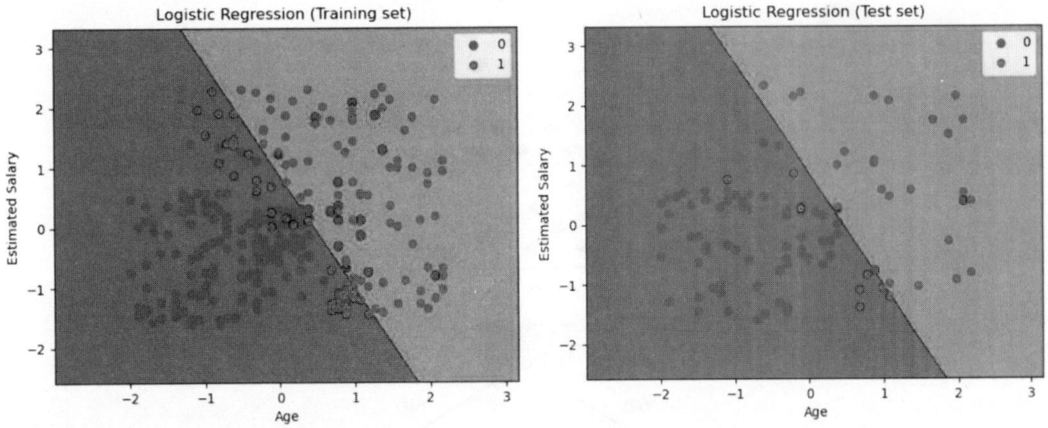

Advantages and Disadvantages

Logistic regression is specifically meant for classification, it is useful in understanding how a set of independent variables affect the outcome of the dependent variable. The main disadvantage of the logistic regression algorithm is that it only works when the predicted variable is binary, it assumes that the data is free of missing values and assumes that the predictors are independent of each other.

Use Cases

- Identifying risk factors for diseases
- Word classification
- Weather Prediction
- Voting Applications

DECISION TREE CLASSIFICATION

Decision Tree concepts have already been discussed under Regression chapter. Readers are advised to refer the concept given there and refresh the knowledge before continuing to work here.

How Decision Tree Classifier works:

The basic idea behind any decision tree algorithm is as follows:

1. Select the best attribute using Attribute Selection Measures (ASM) to split the records.
2. Make that attribute a decision node and breaks the dataset into smaller subsets.

3. Starts tree building by repeating this process recursively for each child until one of the condition will match:
    a. All the tuples belong to the same attribute value.
    b. There are no more remaining attributes.
    c. There are no more instances.

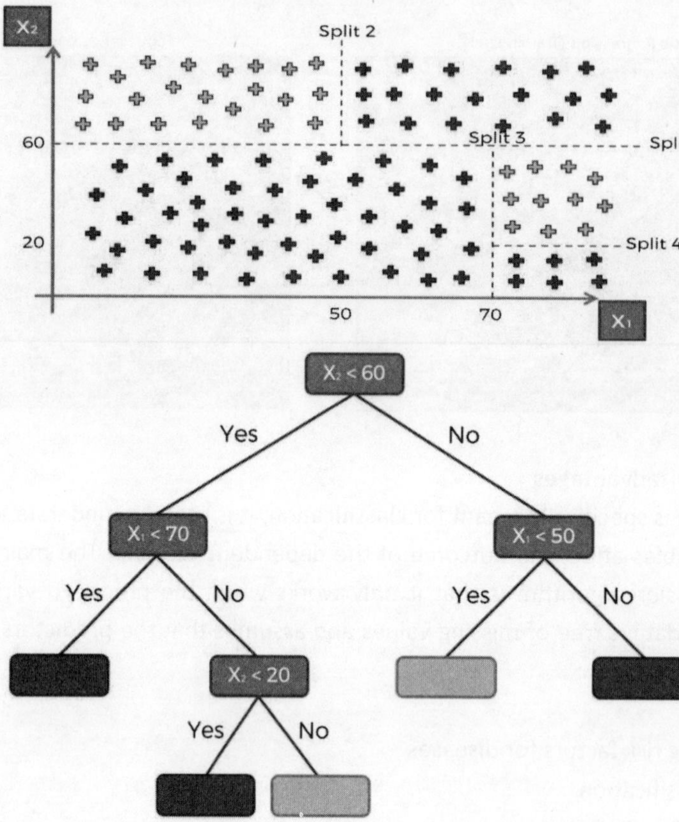

Information Gain

The concept of entropy measures the impurity of the input set. In physics and mathematics, entropy referred as the randomness or the impurity in the system. In information theory, it refers to the impurity in a group of examples. Information gain is the decrease in entropy. Information gain computes the difference between entropy before split and average entropy after split of the dataset based on given attribute values.

Gini index

Another decision tree algorithm CART (Classification and Regression Tree) uses the Gini method to create split points.

$$\text{Gini(D)}=1-\sum_{i=1}^{m} \text{Pi}^2$$

Where, pi is the probability that a tuple in D belongs to class Ci.

The Gini Index considers a binary split for each attribute. You can compute a weighted sum of the impurity of each partition. If a binary split on attribute A partitions data D into D1 and D2, the Gini index of D is:

$$Gini_A(D)=\frac{|D1|}{|D|}Gini(D_1)+\frac{|D2|}{|D|}Gini(D_2)$$

In case of a discrete-valued attribute, the subset that gives the minimum gini index for that chosen is selected as a splitting attribute. In the case of continuous-valued attributes, the strategy is to select each pair of adjacent values as a possible split-point and point with smaller gini index chosen as the splitting point.

$$\Delta Gini(A) = Gini(D) - Gini_A(D).$$

The attribute with minimum Gini index is chosen as the splitting attribute.

Implementation using Python

```
# Fitting Decision Tree Classification to the Training set
from sklearn.tree import DecisionTreeClassifier
classifier = DecisionTreeClassifier(criterion = 'entropy',
random_state = 0)
classifier.fit(X_train, y_train)
```

Optimizing Decision Tree Performance

criterion : optional (default="gini") or Choose attribute selection measure: This parameter allows us to use the different-different attribute selection measure. Supported criteria are "gini" for the Gini index and "entropy" for the information gain.

splitter : string, optional (default="best") or Split Strategy: This parameter allows us to choose the split strategy. Supported strategies are "best" to choose the best split and "random" to choose the best random split.

max_depth : int or None, optional (default=None) or Maximum Depth of a Tree: The maximum depth of the tree. If None, then nodes are expanded until all the leaves contain less than min_samples_split samples. The higher value of maximum depth causes overfitting, and a lower value causes underfitting.

In Scikit-learn, optimization of decision tree classifier performed by only pre-pruning. Maximum depth of the tree can be used as a control variable for pre-pruning. In the following the example, you can plot a decision tree on the same data with max_depth=3. Other than pre-pruning parameters, you can also try other attribute selection measure such as entropy.

Data Visualization in Decision Tree

Print Text Representation

```
from sklearn import datasets
from sklearn.tree import DecisionTreeClassifier
from sklearn import tree
text_representation = tree.export_text(classifier)
print(text_representation)
```

Output:

```
|--- feature_0 <= 0.63
|   |--- feature_1 <= 0.61
|   |   |--- feature_0 <= -0.16
|   |   |   |--- class: 0
|   |   |--- feature_0 > -0.16
|   |   |   |--- feature_1 <= -0.06
|   |   |   |   |--- class: 0
|   |   |   |--- feature_1 >  -0.06
|   |   |   |   |--- feature_1 <= 0.40
|   |   |   |   |   |--- feature_1 <= 0.03
|   |   |   |   |   |   |--- class: 1
|   |   |   |   |   |--- feature_1 >  0.03
```

Plot Tree with *plot_tree*

```
#Visualize with Plot_tree
fig = plt.figure(figsize=(25,20))
_ = tree.plot_tree(classifier,
                   filled=True)
plt.show()
```

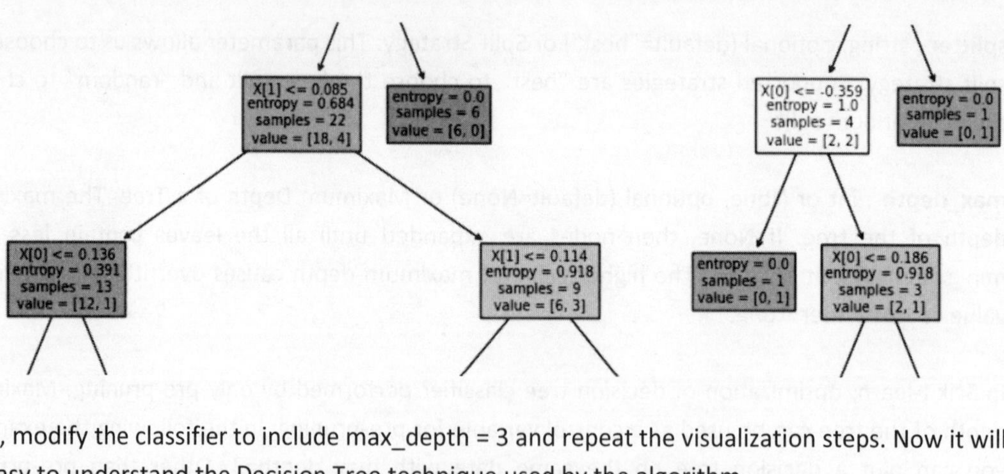

Now, modify the classifier to include max_depth = 3 and repeat the visualization steps. Now it will be easy to understand the Decision Tree technique used by the algorithm.

```
# Fitting Decision Tree Classification to the Training set
from sklearn.tree import DecisionTreeClassifier
classifier = DecisionTreeClassifier(criterion = 'entropy',
random_state = 0, max_depth=3)
```

```
classifier.fit(X_train, y_train)
```

Points to remember:

1. Impurity: Impurity is when we have a traces of one class division into other. This can arise due to following reason
   - We run out of available features to divide the class upon.
   - We tolerate some percentage of impurity (we stop further division) for faster performance. (There is always trade off between accuracy and performance).
2. Entropy: Entropy is degree of randomness of elements or in other words it is measure of impurity.
3. Information Gain: Decision tree at every stage selects the one that gives best information gain. When information gain is 0 means the feature does not divide the working set at all.

RANDOM FOREST CLASSIFICATION

In simple terms, random forest builds multiple decision trees and merges them together to get a more accurate and stable prediction. We have discussed the basic concept of decision tree and random forest in Regression chapter. Readers are advised to read the topic under regression first and then come back here.

Let's understand the concept of classifier with a real life analogy. Virat wants to decide where to go during one-month vacation he has got before the next cricket match series starts. So he asks Rohit who know him best for suggestions. Rohit knows Virat's likes and dislikes of his past travels. Based on the information, he will give Virat some advice. This is a typical decision tree algorithm approach. Rohit created rules to guide his decision about what he should recommend, by using Virat's answers.

Afterwards, Virat starts asking more and more of his friends to advise him and they again ask him different questions they can use to derive some recommendations from. Finally, Virat chooses the places that were recommended the most to him, which is the typical random forest algorithm approach.

Random Forest Classifier is ensemble algorithm. Ensemble algorithms are those which combines more than one algorithms of same or different kind for classifying objects. Random forest classifier creates a set of decision trees from randomly selected subset of training set. It then aggregates the votes from different decision trees to decide the final class of the test object.
Understanding in simple term: Suppose training set is given as: [X1, X2, X3, X4] with corresponding labels as [L1, L2, L3, L4], random forest may create three decision trees taking input of subset for example,

[X1, X2, X3]
[X1, X2, X4]
[X2, X3, X4]

So finally, it predicts based on the majority of votes from each of the decision trees made.
This works well because a single decision tree may be prone to a noise, but aggregate of many decision trees reduce the effect of noise giving more accurate results. Alternatively, the random forest can apply weight concept for considering the impact of result from any decision tree. Tree with high error rate are given low weight value and vise versa. This would increase the decision impact of trees with low error rate.

How the Random Forest Algorithm Works

The following are the basic steps involved in performing the random forest algorithm:

1. Pick N random records from the dataset.
2. Build a decision tree based on these N records.
3. Choose the number of trees you want in your algorithm and repeat steps 1 and 2.
4. In case of a regression problem, for a new record, each tree in the forest predicts a value for Y (output). The final value can be calculated by taking the average of all the values predicted by all the trees in forest. Or, in case of a classification problem, each tree in the forest predicts the category to which the new record belongs. Finally, the new record is assigned to the category that wins the majority vote.

Advantages of using Random Forest

- The random forest algorithm is not biased, since, there are multiple trees and each tree is trained on a subset of data. Basically, the random forest algorithm relies on the power of "the crowd"; therefore the overall biasedness of the algorithm is reduced.
- This algorithm is very stable. Even if a new data point is introduced in the dataset the overall algorithm is not affected much since new data may impact one tree, but it is very hard for it to impact all the trees.
- The random forest algorithm works well when you have both categorical and numerical features.
- The random forest algorithm also works well when data has missing values or it has not been scaled well (although we have performed feature scaling in this article just for the purpose of demonstration).

Disadvantages of using Random Forest

- A major disadvantage of random forests lies in their complexity. They required much more computational resources, owing to the large number of decision trees joined together.
- Due to their complexity, they require much more time to train than other comparable algorithms.

Python Implementation

The following are the basic steps involved in performing the random forest algorithm:

Pick N random records from the dataset.

- Build a decision tree based on these N records.
- Choose the number of trees you want in your algorithm and repeat steps 1 and 2.
- In case of a classification problem, each tree in the forest predicts the category to which the new record belongs. Finally, the new record is assigned to the category that wins the majority vote.

Let's practice an example with program:

```
# Fitting Random Forest Classification to the Training set
from sklearn.ensemble import RandomForestClassifier
classifier = RandomForestClassifier(n_estimators = 10,
criterion = 'entropy', random_state = 0)
classifier.fit(X_train, y_train)
```

Evaluating the Algorithm

For classification problems the metrics used to evaluate an algorithm are accuracy, confusion matrix:

```
# Making the Confusion Matrix
from sklearn.metrics import classification_report,
confusion_matrix, accuracy_score
cm = confusion_matrix(y_test, y_pred)
print("Confusion Matrix: \n",cm)
cr = classification_report(y_test,y_pred)
print("Classification Report: \n",cr)
acc_score = accuracy_score(y_test, y_pred)
print("Accuracy Score: ",acc_score)
```

```
Confusion Matrix:
 [[63  5]
 [ 4 28]]
Classification Report:
              precision    recall  f1-score   support

           0       0.94      0.93      0.93        68
           1       0.85      0.88      0.86        32

    accuracy                           0.91       100
   macro avg       0.89      0.90      0.90       100
weighted avg       0.91      0.91      0.91       100

Accuracy Score:  0.91
```

STOCHASTIC GRADIENT DESCENT

Gradient, in plain terms means slope or slant of a surface. So gradient descent literally means descending a slope to reach the lowest point on that surface.

This is an extension of least squares algorithm and Linear Regression. Lets understand what is gradient descent first.

Gradient Descent

When we fit a line in linear regression, we optimize the intercept and the slope. We saw that in the logistic regression, we optimize the squiggle (the S shaped curved). These are just a few examples of optimization we have seen. There are many more things we optimize. Gradient descent can also optimize all these things and much more that follow least squares method.

Let's take a simple example. We have weight on X-axis and height on Y-axis, as shown below. For simplicity, we take only 3 data points. We draw a best fit line which can be used to predict using following equation:

Predicted height = **Intercept** + **Slope** * Weight

We need to optimize Intercept and Slope. Lets first understand how we can optimize Intercept using Gradient Descent and then we will optimize Intercept and Slope with same logic.

Optimizing Interept for a fixed value of Slope

First, lets take intercept as zero and predict the Height, then slowly increase the values of intercept, keeping the slope constant.

In all the cases, evaluate how well the best fit line fits the data by finding the sum of the squared residuals. In machine learning, sum of the squared is a type of loss function.

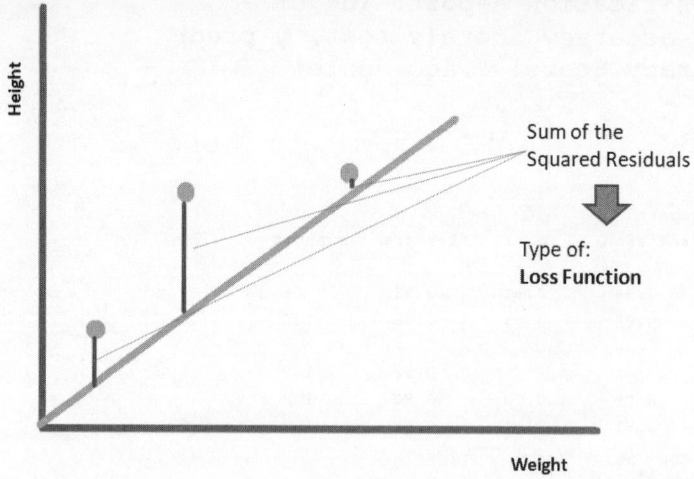

Start calculating the residuals (Observed height – Predicted height) of each point and perform the sum of the squares. In this example, we have 3 datapoints, let's assume we get following residuals: 1.1, 2.4, 0.2, hence:
Sum of squared residuals = $1.1^2 + 2.4^2 + 0.2^2 = 1.21 + 5.76 + 0.04 = 7.01$

Plot this value on a Intercept v Sum of squared residuals. So for intercept = 0, we get sum of squared residual as 7.01. As we keep increasing the values for intercept, the residual values will keep decreasing upto a point and then again it will start increasing:

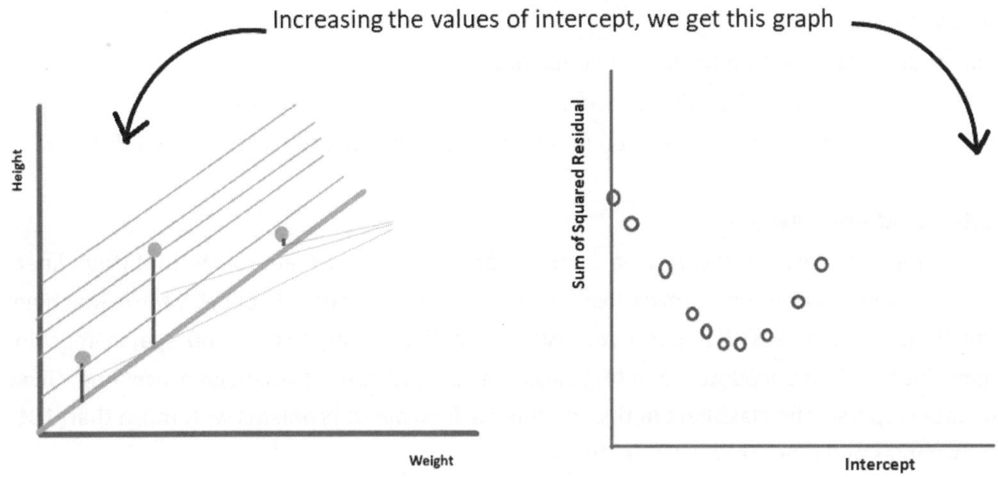

The sum of squared residual and intercept graph will look like a 2 diamensional graph, something like a parabola. We see here that the lowest value of y is where the sum of residual square is lowest. But is it the optimized solution? The gradient descent algorithm is smart enough to optimize the best possible values. Gradient descent only does a few calculations far from the optimal solution and increases the number of calculations closer to the optimal value.

Now, lets talk about how to estimate intercept and slope. We will calculate the loss function for each possible values. This time we get 3-D graph of loss function for different values for the intercept and the slope. The graph would look like a bowl.

The surface of our bowl is called our loss landscape, which is essentially a plot of our loss function. The difference between our loss landscape and your cereal bowl is that your cereal bowl only

exists in three dimensions, while your loss landscape exists in many dimensions, perhaps tens, hundreds, or even thousands of dimensions.
Each position along the surface of the bowl corresponds to a particular loss value given our set of parameters, W (weight matrix) and b (bias vector). Our goal is to try different values of W and b, evaluate their loss, and then take a step towards more optimal values that will (ideally) have lower loss.

Iteratively repeating this process will allow us to navigate our loss landscape, following the gradient of the loss function (the bowl), and find a set of parameters that have minimum loss and high classification accuracy.
The gradient descent algorithm comes in two flavors:

- The standard "vanilla" implementation which we just now discussed
- The optimized "stochastic" version that is more commonly used. Let's discuss this now.

Stochastic Gradient Descent

Stochastic Gradient Descent (SGD) is a simple yet very efficient approach to fitting linear classifiers and regressors under convex loss functions such as (linear) Support Vector Machines and Logistic Regression. SGD has been successfully applied to large-scale and sparse machine learning problems often encountered in text classification and natural language processing. Given that the data is sparse, the classifiers in this module easily scale to problems with more than 10^5 training examples and more than 10^5 features.

Strictly speaking, SGD is merely an optimization technique and does not correspond to a specific family of machine learning models. It is only a way to train a model. Often, an instance of SGDClassifier or SGDRegressor will have an equivalent estimator in the scikit-learn API, potentially using a different optimization technique. For example, using SGDClassifier(loss='log') results in logistic regression, i.e. a model equivalent to LogisticRegression which is fitted via SGD instead of being fitted by one of the other solvers in LogisticRegression. Similarly, SGDRegressor(loss='squared_loss', penalty='l2') and Ridge solve the same optimization problem, via different means.

Let's take an example. Suppose we use 23,000 genes to predit if a person will have disease or not using a Logistic Regression. Then we would have 23,000 derivatives to plug the data into. What if we had 1million samples. In that case, we would have to analyze 1 million dataset of 23,000 derivates. Let's say each step takes 1000 steps then imagine how many iterations, we will have to perform! So, for big data Gradient Descent is slow, that's where Stochastic gradient descent comes as a savior. The stochastic gradient descent takes only one data point from many or one point for each group (leaving out duplicates) which makes fewer datapoints to be taken for analysis. So SGD is useful when there are redundancies in the data.

The advantages of Stochastic Gradient Descent are:

- Efficiency.
- Ease of implementation (lots of opportunities for code tuning).

The disadvantages of Stochastic Gradient Descent include:

- SGD requires a number of hyperparameters such as the regularization parameter and the number of iterations.
- SGD is sensitive to feature scaling.

Python code:

```
from sklearn import linear_model
SGDClf = linear_model.SGDClassifier(max_iter = 1000, tol=1e-
3,penalty = "elasticnet")
SGDClf.fit(X_train, y_train)
y_pred = SGDClf.predict(X_test)
```

Where:

max_iter – int, optional, default = 1000 As name suggest, it represents the maximum number of passes over the epochs i.e. training data.
tol – float or none, optional, default = 1.e-3 This parameter represents the stopping criterion for iterations. Its default value is False but if set to None, the iterations will stop when *l*loss > best_loss - tol for n_iter_no_changesuccessive epochs.

Output:

```
[[50  8]
 [ 9 33]]
```

Stochastic Gradient Descent as Regressor

Stochastic Gradient Descent (SGD) regressor basically implements a plain SGD learning routine supporting various loss functions and penalties to fit linear regression models. Scikit-learn provides SGDRegressor module to implement SGD regression.

```
from sklearn import linear_model
SGDReg =linear_model.SGDRegressor(
   max_iter = 1000,penalty = "elasticnet",loss = 'huber',tol =
1e-3, average = True
)
SGDReg.fit(X_train, y_train)
y_pred = SGDReg.predict(X_test)
print("Coefficient: ",SGDReg.coef_)
print("Intercept: ",SGDReg.intercept_)
```

For detail learning on this model, please refer the official documentation page here: https://scikit-learn.org/stable/modules/sgd.html

BOOSTING ALGORITHM

Unlike many ML models which focus on high quality prediction done by a single model, boosting algorithms seek to improve the prediction power by training a sequence of weak models, each compensating the weaknesses of its predecessors.

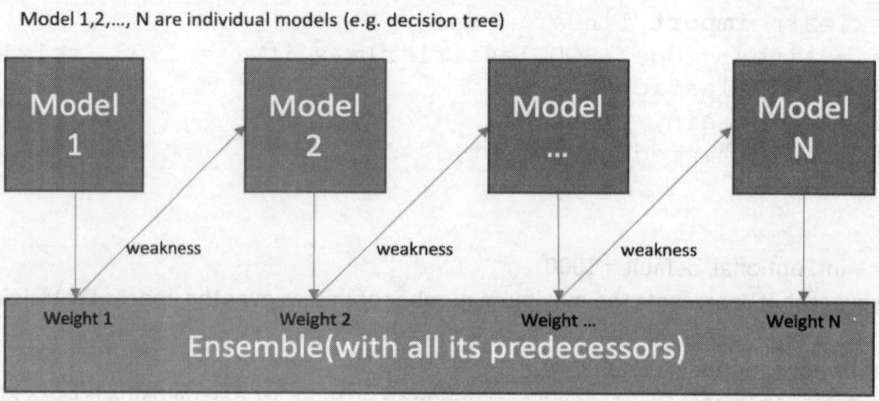

To understand Boosting, it is crucial to recognize that boosting is a generic algorithm rather than a specific model. Boosting needs you to specify a weak model (e.g. regression, shallow decision trees, etc) and then improves it.

With that sorted out, it is time to explore different definitions of weakness and their corresponding algorithms. We will talk about two major algorithms:

- Adaptive Boosting (AdaBoost)
- Gradient Boosting.

AdaBoost

We will use AdaBoost with DecisionTree as that's the most common way to use. Few things to remember:

1. In a Random Forest, each time we create a full sized tress. Some tree might be bigger than others, but there is no predeterminded maximum depth.
2. In contrast, in a Forest of trees made with AdaBoost, the trees are usually just a node with two leaves.

A tree with just one node and 2 leaves is called stump. Stumps are not great at making accurate classifications, as stumps will take only 1 variable to make a decision.

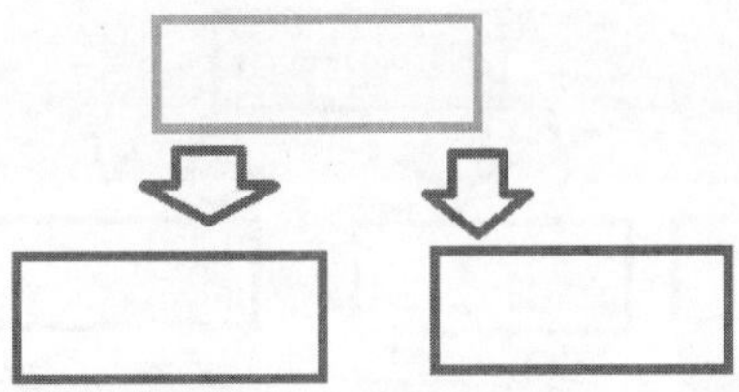

3. So AdaBoost is really a forest of stumps rather than trees and are classified as weak learners – works well for AdaBoost algorithm.
4. In random forest algorithm, each tree votes have same weight hence we take a simple average to find the classification or regression values. In contrast, in a Forest of stumps made with AdaBoost, some stumps get more say in the final classification than others.
5. In random forest, each decision tree is made independently of the other, hence the order in which trees are created doesn't matter. In contrast, in a Forest of stumps, order is important – the error the first stump makes, influences how the second stump is made. And the erros the third stump makes influence how the third stump is made.

Definition of Weakness

AdaBoost is a specific Boosting algorithm developed for classification problems (also called discrete AdaBoost). Let's take below sample dataset. Dataset talks about predicting Heart Disease (Y) based on three attributes (X) – Chest Pain, Blocked Arteries and Patient Weight. To begin with we have to assign a sample weight, since we have 8 rows of data we assign 1/8 weight to all the values. This makes the samples all equally important.

Chest Pain	Blocked Arteries	Patient Weight	Heart Disease	Sample Weight
Yes	Yes	205	Yes	1/8
No	Yes	180	Yes	1/8
Yes	No	210	Yes	1/8
Yes	Yes	167	Yes	1/8
No	Yes	156	No	1/8
No	Yes	125	No	1/8
Yes	No	168	No	1/8
Yes	Yes	172	No	1/8

Creating first stump: First stump is created by finding the variable: Chest Pain (CP), Blocked Arteries (BA) or Patient Weight (PW), that does the best job classifying the samples. We can ignore the weight in step 1 as all the weights are same. Let's create a stump with Chest Pain:

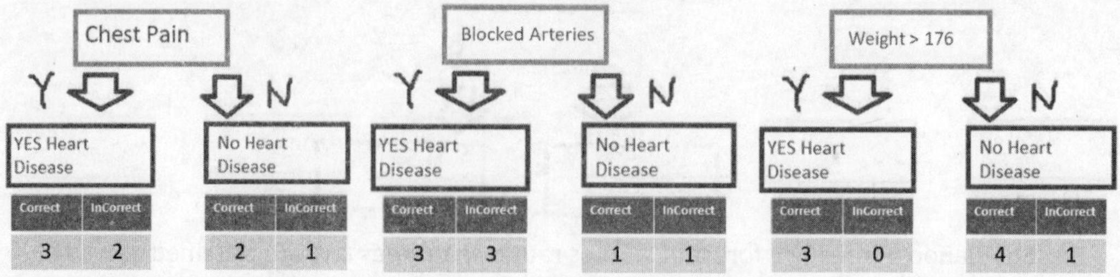

Gini Index	0.47	0.5	0.2

Of the 5 samples with Chest Pain, 3 were correctly classified as Heart Disease and 2 were incorrectly classified as heart disease. On the other hand, of the 3 samples with no Chest Pain, 2 were correctly classified as No Heart Disease and 1 incorrectly as not having heart disease. We repeat the step for Blocked Arteries and Patient Weight. We used DecisionTree technique to find the best weight value to divide the tree.

Calcualte the Gini Index for the 3 stumps: The Gini Index is calculated by subtracting the sum of the squared probabilities of each class (Here: Yes Heart Disease and No Heart Disease) from one. It favors larger partitions.

Formula: $Gini=1-\sum_{i=1}^{C}(p_i)^2$

Gini for Chest Pain: 1 – ((5/8)**2 + (3/8)**2) = 1 – (0.39 + 0.140) = 0.47
Gini for Blocked Arteries: 1 –((4/8)**2+(4/8)**2) = 0.5
Gini for Patient Weight: 1-((7/8)**2 + (1/8)**2) = 1-(0.766+0.016) = 0.2
Note: **2 represents power of 2 (squared value)

Gini index for Patient Weight is the lowest so this will be the first stump in the forest. Next step is to calculate the weight of this stump. The total error for a stump is the sum of the weights associated with the incorrectly classified sample. In this case, it made only 1 incorrect classification (0+1). This, in this case, the total error is 1/8.

Amount of say this stump will have = $\frac{1}{2}\log\left(\frac{1 - \text{Total Error}}{\text{Total Error}}\right)$

When the stump has lower error value, the amount of say will be relative large positive value. If the total error is 0.5, then the amount of say will be 0.
When the total error is 1/8, the amount of say is **0.97**

Now we need to learn how to modify the weights so that the next stump will take the errors that the current stump made into account. In the first attempt, following dataset was incorrectly classified, so now we need to increase its weight so that the next stump will try to classify this correctly and decrease all the other sample weight:

Yes	Yes	167	Yes	1/8

Formula to increase the sample weigt:

$$\text{New Sample Weight} = \text{sample weight} \times e^{\text{amount of say}} = \frac{1}{8} e^{0.97} = \frac{1}{8} \times 2.64 = 0.33$$

Let's understand this better. When the amount of say is relatively large (the previous stump did a good job of classification), then we will scale the previous Sample Weight with a large number. This means the new sample weight will be much larger than the previous weight. When the amount of say is relatively low (last stump didn't do a good job of classifying samples), then the previous Sample Weight is scaled by a relatively small number. This means that the new sample weight will only be a little larger than the previous one.

The incorrectly classified dataset gets get weight of 0.33. Also means rest of the dataset should decrease its weight. We will use below formula (note the decrease sign of amount of say):

$$\text{New Sample Weight} = \text{sample weight} \times e^{-\text{amount of say}} = \frac{1}{8} e^{-\text{amount of say}} = \frac{1}{8} e^{-0.97} = \frac{1}{8} \times 0.38$$

=0.05

The total weight as shown in below table, is not 1 so we need to normalize the weights. To normalize we divide the sample weight by total weight (i.e. 0.68):

Chest Pain	Blocked Arteries	Patient Weight	Heart Disease	Sample Weight	New Weight	Normalized Weight	CumulativeWeight
Yes	Yes	205	Yes	1/8	0.05	0.07	0.07
No	Yes	180	Yes	1/8	0.05	0.07	0.15
Yes	No	210	Yes	1/8	0.05	0.07	0.22
Yes	Yes	167	Yes	1/8	0.33	0.49	0.71
No	Yes	156	No	1/8	0.05	0.07	0.78
No	Yes	125	No	1/8	0.05	0.07	0.85
Yes	No	168	No	1/8	0.05	0.07	0.93
Yes	Yes	172	No	1/8	0.05	0.07	1.00
			Total ->	1	0.68	1.00	

Now, we can use the normalized sample weights to make the second stump in the forest.

In theory we could use the sample weights to calculate the weighted gini indexes to determine which variable should split the next stump. The weigted gini index would put more emphasis on correctly classifying the misclassified dataset by the last stump, since the misclassified dataset has the largest sample weight. Alternatively, instead of using a weighted gini index, we can make a new collection of samples that contains duplicate copies of the samples with the largest sample weights.

We start by making new but empty dataset which is of the same size as the original dataset. We would randomly pick data from the original dataset and put them in the new dataset with replacement, meaning the dataset can be repeated. We randomly pick a number between 0 and 1 and based on the cumulative value from the above table, dataset is picked. For example, if the number is between 0.21 and 0.70, then we would put one with the 0.49 weight (Row #4). We continue the process for 7 more times as we have total of 8 dataset in this example. The rows can be repeated as we will see that the one with higher weight will have more chances of getting picked more than once. Once we have the 8 dataset, we discard the original dataset. This also means with the rows will lower value has maximum chances of getting discarded. Once we have the dataset ready, we begin by giving equal weights to all the dataset again (1/8 value). This doesn't mean that the next stump will not emphasize the need to correctly classify the samples which had the highest weight in previous dataset. Since these values has higher probability of getting repeated in the new dataset, any misclassification of these data would result in higher penalty for being misclassified. Now continue building the stumps.

How does classification of new value is performed?

Divide the stumps into two groups – one which has classified the patient as having the disease and other as the one which classified as No heart disease. Calculate the Amount of say of all the stumps. The group which has the largest value of amount of say will be considered as the class for the new value.

Python Implementation:

```
from sklearn.ensemble import AdaBoostClassifier
classifier = AdaBoostClassifier(n_estimators=4, random_state=0,
algorithm='SAMME')
# fit the model on the whole dataset
classifier.fit(X_train, y_train)
y_pred = classifier.predict(X_test)
```

Gradient Boosting

Gradient boosting is similar to AdaBoost but main difference is Gradient Boost starts by making a single lead, instead of a tree or stump. This lead represents an initial guess for the weights of all the samples.

Implementation for Regressor

In regression, the first step is to predict the average value of all the given variables in Y and then the Gradient Boost builds a tree. Like AdaBoost, this also builds next tree based on the error created by previous tree. These trees are bigger than a stump. We will see example of trees with 4 leaves but in practice, people set the value of leaves between 8 and 32.

Let's look at our dataset:

Height (m)	Favorite Color	Gender	Weight (kg)	Residual
1.6	Blue	Male	88	16.8
1.6	Green	Female	76	4.8
1.5	Blue	Female	56	-15.2
1.8	Red	Male	73	1.8
1.5	Green	Male	77	5.8
1.4	Blue	Female	57	-14.2

We are going to predict Weight of a person based on its Height, Favorite color and Gender.

Step 1 is to calculate the average weight, which is 71.2 in this example. This is the first tree. Next step is to build another tree based on the errors of the first tree. We know that the error is measured by: Observed weight - Predicted weight

We need to calculate the error for each data and add in another column as shown above.

Now we will build a tree using Height, Favorite Color and Gender to predict the residual or the error. In our example, we are allowing upto 4 leaves, so a tree would look like:

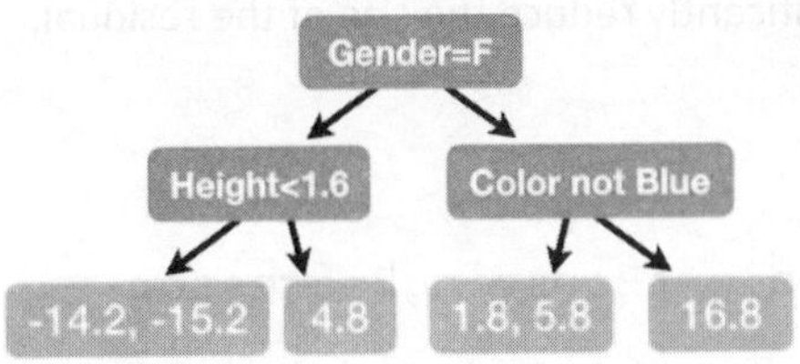

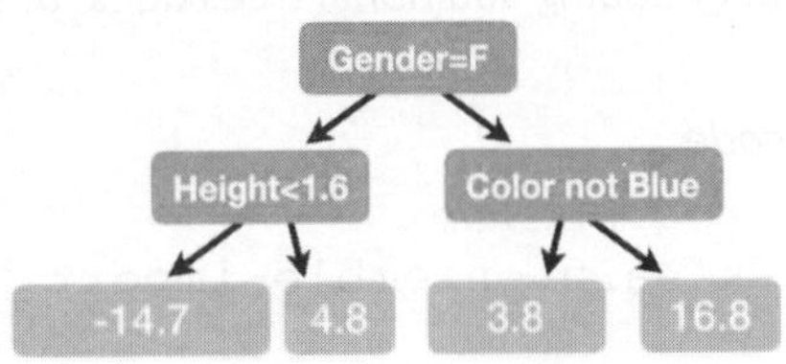

The leaf which has more than 1 value, replaces the value with the average of the data it has.

Based on this we make new predictions to our data. From the tree, we predict the residual so to make the second round of predictions, we add the new residual value to the previously predicted value, which was 71.2.

For the example, H=1.6, C=Blue and Gender M, we get predicted weight as: 71.2 + 16.8 = 88

Exact match, time to be happy? Not yet. This could be because of overfitting, low bias but probably very high variance. To deal with that, Gradiet Boost uses a parameter called as Learning Rate to scale the contribution from the new tree. The Learning Rate value is between 0 and 1.

Let, set Learning Rate to 0.1 , now our predicted weight, for the same example above, will be:

71.2 + 0.1 * 16.8 = 72.9

With the introduction of learning rate, the prediction isn't as good as what we saw earlier, but its still better than our first prediction. Introdution of learning rate is a small step in the right direction.

Let's build another tree. Let's create the updated table with new prediction and calculate the residual value.

Height (m)	Favorite Color	Gender	Weight (kg)	Residual
1.6	Blue	Male	88	15.1
1.6	Green	Female	76	4.3
1.5	Blue	Female	56	-13.7
1.8	Red	Male	73	1.4
1.5	Green	Male	77	5.4
1.4	Blue	Female	57	-12.7

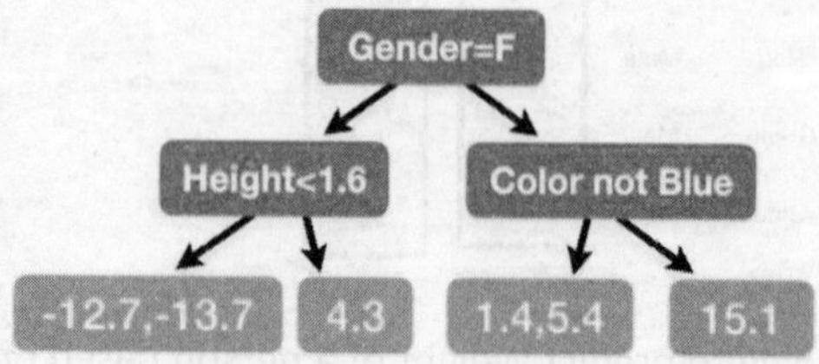

Now we need to make a new tree with the new residual. In this example, the branches are same as before. However, it can be different each time. In this case too, we have ended up with multiple values in the same leaf so we will take average of them. To calculate the new value, we start with the original value and then add the previous residual and now add the residual calculated in this step:

Average weight + Learning Rate * First Tree Result + Learning Rate * Second Tree Result

This takes us a step closer to the actual value. We keep making trees until we reach the maximum specified, or adding additional trees doesnot significantly reduce the size of the residual.

Python code:

```
# for regression
from sklearn.ensemble import GradientBoostingRegressor
model =
GradientBoostingRegressor(n_estimators=3,learning_rate=0.5)
model.fit(X_test,y_train)
```

Implementation for Classifier

For the classifier example, we take the below that to understand the concept:

Likes Popcorn	Age	Favorite Color	Loves Troll 2
Yes	12	Blue	Yes
Yes	87	Green	Yes
No	44	Blue	No
Yes	19	Red	No
No	32	Green	Yes
No	14	Blue	Yes

We have taken the Likes of Popcorn, Age and Favorite color to predict the audience will love Troll2 or not.

In the regressor, we used average value, in Classifier, we use log(odds) as our previous prediction. 4 people loves the movie out of 6 so the initial value is:

Log(4/2) = 0.7 (value upto 4 decimal places: 0.6931)

This is the initial prediction and this is exactly used like Logistic Regression. Just like with Logistic Regression, the easiest way to use the log(odds) for classification is to convert it to a Probability and we do that with a Logistic Function.

Probability of loving troll2 = $\dfrac{e^{\log(\text{odds})}}{1 + e^{\log(\text{odds})}} = \dfrac{e^{\log(4/2)}}{1 + e^{\log(4/2)}} = \boxed{0.7}$

Probability value upto 4 decimal places: 0.6667

Since the probability of Loving Troll 2 is greater than 0.5, we can Classify everyone in the training dataset as someone who loves Troll 2. This is pretty lame because we have 2 dataset which doesn't love the movie.

We can measure how bad the initial prediction is by calculating Pseudo Residuals: Observed – Predicted values.

We will draw this on a graph: The shaded plus and circle signs represent the observed values. Plus indicate those loves the Troll2 and represent probability of 1 and circle indicate those who doesn't love the Troll2 and are represented as probability of 0. The Plus and Circle represent the Observed values and the dotted line represent the Predicted values.

Likes Popcorn	Age	Favorite Color	Loves Troll 2	Residual
Yes	12	Blue	Yes	0.3
Yes	87	Green	Yes	0.3
No	44	Blue	No	-0.7
Yes	19	Red	No	-0.7
No	32	Green	Yes	0.3
No	14	Blue	Yes	0.3

In the residual equation, we put 0 for Observed values of No, 1 for observed value 1 and 0.7 for predicted values. We get residual table as shown above. Now we build a tree, using Likes Popcorn. Age and Favorite color to predict the residuals. Here is the Tree:

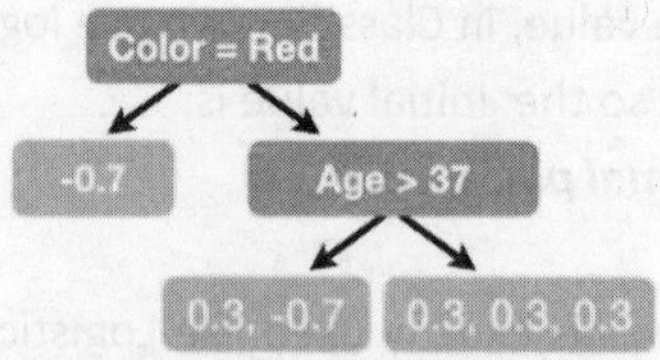

Just like we did for Regression, we will limit the number of leaves that we will allow in the tree. In this example, we will limit the number of leaves to 3. In practical scenario, we limit the number of leaves to be between 8 and 32. Now lets calculate the output values for the leaves. We need to transform the probability value as the predictions are in terms of log and the leaves are derived from a probability. In common practice we use the below formula for the transformation:

$$\frac{\sum \text{Residual}_i}{\sum [\text{Previous Probability}_i \times (1 - \text{Previous Probability}_i)]}$$

i.e sum of residual divided by sum of the product of the previous probability * 1- the same probability.

Let's evaluate each leaf. For the color=Red TRUE [value of -0.7]:

Transformation formula will be Probability from initial step = 0.7, residual from the leave = -0.7. Since the leaf has only 1 value, summation has no meaning here.

$$\frac{-0.7}{0.7 \times (1 - 0.7)} = \boxed{-3.3}$$

Output value for second leaf:

$$\frac{0.3 + -0.7}{(0.7 \times (1 - 0.7)) + (0.7 \times (1 - 0.7))} \quad \frac{0.3 + -0.7}{2(0.7 \times (1 - 0.7))} = -1$$

Output for the third leaf: 1.4

Now we are ready to update our Predictions by combining the initial leaf with the new tree. Just like we did in Regression, the new tree will be scaled by a learning rate. Smaller the learning rate, better will be the result. For our example, let's take a large value just for illustration purpose.

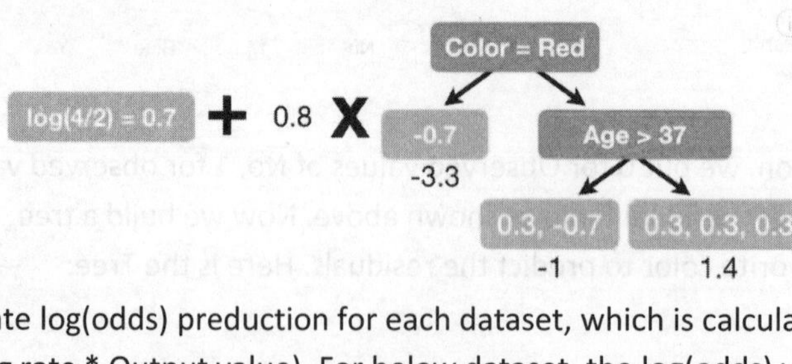

Now, we will calculate log(odds) preduction for each dataset, which is calculated as: Previous prediction +(learning rate * Output value). For below dataset, the log(odds) value will be:

Likes Popcorn	Age	Favorite Color	Loves Troll 2
Yes	12	Blue	Yes

$= 0.7 + (0.8*1.4) = 1.8$

$$\text{Probability} = \frac{e^{1.8}}{1 + e^{1.8}} = 0.9$$

For second data: $\text{log(odds) Prediction} = 0.7 + (0.8 \times -1) = -0.1$

$$\text{Probability} = \frac{e^{-0.1}}{1 + e^{-0.1}} = 0.5$$

Next step is to calculate the residual, just like the previous step but the difference here is that we will use different probability.

Likes Popcorn	Age	Favorite Color	Loves Troll 2	Predicted Prob.	Residual
Yes	12	Blue	Yes	0.9	0.1
Yes	87	Green	Yes	0.5	0.5
No	44	Blue	No	0.5	-0.5
Yes	19	Red	No	0.1	-0.1
No	32	Green	Yes	0.9	0.1
No	14	Blue	Yes	0.9	0.1

Now that we have residual, lets build another tree with 3 leaves:

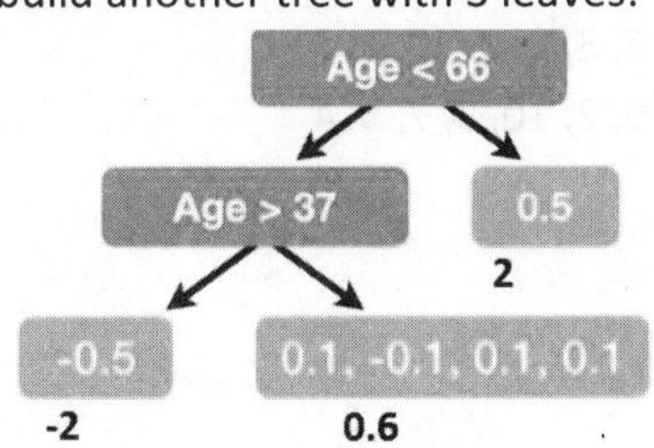

We repeat the complete step till we reach the maximum number of trees specified, or the residual get very very small. When a new value is added then the whole process of going through all the trees we have created is run through. We calculate the final probability and based on the threshold value we can classify the category to which the new value belongs to.

Python Code:

```
# for classification
from sklearn.ensemble import GradientBoostingClassifier
model = GradientBoostingClassifier()
model.fit(X_train,y_train)
```

BAGGING

Bootstrap Aggregation, or Bagging for short, is an ensemble machine learning algorithm that combines the predictions from many decision trees. It is also easy to implement given that it has few key hyperparameters and sensible heuristics for configuring these hyperparameters. Bagging performs well in general and provides the basis for a whole field of ensemble of decision tree algorithms such as the popular random forest and extra trees ensemble algorithms, as well as the lesser-known Pasting, Random Subspaces, and Random Patches ensemble algorithms.

Each base classifier is trained in parallel with a training set which is generated by randomly drawing, with replacement, N examples(or data) from the original training dataset – where N is the size of the original training set. Training set for each of the base classifiers is independent of each other. Many of the original data may be repeated in the resulting training set while others may be left out.

Bagging reduces overfitting (variance) by averaging or voting, however, this leads to an increase in bias, which is compensated by the reduction in variance though. Since Bagging resamples the original training dataset with replacement, some instance(or data) may be present multiple times while others are left out.

Step 1: Build Dataset for different models – Sample with Replacement:
Original training dataset: 1, 2, 3, 4, 5, 6, 7, 8, 9, 10

Resampled training set 1: 2, 3, 3, 5, 6, 1, 8, 10, 9, 1
Resampled training set 2: 1, 1, 5, 6, 3, 8, 9, 10, 2, 7
Resampled training set 3: 1, 5, 8, 9, 2, 10, 9, 7, 5, 4

Bagging Training:

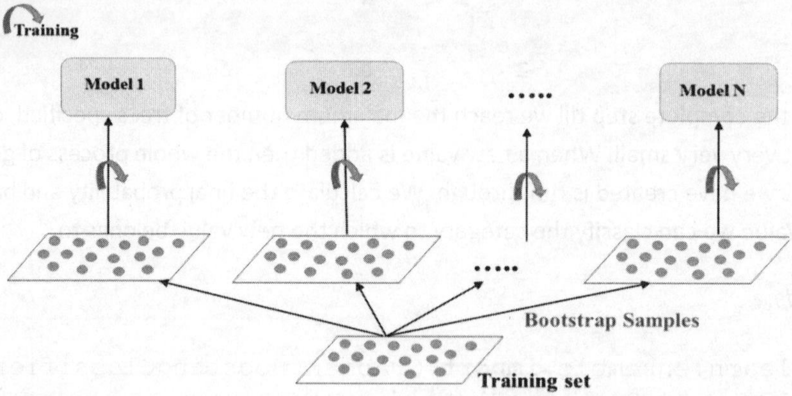

Step 3: Prediction

- Aggregates predictions by majority voting in Classification (BaggingClassifier in scikit-learn).
- Aggregates predictions through averaging in Regression (BaggingRegressor).

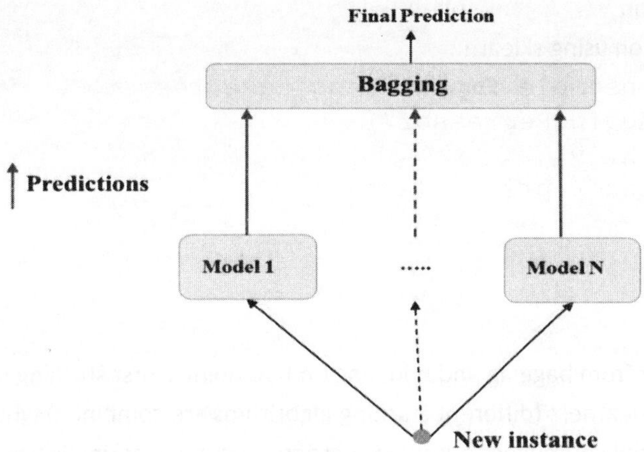

Implementation using Python

Sklearn version should be 0.22.1 or higher. Check the version using:

```
import sklearn
print(sklearn.__version__)
```

Bagging is provided via the BaggingRegressor and BaggingClassifier classes. Both models operate the same way and take the same arguments that influence how the decision trees are created. Randomness is used in the construction of the model. This means that each time the algorithm is run on the same data, it will produce a slightly different model.

Bagging for Classification

Python implementation using sklearn:

```
from sklearn.ensemble import BaggingClassifier
from sklearn.tree import DecisionTreeClassifier
# define the model
base_cls = DecisionTreeClassifier()
num_trees = 100
classifier = BaggingClassifier(base_estimator = base_cls,
                          n_estimators = num_trees,
                          random_state = 1)
# fit the model on the whole dataset
classifier.fit(X_train, y_train)
y_pred = classifier.predict(X_test)
```

Output:

```
Confusion Matrix is:
 [[51  7]
 [ 8 34]]
```

Bagging for Regression

Python implementation using sklearn:

```
from sklearn.ensemble import BaggingRegressor
regressor = BaggingRegressor()
regressor.fit(X, y)
y_pred = regressor.predict(X_test)
```

STACKING

Stacking mainly differ from bagging and boosting on two points. First stacking often considers heterogeneous weak learners (different learning algorithms are combined) whereas bagging and boosting consider mainly homogeneous weak learners. Second, stacking learns to combine the base models using a meta-model whereas bagging and boosting combine weak learners following deterministic algorithms.

For example, for a classification problem, we can choose as weak learners a KNN classifier, a logistic regression and a SVM, and decide to learn a neural network as meta-model. Then, the neural network will take as inputs the outputs of our three weak learners and will learn to return final predictions based on it.

So, assume that we want to fit a stacking ensemble composed of L weak learners. Then we have to follow the steps thereafter:

I. Split the training data in two folds
II. Choose L weak learners and fit them to data of the first fold
III. For each of the L weak learners, make predictions for observations in the second fold
IV. Fit the meta-model on the second fold, using predictions made by the weak learners as inputs

At a high level, we can say that bagging will mainly focus at getting an ensemble model with less variance than its components whereas boosting and stacking will mainly try to produce strong models less biased than their components.

K-NEAREST NEIGHBOR CLASSIFICATION

The K-nearest neighbors (KNN) algorithm is a type of supervised machine learning algorithms. KNN is extremely easy to implement in its most basic form, and yet performs quite complex classification tasks. It is a lazy learning algorithm since it doesn't have a specialized training phase. Rather, it uses all of the data for training while classifying a new data point or instance. KNN is a non-parametric learning algorithm, which means that it doesn't assume anything about the underlying data. This is an extremely useful feature since most of the real world data doesn't really follow any theoretical assumption e.g. linear-separability, uniform distribution, etc.

How the Algorithm works

1. Pick a value for K (i.e. 5).
2. Take the K nearest neighbors of the new data point according to their Euclidean distance.
3. Among these neighbors, count the number of data points in each category and assign the new data point to the category where you counted the most neighbors.

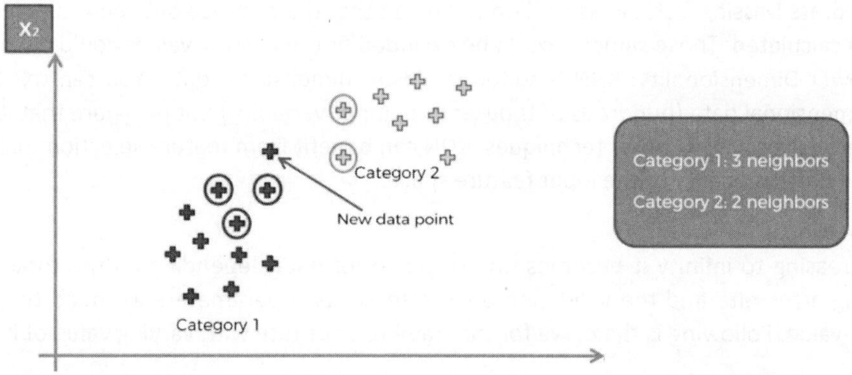

Python Code

```
# Fitting K-NN to the Training set
from sklearn.neighbors import KNeighborsClassifier
classifier = KNeighborsClassifier(n_neighbors = 5, metric =
'minkowski', p = 2)
classifier.fit(X_train, y_train)
```

Evaluating the Algorithm

For classification problems the metrics used to evaluate an algorithm are accuracy, confusion matrix:

```
Confusion Matrix:
 [[64  4]
 [ 3 29]]
Classification Report:
              precision    recall  f1-score   support

           0       0.96      0.94      0.95        68
           1       0.88      0.91      0.89        32

    accuracy                           0.93       100
   macro avg       0.92      0.92      0.92       100
weighted avg       0.93      0.93      0.93       100

Accuracy Score:  0.93
```

Other popular distance measures include:

- Hamming Distance: Calculate the distance between binary vectors (more).
- Manhattan Distance: Calculate the distance between real vectors using the sum of their absolute difference. Also called City Block Distance (more).

- Minkowski Distance: Generalization of Euclidean and Manhattan distance

Best Prepare Data for KNN

- Rescale Data: KNN performs much better if all of the data has the same scale. Normalizing your data to the range [0, 1] is a good idea. It may also be a good idea to standardize your data if it has a Gaussian distribution.
- Address Missing Data: Missing data will mean that the distance between samples can not be calculated. These samples could be excluded or the missing values could be imputed.
- Lower Dimensionality: KNN is suited for lower dimensional data. You can try it on high dimensional data (hundreds or thousands of input variables) but be aware that it may not perform as well as other techniques. KNN can benefit from feature selection that reduces the dimensionality of the input feature space.

How do we choose K factors?

With K increasing to infinity it becomes one single set of data depending on the total majority. The training error rate and the validation error rate are two parameters we need to access on different K-value. Following is the curve for the training error rate with varying value of K:

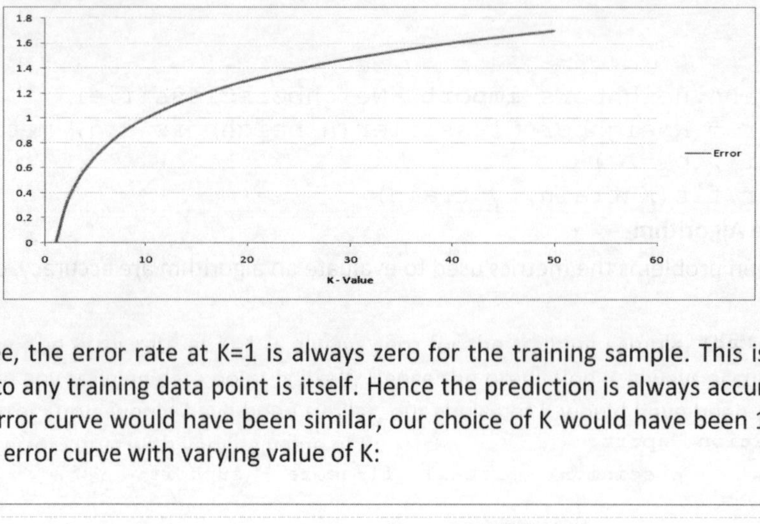

As you can see, the error rate at K=1 is always zero for the training sample. This is because the closest point to any training data point is itself. Hence the prediction is always accurate with K=1. If validation error curve would have been similar, our choice of K would have been 1. Following is the validation error curve with varying value of K:

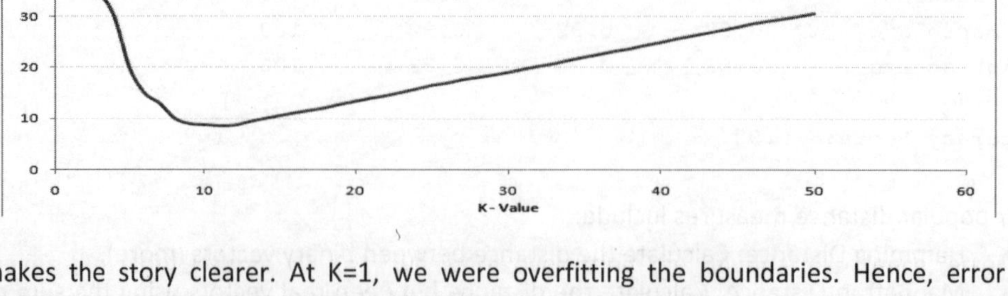

This makes the story clearer. At K=1, we were overfitting the boundaries. Hence, error rate initially decreases and reaches minima. After the minima point, it then increases with increasing K.

To get the optimal value of K, you can segregate the training and validation from the initial dataset. Now plot the validation error curve to get the optimal value of K. This value of K should be used for all predictions.

Curse of Dimensionality

KNN works well with a small number of input variables (p), but struggles when the number of inputs is very large. Each input variable can be considered a dimension of a p-dimensional input space. For example, if you had two input variables x1 and x2, the input space would be 2-dimensional. As the number of dimensions increases the volume of the input space increases at an exponential rate. In high dimensions, points that may be similar may have very large distances. All points will be far away from each other and our intuition for distances in simple 2 and 3-dimensional spaces breaks down. This might feel unintuitive at first, but this general problem is called the "Curse of Dimensionality".

NAÏVE BAYES CLASSIFICATION

This is a classification technique based on an assumption of independence between predictors or what's known as Bayes' theorem. In simple terms, a Naive Bayes classifier assumes that the presence of a particular feature in a class is unrelated to the presence of any other feature.

For example, a fruit may be considered to be an apple if it is red, round, and about 3 inches in diameter. Even if these features depend on each other or upon the existence of the other features, a Naive Bayes Classifier would consider all of these properties to independently contribute to the probability that this fruit is an apple.

Bayes theorem provides a way of calculating posterior probability P(c|x) from P(c), P(x) and P(x|c). The expression for Posterior Probability is as follows:

Likelihood

Class Prior Probability

$$P(c \mid x) = \frac{P(x \mid c)P(c)}{P(x)}$$

Posterior Probability

Predictor Prior Probability

$$P(c \mid X) = P(x_1 \mid c) \times P(x_2 \mid c) \times \cdots \times P(x_n \mid c) \times P(c)$$

Here,

- P(c|x) is the posterior probability of class (target) given predictor (attribute).
- P(c) is the prior probability of class.
- P(x|c) is the likelihood which is the probability of predictor given class.
- P(x) is the prior probability of predictor.

Example: Let's work through an example to understand this better. So, here I have a training data set of weather namely, sunny, overcast and rainy, and corresponding binary variable 'Play'. Now, we need to classify whether players will play or not based on weather conditions. Let's follow the below steps to perform it.

Step 1: Convert the data set to the frequency table
Step 2: Create a Likelihood table by finding the probabilities like Overcast probability = 0.29 and probability of playing is 0.64.
Step 3: Now, use the Naive Bayesian equation to calculate the posterior probability for each class. The class with the highest posterior probability is the outcome of the prediction.

Weather	Play
Sunny	No
Overcast	Yes
Rainy	Yes
Sunny	Yes
Sunny	Yes
Overcast	Yes
Rainy	No
Rainy	No
Sunny	Yes
Rainy	Yes
Sunny	No
Overcast	Yes
Overcast	Yes
Rainy	No

Frequency Table		
Weather	No	Yes
Overcast		4
Rainy	3	2
Sunny	2	3
Grand Total	5	9

Likelihood table				
Weather	No	Yes		
Overcast		4	=4/14	0.29
Rainy	3	2	=5/14	0.36
Sunny	2	3	=5/14	0.36
All	5	9		
	=5/14	=9/14		
	0.36	0.64		

Problem: Players will play if the weather is sunny, is this statement correct?
We can solve it using above discussed method, so P(Yes | Sunny) = P(Sunny | Yes) * P(Yes) / P (Sunny)
Here we have P (Sunny |Yes) = 3/9 = 0.33, P(Sunny) = 5/14 = 0.36, P(Yes)= 9/14 = 0.64
Now, P (Yes | Sunny) = 0.33 * 0.64 / 0.36 = 0.60, which has higher probability.

Naive Bayes uses a similar method to predict the probability of different class based on various attributes. This algorithm is mostly used in text classification and with problems having multiple classes.

How Naïve Bayes theorem
To understand the algorithm, we will use same dataset 5_Ads_Success.csv and select EstimatedSalary and Age as the independent variables to predict Purchase decision.
Step 1: Convert the data into frequency distribution table.
Step 2: Create Likelihood table by finding the probabilities
Step 3: Use Naive Bayesian equation to calculate the posterior probability for each class. The class with the highest posterior probability is the outcome of prediction.
Let's plot the EstimatedSalary on the Y-axis and Age on the X-axis:

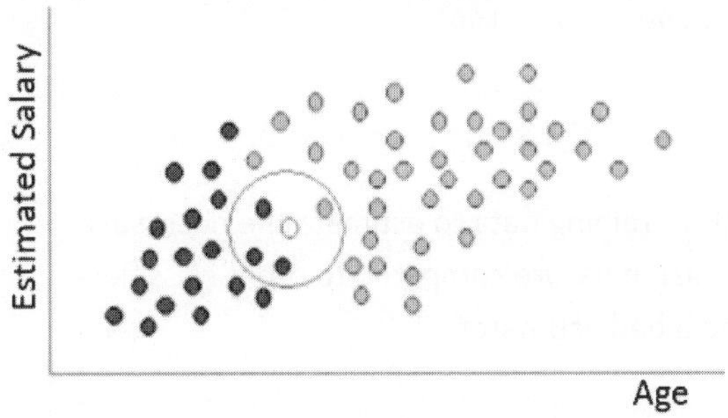

Problem:

- Green circle represents the training set data indicating Purchased
- Red circle represents the training set data indicating NOT Purchased
- White circle is the input data which we need to classify if Purchased or Not.

To measure this likelihood, we draw a circle around X which encompasses a number (to be chosen a priori) of points irrespective of their class labels.

Step 1: To find Posterior probability if Purchased

a. Likelihood that new data is Purchased (look into the circle and ignore Not Purchased) = Similar points / Total points = 1/20
b. Prior Probability of Purchased = Total Green/Total circle = 20/30
c. Predictor Prior Probability of Purchased (We will look into the circle assuming the points in the circle have the same characteristics) = Similar points/Total = 4/30
d. Posterior probability of purchased = a * b / c = 1/20*20/30*30/4 = ¼= 0.25

Step 2: To find Posterior probability if Not Purchased

a. Likelihood that new data is Not Purchased = 3/10
e. Prior Probability of Not Purchased = Total Red/Total circle = 10/30
b. Predictor Prior Probability of Not Purchased = Similar points/Total = 4/30
c. Posterior probability of Not purchased = a * b / c =3/10*10/30*30/4 = ¾=0.75

Step 3: Compare the probabilities

- The new data-point is more likely to exhibit Not Purchased behavior (75%).

```
# Fitting Naive Bayes to the Training set
from sklearn.naive_bayes import GaussianNB
classifier = GaussianNB()
```

```
classifier.fit(X_train, y_train)
```

```
Confusion Matrix:
 [[65  3]
 [ 7 25]]
Classification Report:
              precision    recall  f1-score   support

           0       0.90      0.96      0.93        68
           1       0.89      0.78      0.83        32

    accuracy                           0.90       100
   macro avg       0.90      0.87      0.88       100
weighted avg       0.90      0.90      0.90       100

Accuracy Score:  0.9
```

Advantages and Disadvantages

The Naive Bayes classifier requires a small amount of training data to estimate the necessary parameters to get the results. They are extremely fast in nature compared to other classifiers. The only disadvantage is that they are known to be a bad estimator.

Use Cases:

- Disease Predictions
- Document Classification
- Spam Filters
- Sentiment Analysis

PRINCIPAL COMPONENT ANALYSIS (PCA)

Principal Component Analyis is actually a statistical procedure to convert a set of observation of possibly correlated variables into a set of values of linearly uncorrelated variables to get a better and faster result in the analysis. We call PCA as a dimension reduction process but there is no guarantee that the dimension is interpretable.

Each of the principal components is chosen in such a way so that it would describe most of the still available variance and all these principal components are orthogonal to each other. In all principal components first principal component has maximum variance and we can choose to ignore less significant components from the analysis. Let's take an example and see how PCA reduces attribute space from a large number of variables to a smaller number of factors.

Examplanation

We will look at PCA algorithm one step at a time using Singular Value Decomposition (SVD). This will help us to get deeper insigh into the data. Let's start with a simple dataset, a 2-D dataset – marks obtained in a unit test in two subjects by 6 students of a class. Dataset sample:

	Student 1	Student 2	Student 3	Student 4	Student 5	Student 6
Maths	10	11	8	3	2	1
Science	6	4	5	3	2.8	1

If we measure only 1 subject, we can plot the data in a number line (1D that is). If we take only Maths as the only subject, we can see that the students 4,5 and 6 are similar and have scored low and the students 1,2 and 3 are similar and have scored relatively higher marks.
If we take into account both the values(X), we can ploton X and Y, a graph will something like:

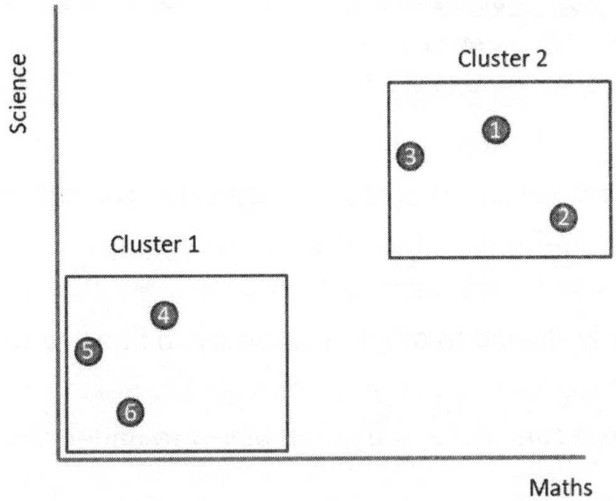

If we measure three variables, we would get a 3D graph. We will discuss higher Dimensions of the graph little later. Our goal is to find which data has more say in the separation of the dataset. It can happen that when we take 4 attributes, only 2 attributes have impact of 90% in that case we can choose to drop two other attributes which are less significant.
Coming back to 2D example here, following steps we follow to arrive at principal components:

Step 1: Plot the graph on the 2D. The number of diamensions will be the minimum of number of attributes or samples. In this case, number of samples is 6 and number of attributes is 2 hence we have 2D graph.

Step 2: Calculate the average measurement for Subject Maths (on X Axis) and Subject Science (Y-axis). Find the Average (X,Y) point on the graph.

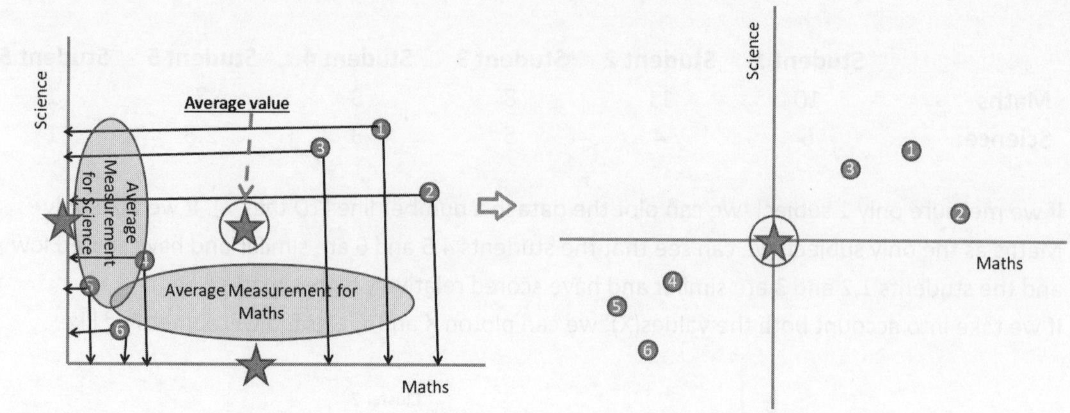

Step 3: Now we will shift the data such that the average value coincide with the origin (0,0). Understand that the relative positions of the data will not change.

Step 4: Now that the center is aligned to origin, we can try to fit a line to it. To get the best fit line, PCA will start by drawing a random line that goes through the origin and then we rotate the line until it fits the data as well is it can. Refer the graph below to understand it better:

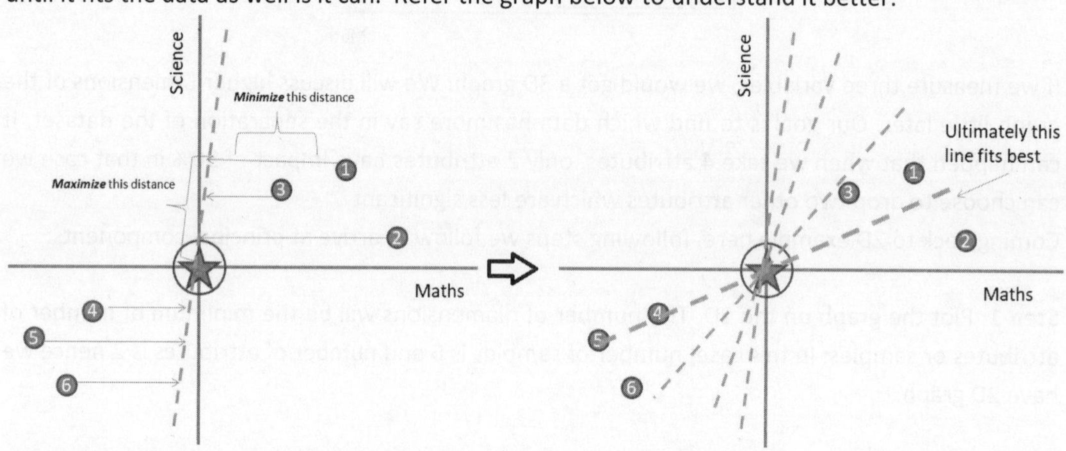

To quantify how good this line fits the data, PCA projects the data onto it and then it can either measure the distances from the data to the line and try to find the line that minimizes those distances or it can try to find the line that maximizes the distances from the projected points to the origin. These two conditions are equivalent. The distance between the line and the point is the perdendicular line, if you look at these two distances in the below figure:

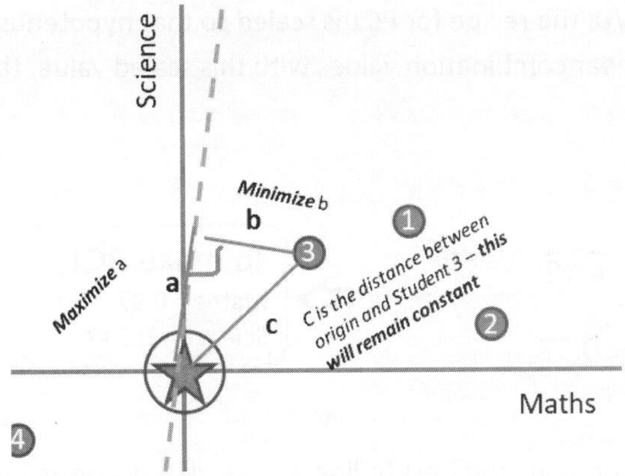

When the line fits better, the line b as shown in above picture shrinks. The line will fit the best if the b takes the smallest possible values (goal is to minimize this distance). As we shrink b, the a will increase. To test this, lets the above picture again. Since b, is perpendicular to the fit line, triangle with sides: a,b and c forms a right angled triangle with c as the hypotenuse. C is the distance between point and the origin which is not going to change. The equation becomes:

$$a^2 + b^2 = c^2$$

We can see that if b decreases, then to keep the value of c unchanged, we have to increase the value of a. So we need to minimize b and maximize a to best fit the line. Let's say we have a1 for datapoint 1, a2 for datapoint 2, ... soon till a6 for datapoint 6.

Step 5: Square all the measured distances to find total distance:

$$\text{Sum of squared distances (SS Distances)} = a1^2 + a2^2 + a3^2 + a4^2 + a5^2 + a6^2$$

We sum up the squared distances from the projected points to the origin. We repeat the process until we end up with the line with the largest sum of squared distances between the projected points and the origin.The best fit line that we end up creating using this technique is called **Principal Component 1** (PC1 for short).

Step 6: Calculate the slope of PC1. In our example, the slope comes to 0.25

Slope = Distance on Y / Distance on X = 0.25 = ¼

In other words, every 4 units that we go out along Maths axis (x-Axis), we go up 1 unit along the Science axis (Y-axis). That means the data are mostly spread out along the Maths axis and only a little bit spread out along the Science axis. The ratio of Maths to Science tells us that Maths is more important when it comes to describe how the students' results are spread out.

The ratio of 4:1 for maths and science is called a "linear combination" of Maths and Science.

Step 7: Scale the values using the linear combination.

Using Pythogorous theorem, we can calculate the hypotenuse: 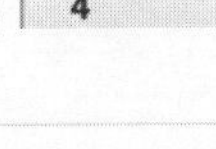

When we do PCA with SVD, the recipe for PC1 is scaled so that hypotenuse length becomes 1. We need to divide the linear combination values with this scaled value, the final numbers will look like:

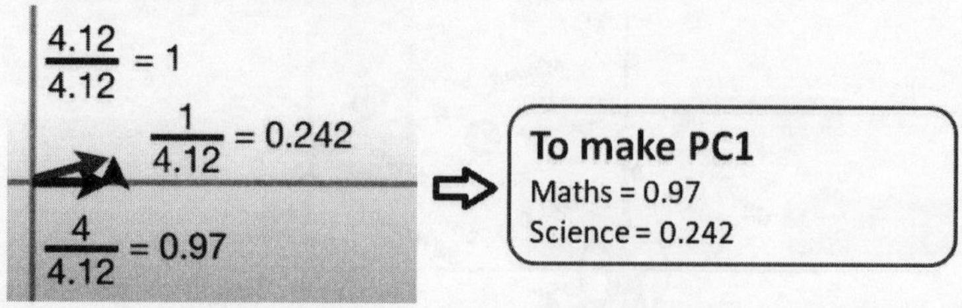

Step 8: The 1 unit of vector along the best fit line we calculated, consisting of 0.97 parts of Maths axis and 0.242 part of Science axis, is called the Singular Vector or the Eigenvector for PC1. The proportion we calculated are called Loading Scores.
The sum of the squared distances for the best fit line is called as Eigenvalue for PC1.
The square root of Eigenvalue for PC1 is called as Singular Value for PC1.

Step 9: Because this is just a 2D graph, the PC2 is simply the line through the origin and is perpendicular to PC1, without any further optimization that has to be done.

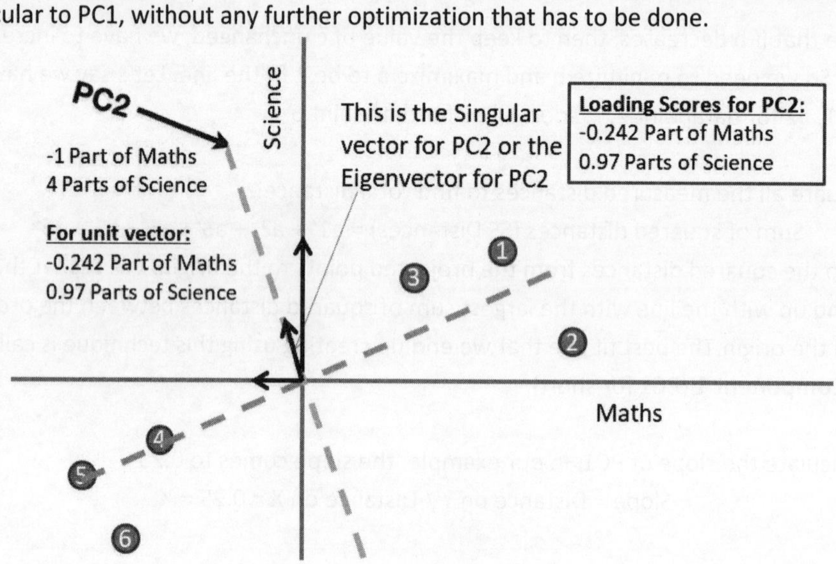

This tells us that, in terms of how the values are projected onto PC2, Science axis is 4 times more important than Maths axis.

The Eigenvalue for PC2 is the sum of squares of the distances between the projected points and the origin.

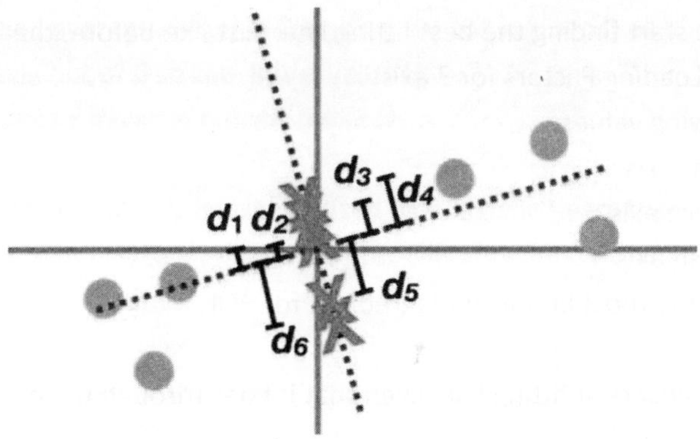

To draw the final PCA plot, we rotate everything so that the PC1 becomes the Horizontal axis and we use the projected points to find where the samples go in the PCA plot. We just completed PCA with Singular Value Decomposition.

Step 10: Let's calculate variation.

$$\frac{\text{SS(distances for PC1)}}{n-1} = \text{Variation for PC1}$$

$$\frac{\text{SS(distances for PC2)}}{n-1} = \text{Variation for PC2}$$

Assume the variation for PC1 = 15 and the variation for PC2=3. So the total variation around both PCs = 15+3 = 18

PC1 accounts for 15/18 = 83% of the total variation around the PCs. PC2 accounts for 17% of the total variation.

Step 11: Draw a Scree plot. A Scree plot is a graphical representation of the percentages of variation that each PCs account for.

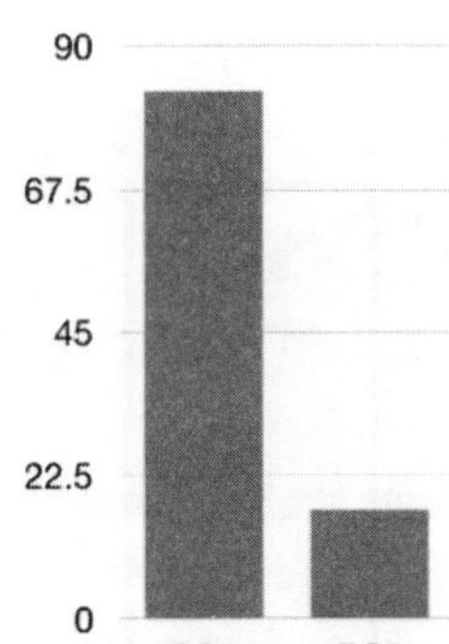

Let's extend this concept for more than 2D. In the next example, we take PCA with 3 variables. Let's introduce marks in English language as well. Now the graph will be a 3D graph. So we center the data to origin. We start finding the best fitting line. Just like before, the best fitting line is PC1. We will calculate the Loading Factors for 3 axis:

Lets say, we get following values:

0.62 for Maths axis
0.15 for Science axis
0.77 for English axis

In this case, English is the most important ingredient for PC1.

We now find PC2, the nest best fitting line given that it goes through the origin and it is perpendicular to PC1.

The loading factors for PC2 now will be:

0.77 for Maths axis
0.62 for Science axis
0.15 for English axis

For PC2, Maths become the most important factor.

Lastly we find PC3, that best fitting line that goes through the origin and is perpendicular to PC1 and PC2. If we have more attributes, we would have just kept on finding more and more principal components by adding perpendicular lines and rotating them. In theory, we have 1 PC per variable but in practical the number of PCs is either the number of variables or the number of samples, whichever is smaller.

Once we have all the principal components figured out, we can use the Eigenvalues (SS Distances) to determine the proportion of variation that each PC accounts for. Let's say, our 3 variable case, PC1 accounts for 79% of the variation, PC2 accounts for 15% of the variation and PC3 accounts for 6% of the variation.

The Screen Plot:

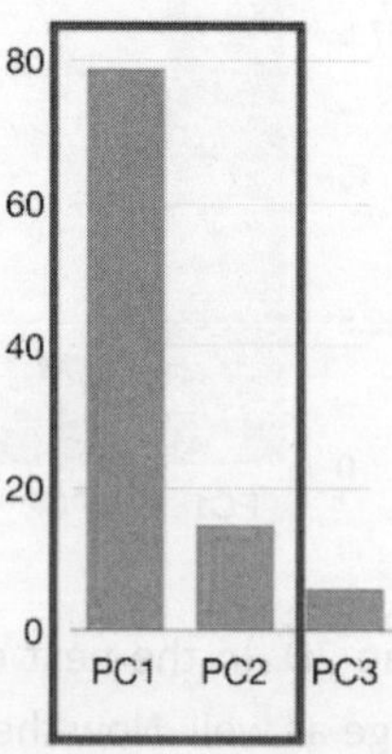

The PC1 and PC2 togather accounts for vast majority of variation. That's means, in this case, a 2D graph just using PC1 and PC2 would be a good approximation of this 3D graph since, it would account for 94% of the variation of data. To convert 3D to 2D graph, we strip away everything except data and PC1 and PC2. Then project the samples on PC1 and PC2.

Uses of PCA:

- It is used to find inter-relation between variables in the data.
- It is used to interpret and visualize data using Scree plot.
- As number of variables are decreasing it makes further analysis simpler.
- It's often used to visualize genetic distance and relatedness between populations.

Python Implementation

Every step that we do in a Classification algorithms hold true here as well. In our exampl, the preprocessing steps that hav been done till Standard Scaler Feature Scaling holds true. We need to perform additiona step of PCA after Standard Scaler and before we train the model. We will use Logistic Regression along with PCA analysis in the example below:

```
# Applying PCA function on training
# and testing set of X component
from sklearn.decomposition import PCA

pca = PCA(n_components = 2)
X_train = pca.fit_transform(X_train)
X_test = pca.transform(X_test)

explained_variance = pca.explained_variance_ratio_
print("Explained Variance: ", explained_variance)

# Fitting Logistic Regression To the training set
from sklearn.linear_model import LogisticRegression
classifier = LogisticRegression(random_state = 0)
classifier.fit(X_train, y_train)
```

```
Explained Variance:   [0.57095752 0.42904248]
Confusion Matrix:
 [[65  3]
 [ 8 24]]
```

We end our discussion on classification models here. In the next step, lets understand how to select the best classification model.

CHOOSING THE RIGHT CLASSIFICATION ALGORITHM

Let's understand ***False positive and False negative*** concepts. A false positive error, or in short a false positive, commonly called a "false alarm", is a result that indicates a given condition exists, when it does not. For example, in the case of "The Boy Who Cried Wolf", the condition tested for was "is there a wolf near the herd?"; the shepherd at first wrongly indicated there was one, by calling "Wolf, wolf!". A false positive error is a type I error where the test is checking a single condition, and wrongly gives an affirmative (positive) decision.

A false negative error, or in short a false negative, is a test result that indicates that a condition does not hold, while in fact it does. I.e., erroneously no effect has been inferred. An example is a truly guilty prisoner who is acquitted of a crime. The condition "the prisoner is guilty" holds (the prisoner is guilty). But the test (a trial in a court of law) failed to realize this, and wrongly decided the prisoner was not guilty, falsely concluding a negative about the condition. A false negative error is a type II error occurring in a test where a single condition is checked for and the result of the test is erroneously that the condition is absent.

Confusion Matrix: A confusion matrix is a table that is often used to describe the performance of a classification model (or "classifier") on a set of test data for which the true values are known. The confusion matrix itself is relatively simple to understand, but the related terminology can be confusing.

n=165	**Predicted: NO**	**Predicted: YES**
Actual: NO	50	10
Actual: YES	5	100

n=165	**Predicted: NO**	**Predicted: YES**	
Actual: NO	TN = 50	FP = 10	60
Actual: YES	FN = 5	TP = 100	105
	55	110	

What can we learn from this matrix?

- There are two possible predicted classes: "yes" and "no". If we were predicting the presence of a disease, for example, "yes" would mean they have the disease, and "no" would mean they don't have the disease.
- The classifier made a total of 165 predictions (e.g., 165 patients were being tested for the presence of that disease).
- Out of those 165 cases, the classifier predicted "yes" 110 times, and "no" 55 times.
- In reality, 105 patients in the sample have the disease, and 60 patients do not.

Let's now define the most basic terms, which are whole numbers (not rates):

- true positives (TP): These are cases in which we predicted yes (they have the disease), and they do have the disease.
- true negatives (TN): We predicted no, and they don't have the disease.
- false positives (FP): We predicted yes, but they don't actually have the disease. (Also known as a "Type I error.")
- false negatives (FN): We predicted no, but they actually do have the disease. (Also known as a "Type II error.")

This is a list of rates that are often computed from a confusion matrix for a binary classifier:

- Accuracy: Overall, how often is the classifier correct?

- (TP+TN)/total = (100+50)/165 = 0.91
- Misclassification Rate: Overall, how often is it wrong?
    - (FP+FN)/total = (10+5)/165 = 0.09
    - equivalent to 1 minus Accuracy
    - also known as "Error Rate"
- True Positive Rate (***Sensitivity***): When it's actually yes, how often does it predict yes?
    - TP/actual yes = 100/105 = 0.95
    - also known as "Sensitivity" or "Recall"
- False Positive Rate: When it's actually no, how often does it predict yes?
    - FP/actual no = 10/60 = 0.17
- ***Specificity***: When it's actually no, how often does it predict no?
    - TN/actual no = 50/60 = 0.83
    - equivalent to 1 minus False Positive Rate
- ***Precision***: When it predicts yes, how often is it correct?
    - TP/predicted yes = 100/110 = 0.91
- ***Prevalence***: How often does the yes condition actually occur in our sample?
    - actual yes/total = 105/165 = 0.64

Accuracy Paradox

n=200	Predicted: NO	Predicted: YES
Actual: NO	25	65
Actual: YES	10	100

Classification model based solution
Accuracy =125/200 = 60.25%

n=200	Predicted: NO	Predicted: YES
Actual: NO	0	35
Actual: YES	0	165

No model used, default Prediction is YES
Predicted Yes for all values
Accuracy = 165/200 = 82.5%

In the above example, the second table gives better accuracy which doesn't use any model instead predicts YES for all data. This shouldn't have been the case. Hence we can not rely on just accuracy metric. This is a good time to introduce few other terms:

Positive Predictive Value: This is very similar to precision, except that it takes prevalence into account. In the case where the classes are perfectly balanced (meaning the prevalence is 50%), the positive predictive value (PPV) is equivalent to precision.

$$\text{PPV} = \frac{\text{number of true positives}}{\text{number of true positives} + \text{number of false positives}} = \frac{\text{number of true positives}}{\text{number of positive calls}} = \frac{\text{sensitivity} \times \text{prevalence}}{\text{sensitivity} \times \text{prevalence} + (1 - \text{specificity}) \times (1 - \text{prevalence})}$$

The complement of the PPV is the false discovery rate (FDR): 1-PPV

Cumulative Accuracy Profile (CAP) Curve: Imagine that you as a data scientist work in a company that want to promote its new product so they will send an email with their offer to all the customers and usually 10% of the customer responses and actually buys the product so they though that that will be the case for this time and that scenario is called the Random Scenario.
Inspect your historical data and take a group of customers who actually bought the offer and try to extract those information [browsing device type (mobile or laptop), Age, Salary, Savings].

Measure those factors and try to discover which of them affects the number of Purchased products or in other words fit the data to a Logistic Regression model. Make a prediction of which customers are more likely to purchase the product. Then by measuring the response of those targeted group represented in that curve 'CAP Curve'.

We definitely can notice the improvement; when you contacted 20,000 targeted customers you got about 5,000 positive responses where in scenario#1 by contacting the same number of customers, you got only 2,000 positive responses.

The idea here is to compare your model to the random scenario and you can take it to the next level by building another model maybe a Support Vector Machine (SVM)/ Kernel SVM model to compare it with your current logistic regression model.

Hypothetically we can draw the so called The Perfect Model which represents a model which is kind of impossible to build unless you have some sort of a Crystal Ball. It shows that when sending the offer to 10,000 possible customers you got a perfect positive response where all contacted people bought the product.

Now let's draw them on the plot.

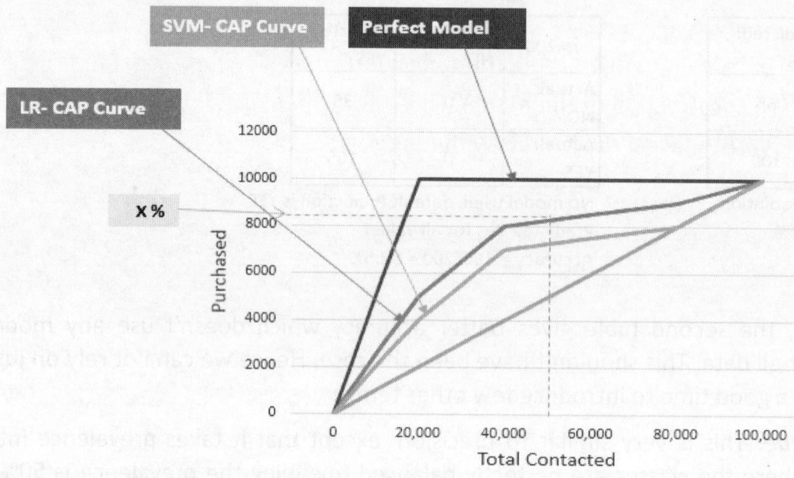

There are 2 approaches to analyze the graph:

First —

- Calculate area under the Perfect Model Curve (aP)
- Calculate area under the Perfect Model Curve (aR)
- Calculate Accuracy rate(AR) = aR/ aP; as (AR)~1 (The better is your model) and as (AR)~0 (The worse is your model)

Second —

- Draw a line from the 50% point (50,000) in the Total Contacted axis up to the Model CAP Curve
- Then from that intersection point, Project it to the Purchased axis
- This X% value represents how good your model is:

- If X < 60% then you have a rubbish model
- If 60% < X < 70% then you have a poor model
- If 70% < X < 80% then you have a good model
- If 80% < X < 90% then you have a very good model
- If 90% < X < 100% then your model is too good to be true! This usually happens due Overfitting which is definitely not a good thing as your model will be good in classifying only the data it is trained on but very poor with new unseen instances.

MODEL EVALUATION

We suggest using following 3 steps process to build and test your models:

1. Need a way to choose between models: different model types, tuning parameters, and features
2. Use a model evaluation procedure to estimate how well a model will generalize to out-of-sample data
3. Requires a model evaluation metric to quantify the model performance

Model evaluation procedures

1. Training and testing on the same data
    a. Rewards overly complex models that "overfit" the training data and won't necessarily generalize
2. Train/test split
    a. Split the dataset into two pieces, so that the model can be trained and tested on different data
    b. Better estimate of out-of-sample performance, but still a "high variance" estimate
    c. Useful due to its speed, simplicity, and flexibility
3. K-fold cross-validation
    a. Systematically create "K" train/test splits and average the results together
    b. Even better estimate of out-of-sample performance
    c. uns "K" times slower than train/test split

Model Evaluation Metric

```
#Pima Indian Diabetes dataset from the UCI Machine Learning
Repository
# read the data into a Pandas DataFrame
import pandas as pd
url =
'https://raw.githubusercontent.com/swapnilsaurav/Dataset/master
/pima-indians-diabetes.csv'
col_names = ['pregnant', 'glucose', 'bp', 'skin', 'insulin',
'bmi', 'pedigree', 'age','label']
pima = pd.read_csv(url, header=None, names=col_names)
# print the first 5 rows of data from the dataframe
print("Dataset:\n",pima.head())
```

```
# label -> 1: diabetes 0: no diabetes
# pregnant -> number of times pregnant

# define X and y
feature_cols = ['pregnant', 'insulin', 'bmi', 'age']

# X is a matrix, hence we use [] to access the features we want
in feature_cols
X = pima[feature_cols]

# y is a vector, hence we use dot to access 'label'
y = pima.label

# split X and y into training and testing sets
from sklearn.model_selection import train_test_split
X_train, X_test, y_train, y_test = train_test_split(X, y,
random_state=0)
# train a logistic regression model on the training set
from sklearn.linear_model import LogisticRegression

# instantiate model
logreg = LogisticRegression()

'''
LogisticRegression(C=1.0, class_weight=None, dual=False,
fit_intercept=True, intercept_scaling=1, max_iter=100,
multi_class='ovr', n_jobs=1, penalty='l2', random_state=None,
solver='liblinear', tol=0.0001, verbose=0, warm_start=False)
'''

# fit model
logreg.fit(X_train, y_train)
# make class predictions for the testing set
y_pred_class = logreg.predict(X_test)

# Calculate accuracy
from sklearn import metrics
print("Classification accuracy:
",metrics.accuracy_score(y_test, y_pred_class))

#Null accuracy: accuracy that could be achieved by always
predicting the most frequent class
# examine the class distribution of the testing set (using a
Pandas Series method)
print("Null Accuracy:\n",y_test.value_counts())

# calculate the percentage of ones
```

```
# because y_test only contains ones and zeros, we can simply
calculate the mean = percentage of ones
print("The percentage of ones: \n",y_test.mean())

# calculate null accuracy in a single line of code
# only for binary classification problems coded as 0/1
print("Null accuracy (A dumb model that always predicts 0):
",max(y_test.mean(), 1 - y_test.mean()))

# calculate null accuracy (for multi-class classification
problems)
print("Null Accuracy for Multi-
class:",y_test.value_counts().head(1) / len(y_test))

###Confusion Matrix
from sklearn.metrics import confusion_matrix
cm = confusion_matrix(y_test,y_pred_class)
print("Confusion Matrix is: \n",cm)
# print the first 25 true and predicted responses
print('True', y_test.values[0:25])
print('Pred', y_pred_class[0:25])

#[row, column]
TP = cm[1, 1]
TN = cm[0, 0]
FP = cm[0, 1]
FN = cm[1, 0]

# Metrics computed from a confusion matrix
# use float to perform true division, not integer division
print((TP + TN) / float(TP + TN + FP + FN))
print("accuracy_score: ",metrics.accuracy_score(y_test,
y_pred_class))

#how often is the classifier incorrect?
classification_error = (FP + FN) / float(TP + TN + FP + FN)
print("classification_error:",classification_error)
print("Error Score: ",1 - metrics.accuracy_score(y_test,
y_pred_class))

#Sensitivity: When the actual value is positive, how often is
the prediction correct?
sensitivity = TP / float(FN + TP)
print("sensitivity: ",sensitivity)
#How "sensitive" is the classifier to detecting positive
instances?
#Also known as "True Positive Rate" or "Recall"
print("recall_score: ",metrics.recall_score(y_test,
```

```
y_pred_class))

#Specificity: When the actual value is negative, how often is
the prediction correct?
specificity = TN / (TN + FP)
print("specificity: ",specificity)

#False Positive Rate: When the actual value is negative, how
often is the prediction incorrect?
false_positive_rate = FP / float(TN + FP)
print("false_positive_rate: ",false_positive_rate)
print(1 - specificity)

#Precision: When a positive value is predicted, how often is
the prediction correct?
#How "precise" is the classifier when predicting positive
instances?
precision = TP / float(TP + FP)
print("precision: ",precision)
print("precision: ",metrics.precision_score(y_test,
y_pred_class))

#Adjusting the classification threshold
# print the first 10 predicted responses
# 1D array (vector) of binary values (0, 1)
logreg.predict(X_test)[0:10]
# print the first 10 predicted probabilities of class
membership
logreg.predict_proba(X_test)[0:10]
#There is a 0.5 classification threshold

# print the first 10 predicted probabilities for class 1
logreg.predict_proba(X_test)[0:10, 1]
# store the predicted probabilities for class 1
y_pred_prob = logreg.predict_proba(X_test)[:, 1]

# histogram of predicted probabilities
import matplotlib.pyplot as plt
# 8 bins
plt.hist(y_pred_prob, bins=8)

# x-axis limit from 0 to 1
plt.xlim(0,1)
plt.title('Histogram of predicted probabilities')
plt.xlabel('Predicted probability of diabetes')
plt.ylabel('Frequency')
plt.show()
```

Plotting ROC Curve: Receiver Operating Characteristic (ROC)

Its difficult to create confusion matrix for all possible values to evaluate hence we use ROC cusrve. ROC curve can help you to choose a threshold that balances sensitivity and specificity in a way that makes sense for your particular context. You can't actually see the thresholds used to generate the curve on the ROC curve itself.

```
#see how sensitivity and specificity are affected by various
thresholds, without actually changing the threshold
# IMPORTANT: first argument is true values, second argument is
predicted probabilities

# we pass y_test and y_pred_prob
# we do not use y_pred_class, because it will give incorrect
results without generating an error
# roc_curve returns 3 objects fpr, tpr, thresholds
# fpr: false positive rate
# tpr: true positive rate
fpr, tpr, thresholds = metrics.roc_curve(y_test, y_pred_prob)

plt.plot(fpr, tpr)
plt.xlim([0.0, 1.0])
plt.ylim([0.0, 1.0])
plt.rcParams['font.size'] = 12
plt.title('ROC curve for diabetes classifier')
plt.xlabel('False Positive Rate (1 - Specificity)')
plt.ylabel('True Positive Rate (Sensitivity)')
plt.grid(True)
plt.show()

# define a function that accepts a threshold and prints
sensitivity and specificity
def evaluate_threshold(threshold):
    print('Sensitivity:', tpr[thresholds > threshold][-1])
    print('Specificity:', 1 - fpr[thresholds > threshold][-1])

evaluate_threshold(0.5)
evaluate_threshold(0.3)
```

AUC

AUC is the percentage of the ROC plot that is underneath the curve. The AUC represents a model's ability to discriminate between positive and negative classes. An area of 1.0 represents a model that made all predictions perfectly (Higher value = better classifier). An area of 0.5 represents a model as good as random. AUC is useful as a single number summary of classifier performance.

```
# IMPORTANT: first argument is true values, second argument is
```

```
predicted probabilities
print("AUC:",metrics.roc_auc_score(y_test, y_pred_prob))
```

AUC: 0.7227047146401985

Higher the area, better the model is.

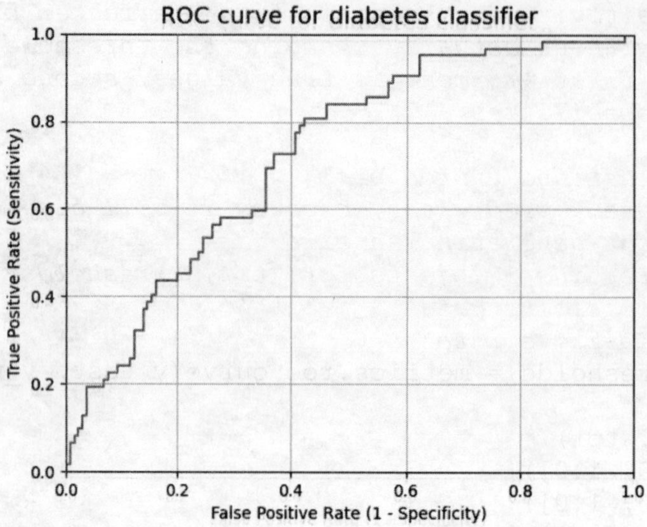

APPLICATIONS

- Email spam classification
- Bank customers loan pay willingness prediction.
- Cancer tumor cell identification.
- Sentiment analysis
- Drugs classification
- Facial keypoints detection
- Pedestrian detection in automotive car driving.

By now, I am sure, you would have an idea of classification machine learning algorithms. If you are keen to master machine learning, start right away. Take up problems, develop a physical understanding of the process, apply these codes and see the fun!

* * *

UNIT 18: CLUSTERING ALGORITHMS

Clustering or cluster analysis is an unsupervised learning problem. It is often used as a data analysis technique for discovering interesting patterns in data, such as groups of customers based on their behavior. There are many clustering algorithms to choose from and no single best clustering algorithm for all cases. Instead, it is a good idea to explore a range of clustering algorithms and different configurations for each algorithm.

It is crucial to understand customer behavior in any industry. Let's say chief marketing officer of your company comes to you and asks you – "Can you tell me which existing customers should we target for our new product?" To answer such questions, we need to segment the customers so that we can tailor and build targeted strategies. This is where the concept of clustering is useful.

Problems like segmenting customers are often deceptively tricky because we are not working with any target variable in mind. We are officially in the land of unsupervised learning where we need to figure out patterns and structures without a set outcome in mind. That's why concept of clustering falls under unsupervised learning.

Clustering is the task of dividing the population or data points into a number of groups such that data points in the same groups are more similar to other data points in the same group than those in other groups. In simple words, the aim is to segregate groups with similar traits and assign them into clusters.

Let's understand this with an example. Suppose, you are head of a retail store chain, which has 200 stores across the country. You sell many products like apparel, accessories, home care, beauty and cosmetics and grocery. You will have to plan the quantity and types of products you want these stores to sell. Can we have one strategy for all the stores? No, because the customer preferences would vary from store to store. Stores located in upscale area will carry different products than those near a college. Is it possible for you to look at details of each store and devise a unique business strategy for each one of them? Even this is not possible because managing 200 stores * number of products will make your life difficult. Then what do we do? What you can do is to cluster all of your stores into say 10 groups based on the purchasing habits of customers coming into the stores and use a separate strategy for these 10 groups. Now our decision points has reduced from 200 to just 10. This is what we call clustering.

The general idea of a clustering algorithm is to partition a given dataset into distinct, exclusive clusters so that the data points in each group are quite similar to each other and are meaningful. Clustering falls into the unsupervised learning algorithms. Meaningfulness purely depends on the intention behind the purpose of the group's formations.

Let's look at another example. Suppose we have 100 articles and we want to group them into different categories. Let's consider the below categories: Sports articles, Business articles and Entertainment articles. When we group all the 100 articles into the above 3 categories, all the articles belong to the sports category will be same, In the sense, the content in the sports articles belongs to sports category. When you pick an article from sports category and the other article from business articles, content-wise they will be completely different. This summarizes the rule of thumb condition to form clusters

Types of Clustering

Broadly speaking, clustering can be divided into two subgroups :

- Hard Clustering: In hard clustering, each data point either belongs to a cluster completely or not. For example, in the above example each store is put into one group out of the 10 groups.
- Soft Clustering: In soft clustering, instead of putting each data point into a separate cluster, a probability or likelihood of that data point to be in those clusters is assigned. For example, from the above scenario each store is assigned a probability to be in either of 10 clusters of the retail store.

Types of clustering algorithms

Since the task of clustering is subjective, the means that can be used for achieving this goal are plenty. Every methodology follows a different set of rules for defining the 'similarity' among data points. In fact, there are more than 100 clustering algorithms known. But few of the algorithms are used popularly, let's look at them in detail:

- **Connectivity models**: As the name suggests, these models are based on the notion that the data points closer in data space exhibit more similarity to each other than the data points lying farther away. These models can follow two approaches. In the first approach, they start with classifying all data points into separate clusters & then aggregating them as the distance decreases. In the second approach, all data points are classified as a single cluster and then partitioned as the distance increases. Also, the choice of distance function is subjective. These models are very easy to interpret but lacks scalability for handling big datasets. Examples of these models are hierarchical clustering algorithm and its variants.
- **Centroid models**: These are iterative clustering algorithms in which the notion of similarity is derived by the closeness of a data point to the centroid of the clusters. K-Means clustering algorithm is a popular algorithm that falls into this category. In these models, the no. of clusters required at the end have to be mentioned beforehand, which makes it important to have prior knowledge of the dataset. These models run iteratively to find the local optima.
- **Distribution models**: These clustering models are based on the notion of how probable is it that all data points in the cluster belong to the same distribution (For example: Normal,

Gaussian). These models often suffer from overfitting. A popular example of these models is Expectation-maximization algorithm which uses multivariate normal distributions.

- **Density Models**: These models search the data space for areas of varied density of data points in the data space. It isolates various different density regions and assign the data points within these regions in the same cluster. Popular examples of density models are DBSCAN and OPTICS.

We will learn two of the most popular clustering algorithms in detail – K Means clustering and Hierarchical clustering.

K-MEANS

K-Means clustering approach is very popular in a variety of domains. In biology it is often used to find structure in DNA-related data or subgroups of similar tissue samples to identify cancer cohorts. In marketing, K-Means is often used to create market/customer/product segments. One of the first steps in building a K-Means clustering work is to define the number of clusters to work with. Subsequently, the algorithm assigns each individual data point to one of the clusters in a random fashion. Details Steps involved in K-means are:

1. Choose the K-number of clusters. Each data point is randomly assigned to a cluster.
2. Select random K points, the initial set of centroids (not necessarily from the dataset)
3. Assign each data point to the closet centroid that forms K clusters
4. Compute and place the new centroids of each cluster
5. Reassign each data point to the new closest centroid.
6. If there is any reassignment of clusters, go to Step 4 or else Stop.

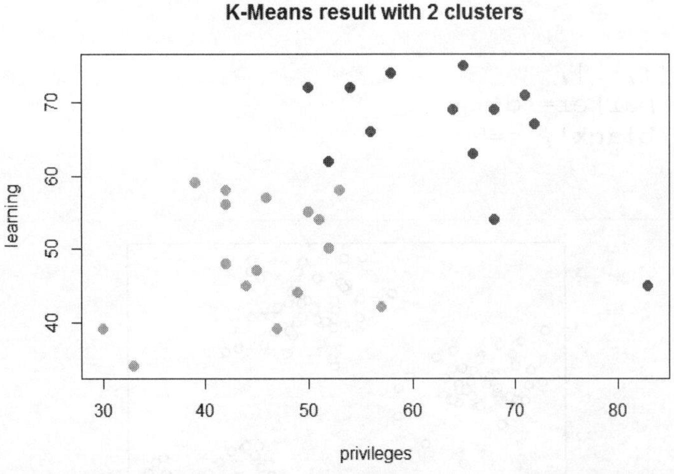

The underlying idea of the algorithm is that a good cluster is the one which contains the smallest possible within-cluster variation of all observations in relation to each other. The most common way to define this variation is using the squared Euclidean distance. This process of identifying groups of similar data points can be a relatively complex task since there is a very large number of ways to partition data points into clusters. Each cluster is represented by a prototype, which can either be the centroid (average) of similar points with continuous features, or the medoid (the most representative or most frequently occurring point) in the case of categorical features.

Python Implementation

Python's Sklearn library provides a great sample dataset generator which will help you to create your own custom dataset. It's fast and very easy to use. The make_blobs function is a part of sklearn.datasets.samples_generator. All methods in the package, help us to generate data samples or datasets. n_features determined how many columns or features the generated datasets will have. In machine learning, features correspond to numerical characteristics data. For example, in Iris Dataset, there are 4 features (Sepal Length, Sepal Width, Petal Length and Petal Width) so there are 4 numerical columns in the dataset. So by increasing n_features in make_blobs, we are adding more features hence increase the complexity of generated dataset. Centers corresponds to number of classes generated in the data. It uses centers as a term because samples that belong to same class, tend to gather close to a center (coordinate).
X variable will store the feature values and y will have the group(center).

```
import matplotlib.pyplot as plt
from sklearn.datasets import make_blobs

# create dataset
X, y = make_blobs(
   n_samples=150, n_features=2,
   centers=3, cluster_std=0.5,
   shuffle=True, random_state=0
)

# plot
plt.scatter(
   X[:, 0], X[:, 1],
   c='white', marker='o',
   edgecolor='black', s=50
)
plt.show()
```

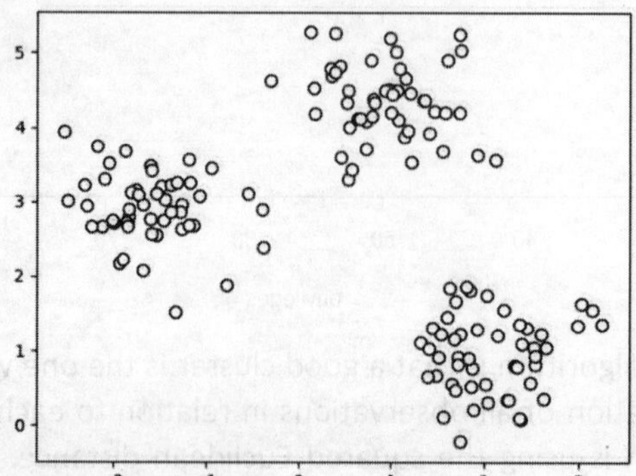

The dataset that we just created consists of 150 randomly generated points that are roughly grouped into three regions with higher density, which is visualized via a two-dimensional scatterplot. In real-world applications of clustering, we do not have any ground truth category information (information provided as empirical evidence as opposed to inference) about those samples; otherwise, it would fall into the category of supervised learning.

Applying the algorithm:

```
from sklearn.cluster import KMeans
km = KMeans(
    n_clusters=3, init='random',
    n_init=10, max_iter=300,
    tol=1e-04, random_state=0
)
y_km = km.fit_predict(X)
```

Using the above code, we set the number of desired clusters to 3. We set n_init=10 to run the k-means clustering algorithms 10 times independently with different random centroids to choose the final model as the one with the lowest SSE. Via the max_iter parameter, we specify the maximum number of iterations for each single run (here, 300).

Note that the k-means implementation in scikit-learn stops early if it converges before the maximum number of iterations is reached. However, it is possible that k-means does not reach convergence for a particular run, which can be problematic (computationally expensive) if we choose relatively large values for max_iter.

One way to deal with convergence problems is to choose larger values for tol, which is a parameter that controls the tolerance with regard to the changes in the within-cluster sum-squared-error to declare convergence. In the preceding code, we chose a tolerance of 1e-04 (= 0.0001).

A problem with k-means is that one or more clusters can be empty. However, this problem is accounted for in the current k-means implementation in scikit-learn. If a cluster is empty, the algorithm will search for the sample that is farthest away from the centroid of the empty cluster. Then it will reassign the centroid to be this farthest point.

Visualizing the Clusters

Now that we have predicted the cluster labels y_km, let's visualize the clusters that k-means identified in the dataset together with the cluster centroids. These are stored under the cluster_centers_ attribute of the fitted KMeans object:

```
#Visualize the clusters: plot the 3 clusters
plt.scatter(
    X[y_km == 0, 0], X[y_km == 0, 1],
    s=50, c='lightgreen',
    marker='s', edgecolor='black',
    label='cluster 1'
)
```

```
plt.scatter(
    X[y_km == 1, 0], X[y_km == 1, 1],
    s=50, c='orange',
    marker='o', edgecolor='black',
    label='cluster 2'
)

plt.scatter(
    X[y_km == 2, 0], X[y_km == 2, 1],
    s=50, c='lightblue',
    marker='v', edgecolor='black',
    label='cluster 3'
)

# plot the centroids
plt.scatter(
    km.cluster_centers_[:, 0], km.cluster_centers_[:, 1],
    s=250, marker='*',
    c='red', edgecolor='black',
    label='centroids'
)
plt.legend(scatterpoints=1)
plt.grid()
plt.show()
```

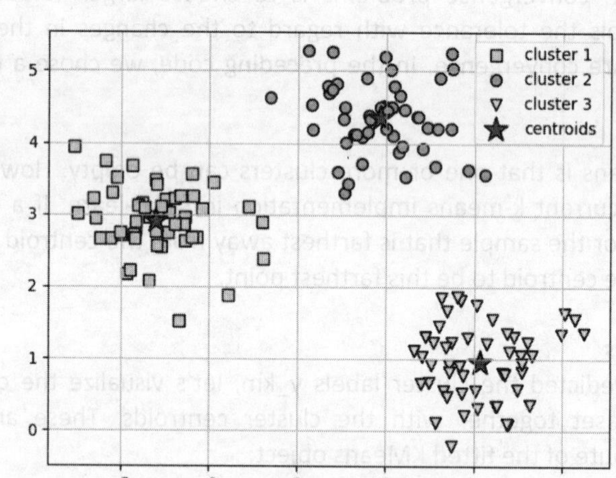

Finding Best Value For K

As mentioned before, one of the key decisions to be made when performing K-Means clustering is to decide on the numbers of clusters to use. In practice, there is no easy answer and it's important to try different ways and numbers of clusters to decide which options is the most useful, applicable or interpretable solution. However, one solution often used to identify the optimal number of clusters is called the Elbow method and it involves observing a set of possible numbers of clusters relative to how they minimize the within-cluster sum of squares. In other words, the Elbow method examines the within-cluster dissimilarity as a function of the number of clusters.

The elbow method is a useful graphical tool to estimate the optimal number of clusters k for a given task. Intuitively, we can say that, if k increases, the within-cluster SSE ("distortion") will decrease. This is because the samples will be closer to the centroids they are assigned to.
The idea behind the elbow method is to identify the value of k where the distortion begins to decrease most rapidly, which will become clearer if we plot the distortion for different values of k:

```
# calculate distortion for a range of number of cluster
distortions = []
max_k = 15
for i in range(1, max_k):
    km = KMeans(
        n_clusters=i, init='random',
        n_init=10, max_iter=300,
        tol=1e-04, random_state=0
    )
    km.fit(X)
    distortions.append(km.inertia_)
# plot
plt.plot(range(1, max_k), distortions, marker='o')
plt.xlabel('# of Clusters')
plt.ylabel('Distortion')
plt.show()
```

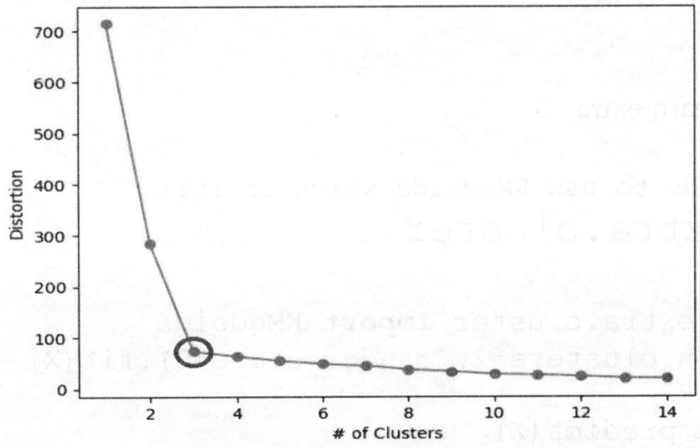

As we can see in the resulting plot, the elbow is located at k = 3, which is evidence that k = 3 is indeed a good choice for this dataset.

Further read, visit official documentation available here: https://scikit-learn.org/stable/modules/generated/sklearn.cluster.KMeans.html

PARTITIONING AROUND MEDOIDS (PAM)

The K-means technique is fast, and doesn't require calculating all of the distances between each observation and every other observation. It can be written to efficiently deal with very large data sets, so it may be useful in cases where other methods fail. On the down side, if you rearrange your data, it's very possible that you'll get a different solution every time you change the ordering of your data.

The sklearn library provides a modern alternative to k-means clustering, known as pam, which is an acronym for "Partitioning around Medoids". The term medoid refers to an observation within a cluster for which the sum of the distances between it and all the other members of the cluster is a minimum. PAM requires that you know the number of clusters that you want (like k-means clustering), but it does more computation than k-means in order to insure that the medoids it finds are truly representative of the observations within a given cluster.

K-means aims to minimize the total squared error from a central position in each cluster. These central positions are called centroids. On the other hand, k-medoids attempts to minimize the sum of dissimilarities between objects labeled to be in a cluster and one of the objects designated as the representative of that cluster. These representatives are called medoids.

In contrast to the k-means algorithm that the centroids are central, average positions that might not be data points in the set, k-medoids chooses medoids from the data points in the set.

Implementation using Python

At the time of writing this piece, the KMedoid algorithm was not made part of standard sklearn. To use the inbuild PAM implementation, we need to install sklearn_extra by using following command:

```
pip install scikit-learn-extra
```

Now we are ready to use KMedoids which is in:

sklearn_extra.cluster

```
from sklearn_extra.cluster import KMedoids
km =KMedoids(n_clusters=2, random_state=0).fit(X)

y_km = km.fit_predict(X)
```

Elbow method for K:

```
# calculate distortion for a range of number of cluster
distortions = []
max_k = 15
for i in range(1, max_k):
    km = KMedoids(
        n_clusters=i, random_state=0
    )
```

```
km.fit(X)
distortions.append(km.inertia_)
```

Example: Multiple k-values for a same set of data

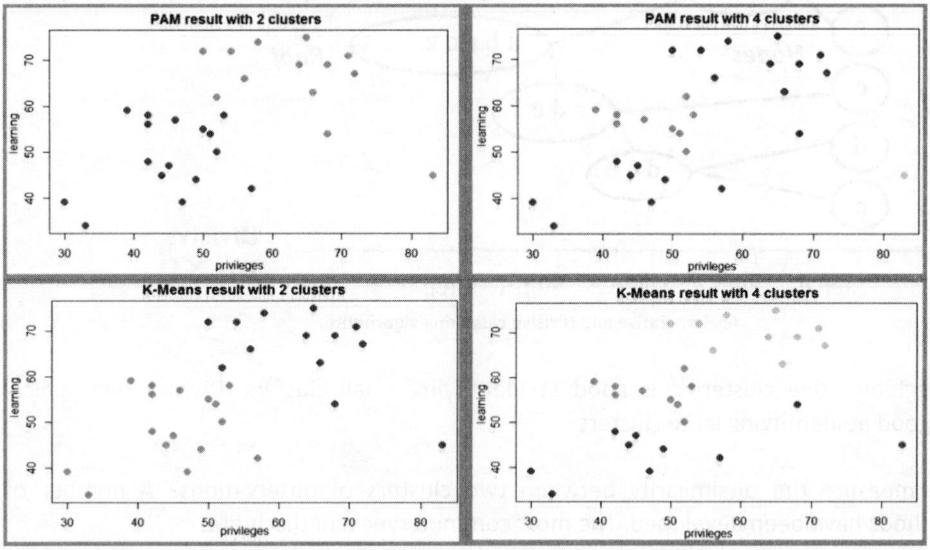

Now, let's look at another algorithm for clustering.

HEIRARCHICAL CLUSTERING

Hierarchical clustering is an alternative approach to k-means clustering for identifying groups in the dataset and does not require to pre-specify the number of clusters to generate. It refers to a set of clustering algorithms that build tree-like clusters by successively splitting or merging them. This hierarchical structure is represented using a tree. Hierarchical clustering methods use a distance similarity measure to combine or split clusters. The recursive process continues until there is only one cluster left or we cannot split more clusters. We can use a dendrogram to represent the hierarchy of clusters. Hierarchical classifications produced by either Agglomerative (Bottom up approach) or Divisive (Top down approach).

Agglomerative clustering: It's also known as AGNES (Agglomerative Nesting). It works in a bottom-up manner. Each object is initially considered as a single-element cluster (leaf). At each step of the algorithm, the two clusters that are the most similar are combined into a new bigger cluster (nodes). This procedure is iterated until all points are member of just one single big cluster (root). The result is a tree which can be plotted as a dendrogram.

Divisive hierarchical clustering: It's also known as DIANA (Divise Analysis) and it works in a top-down manner. The algorithm is an inverse order of AGNES. It begins with the root, in which all objects are included in a single cluster. At each step of iteration, the most heterogeneous cluster is divided into two. The process is iterated until all objects are in their own cluster.

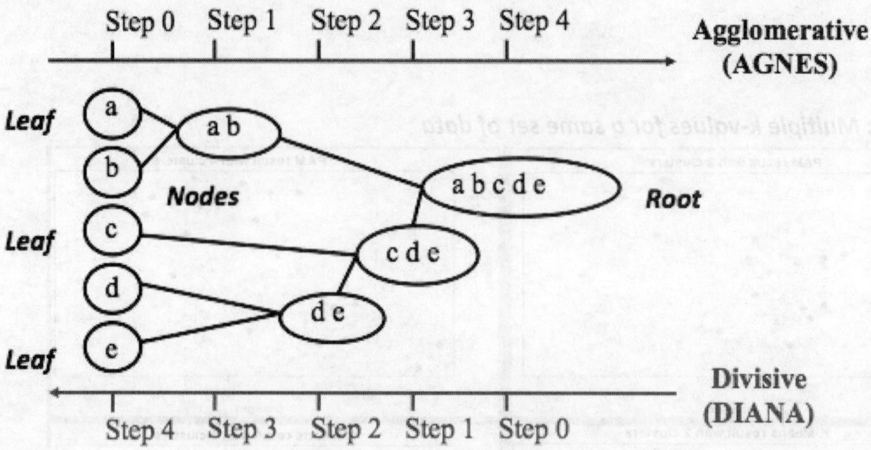

Agglomerative and Divisive clustering algorithms

Note that agglomerative clustering is good at identifying small clusters. Divisive hierarchical clustering is good at identifying large clusters.

How do we measure the dissimilarity between two clusters of observations? A number of different methods have been developed. The most common types methods are:

- Maximum or complete linkage clustering: It computes all pairwise dissimilarities between the elements in cluster 1 and the elements in cluster 2, and considers the largest value (i.e., maximum value) of these dissimilarities as the distance between the two clusters. It tends to produce more compact clusters.
- Minimum or single linkage clustering: It computes all pairwise dissimilarities between the elements in cluster 1 and the elements in cluster 2, and considers the smallest of these dissimilarities as a linkage criterion. It tends to produce long, "loose" clusters.
- Mean or average linkage clustering: It computes all pairwise dissimilarities between the elements in cluster 1 and the elements in cluster 2, and considers the average of these dissimilarities as the distance between the two clusters.
- Centroid linkage clustering: It computes the dissimilarity between the centroid for cluster 1 (a mean vector of length p variables) and the centroid for cluster 2.
- Ward's minimum variance method: It minimizes the total within-cluster variance. This method does not directly define a measure of distance between two points or clusters. It is an ANOVA based approach. At each stage, those two clusters merge, which provides the smallest increase in the combined error sum of squares from one-way univariate ANOVAs that can be done for each variable with groups defined by the clusters at that stage of the process.

The different approaches produce different dendrograms. Its left to the readers to plot and check different dendrograms. The code for the plotting and interpreting the dendrogram is given later in this section.

Preparing the Dataset

Let's see the implementation in Python. Step 1 is to prepare for the dataset. We'll use the *USArrests dataset*, which contains statistics in arrests per 100,000 residents for assault, murder, and rape in each of the 50 US states in 1973. It includes also the percent of the population living in urban areas. Below code is common for both Agglomerative and Divisive hierarchical clustering algorithms.

```
import pandas as pd
import numpy as np
import matplotlib.pyplot as plt
data =
pd.read_csv('https://raw.githubusercontent.com/swapnilsaurav/Ma
chineLearning/master/USArrests.csv')
print("Sample Data: \n",data.head())
X=data.iloc[:,1:]
```

```
Sample Data:
        State  Murder  Assault  UrbanPop  Rape
0     Alabama    13.2      236        58  21.2
1      Alaska    10.0      263        48  44.5
2     Arizona     8.1      294        80    31
3    Arkansas     8.8      190        50  19.5
4  California     9.0      276        91  40.6
```

Before applying Hierarchical Clustering, we have to normalize the data so that the scale of each variable is the same. If the scale of the variables is not the same, the model might become biased towards the variables with a higher magnitude. So, let's first normalize the data and bring all the variables to the same scale:

```
from sklearn.preprocessing import normalize
data_scaled = normalize(X)
data_scaled = pd.DataFrame(data_scaled)
print("Normalize Sample Data: \n",data_scaled.head())
```

Hierarchical agglomerative clustering methods, starts out by putting each observation into its own separate cluster. It then examines all the distances between all the observations and pairs together the two closest ones to form a new cluster. This is a simple operation, since hierarchical methods require a distance matrix, and it represents exactly what we want - the distances between individual observations. So finding the first cluster to form simply means looking for the smallest number in the distance matrix and joining the two observations that the distance corresponds to into a new cluster. Now there is one less cluster than there are observations. To determine which observations will form the next cluster, we need to come up with a method for finding the distance between an existing cluster and individual observations.

Choosing the Number of Clusters in Hierarchical Clustering

To get the number of clusters for hierarchical clustering, we make use of an awesome concept called a Dendrogram. A dendrogram is a tree-like diagram that records the sequences of merges or splits. Let's take an example to understand the concept of dendogram.

Suppose a teacher wants to divide her students into different groups. She has the marks scored by each student in an assignment and based on these marks, she wants to segment them into groups. There's no fixed target here as to how many groups to have. We will try to apply hierarchical clustering here and segment the students into different groups.

Let's take a sample of 5 students:

RollNo	1	2	3	4	5
Marks	10	7	28	20	35

Creating a Proximity Matrix

First, we will create a proximity matrix which will tell us the distance between each of these points. Since we are calculating the distance of each point from each of the other points, we will get a square matrix of shape n X n (where n is the number of observations).

Let's make the 5 x 5 proximity matrix for our example:

The diagonal elements of this matrix will always be 0 as the distance of a point with itself is always 0. We will use the Euclidean distance formula to calculate the rest of the distances. So, let's say we want to calculate the distance between point 1 and 2: $\sqrt{(10-7)^2} = \sqrt{9} = 3$

Similarly, we can calculate all the distances and fill the proximity matrix.

RollNo	**1**	**2**	**3**	**4**	**5**
1	0	3	18	10	25
2	3	0	21	13	28
3	18	21	0	8	7
4	10	13	8	0	15
5	25	28	7	15	0

Performing Agglomerative Hierarchical Clustering.

Step 1: First, we assign all the points to an individual cluster.

Step 2: Next, we will look at the smallest distance in the proximity matrix and merge the points with the smallest distance. We then update the proximity matrix. Here, the smallest distance is 3 and hence we will merge point 1 and 2. Here, we have taken the maximum of the two marks (7, 10) to replace the marks for this cluster. Instead of the maximum, we can also take the minimum value or the average values as well. Now, we will again calculate the proximity matrix for these clusters.

Group	{1,2}	3	4	5
Marks	10	28	20	35

RollNo	**{1,2}**	**3**	**4**	**5**
{1,2}	0	18	10	25
3	18	0	8	7
4	10	8	0	15
5	25	7	15	0

Step 3: We will repeat step 2 until only a single cluster is left.
We started with 5 clusters and finally have a single cluster. This is how agglomerative hierarchical clustering works.

Finding number of clusters

We started by merging sample 1 and 2 and the distance between these two samples was 3 (refer to the first proximity matrix in the previous section). Let's plot this in the dendrogram as shown on the left image. Here, we can see that we have merged sample 1 and 2. The vertical line represents the distance between these samples. Similarly, we plot all the steps where we merged the clusters and finally, we get a dendrogram like the image on the right.

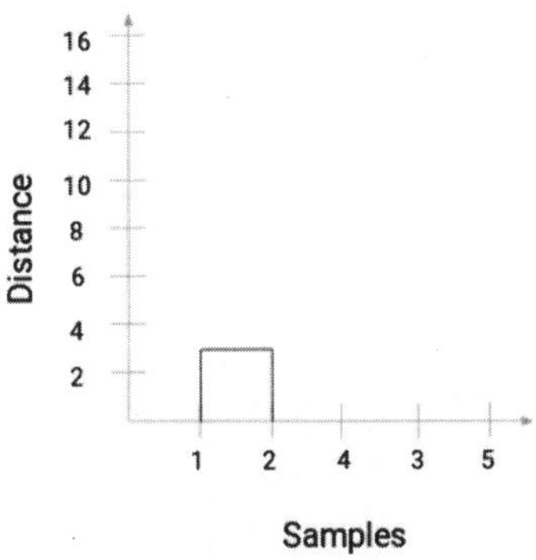

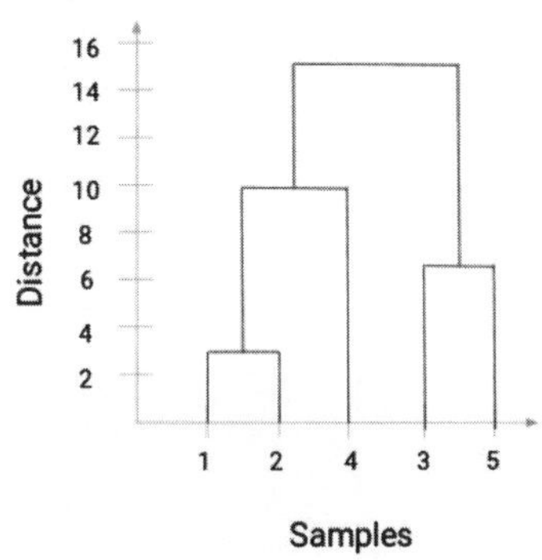

We can clearly visualize that more the distance of the vertical lines in the dendrogram, more the distance between those clusters. Now, we can set a threshold distance and draw a horizontal line (Generally, we try to set the threshold in such a way that it cuts the tallest vertical line). Let's set this threshold as 12 and draw a horizontal line:

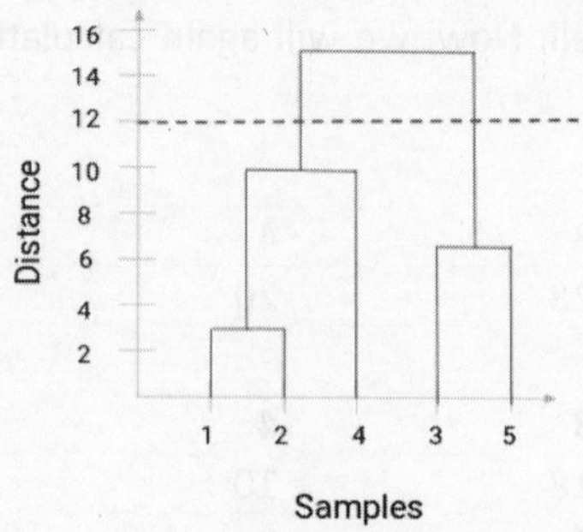

The number of clusters will be the number of vertical lines which are being intersected by the line drawn using the threshold. In the above example, since the red line intersects 2 vertical lines, we will have 2 clusters. One cluster will have a sample (1,2,4) and the other will have a sample (3,5). This is how we can decide the number of clusters using a dendrogram in Hierarchical Clustering.

```
#draw the dendrogram
import scipy.cluster.hierarchy as shc
plt.figure(figsize=(10, 7))
plt.title("Dendrograms")
dend = shc.dendrogram(shc.linkage(data_scaled, method='ward'))
plt.show()
plt.figure(figsize=(10, 7))
plt.title("Dendrograms")
dend = shc.dendrogram(shc.linkage(data_scaled, method='ward'))
plt.axhline(y=0.8, color='r', linestyle='--')
plt.show()
```

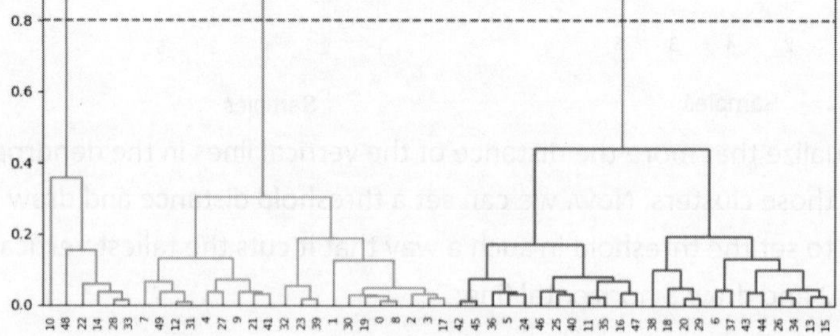

We have three clusters as this line cuts the dendrogram at three points. Let's now apply hierarchical clustering for 3 clusters:

```
from sklearn.cluster import AgglomerativeClustering
```

```
cluster = AgglomerativeClustering(n_clusters=3,
affinity='euclidean', linkage='ward')
cluster.fit_predict(data_scaled)
#Visualize the three clusters - Murder v Assualt
plt.figure(figsize=(10, 7))
plt.scatter(data_scaled[0], data_scaled[1], c=cluster.labels_)
plt.show()
```

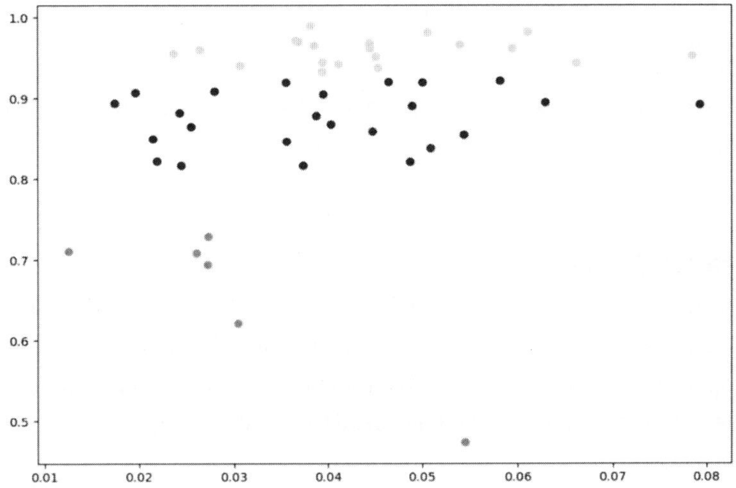

OTHER CLUSTERING ALGORITHMS

There are many types of clustering algorithms. Many algorithms use similarity or distance measures between examples in the feature space in an effort to discover dense regions of observations. As such, it is often good practice to scale data prior to using clustering algorithms. Some clustering algorithms require you to specify or guess at the number of clusters to discover in the data, whereas others require the specification of some minimum distance between observations in which examples may be considered "close" or "connected."

As such, cluster analysis is an iterative process where subjective evaluation of the identified clusters is fed back into changes to algorithm configuration until a desired or appropriate result is achieved.

Some of the other popular algorithms is as follows:

1. Affinity Propagation
2. Agglomerative Clustering
3. BIRCH
4. DBSCAN

5. Mini-Batch K-Means
6. Mean Shift
7. OPTICS
8. Spectral Clustering
9. Mixture of Gaussians

Each algorithm offers a different approach to the challenge of discovering natural groups in data. There is no best clustering algorithm, and no easy way to find the best algorithm for your data without using controlled experiments.

CLUSTERING DATASET

Python's Sklearn library provides a great sample dataset generator which will help you to create your own custom dataset. There are many functions which generate the dataset. Let's understand some of them:

Blobs Classification Problem

The ***make_blobs()*** function can be used to generate blobs of points with a Gaussian distribution. You can control how many blobs to generate and the number of samples to generate, as well as a host of other properties. The problem is suitable for linear classification problems given the linearly separable nature of the blobs. We have used this in KMean algorithm.

```
from sklearn.datasets import make_blobs
# generate 2d classification dataset
X, y = make_blobs(n_samples=100, centers=3, n_features=2)
```

Moons Classification Problem

The make_moons() function is for binary classification and will generate a swirl pattern, or two moons. You can control how noisy the moon shapes are and the number of samples to generate. This test problem is suitable for algorithms that are capable of learning nonlinear class boundaries.

```
from sklearn.datasets import make_moons
X, y = make_moons(n_samples=100, noise=0.1)
```

Circles Classification Problem

The make_circles() function generates a binary classification problem with datasets that fall into concentric circles. Again, as with the moons test problem, you can control the amount of noise in the shapes. This test problem is suitable for algorithms that can learn complex non-linear manifolds.

```
from sklearn.datasets import make_circles
```

```
# generate 2d classification dataset
X, y = make_circles(n_samples=100, noise=0.05)
```

Regression Test Problems

Regression is the problem of predicting a quantity given an observation. The make_regression() function will create a dataset with a linear relationship between inputs and the outputs. You can configure the number of samples, number of input features, level of noise, and much more. This dataset is suitable for algorithms that can learn a linear regression function.

```
from sklearn.datasets import make_regression
# generate regression dataset
X, y = make_regression(n_samples=100, n_features=1, noise=0.1)
```

CLUSTERING ALGORITHMS

We will use same dataset which different dataset for the rest of the algorithms. We will use the make_classification() function to create a test binary classification dataset.

The dataset will have 1,000 examples, with two input features and one cluster per class. The clusters are visually obvious in two dimensions so that we can plot the data with a scatter plot and color the points in the plot by the assigned cluster. This will help to see, at least on the test problem, how "well" the clusters were identified.

```
# dummy classification dataset
from numpy import where
from sklearn.datasets import make_classification
from matplotlib import pyplot
# define dataset
X, y = make_classification(n_samples=1000, n_features=2,
n_informative=2, n_redundant=0, n_clusters_per_class=1,
random_state=4)
# create scatter plot for samples from each class
for class_value in range(2):
    # get row indexes for samples with this class
    row_ix = where(y == class_value)
    # create scatter of these samples
    pyplot.scatter(X[row_ix, 0], X[row_ix, 1])
# show the plot
pyplot.show()
```

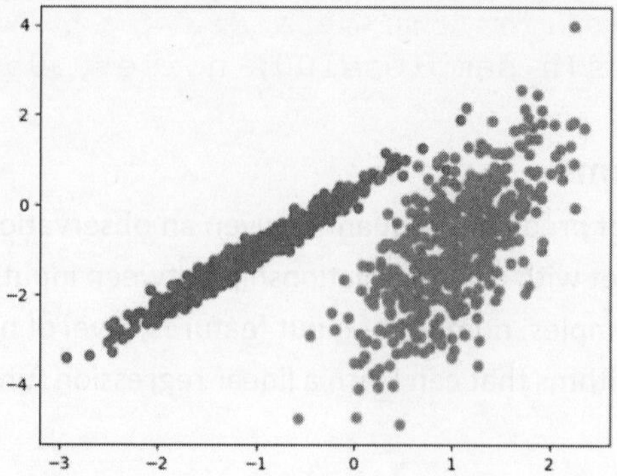

Algorithm 1: Affinity Propagation

Affinity Propagation involves finding a set of exemplars that best summarize the data. We devised a method called "affinity propagation," which takes as input measures of similarity between pairs of data points. Real-valued messages are exchanged between data points until a high-quality set of exemplars and corresponding clusters gradually emerges.

```
# affinity propagation clustering
from numpy import unique
from numpy import where
from sklearn.datasets import make_classification
from sklearn.cluster import AffinityPropagation
from matplotlib import pyplot
# define dataset
X, _ = make_classification(n_samples=1000, n_features=2,
n_informative=2, n_redundant=0, n_clusters_per_class=1,
random_state=4)
# define the model
model = AffinityPropagation(damping=0.9)
# fit the model
model.fit(X)
# assign a cluster to each example
yhat = model.predict(X)
# retrieve unique clusters
clusters = unique(yhat)
# create scatter plot for samples from each cluster
for cluster in clusters:
   # get row indexes for samples with this cluster
   row_ix = where(yhat == cluster)
   # create scatter of these samples
   pyplot.scatter(X[row_ix, 0], X[row_ix, 1])
# show the plot
pyplot.show()
```

Algorithm 2: Agglomerative Clustering

Agglomerative clustering involves merging examples until the desired number of clusters is achieved.

```
from sklearn.cluster import AgglomerativeClustering
# define dataset
X, _ = make_classification(n_samples=1000, n_features=2,
n_informative=2, n_redundant=0, n_clusters_per_class=1,
random_state=4)
# define the model
model = AgglomerativeClustering(n_clusters=2)
# fit model and predict clusters
yhat = model.fit_predict(X)

# retrieve unique clusters
clusters = unique(yhat)
```

Algorithm 3: BIRCH

BIRCH Clustering (BIRCH is short for Balanced Iterative Reducing and Clustering using Hierarchies) involves constructing a tree structure from which cluster centroids are extracted. BIRCH incrementally and dynamically clusters incoming multi-dimensional metric data points to try to produce the best quality clustering with the available resources (i. e., available memory and time constraints).

```
from sklearn.cluster import Birch
from matplotlib import pyplot
# define dataset
X, _ = make_classification(n_samples=1000, n_features=2,
n_informative=2, n_redundant=0, n_clusters_per_class=1,
random_state=4)
# define the model
model = Birch(threshold=0.01, n_clusters=2)
# fit the model
model.fit(X)
# assign a cluster to each example
yhat = model.predict(X)
# retrieve unique clusters
clusters = unique(yhat)
```

Algorithm 4: DBSCAN

DBSCAN Clustering (where DBSCAN is short for Density-Based Spatial Clustering of Applications with Noise) involves finding high-density areas in the domain and expanding those areas of the feature space around them as clusters.

```
from sklearn.cluster import DBSCAN
from matplotlib import pyplot
```

```
# define dataset
X, _ = make_classification(n_samples=1000, n_features=2,
n_informative=2, n_redundant=0, n_clusters_per_class=1,
random_state=4)
# define the model
model = DBSCAN(eps=0.30, min_samples=9)
# fit model and predict clusters
yhat = model.fit_predict(X)
# retrieve unique clusters
clusters = unique(yhat)
```

Algorithm 5: Mini-Batch K-Means

Mini-Batch K-Means is a modified version of k-means that makes updates to the cluster centroids using mini-batches of samples rather than the entire dataset, which can make it faster for large datasets, and perhaps more robust to statistical noise.

```
from sklearn.cluster import MiniBatchKMeans
from matplotlib import pyplot
# define dataset
X, _ = make_classification(n_samples=1000, n_features=2,
n_informative=2, n_redundant=0, n_clusters_per_class=1,
random_state=4)
# define the model
model = MiniBatchKMeans(n_clusters=2)
# fit the model
model.fit(X)
# assign a cluster to each example
yhat = model.predict(X)
# retrieve unique clusters
clusters = unique(yhat)
```

Algorithm 6: Mean Shift

Mean shift clustering involves finding and adapting centroids based on the density of examples in the feature space.

```
from sklearn.cluster import MeanShift
from matplotlib import pyplot
# define dataset
X, _ = make_classification(n_samples=1000, n_features=2,
n_informative=2, n_redundant=0, n_clusters_per_class=1,
random_state=4)
# define the model
model = MeanShift()
# fit model and predict clusters
yhat = model.fit_predict(X)
```

```
# retrieve unique clusters
clusters = unique(yhat)
```

Algorithm 7: OPTICS

OPTICS clustering (where OPTICS is short for Ordering Points To Identify the Clustering Structure) is a modified version of DBSCAN described above.

```
from sklearn.cluster import OPTICS
from matplotlib import pyplot
# define dataset
X, _ = make_classification(n_samples=1000, n_features=2,
n_informative=2, n_redundant=0, n_clusters_per_class=1,
random_state=4)
# define the model
model = OPTICS(eps=0.8, min_samples=10)
# fit model and predict clusters
yhat = model.fit_predict(X)
# retrieve unique clusters
clusters = unique(yhat)
```

Algorithm 8: Spectral Clustering

Spectral Clustering is a general class of clustering methods, drawn from linear algebra.

```
from sklearn.cluster import SpectralClustering
from matplotlib import pyplot
# define dataset
X, _ = make_classification(n_samples=1000, n_features=2,
n_informative=2, n_redundant=0, n_clusters_per_class=1,
random_state=4)
# define the model
model = SpectralClustering(n_clusters=2)
# fit model and predict clusters
yhat = model.fit_predict(X)
# retrieve unique clusters
clusters = unique(yhat)
```

Algorithm 9: Gaussian Mixture Model

A Gaussian mixture model summarizes a multivariate probability density function with a mixture of Gaussian probability distributions as its name suggests.

```
from sklearn.mixture import GaussianMixture
from matplotlib import pyplot
# define dataset
X, _ = make_classification(n_samples=1000, n_features=2,
```

```
n_informative=2, n_redundant=0, n_clusters_per_class=1,
random_state=4)
# define the model
model = GaussianMixture(n_components=2)
# fit the model
model.fit(X)
# assign a cluster to each example
yhat = model.predict(X)
# retrieve unique clusters
clusters = unique(yhat)
```

That's all we have in Clustering. Let's move to next topic.

***

UNIT 19: ASSOCIATION ALGORITHMS

The association rule learning is a rule-based machine learning approach that generates the relationship between variables in a dataset. It has major applications in the retail industry including E-Commerce retail businesses. Using this strategy, the products sold in an association can be explored and can be offered to customers to buy together. For example, it can be discovered that if the customers have bought onion and potato together, then most likely they have bought tomato also. It can be given a rule in the form of :

{onion, potato} -> tomato

These rules are called association rules. The Association Learning methods discover these types of rules from the dataset comprising the list of transactions.
The association rule learning has three popular algorithms – Apriori, Eclat, and FP-Growth.

APRIORI ALGORITHM

Apriori is a popular algorithm used in market basket analysis. This algorithm is used with relational databases for frequent itemset mining and association rule learning. It uses a bottom-up approach where frequent items are extended one item at a time and groups of candidates are tested against the available dataset. This process continues until no further extensions are found.

Let's understand how Apriori works. We know that Apriori works to find Frequent Item Sets. Lets take an example of below transaction list:

Transactions	Item 1	Item 2	Item 3
1	Milk	Sugar	Coffee
2	Milk	Sugar	Coffee
3	Milk	Sugar	Coffee
4	Milk	Sugar	
5	Milk	Sugar	
6	Milk	Sugar	

In the above 6 transactions, we see that Milk and Sugar are bought together 100% of the times. To write this we use IF (or Antecedent or Left Hand Side) and THEN (or Consequent or Right Hand Side). If Milk is bought Then Sugar is also bought. If Milk and Sugar are bought Then 50% of the time (3/6), Coffee is also bought. We write all the possible combinations like below:

{Coffee} => {Milk}
{Milk, Sugar} => {Coffee}

Apriori works on the concept that all subsets of a frequent item sets must be frequent and also for any infrequent item set, all its supersets must be infrequent too.

Apriori Algorithm uses the concept of Support, Confidence and Lift where,

- Support refers to the default popularity of an item and is calculated by finding number of transactions containing a particular item divided by total number of transactions.
- Confidence refers to the likelihood that an item B is also bought if item A is bought. It can be calculated by finding the number of transactions where A and B are bought together, divided by total number of transactions where A is bought.
- Lift(A -> B) refers to the increase in the ratio of sale of B when A is sold. Lift(A –> B) can be calculated by dividing Confidence(A -> B) divided by Support(B).

$$\text{Support (Item I)} = \frac{(Total\ Number\ of\ transactions\ with\ Item\ I)}{(Total\ number\ of\ transactions)}$$

$$\text{Confidence (Item } I_1 \rightarrow \text{Item } I_2) = \frac{No.\ of\ transactions\ with\ I_1\ and\ I_2}{No.\ of\ transactions\ with\ I_1}$$

$$\text{Lift (Item } I_1 \rightarrow \text{Item } I_2) = \frac{Confidence(Item\ I_1 \rightarrow I_2)}{Supprt(Item\ I_2)}$$

In our example:
Support(Coffee) = 3/6 = 0.5
Confidence of ({Coffee} => {Milk}) = 3/3 = 1
Confidence of ({Milk} => {Coffee}) = 3/6 = 0.5

In confidence example, we are only taking the Antecedent into consideration to know the confidence but we ignore the popularity of Consequent, hence we use Lift:
Lift({Coffee} => {Milk}) = Confidence of ({Coffee} => {Milk}) /(3/6) = 1*6/3 = 2

If Lift > 1, indicate that RHS (Consequent) is likely to be bought with LHS. Less than 1 would mean it is less likely to be bought with LHS.

Conviction: There is a another concept we talk about here. Conviction (X => Y) compares the probability that X appears without Y if they were dependent with the actual frequency of the appearance of X without Y. In that respect it is similar to lift, however, it contrast to lift it is a directed measure. Furthermore, conviction is monotone in confidence and lift.

Conviction(X=>Y) = (1-Support(Y) / (1-Confidence(X=>Y)

The steps of working of the apriori algorithm can be given as:

- Define the minimum support and confidence for the association rule
- Take all the subsets in the transactions with higher support than the minimum support
- Take all the rules of these subsets with higher confidence than minimum confidence
- Sort the association rules in the decreasing order of lift.
- Visualize the rules along with confidence and support.

At a high level, Apriori is a 2 step process: Frequent Itemset generation, and Rule Generation

Python Implementation

The algorithm in the apyori package is implemented in such a way that the input to the algorithm is a list of lists rather than a data frame. So we need to convert the data into a list of lists.

```
# Importing the libraries
import pandas as pd

# Data Preprocessing
dataset =
pd.read_csv('https://raw.githubusercontent.com/swapnilsaurav/MachineLearning/master/Market_Basket_Optimisation.csv', header =
None)
print("Dataset: \n",dataset.head())
transactions = []
for i in range(0, len(dataset)):
    transactions.append([str(dataset.values[i,j]) for j in
range(0, 20)])

# Training Apriori on the dataset
from apyori import apriori
rules = apriori(transactions, min_support = 0.003,
min_confidence = 0.2, min_lift = 3, min_length = 2)

# Visualising the results
results = list(rules)
print("Result: ",results)
```

- min_support: The minimum support of relations (float)
- min_confidence: The minimum confidence of relations (float)
- min_lift: The minimum lift of relations (float)
- min_length: The minimum number of items in a rule
- max_length: The maximum number of items in a rule

The optimum values for min_support,min_confidence and min_lift arguments can be set by trying out different values and checking the association rules whether the arguments produced a valid association between items or not.

The apriori algorithm automatically sorts the associations' rules based on relevance, thus the topmost rule has the highest relevance compared to the other rules returned by the algorithm. Let's have a look at the first and most relevant association rule from the given dataset.

```
print("First Association: \n",associations[0])
```

```
First Association:
 RelationRecord(items=frozenset({'chicken', 'light cream'}), support=0.004532728969470737,
  ordered_statistics=[OrderedStatistic(items_base=frozenset({'light cream'}),
 items_add=frozenset({'chicken'}), confidence=0.29059829059829057, lift=4.84395061728395)])
```

Rule one is the most relevant rule that the algorithm identified from the given dataset.

- The first output specifies the association between two products 'chicken' and 'light cream'.
- The two products have the support of 0.0045. i,e.
- support('chicken', 'light cream') =0.0045

Also from the output,

- confidence('light cream','light cream')=0.29

This implies that if a person buys light cream he or she is 29% likely to buy chicken as well. The lift of 4.84 shows the relevance of the rule since we have only chosen the rules with a minimum relevance of 3.

Lift basically tells us that the likelihood of buying a Chicken and Light Cream together is 4.84 times more than the likelihood of just buying the ketchup. A Lift of 1 means there is no association between products A and B. Lift of greater than 1 means products A and B are more likely to be bought together. Finally, Lift of less than 1 refers to the case where two products are unlikely to be bought together.

ECLAT

Eclat (Equivalence Class Transformation) is an improved version of Apriori. The frequent Itemset generation in Apriori can be computationally expensive process, and that's where Eclat comes into picture. Eclat is depth first search algorithm. Let's understand with an example:

Transactions	Item 1	Item 2	Item 3
1	Milk	Sugar	Coffee
2	Milk	Sugar	Coffee
3	Milk	Sugar	Coffee
4	Milk	Sugar	
5	Milk	Sugar	
6	Milk	Sugar	

We take same example discussed earlier. Eclat algorithm starts with MinSup (or Support Thresold) provided by the user. Lets say, in this case, we provide MinSup as 33.33% (or 2 Transactions).

Each itemset is annoted with support, for example:

ItemSet	Support
Milk	6
Sugar	6
Coffee	3
Milk, Sugar	6
Sugar, Coffee	3
Milk, Coffee	3
Milk, Sugar, Coffee	3

All the itemset is selected as we have minsup as 2. If we increase it to 4, all the transactions with support value less than 4 will be rejected. That's how we are able to improve upon the Apriori algorithm. Eclat arranges the content in increasing or decreasing order or the lexical order before using it. Its advantages are:

1. Since Eclat uses depth first search, it reduces memory requirements
2. It reduces the scan time aswe have a smaller itemset now

Eclat can become expensive to maintain.

At the time of writing this, the Eclat algorithm is still not put in the main package. You can download/copy the code from following location:
https://github.com/swapnilsaurav/MachineLearning/blob/master/EclatCode.py

Put this program in a file named éclat.py
Now we will write following code to execute the model. Instead of the Item name, we have used the Item code in the market basket list.

```
# Importing the libraries
import pandas as pd

# Data Preprocessing
#suggested min support range for this dataset: [0.6 0.02]
dataset =
pd.read_csv('https://raw.githubusercontent.com/swapnilsaurav/Da
taset/master/EclatDataset.csv', header = None)
print("Dataset: \n",dataset.head())
transactions = []
for i in range(0, len(dataset)):
    transactions.append([str(dataset.values[i,j]) for j in
range(0, 20)])

# Training Apriori on the dataset
from eclat import eclat
rules = eclat(transactions, min_support = 0.2)
```

```
# Visualising the results
results = list(rules)
print("Result: ",results)
```

Sample Output:

```
Data transformed into vertical bitvector representation with shape:  (97, 8416)
Running Eclat in recursive: number of itemsets found: 24063
728, ('1', '23', '31', '38', '41', '57', '67', '90', '97', '104'): 1728, ('1', '23', '38'
```

FP-GROWTH

Frequency Pattern-growth (FP-growth) is an improved version of the Apriori Algorithm. Using Apriori required multiple scans of the database to check the support count of each item and itemsets. The FP-Growth algorithm only scans the database twice and used a tree structure (FP-tree) to store all the information. The root represents null, each node represents an item, while the association of the nodes is the itemsets with the order maintained while forming the tree. The FP-tree is concise and is used to directly generating large itemsets. Once an FP-tree has been constructed, it uses a recursive divide-and-conquer approach to mine the frequent itemsets.

Steps in FP-tree:

Step 1: Deduce the ordered frequent items. For items with the same frequency, the order is given by the alphabetical order.

Step 2: Construct the FP-tree from the above data

Step 3: From the FP-tree above, construct the FP-conditional tree for each item (or itemset).

Step 4: Determine the frequent patterns.

Let's take a look at an example of how to generate an FP-tree.

Deduce the ordered frequent items and tabulate them (as shown in the table below):

Transactions	Item 1	Item 2	Item 3
1	Milk (M)	Sugar (S)	Coffee (C)
2	Milk (M)	Tea (T)	Coffee (C)
3	Milk (M)	Sugar (S)	Tea (T)
4	Milk (M)	Sugar (S)	Bread (B)
5	Milk (M)	Sugar (S)	
6	Milk (M)	Sugar (S)	

Item	Frequency
M	6
S	5
C	2
T	2
B	1

Threshold = 2

Item	Frequency
M	6
S	5
C	2
T	2

Construct the FP-tree: Find all frequent itemsets with support ≥2.

Transactions	Items	Ordered Frequent Items
1	M, S, C	M, S, C
2	M, T, C	M, C, T
3	M, S, T	M, S, T
4	M, S, B	M, S
5	M, S	M, S
6	M, S	M, S

Before constructing the FP-tree, reorder the transaction based on their item frequency. When start constructing the FP-tree, we need to create a header table that records the location of all item node with a link list. Each time a new node is added to the tree, it needs to be linked to the last node with the same item.

Now, all the Ordered-Item sets are inserted into a Tree Data Structure.

a) Inserting the set {MSC}: Transaction 1

b) Inserting {MCT}: Transaction 2

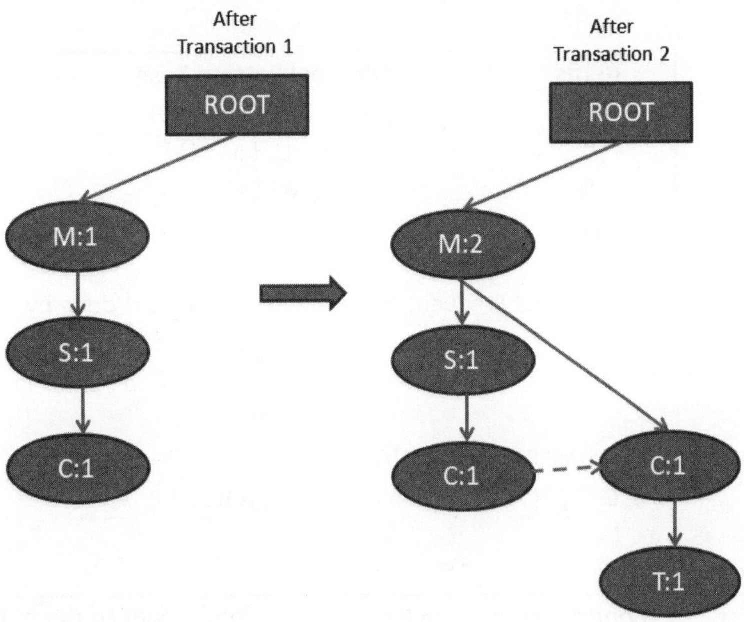

c) Inserting the set {MST}: Transaction 3

d) Inserting {MS}: Transaction 4

e) Inserting {MS}: Transaction 5

f) Inserting {MS}: Transaction 6

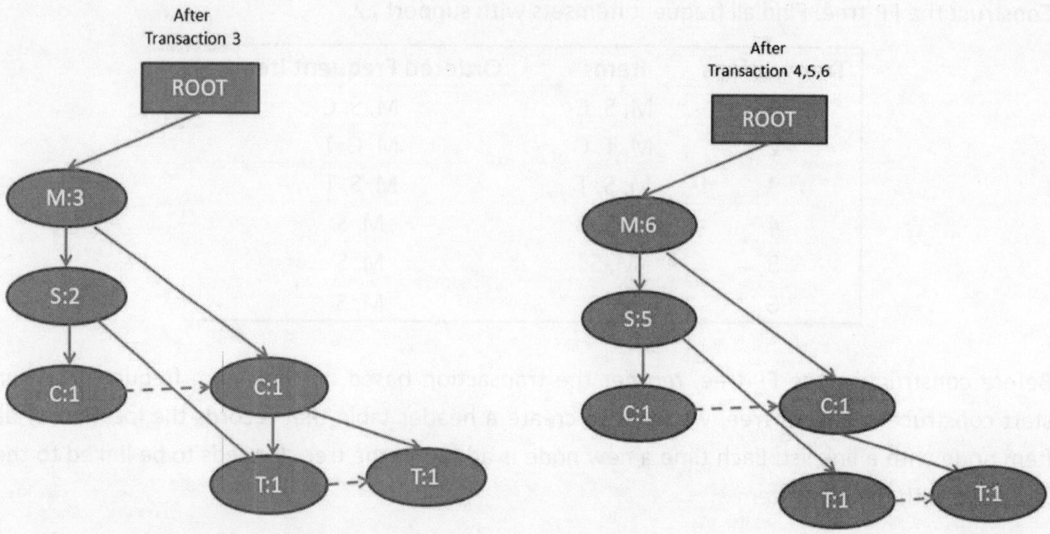

Determine the frequent patterns.

Now, for each item, the Conditional Pattern Base is computed which is path labels of all the paths which lead to any node of the given item in the frequent-pattern tree. Note that the items in the below table are arranged in the ascending order of their frequencies.

Items	Conditional Pattern Base
T	{ { M, S : 1} , { M, C : 1}}
C	{ { M, S : 1}, { M : 1} }
S	{ { M : 5} }
M	

Now for each item the Conditional Frequent Pattern Tree is built. It is done by taking the set of elements which is common in all the paths in the Conditional Pattern Base of that item and calculating it's support count by summing the support counts of all the paths in the Conditional Pattern Base.

Example: If we had a Conditional Pattern like this:

K	{ { A, B ,C : 1} , { A, B : 1} }	{ A,B : 2 }

Coming back to our example:

Items	Conditional Pattern Base	Conditional Frequent Pattern Tree
T	{ { M ,S : 1} , { M, C : 1} }	{ M : 2 }
C	{ { M, S : 1} , { M : 1}}	{ M : 2 }
S	{ { M : 5} }	{ M : 5 }
M		

From the Conditional Frequent Pattern tree, the Frequent Pattern rules are generated by pairing the items of the Conditional Frequent Pattern Tree set to the corresponding to the item as given in the below table. All the possible patterns are generated.

Example: If we had a Conditional Pattern like this:

K	{ A,B : 2 }	{ <A,B,K : 3>, <A,K : 3>, <B,K : 3> }

Coming back to our example:

Items	Conditional Pattern Base
T	{< M, T : 2> }
C	{< M, C : 2> }
S	{< M, S : 5> }
M	

For each row, two types of association rules can be inferred for example for the first row which contains the element, the rules T -> M and M -> T can be inferred. To determine the valid rule, the confidence of both the rules is calculated and the one with confidence greater than or equal to the minimum confidence value is retained.

All possible itemsets: {M,T}, {M, C}, {M,S}. If we take minimum confidence level as 3, then possible itemset will be {M,S}.

Code for complete implementation of FP Growth algorithm by Eric Naeseth is available at:
https://github.com/enaeseth/python-fp-growth/blob/master/fp_growth.py

***

UNIT 20: TIME SERIES

As the name suggests, Time Series (TS) is a collection of data points collected at constant time intervals, e,g daily, weekly, monthly, etc. These are analyzed to determine the long term trend so as to forecast the future or perform some other form of analysis. Depending on the frequency of observations, a time series may typically be hourly, daily, weekly, monthly, quarterly and annual. Sometimes, you might have seconds and minute-wise time series as well, like, number of clicks and user visits every minute etc. Time series forecasting has enormous commercial significance to a business and things like demand and sales, number of visitors to a website, stock price etc are essentially time series data.

There are two main differences between Time Series problem statement and a regular regression problem:

- It is time dependent. So the basic assumption of a linear regression model that the observations are independent doesn't hold in this case.
- Along with an increasing or decreasing trend, most TS have some form of seasonality trends, i.e. variations specific to a particular time frame. For example, if you see the sales of a woolen jacket over time, you will invariably find higher sales in winter seasons.

Because of the inherent properties of a TS, there are various steps involved in analyzing it. These are discussed in detail below. Lets start by loading a TS object in Python. Please note that the aim of this chapter is to familiarize you with the various techniques used for TS in general. The example considered here is just for illustration and will focus on coverage a breadth of topics and not making a very accurate forecast.

We'll be using the popular AirPassengers dataset for this.

```
#Import packages
from dateutil.parser import parse
import matplotlib as mpl
import matplotlib.pyplot as plt
import seaborn as sns
import numpy as np
import pandas as pd
plt.rcParams.update({'figure.figsize': (10, 7), 'figure.dpi':
120})
#Import time series data
df =
pd.read_csv('https://raw.githubusercontent.com/swapnilsaurav/Da
taset/master/AirPassengers.csv', parse_dates=['Month'])
print(df.head())
```

The data contains a particular month and number of passengers travelling in that month. Let's convert it into a Time series object and use the Month column as our index.

Visualize the dataset

```
#Visualizing a time series
# Draw Plot
def plot_df(df, x, y, title="", xlabel='Month',
ylabel='Passenger', dpi=100):
    plt.figure(figsize=(16,5), dpi=dpi)
    plt.plot(x, y, color='tab:red')
    plt.gca().set(title=title, xlabel=xlabel, ylabel=ylabel)
    plt.show()

plot_df(df, x=df.index, y=df["#Passengers"], title='Monthly Air
Travel Passengers')
plt.show()

###
# Prepare data
df['year'] = [d.year for d in df.Month]
df['month'] = [d.strftime('%b') for d in df.Month]
years = df['year'].unique()

# Draw Plot
fig, axes = plt.subplots(1, 2, figsize=(20,7), dpi= 80)
sns.boxplot(x='year', y='#Passengers', data=df, ax=axes[0])
sns.boxplot(x='month', y='#Passengers',
data=df.loc[~df.year.isin([1949, 1960]), :])

# Set Title
axes[0].set_title('Year-wise Box Plot\n(The Trend)',
fontsize=18);
axes[1].set_title('Month-wise Box Plot\n(The Seasonality)',
fontsize=18)
plt.show()
```

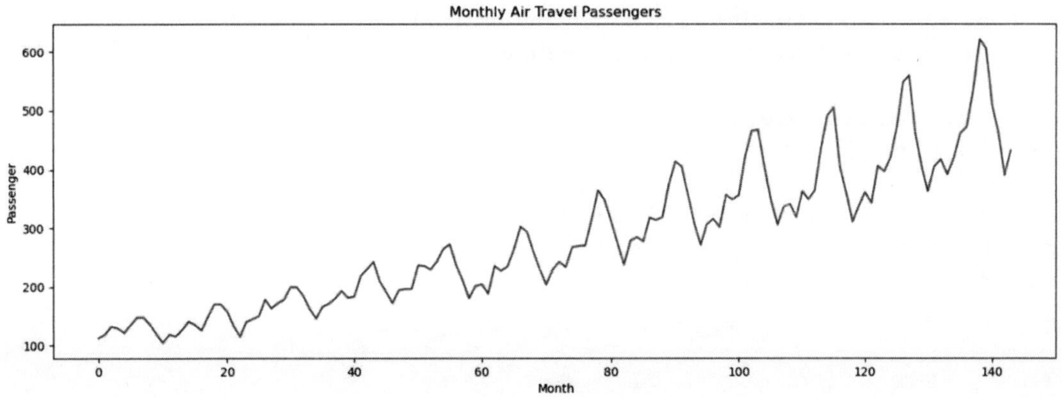

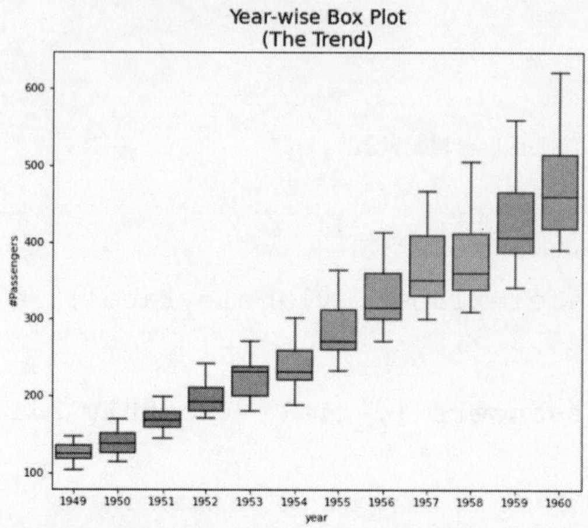

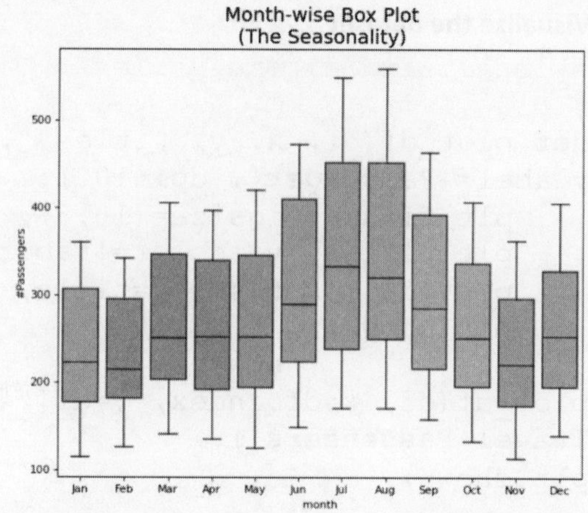

The boxplots make the year-wise and month-wise distributions evident. Also, in a month-wise boxplot, the months of July and August clearly has higher passengers travelling, which can be attributed to the holiday/vacation season.

Explore the dataset

There is some noise in realizing the forward trend here. There are some methods to model these trends and then remove them from the series. Some of the common ones are:

- Smoothing: using rolling/moving average
- Aggression: by taking the mean for a certain time period (year/month)

Moving averages are a simple and common type of smoothing used in time series analysis and time series forecasting. Calculating a moving average involves creating a new series where the values are comprised of the average of raw observations in the original time series. Moving averages can remove seasonal patterns to reveal underlying trends.

```
#Import Datatime
from datetime import datetime
df['Month']=pd.to_datetime(df['Month'])
df.set_index('Month', inplace=True)
#convert to time series:
ts = df['#Passengers']
ts_log = np.log(ts)
#Pandas has a function for rolling estimate
moving_avg = ts_log.rolling(12).mean()
plt.plot(ts_log, color="red")
plt.plot(moving_avg, color="blue")
plt.show()

#Specify the index as a String constant
print(ts['1949-01-01'])
print(ts[datetime(1949,1,1)])
```

```
#Get range
print(ts['1949-01-01':'1949-12-01'])
```

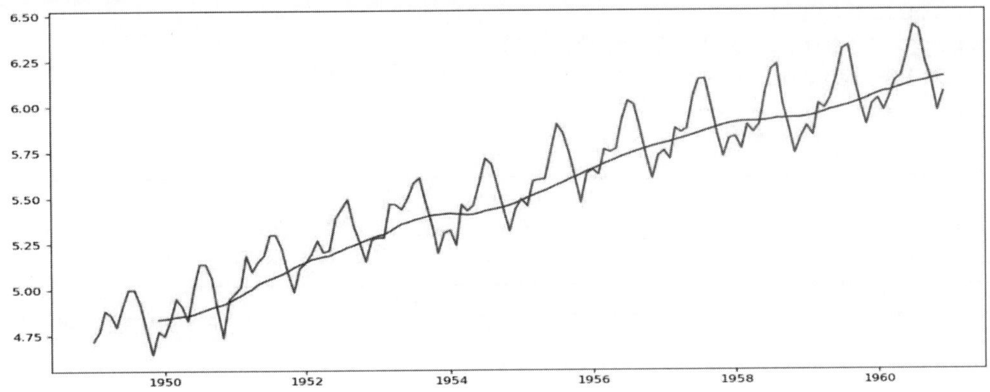


```
112
112
Month
1949-01-01    112
1949-02-01    118
1949-03-01    132
1949-04-01    129
1949-05-01    121
1949-06-01    135
1949-07-01    148
1949-08-01    148
1949-09-01    136
1949-10-01    119
1949-11-01    104
1949-12-01    118
Name: #Passengers, dtype: int64
```

Patterns in a time series

A trend is observed when there is an increasing or decreasing slope observed in the time series. Whereas seasonality is observed when there is a distinct repeated pattern observed between regular intervals due to seasonal factors. It could be because of the month of the year, the day of the month, weekdays or even time of the day. However, it is not mandatory that all time series must have a trend and/or seasonality. A time series may not have a distinct trend but have a seasonality. The opposite can also be true. So, a time series may be imagined as a combination of the **trend**, **seasonality** and the **error** terms.

```
from statsmodels.tsa.seasonal import  seasonal_decompose
decomposition = seasonal_decompose(ts_log)
trend = decomposition.trend
seasonal = decomposition.seasonal
error = decomposition.resid
plt.subplot(411)
plt.plot(ts_log,label="Original")
plt.subplot(412)
```

```
plt.plot(trend,label="Trend")
plt.subplot(413)
plt.plot(seasonal,label="Seasonal")
plt.subplot(414)
plt.plot(error,label="Residual")
plt.tight_layout()
plt.show()
```

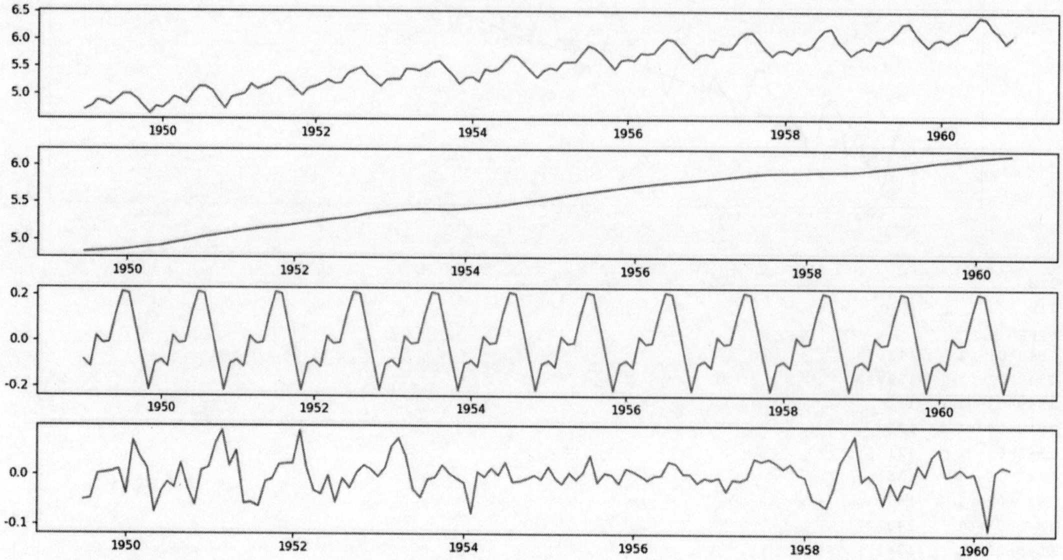

Depending on the nature of the trend and seasonality, a time series can be modeled as an additive or multiplicative, wherein, each observation in the series can be expressed as either a sum or a product of the components:

Additive time series:

Value = Base Level + Trend + Seasonality + Error

Multiplicative Time Series:

Value = Base Level x Trend x Seasonality x Error

```
# Multiplicative Decomposition
result_mul = seasonal_decompose(ts, model='multiplicative',
extrapolate_trend='freq')

# Additive Decomposition
result_add = seasonal_decompose(ts, model='additive',
extrapolate_trend='freq')

# Plot
plt.rcParams.update({'figure.figsize': (10,10)})
result_mul.plot().suptitle('Multiplicative Decompose',
```

```
fontsize=12)
result_add.plot().suptitle('Additive Decompose', fontsize=12)
plt.show()
```

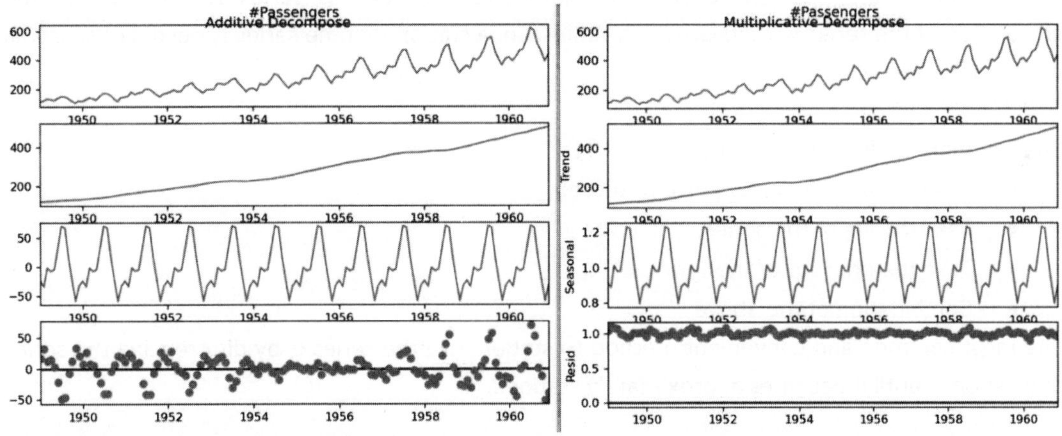

If you look at the residuals of the additive decomposition, it looks quite random, which is good. The multiplicative decomposition, however, looks straight line, not much variation. So ideally, additive decomposition should be preferred for this particular series.

```
# Extract the Components ----
# Actual Values = Product of (Seasonal * Trend * Resid)
df_reconstructed = pd.concat([result_mul.seasonal,
result_mul.trend, result_mul.resid, result_mul.observed],
axis=1)
df_reconstructed.columns = ['seas', 'trend', 'resid',
'actual_values']
print("Reconstructed data: \n",df_reconstructed.head())
```

```
Reconstructed data:
                seas       trend     resid  actual_values
Month
1949-01-01  0.911256  118.588481  1.036418          112.0
1949-02-01  0.890342  119.734169  1.106896          118.0
1949-03-01  1.012397  120.879856  1.078621          132.0
1949-04-01  0.980719  122.025544  1.077940          129.0
1949-05-01  0.979495  123.171232  1.002938          121.0
```

Another aspect to consider is the cyclic behaviour. It happens when the rise and fall pattern in the series does not happen in fixed calendar-based intervals. Care should be taken to not confuse 'cyclic' effect with 'seasonal' effect. If the patterns are not of fixed calendar based frequencies, then it is cyclic. Unlike the seasonality, cyclic effects are typically influenced by the business and other socio-economic factors.

Stationary and Non-Stationary Time Series

Stationarity is a property of a time series. A stationary series is one where the values of the series is not a function of time. That is, the statistical properties of the series like mean, variance and autocorrelation are constant over time. Autocorrelation of the series is nothing but the correlation of the series with its previous values. So, a stationary time series is devoid of seasonal effects as well.

You can make series stationary by:

- Differencing the Series (once or more)
- Take the log of the series
- Take the nth root of the series
- Combination of the above

The most common and convenient method to stationarize the series is by differencing the series at least once until it becomes approximately stationary.

What is differencing?

If Y_t is the value at time 't', then the first difference of Y = Yt – Y(t-1). In simpler terms, differencing the series is nothing but subtracting the previous value by the current value.

If the first difference doesn't make a series stationary, you can go for the second differencing. And so on.

For example, consider the following series: **[1, 5, 4, 10, 12, 8, 20]**

First differencing gives: [5-1, 4-5, 10-4, 12-10, 8-12, 20-8] = **[4, -1, 6, 2, -4, 12]**

Second differencing gives: [-1-4, 6-(-1), 2-6, -4-2,12-(-4)] = **[-5, 7, -4,-6, 16]**

Why make a non-stationary series stationary before forecasting?

Forecasting a stationary series is relatively easy and the forecasts are more reliable. An important reason is, autoregressive forecasting models are essentially linear regression models that utilize the lag(s) of the series itself as predictors. We know that linear regression works best if the predictors (X variables) are not correlated against each other. So, stationarizing the series solves this problem since it removes any persistent autocorrelation, thereby making the predictors (lags of the series) in the forecasting models nearly independent.

How to test for stationarity?

The stationarity of a series can be established by looking at the plot of the series. Another method is to split the series into 2 or more contiguous parts and computing the summary statistics like the mean, variance and the autocorrelation. If the stats are quite different, then the series is not likely to be stationary.

Nevertheless, you need a method to quantitatively determine if a given series is stationary or not. This can be done using statistical tests called 'Unit Root Tests'. There are multiple variations of this, where the tests check if a time series is non-stationary and possess a unit root.

There are multiple implementations of Unit Root tests like:

- Augmented Dickey Fuller test (ADH Test)
- Kwiatkowski-Phillips-Schmidt-Shin – KPSS test (trend stationary)
- Philips Perron test (PP Test)

The most commonly used is the ADF test, where the null hypothesis is the time series possesses a unit root and is non-stationary. So, id the P-Value in ADH test is less than the significance level (0.05), you reject the null hypothesis.
The KPSS test, on the other hand, is used to test for trend stationarity. The null hypothesis and the P-Value interpretation is just the opposite of ADH test. The below code implements these two tests using statsmodels package in python.

```
from statsmodels.tsa.stattools import adfuller, kpss

# ADF Test
result = adfuller(ts, autolag='AIC')
print(f'ADF Statistic: {result[0]}')
print(f'p-value: {result[1]}')
if result[1] > 0.05:
    print("We reject the Null hypothesis using ADF test. The 
time series is stationary")
else:
    print("Using ADF test, we conclude that time series 
possesses a unit root and is non-stationary")
for key, value in result[4].items():
    print('Critial Values:')
    print(f'   {key}, {value}')

# KPSS Test
result = kpss(ts, regression='c')
print('\nKPSS Statistic: %f' % result[0])
print('p-value: %f' % result[1])
if result[1] > 0.05:
    print("We reject the Null hypothesis using KPSS test. The 
time series is non-stationary")
else:
    print("Using KPSS test, we conclude that time series is 
stationary")
for key, value in result[3].items():
    print('Critial Values:')
    print(f'   {key}, {value}')
```

```
ADF Statistic: 0.8153688792060406
 p-value: 0.9918802434376409
We reject the Null hypothesis using ADF test. The time series is stationary
Critial Values:
   1%, -3.4816817173418295
Critial Values:
   5%, -2.8840418343195267
Critial Values:
   10%, -2.578770059171598
KPSS Statistic: 1.052175
p-value: 0.010000
Using KPSS test, we conclude that time series is stationary
Critial Values:
   10%, 0.347
Critial Values:
   5%, 0.463
Critial Values:
   2.5%, 0.574
Critial Values:
   1%, 0.739
```

How to detrend a time series?

Detrending a time series is to remove the trend component from a time series. There are multiple approaches.

1. Subtract the line of best fit from the time series. The line of best fit may be obtained from a linear regression model with the time steps as the predictor. For more complex trends, you may want to use quadratic terms (x^2) in the model.
2. Subtract the trend component obtained from time series decomposition we saw earlier.
3. Subtract the mean
4. Apply a filter like Baxter-King filter(statsmodels.tsa.filters.bkfilter) or the Hodrick-Prescott Filter (statsmodels.tsa.filters.hpfilter) to remove the moving average trend lines or the cyclical components.

Let's implement the first two methods.

```
from scipy import signal
detrended = signal.detrend(ts)
plt.plot(detrended)
plt.title('Passenger Count detrended by subtracting the least squares fit', fontsize=16)
plt.show()
#2
detrended = ts - result_add.trend
plt.plot(detrended)
plt.title('Passenger Count detrended by subtracting the trend component', fontsize=16)
plt.show()
```

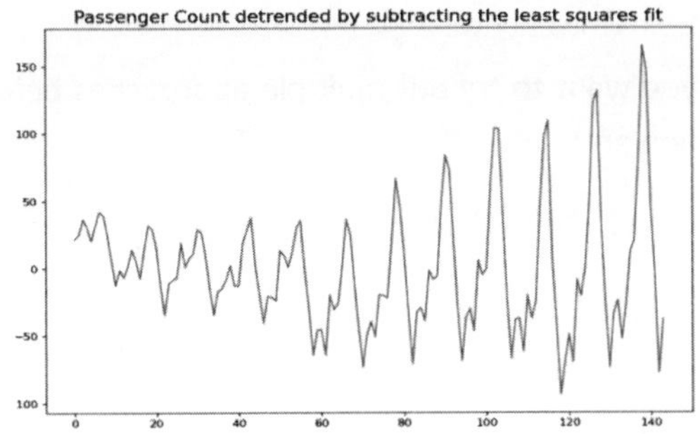

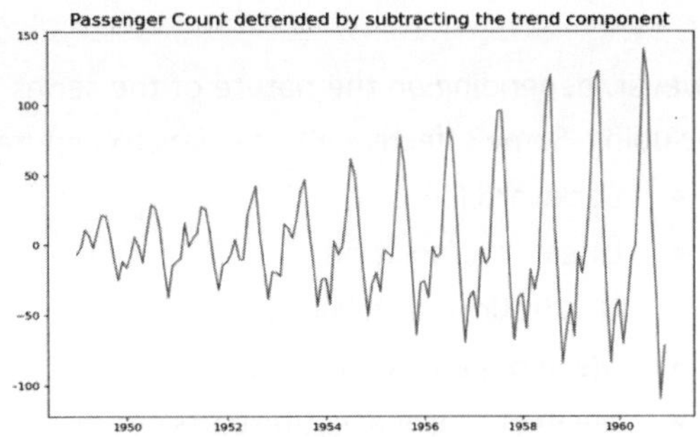

Deseasonalize a time series

1. Take a moving average with length as the seasonal window. This will smoothen in series in the process.
2. Seasonal difference the series (subtract the value of previous season from the current value)
3. Divide the series by the seasonal index obtained from STL decomposition

If dividing by the seasonal index does not work well, try taking a log of the series and then do the deseasonalizing. You can later restore to the original scale by taking an exponential.

```
# Deseasonalize
deseasonalized = ts / result_add.seasonal
# Plot
plt.plot(deseasonalized)
plt.title('Airline Passenger Count Deseasonalized',
fontsize=16)
plt.show()
```

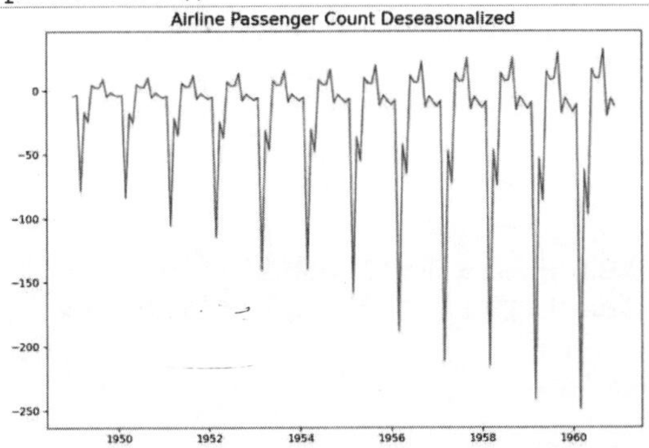

How to treat missing values in a time series?

Sometimes, your time series will have missing dates/times. It could so happen the measurement was zero on those days, in which case, case you may fill up those periods with zero.

Secondly, when it comes to time series, you should typically NOT replace missing values with the mean of the series, especially if the series is not stationary. What you could do instead for a quick and dirty workaround is to forward-fill the previous value.

However, depending on the nature of the series, you want to try out multiple approaches before concluding. Some effective alternatives to imputation are:

- Backward Fill
- Linear Interpolation
- Quadratic interpolation
- Mean of nearest neighbors
- Mean of seasonal couterparts

Our dataset doesn't have any missing value so this is applicable here. But for reference, the code for implementing missing values is given below:

```
from sklearn.metrics import mean_squared_error
#Create a copy of the original df with missing data as ts_missing
df_missing = pd.read_csv('datasets/ts_missings.csv',
parse_dates=['Month'], index_col='Month')
## 1. Actual -------------------------------
df.plot(title='Actual', ax=axes[0], label='Actual', color='red',
style=".-")
df_missing.plot(title='Actual', ax=axes[0], label='Actual',
color='green', style=".-")
axes[0].legend(["Missing Data", "Available Data"])

## 2. Forward Fill --------------------------
df_ffill = df.ffill()
error = np.round(mean_squared_error(df['#Passengers'],
df_ffill['#Passengers']), 2)
df_ffill['#Passengers'].plot(title='Forward Fill (MSE: ' +
str(error) +")", ax=axes[1], label='Forward Fill', style=".-")

## 3. Backward Fill -------------------------
df_bfill = df.bfill()
error = np.round(mean_squared_error(df['#Passengers'],
df_bfill['#Passengers']), 2)
df_bfill['#Passengers'].plot(title="Backward Fill (MSE: " +
str(error) +")", ax=axes[2], label='Back Fill', color='firebrick',
style=".-")

## 4. Linear Interpolation ------------------
df['rownum'] = np.arange(df.shape[0])
df_nona = df.dropna(subset = ['#Passengers'])
f = interp1d(df_nona['rownum'], df_nona['#Passengers'])
df['linear_fill'] = f(df['rownum'])
error = np.round(mean_squared_error(df['value'],
df['linear_fill']), 2)
df['linear_fill'].plot(title="Linear Fill (MSE: " + str(error)
+")", ax=axes[3], label='Cubic Fill', color='brown', style=".-")
```

```
## 5. Cubic Interpolation --------------------
f2 = interp1d(df_nona['rownum'], df_nona['#Passengers'],
kind='cubic')
df['cubic_fill'] = f2(df['rownum'])
error = np.round(mean_squared_error(df['value'],
df['cubic_fill']), 2)
df['cubic_fill'].plot(title="Cubic Fill (MSE: " + str(error) +")",
ax=axes[4], label='Cubic Fill', color='red', style=".-")

# Interpolation References:
#
https://docs.scipy.org/doc/scipy/reference/tutorial/interpolate.ht
ml
# https://docs.scipy.org/doc/scipy/reference/interpolate.html

## 6. Mean of 'n' Nearest Past Neighbors ------
def knn_mean(ts, n):
    out = np.copy(ts)
    for i, val in enumerate(ts):
        if np.isnan(val):
            n_by_2 = np.ceil(n/2)
            lower = np.max([0, int(i-n_by_2)])
            upper = np.min([len(ts)+1, int(i+n_by_2)])
            ts_near = np.concatenate([ts[lower:i], ts[i:upper]])
            out[i] = np.nanmean(ts_near)
    return out

df['knn_mean'] = knn_mean(df.value.values, 8)
error = np.round(mean_squared_error(df['#Passengers'],
df['knn_mean']), 2)
df['knn_mean'].plot(title="KNN Mean (MSE: " + str(error) +")",
ax=axes[5], label='KNN Mean', color='tomato', alpha=0.5, style=".-
")

## 7. Seasonal Mean ---------------------------
def seasonal_mean(ts, n, lr=0.7):
    """
    Compute the mean of corresponding seasonal periods
    ts: 1D array-like of the time series
    n: Seasonal window length of the time series
    """
    out = np.copy(ts)
    for i, val in enumerate(ts):
        if np.isnan(val):
            ts_seas = ts[i-1::-n]  # previous seasons only
            if np.isnan(np.nanmean(ts_seas)):
                ts_seas = np.concatenate([ts[i-1::-n], ts[i::n]])
# previous and forward
            out[i] = np.nanmean(ts_seas) * lr
    return out
```

```
df['seasonal_mean'] = seasonal_mean(df.value, n=12, lr=1.25)
error = np.round(mean_squared_error(df['#Passengers'],
df['seasonal_mean']), 2)
df['seasonal_mean'].plot(title="Seasonal Mean (MSE: " + str(error)
+")", ax=axes[6], label='Seasonal Mean', color='blue', alpha=0.5,
style=".-")
```

Autocorrelation and Partial autocorrelation functions

Autocorrelation is simply the correlation of a series with its own lags. If a series is significantly autocorrelated, that means, the previous values of the series (lags) may be helpful in predicting the current value. Partial Autocorrelation also conveys similar information but it conveys the pure correlation of a series and its lag, excluding the correlation contributions from the intermediate lags.

```
from statsmodels.tsa.stattools import acf, pacf
from statsmodels.graphics.tsaplots import plot_acf, plot_pacf

# Calculate ACF and PACF upto 50 lags
# acf_50 = acf(df.value, nlags=50)
# pacf_50 = pacf(df.value, nlags=50)

# Draw Plot
fig, axes = plt.subplots(1,2,figsize=(16,3), dpi= 100)
plot_acf(df["#Passengers"].tolist(), lags=50, ax=axes[0])
plot_pacf(df["#Passengers"].tolist(), lags=50, ax=axes[1])
plt.show()
```

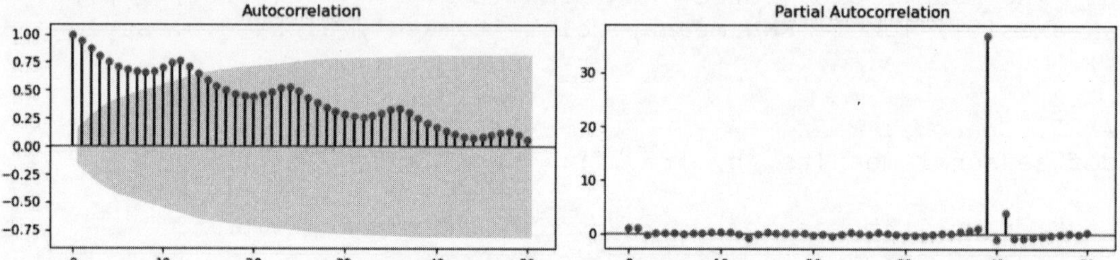

Lag Plots

A Lag plot is a scatter plot of a time series against a lag of itself. It is normally used to check for autocorrelation. If there is any pattern existing in the series, the series is autocorrelated. If there is no such pattern, the series is likely to be random white noise.

In below example, the plots get more and more scattered as the n_lag increases.

```
from pandas.plotting import lag_plot
```

```
plt.rcParams.update({'ytick.left' : False, 'axes.titlepad':10})

# Plot
fig, axes = plt.subplots(1, 4, figsize=(10,3), sharex=True,
sharey=True, dpi=100)
for i, ax in enumerate(axes.flatten()[:4]):
    lag_plot(ts, lag=i+1, ax=ax, c='firebrick')
    ax.set_title('Lag ' + str(i+1))

fig.suptitle('Lag Plots of Airline Passengers Count', y=1.05)
plt.show()
```

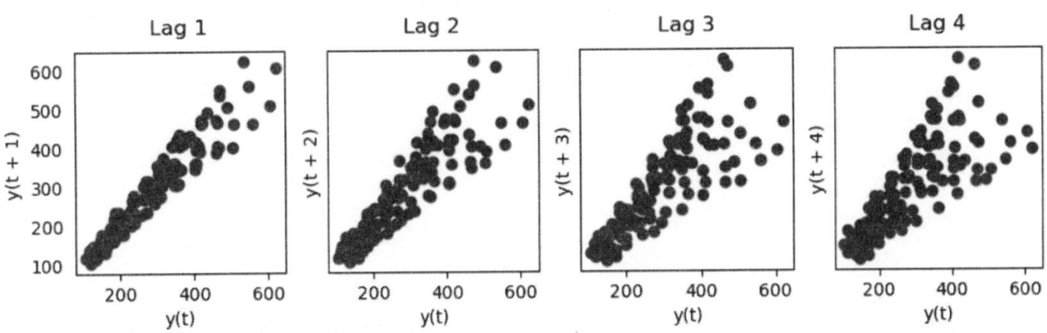

Estimate the forecastability of a time series

The more regular and repeatable patterns a time series has, the easier it is to forecast. The 'Approximate Entropy' can be used to quantify the regularity and unpredictability of fluctuations in a time series. The higher the approximate entropy, the more difficult it is to forecast it.

Another better alternate is the 'Sample Entropy'. Sample Entropy is similar to approximate entropy but is more consistent in estimating the complexity even for smaller time series. For example, a random time series with fewer data points can have a lower 'approximate entropy' than a more 'regular' time series, whereas, a longer random time series will have a higher 'approximate entropy'.

```
def ApEn(U, m, r):
    """Compute Aproximate entropy"""
    def _maxdist(x_i, x_j):
        return max([abs(ua - va) for ua, va in zip(x_i, x_j)])

    def _phi(m):
        x = [[U[j] for j in range(i, i + m - 1 + 1)] for i in
range(N - m + 1)]
        C = [len([1 for x_j in x if _maxdist(x_i, x_j) <= r]) /
(N - m + 1.0) for x_i in x]
        return (N - m + 1.0)**(-1) * sum(np.log(C))
```

```
    N = len(U)
    return abs(_phi(m+1) - _phi(m))
print(ApEn(ts, m=2, r=0.2*np.std(ts)))          # 0.645126

def SampEn(U, m, r):
    """Compute Sample entropy"""
    def _maxdist(x_i, x_j):
        return max([abs(ua - va) for ua, va in zip(x_i, x_j)])

    def _phi(m):
        x = [[U[j] for j in range(i, i + m - 1 + 1)] for i in
range(N - m + 1)]
        C = [len([1 for j in range(len(x)) if i != j and
_maxdist(x[i], x[j]) <= r]) for i in range(len(x))]
        return sum(C)

    N = len(U)
    return -np.log(_phi(m+1) / _phi(m))
print(SampEn(ts, m=2, r=0.2*np.std(ts)))          # 0.625142
```

How to use Granger Causality test to know if one time series is helpful in forecasting another

Granger causality test is used to determine if one time series will be useful to forecast another. Granger causality test is based on the idea that if X causes Y, then the forecast of Y based on previous values of Y AND the previous values of X should outperform the forecast of Y based on previous values of Y alone. So, understand that Granger causality should not be used to test if a lag of Y causes Y. Instead, it is generally used on exogenous (not Y lag) variables only.

statsmodel package has the implementation. It accepts a 2D array with 2 columns as the main argument. The values are in the first column and the predictor (X) is in the second column.

The Null hypothesis is: the series in the second column, does not Granger cause the series in the first. If the P-Values are less than a significance level (0.05) then you reject the null hypothesis and conclude that the said lag of X is indeed useful.

The second argument maxlag says till how many lags of Y should be included in the test.

```
from statsmodels.tsa.stattools import grangercausalitytests
result_test = grangercausalitytests(df[['#Passengers',
'year']], maxlag=2)
print("Result of Granger Causality Test: \n", result_test)
```

Output:

```
Granger Causality
number of lags (no zero) 1
ssr based F test:         F=23.9219 , p=0.0000  , df_denom=140, df_num=1
ssr based chi2 test:   chi2=24.4346 , p=0.0000  , df=1
likelihood ratio test: chi2=22.5580 , p=0.0000  , df=1
parameter F test:         F=23.9219 , p=0.0000  , df_denom=140, df_num=1

Granger Causality
number of lags (no zero) 2
ssr based F test:         F=39.3812 , p=0.0000  , df_denom=137, df_num=2
ssr based chi2 test:   chi2=81.6369 , p=0.0000  , df=2
likelihood ratio test: chi2=64.4959 , p=0.0000  , df=2
parameter F test:         F=39.3812 , p=0.0000  , df_denom=137, df_num=2
```

In the above case, the P-Values are Zero for all tests. So the 'Year' indeed can be used to forecast the Air Passengers.
We have completed the analysis, next step is to begin forecasting.

FORECASTING USING TIME SERIES

Using ARIMA model, you can forecast a time series using the series past values. In this section, we will build an optimal ARIMA model from scratch and extend it to Seasonal ARIMA (SARIMA) and SARIMAX models. You will also see how to build autoarima models in python.

Forecasting a time series can be broadly divided into two types:

- If you use only the previous values of the time series to predict its future values, it is called Univariate Time Series Forecasting.
- If you use predictors other than the series (a.k.a exogenous variables) to forecast it is called Multi Variate Time Series Forecasting.

In this chapter, we will focus on a particular type of forecasting method called ARIMA modeling. ARIMA, short for 'AutoRegressive Integrated Moving Average', is a forecasting algorithm based on the idea that the information in the past values of the time series can alone be used to predict the future values.

Introduction to ARIMA Models

ARIMA, short for 'Auto Regressive Integrated Moving Average' is actually a class of models that 'explains' a given time series based on its own past values, that is, its own lags and the lagged forecast errors, so that equation can be used to forecast future values.

Any 'non-seasonal' time series that exhibits patterns and is not a random white noise can be modeled with ARIMA models. An ARIMA model is characterized by 3 terms: p, d, q where,

p is the order of the AR term
q is the order of the MA term
d is the number of differencing required to make the time series stationary

If a time series, has seasonal patterns, then you need to add seasonal terms and it becomes SARIMA, short for 'Seasonal ARIMA'.

The first step to build an ARIMA model is to make the time series stationary. The value of d, is the minimum number of differencing needed to make the series stationary. And if the time series is already stationary, then d = 0.
'p' is the order of the 'Auto Regressive' (AR) term. It refers to the number of lags of Y to be used as predictors. And 'q' is the order of the 'Moving Average' (MA) term. It refers to the number of lagged forecast errors that should go into the ARIMA Model.

A pure Auto Regressive (AR only) model is one where Yt depends only on its own lags. That is, Yt is a function of the 'lags of Yt'.

$$Y_t = \alpha + \beta_1 Y_{t-1} + \beta_2 Y_{t-2} + .. + \beta_p Y_{t-p} + \epsilon_1$$

Likewise a pure Moving Average (MA only) model is one where Yt depends only on the lagged forecast errors.

$$Y_t = \alpha + \epsilon_t + \phi_1 \epsilon_{t-1} + \phi_2 \epsilon_{t-2} + .. + \phi_q \epsilon_{t-q}$$

where the error terms are the errors of the autoregressive models of the respective lags. The errors Et and E(t-1) are the errors from the following equations:

$$Y_t = \beta_1 Y_{t-1} + \beta_2 Y_{t-2} + .. + \beta_0 Y_0 + \epsilon_t$$

$$Y_{t-1} = \beta_2 Y_{t-2} + \beta_3 Y_{t-3} + .. + \beta_0 Y_0 + \epsilon_{t-1}$$

An ARIMA model is one where the time series was differenced at least once to make it stationary and you combine the AR and the MA terms. So the equation becomes:

$$Y_t = \alpha + \beta_1 Y_{t-1} + \beta_2 Y_{t-2} + .. + \beta_p Y_{t-p} \epsilon_t + \phi_1 \epsilon_{t-1} + \phi_2 \epsilon_{t-2} + .. + \phi_q \epsilon_{t-q}$$

ARIMA model in words:
Predicted Yt = Constant + Linear combination Lags of Y (upto p lags) + Linear Combination of Lagged forecast errors (upto q lags)
The objective, therefore, is to identify the values of p, d and q.

Finding the order of differencing (d) in ARIMA model
The right order of differencing is the minimum differencing required to get a near-stationary series which roams around a defined mean and the ACF plot reaches to zero fairly quick. If the

autocorrelations are positive for many number of lags (10 or more), then the series needs further differencing. On the other hand, if the lag 1 autocorrelation itself is too negative, then the series is probably over-differenced.

In the event, you can't really decide between two orders of differencing, then go with the order that gives the least standard deviation in the differenced series.

IMPLEMENTING THE FORECAST

Training has been done with an ARIMA model. Techniques like moving average and differencing were used to convert the available time series into a stationary time series. ACF and PACF was plotted and the appropriate values of p, d and q for ARIMA were found.

```
import numpy as np
import pandas as pd
from datetime import datetime as dt
from statsmodels.tsa.stattools import adfuller, acf, pacf
from statsmodels.tsa.arima_model import ARIMA
import math
import matplotlib.pyplot as plt
from matplotlib.pylab import rcParams
rcParams['figure.figsize'] = 15, 6

data =
pd.read_csv('https://raw.githubusercontent.com/swapnilsaurav/Da
taset/master/AirPassengers.csv')
print("Column Month: \n",data['Month'].head())
#Adding default date as 15
data['Month'] = data['Month'].apply(lambda x: dt(int(x[:4]),
int(x[5:]), 15))
#Now set index as Month
data = data.set_index('Month')
print("Formatted dataset: \n",data.head())

#Time series dataset
ts = data['#Passengers']
plt.plot(ts)
plt.show()
```

```
Column Month:
 0     1949-01
1     1949-02
2     1949-03
3     1949-04
4     1949-05
Name: Month, dtype: object
Formatted dataset:
                #Passengers
Month
1949-01-15            112
1949-02-15            118
1949-03-15            132
1949-04-15            129
1949-05-15            121
```

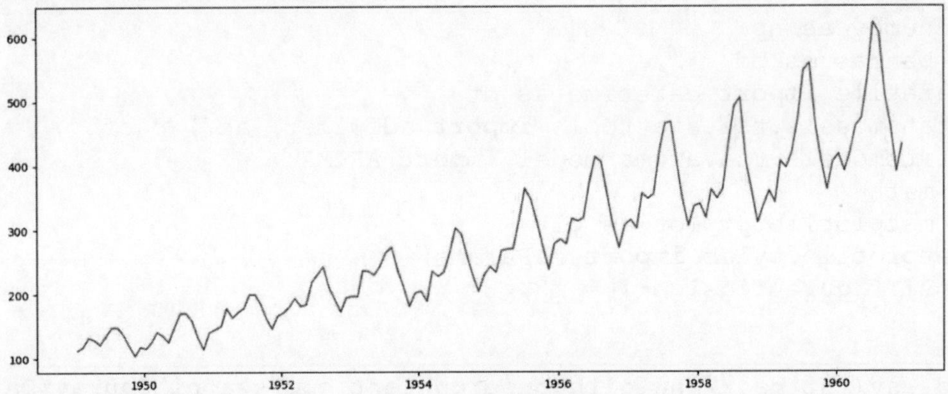

We can clearly observe seasonality and trend in the above graph as discussed in the earlier sections.

Test for stationarity:

Refer the stationary section discussed before, where we performed ADF test. The null hypothesis of the ADF test is that the time series is non-stationary. So, if the p-value of the test is less than the significance level (0.05) then you reject the null hypothesis and infer that the time series is indeed stationary.

Back to checking stationarity, we'll be using the rolling statistics plots along with Dickey-Fuller test results a lot so I have defined a function which takes a TS as input and generated them for us.

```
ts_log = np.log(ts)

def test_stationarity(timeseries):
    # Determing rolling statistics
    rolmean = timeseries.rolling(window=52,
center=False).mean()
    rolstd = timeseries.rolling(window=52, center=False).std()
```

```
    # Plot rolling statistics:
    orig = plt.plot(timeseries, color='blue', label='Original')
    mean = plt.plot(rolmean, color='red', label='Rolling Mean')
    std = plt.plot(rolstd, color='black', label='Rolling Std')
    plt.legend(loc='best')
    plt.title('Rolling Mean & Standard Deviation')
    plt.show()

    # Perform Dickey-Fuller test:
    print('Results of Dickey-Fuller Test:')
    dftest = adfuller(timeseries, autolag='AIC')
    dfoutput = pd.Series(dftest[0:4], index=['Test Statistic',
'p-value', '#Lags Used', 'Number of Observations Used'])
    for key, value in dftest[4].items():
        dfoutput['Critical Value (%s)' % key] = value
    print(dfoutput)

test_stationarity(data['#Passengers'])
```

Choosing the critical value at 0.05, we observe that in the above conducted Dickey-Fuller test for checking if the time series is stationary. Below data indicates mathematically that the time series is not stationary:

```
Results of Dickey-Fuller Test:
Test Statistic                    0.815369
p-value                           0.991880
#Lags Used                       13.000000
Number of Observations Used     130.000000
Critical Value (1%)              -3.481682
Critical Value (5%)              -2.884042
Critical Value (10%)             -2.578770
dtype: float64
```

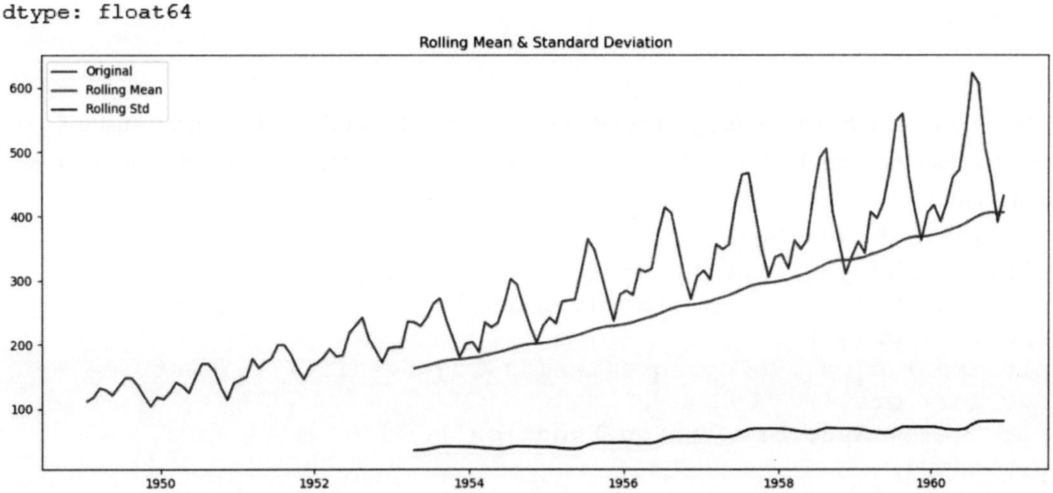

Convert into Stationary:

```
#Convert into Stationarity by taking log of the value
passenger_log_data = data['#Passengers'].apply(lambda x:
math.log(x)).diff(1)
ts_log_mv_diff = passenger_log_data.rolling(2).mean()
ts_log_mv_diff.dropna(inplace = True)
print("Dataset: \n",ts_log_mv_diff.head())
test_stationarity(ts_log_mv_diff)
```

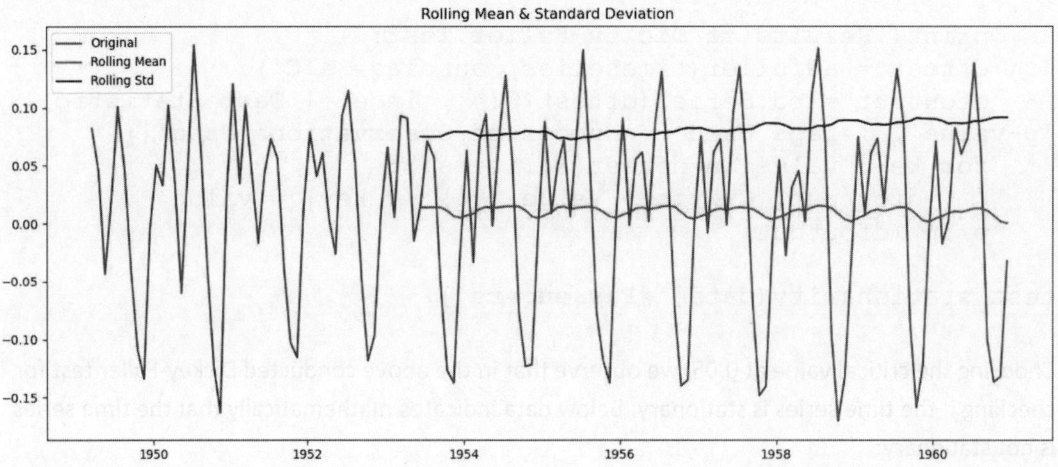

Visually, the above series seems stationary and can be confirmed for the same with Dickey-Fuller test below:

```
Results of Dickey-Fuller Test:
Test Statistic                 -3.167907
p-value                         0.021919
#Lags Used                     11.000000
Number of Observations Used   130.000000
Critical Value (1%)            -3.481682
Critical Value (5%)            -2.884042
Critical Value (10%)           -2.578770
dtype: float64
```

We can see from the above test result that p-value is lesser than 0.05 and the test statistic is greater than the critical value at 5%. We can thus decisively conclude that the time series is now stationary.

```
plt.plot(np.arange(0,11), acf(ts_log_mv_diff, nlags = 10))
plt.axhline(y=0,linestyle='--',color='gray')
plt.axhline(y=-7.96/np.sqrt(len(ts_log_mv_diff)),linestyle='--
',color='gray')
plt.axhline(y=7.96/np.sqrt(len(ts_log_mv_diff)),linestyle='--
',color='gray')
plt.title('Autocorrelation Function')
plt.show()
```

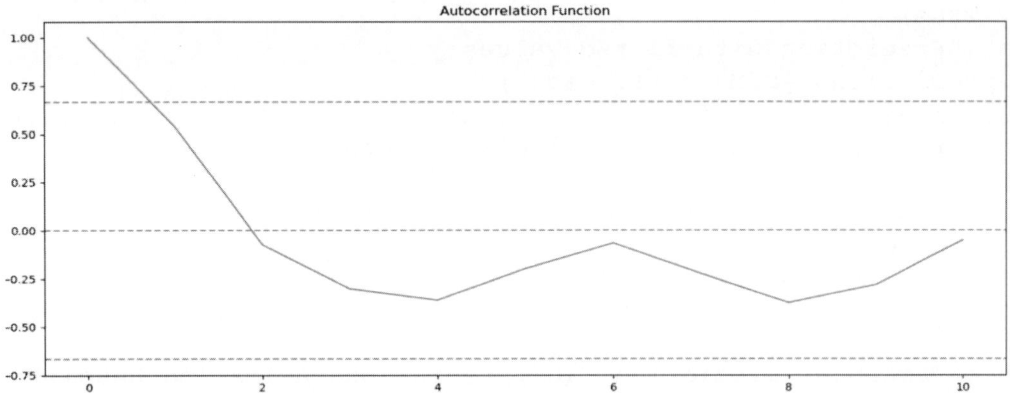

The ACF curve crosses the upper confidence value when the lag value is between 0 and 1. Thus optimal value of q in the ARIMA model must be 0 or 1.

```
plt.plot(np.arange(0,11), pacf(ts_log_mv_diff, nlags = 10))
plt.axhline(y=0,linestyle='--',color='gray')
plt.axhline(y=-7.96/np.sqrt(len(ts_log_mv_diff)),linestyle='--
',color='gray')
plt.axhline(y=7.96/np.sqrt(len(ts_log_mv_diff)),linestyle='--
',color='gray')
plt.title('Partial Autocorrelation Function')
plt.show()
```

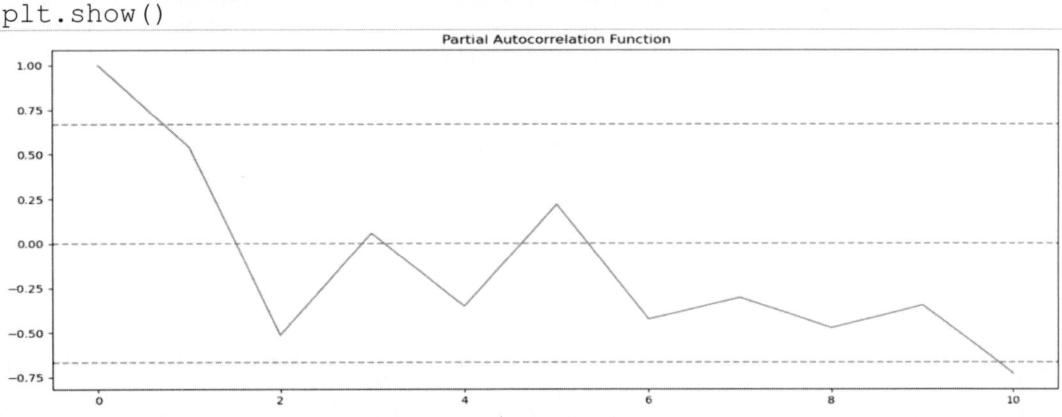

The PACF curve drops to 0 between lag values 1 and 2. Thus optimal value of p in the ARIMA model is 1 or 2.

Building the Model:

```
model = ARIMA(ts_log, order=(1, 1, 0))
results_ARIMA = model.fit(disp=-1)
plt.plot(ts_log_mv_diff)
plt.plot(results_ARIMA.fittedvalues, color='red')
plt.title('RSS: %.4f'% sum((results_ARIMA.fittedvalues[1:] -
ts_log_mv_diff)**2))
predictions_ARIMA_diff = pd.Series(results_ARIMA.fittedvalues,
```

```
copy=True)
print("Prediction with fitted values:
\n",predictions_ARIMA_diff.head())
predictions_ARIMA_diff_cumsum = predictions_ARIMA_diff.cumsum()
print("Prediction with CumulativeSum values:
\n",predictions_ARIMA_diff_cumsum.head())
predictions_ARIMA_log = pd.Series(ts_log.iloc[0],
index=ts_log.index)
predictions_ARIMA_log =
predictions_ARIMA_log.add(predictions_ARIMA_diff_cumsum,fill_va
lue=0)
print("Passenger Prediction: \n",predictions_ARIMA_log.head())

#Calculating the accuracy
predictions_ARIMA = np.exp(predictions_ARIMA_log)
plt.plot(ts)
plt.plot(predictions_ARIMA)
plt.title('RMSE: %.4f'% np.sqrt(sum((predictions_ARIMA-
ts)**2)/len(ts)))
```

```
Prediction with fitted values:
 Month
1949-02-15     0.009676
1949-03-15     0.018164
1949-04-15     0.030130
1949-05-15     0.003154
1949-06-15    -0.005039
dtype: float64
```

```
Prediction with CumulativeSum values:
 Month
1949-02-15     0.009676
1949-03-15     0.027839
1949-04-15     0.057969
1949-05-15     0.061123
1949-06-15     0.056084
dtype: float64
```

```
Passenger Prediction:
 Month
1949-01-15     4.718499
1949-02-15     4.728175
1949-03-15     4.746338
1949-04-15     4.776468
1949-05-15     4.779622
dtype: float64
```

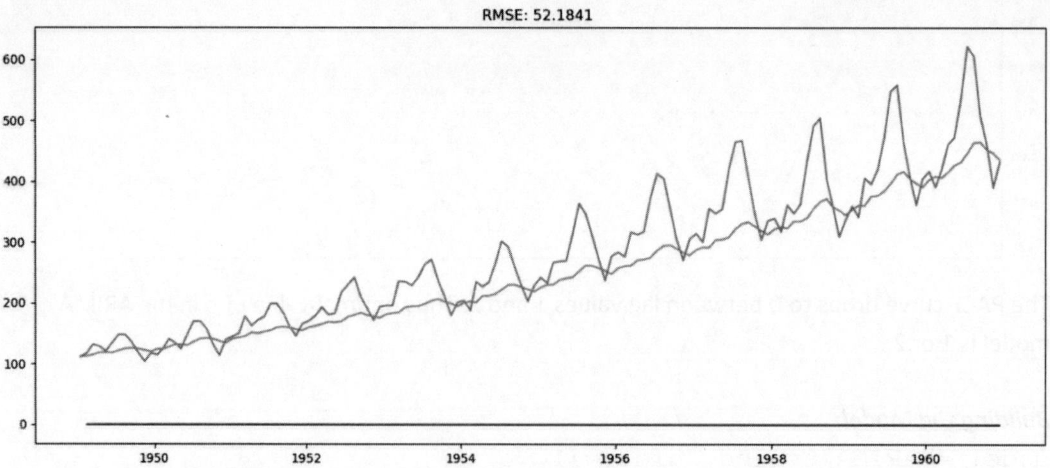

The green (almost straight line) curve is our prediction which has an RMSE of 52.1841. While our model is good at predicting the trend, it fails in capturing the seasonality.

***

UNIT 21: DEPLOY ML MODELS USING FLASK

In this chapter, we will learn how to deploy our model using Flask. The whole process is made up of 3 steps:

1. Create the Machine Learning (ML) Model
2. Creating Flask Application
3. Creating API to pass the values to ML model

CREATING THE MACHINE LEARNING MODEL

Below example is taken from our Simple Regression Model (I have written this is: ml.py file)

```
import pandas as pd
import matplotlib.pyplot as plt

slr_df =
pd.read_csv("https://raw.githubusercontent.com/swapnilsaurav/Da
taset/master/student_scores.csv")
print("Columns in the dataset: \n",slr_df.columns)
#Display first 5 records
slr_df.head()
#Size of the dataset
print("Size of the dataset: ", slr_df.shape)
#Get the statistics
slr_df.describe()
#Scatter plot for complete dataset
plt.scatter(slr_df['Hours'], slr_df['Scores'])
plt.show()

#Getting X and Y values
X=slr_df[['Hours']]
y=slr_df[['Scores']]

#Prediction Model
from sklearn.linear_model import LinearRegression
regressor = LinearRegression()
regressor.fit(X, y)

#Regression Score
print("Score of the Model: ",regressor.score(X,y))
#Predict for a given value
y_pred = regressor.predict([[7.5]])
print("Predicted value for given data: ", y_pred)
#intercept value: c
print("Intercept value: ",regressor.intercept_)
```

```
#coef as m
print("Coefficient value: ",regressor.coef_)
```

Now our simple linear regression model is ready, let's go towards model persistence and save the above as .pkl file

To make the model persistence, add below code to the above lines of code:

```
#pip install joblib
import joblib
joblib.dump(regressor,"linear_reg.pkl")
```

Now our model is saved and can be reused by loading the same again anytime.

Let's build a Web API using Flask and understand the process to achieve the same in a simple manner.

INTRODUCTION TO FLASK

You will have to install Flask yourself, if not already installed, with — **pip install flask**.

Detailed Flask is available in our book – Learn and Practice Python. For demonstration, here's the Flask code to create a very simple web server.

My filename is fl.py

```
from flask import Flask
app = Flask(__name__)
@app.route("/")
def hello():
    return "Hello World!"
if __name__ == '__main__':
    app.run(debug=True)
```

Output:

```
 * Serving Flask app "fl" (lazy loading)
 * Environment: production
   WARNING: This is a development server. Do not use it in a production deployment.
   Use a production WSGI server instead.
 * Debug mode: on
 * Restarting with stat
 * Debugger is active!
 * Debugger PIN: 121-273-934
 * Running on http://127.0.0.1:5000/ (Press CTRL+C to quit)
127.0.0.1 - - [27/Oct/2020 15:39:15] "GET / HTTP/1.1" 200 -
```

Open http://127.0.0.1:5000/

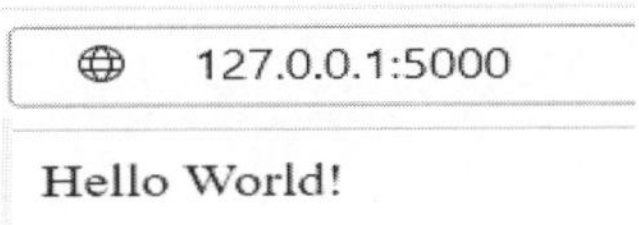

Let's review what the executed code is doing.

After importing, we create an instance of the Flask class and pass in the __name__ variable that Python fills in for us. This variable will be "__main__", if this file is being directly run through Python as a script. If we import the file instead, the value of __name__ will be the name of the file where we did the import. For instance, if we had test.py and run.py, and we imported test.py into run.py the __name__ value of test.py will be test.

Above our hello method definition, there's the @app.route("/") line. The @ denotes a decorator, which allows the function, property, or class it's precedes to be dynamically altered.

The hello method is where we put the code to run whenever the route of our app or API hits the top level route: /.

If our __name__ variable is __main__, indicating that we ran the file directly instead of importing it, then it will start the Flask app which will run and wait for web requests until the process ends.

CREATING THE API

The prediction API takes our data, the number of hours, and pass that into our predict method of our model.

We have created predict.py file:

```
from flask import Flask,jsonify,request
import joblib
app = Flask(__name__)

@app.route("/", methods=['POST','GET'])
def index():
    if(request.method == 'POST'):
        data = request.get_json()
        Score_Pred = float(data["Hours"])
        print("Score_pred: ",Score_Pred)
        lin_reg = joblib.load("./linear_reg.pkl")
        return
jsonify(lin_reg.predict([[Score_Pred]]).tolist())
    else:
        return  jsonify({"about":"Hello World"})
```

```
if __name__ == '__main__':
    app.run(debug=True)
```

Similar to the code above that introduced Flask, we're calling the @app.route decorator.
In our route method definition, we restrict the request methods to be GET/POST and if so, we get the JSON of the request body so we can access its data. With that variable, we access the key of the data we want — area and parse it into a float. We also load our model into memory from the persisted file.
If there were no errors parsing the data then we pass the parsed variable into the predict method of our linear regression model; the variable was pulled into memory when we loaded our Flask app at startup. Next, we have to change the output of the predict method to a list since, without it, we'd get an error: Object of type 'ndarray' is not JSON serializable. We then call the [jsonify](http://flask.pocoo.org/docs/0.12/api/#flask.json.jsonify) method of Flask to send the response data as JSON.

Now we can run our API (in PyCharm you can just right-click anywhere in the script and click "Run"). With our API running we can execute thecode to call it.

Our filename: req_pred.py:

```
import requests
import json
data = {"Hours": 4.5}
response = requests.post("{}/".format("http://127.0.0.1:5000"),
json =data)
print("The Score predicted is "+ str(response.json()))
```

Now, we can see the output on our terminal.

```
The Score predicted is [[48.03782720297045]]
```

In this chapter, we learned what Flask is, how to use it to create APIs, and most importantly how to apply this knowledge to create APIs for interacting with machine learning models.

This is the end of this book. I hope you enjoyed and learnt to program Machine Learning concepts. You can always send your feedback to the author at: ekapresshyderabad@gmail.com

***

APPENDIX 1: Z TABLE

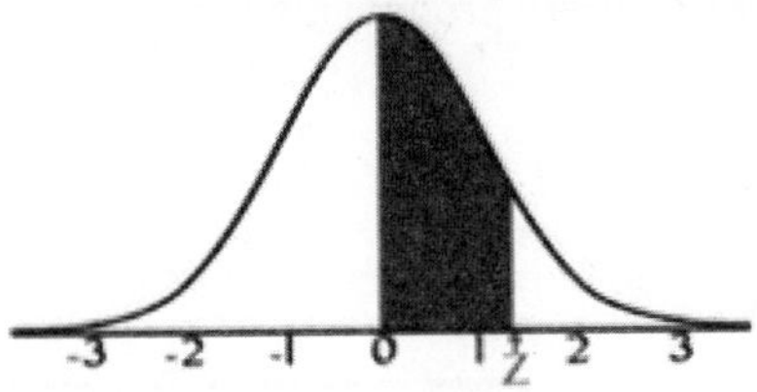

STANDARD NORMAL TABLE (Z)

Entries in the table give the area under the curve between the mean and *z* standard deviations above the mean. For example, for *z* = 1.25 the area under the curve between the mean (0) and *z* is 0.3944.

z	0.00	0.01	0.02	0.03	0.04	0.05	0.06	0.07	0.08	0.09
0.0	0.0000	0.0040	0.0080	0.0120	0.0160	0.0190	0.0239	0.0279	0.0319	0.0359
0.1	0.0398	0.0438	0.0478	0.0517	0.0557	0.0596	0.0636	0.0675	0.0714	0.0753
0.2	0.0793	0.0832	0.0871	0.0910	0.0948	0.0987	0.1026	0.1064	0.1103	0.1141
0.3	0.1179	0.1217	0.1255	0.1293	0.1331	0.1368	0.1406	0.1443	0.1480	0.1517
0.4	0.1554	0.1591	0.1628	0.1664	0.1700	0.1736	0.1772	0.1808	0.1844	0.1879
0.5	0.1915	0.1950	0.1985	0.2019	0.2054	0.2088	0.2123	0.2157	0.2190	0.2224
0.6	0.2257	0.2291	0.2324	0.2357	0.2389	0.2422	0.2454	0.2486	0.2517	0.2549
0.7	0.2580	0.2611	0.2642	0.2673	0.2704	0.2734	0.2764	0.2794	0.2823	0.2852
0.8	0.2881	0.2910	0.2939	0.2969	0.2995	0.3023	0.3051	0.3078	0.3106	0.3133
0.9	0.3159	0.3186	0.3212	0.3238	0.3264	0.3289	0.3315	0.3340	0.3365	0.3389
1.0	0.3413	0.3438	0.3461	0.3485	0.3508	0.3513	0.3554	0.3577	0.3529	0.3621
1.1	0.3643	0.3665	0.3686	0.3708	0.3729	0.3749	0.3770	0.3790	0.3810	0.3830
1.2	0.3849	0.3869	0.3888	0.3907	0.3925	0.3944	0.3962	0.3980	0.3997	0.4015
1.3	0.4032	0.4049	0.4066	0.4082	0.4099	0.4115	0.4131	0.4147	0.4162	0.4177
1.4	0.4192	0.4207	0.4222	0.4236	0.4251	0.4265	0.4279	0.4292	0.4306	0.4319
1.5	0.4332	0.4345	0.4357	0.4370	0.4382	0.4394	0.4406	0.4418	0.4429	0.4441
1.6	0.4452	0.4463	0.4474	0.4484	0.4495	0.4505	0.4515	0.4525	0.4535	0.4545
1.7	0.4554	0.4564	0.4573	0.4582	0.4591	0.4599	0.4608	0.4616	0.4625	0.4633
1.8	0.4641	0.4649	0.4656	0.4664	0.4671	0.4678	0.4686	0.4693	0.4699	0.4706
1.9	0.4713	0.4719	0.4726	0.4732	0.4738	0.4744	0.4750	0.4756	0.4761	0.4767
2.0	0.4772	0.4778	0.4783	0.4788	0.4793	0.4798	0.4803	0.4808	0.4812	0.4817
2.1	0.4821	0.4826	0.4830	0.4834	0.4838	0.4842	0.4846	0.4850	0.4854	0.4857
2.2	0.4861	0.4864	0.4868	0.4871	0.4875	0.4878	0.4881	0.4884	0.4887	0.4890
2.3	0.4893	0.4896	0.4898	0.4901	0.4904	0.4906	0.4909	0.4911	0.4913	0.4916
2.4	0.4918	0.4920	0.4922	0.4925	0.4927	0.4929	0.4931	0.4932	0.4934	0.4936
2.5	0.4938	0.4940	0.4941	0.4943	0.4945	0.4946	0.4948	0.4949	0.4951	0.4952
2.6	0.4953	0.4955	0.4956	0.4957	0.4959	0.4960	0.4961	0.4962	0.4963	0.4964
2.7	0.4965	0.4966	0.4967	0.4968	0.4969	0.4970	0.4971	0.4972	0.4973	0.4974
2.8	0.4974	0.4975	0.4976	0.4977	0.4977	0.4978	0.4979	0.4979	0.4980	0.4981
2.9	0.4981	0.4982	0.4982	0.4983	0.4984	0.4984	0.4985	0.4985	0.4986	0.4986
3.0	0.4987	0.4987	0.4987	0.4988	0.4988	0.4989	0.4989	0.4989	0.4990	0.4990
3.1	0.4990	0.4991	0.4991	0.4991	0.4992	0.4992	0.4992	0.4992	0.4993	0.4993
3.2	0.4993	0.4993	0.4994	0.4994	0.4994	0.4994	0.4994	0.4995	0.4995	0.4995
3.3	0.4995	0.4995	0.4995	0.4996	0.4996	0.4996	0.4996	0.4996	0.4996	0.4997
3.4	0.4997	0.4997	0.4997	0.4997	0.4997	0.4997	0.4997	0.4997	0.4997	0.4998

APPENDIX 2: t Distribution

Numbers in each row of the table are values on a *t*-distribution with (*df*) degrees of freedom for selected right-tail (greater-than) probabilities (*p*).

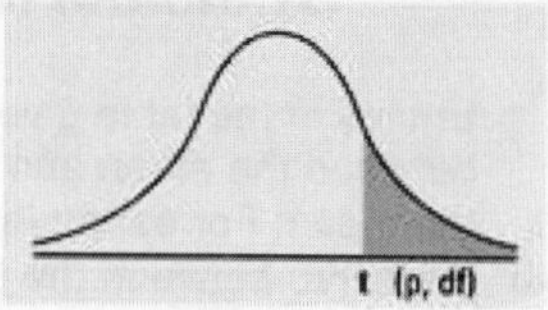

df/p	0.40	0.25	0.10	0.05	0.025	0.01	0.005	0.0005
1	0.324920	1.000000	3.077684	6.313752	12.70620	31.82052	63.65674	636.6192
2	0.288675	0.816497	1.885618	2.919986	4.30265	6.96456	9.92484	31.5991
3	0.276671	0.764892	1.637744	2.353363	3.18245	4.54070	5.84091	12.9240
4	0.270722	0.740697	1.533206	2.131847	2.77645	3.74695	4.60409	8.6103
5	0.267181	0.726687	1.475884	2.015048	2.57058	3.36493	4.03214	6.8688
6	0.264835	0.717558	1.439756	1.943180	2.44691	3.14267	3.70743	5.9588
7	0.263167	0.711142	1.414924	1.894579	2.36462	2.99795	3.49948	5.4079
8	0.261921	0.706387	1.396815	1.859548	2.30600	2.89646	3.35539	5.0413
9	0.260955	0.702722	1.383029	1.833113	2.26216	2.82144	3.24984	4.7809
10	0.260185	0.699812	1.372184	1.812461	2.22814	2.76377	3.16927	4.5869
11	0.259556	0.697445	1.363430	1.795885	2.20099	2.71808	3.10581	4.4370
12	0.259033	0.695483	1.356217	1.782288	2.17881	2.68100	3.05454	43178
13	0.258591	0.693829	1.350171	1.770933	2.16037	2.65031	3.01228	4.2208
14	0.258213	0.692417	1.345030	1.761310	2.14479	2.62449	2.97684	4.1405
15	0.257885	0.691197	1.340606	1.753050	2.13145	2.60248	2.94671	4.0728
16	0.257599	0.690132	1.336757	1.745884	2.11991	2.58349	2.92078	4.0150
17	0.257347	0.689195	1.333379	1.739607	2.10982	2.56693	2.89823	3.9651
18	0.257123	0.688364	1.330391	1.734064	2.10092	2.55238	2.87844	3.9216
19	0.256923	0.687621	1.327728	1.729133	2.09302	2.53948	2.86093	3.8834
20	0.256743	0.686954	1.325341	1.724718	2.08596	2.52798	2.84534	3.8495
21	0.256580	0.686352	1.323188	1.720743	2.07961	2.51765	2.83136	3.8193
22	0.256432	0.685805	1.321237	1.717144	2.07387	2.50832	2.81876	3.7921
23	0.256297	0.685306	1.319460	1.713872	2.06866	2.49987	2.80734	3.7676
24	0.256173	0.684850	1.317836	1.710882	2.06390	2.49216	2.79694	3.7454
25	0.256060	0.684430	1.316345	1.708141	2.05954	2.48511	2.78744	3.7251
26	0.255955	0.684043	1.314972	1.705618	2.05553	2.47863	2.77871	3.7066
27	0.255858	0.683685	1.313703	1.703288	2.05183	2.47266	2.77068	3.6896
28	0.255768	0.683353	1.312527	1.701131	2.04841	2.46714	2.76326	3.6739
29	0.255684	0.683044	1.311434	1.699127	2.04523	2.46202	2.75639	3.6594
30	0.255605	0.682756	1.310415	1.697261	2.04227	2.45726	2.75000	3.6460
z	0.253347	0.674490	1.281552	1.644854	1.95996	2.32635	2.57583	3.2905
CI	———	———	80%	90%	95%	98%	99%	99.9%

APPENDIX 3: CHI SQUARE TABLE (RIGHT TAIL)

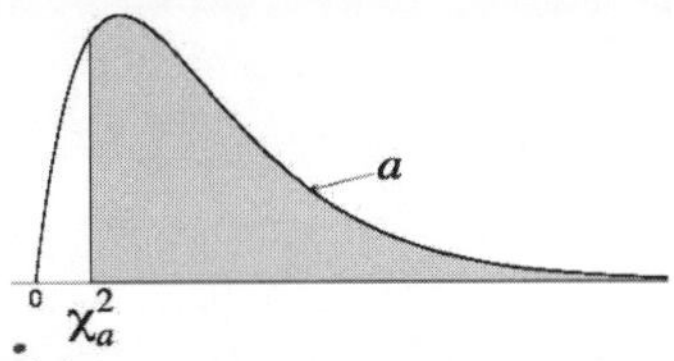

df	$\chi^2_{0.9995}$	$\chi^2_{0.999}$	$\chi^2_{0.995}$	$\chi^2_{0.990}$	$\chi^2_{0.975}$	$\chi^2_{0.95}$	$\chi^2_{0.90}$	$\chi^2_{0.85}$	$\chi^2_{0.80}$
1	0.000	0.000	0.000	0.000	0.001	0.004	0.016	0.036	0.064
2	0.001	0.002	0.010	0.020	0.051	0.103	0.211	0.325	0.446
3	0.015	0.024	0.072	0.115	0.216	0.352	0.584	0.798	1.005
4	0.064	0.091	0.207	0.297	0.484	0.711	1.064	1.366	1.649
5	0.158	0.210	0.412	0.554	0.831	1.145	1.610	1.994	2.343
6	0.299	0.381	0.676	0.872	1.237	1.635	2.204	2.661	3.070
7	0.485	0.598	0.989	1.239	1.690	2.167	2.833	3.358	3.822
8	0.710	0.857	1.344	1.646	2.180	2.733	3.490	4.078	4.594
9	0.972	1.152	1.735	2.088	2.700	3.325	4.168	4.817	5.380
10	1.265	1.479	2.156	2.558	3.247	3.940	4.865	5.570	6.179
11	1.587	1.834	2.603	3.053	3.816	4.575	5.578	6.336	6.989
12	1.934	2.214	3.074	3.571	4.404	5.226	6.304	7.114	7.807
13	2.305	2.617	3.565	4.107	5.009	5.892	7.042	7.901	8.634
14	2.697	3.041	4.075	4.660	5.629	6.571	7.790	8.696	9.467